Praise for *Ghosts of a Holy War*

"In this groundbreaking account of the origins of the Arab-Israeli conflict, Yardena Schwartz tells a compelling story of how one American's tragic life converged with a seminal moment in history. Focusing on the ancient city of Hebron, *Ghosts of a Holy War* masterfully weaves together past and present, the historical and the personal. With a keen reporter's eye, Schwartz reveals the best and the worst in both sides of the conflict. If you are going to read one book to help you understand the current Middle East tragedy, this is it."

—**Yossi Klein Halevi**, senior fellow, Shalom Hartman Institute, and author of the *New York Times* bestseller *Letters to My Palestinian Neighbor*

"With meticulous archival research and journalistic skill, and aided by a fascinating trove of letters left by a doomed young American, Yardena Schwartz gives us a valuable account of one of the key tragedies in the meeting between Jews and Arabs in Palestine. *Ghosts of a Holy War* fills in a missing piece in our understanding of a conflict that continues to echo worldwide, reminding us of the human characters at the heart of global dramas."

—**Matti Friedman**, author of *Who by Fire: Leonard Cohen in the Sinai*

"The Hebron massacre is a pivotal event in the history of the Jewish-Arab confrontation, one with profound resonance with our own troubled time. Yardena Schwartz has written an engaging, accessible, and deeply personal account of the massacre and its enduring legacy in the post–10/7 Middle East."

—**Oren Kessler**, author of *Palestine 1936: The Great Revolt and the Roots of the Middle East Conflict*, winner of the 2024 Sami Rohr Prize for Jewish Literature

"Important, timely, deeply researched, and beautifully written. Yardena Schwartz has made a key contribution to understanding the roots of the Israeli-Palestinian conflict. A family story is seamlessly woven into the political narrative, which explains comprehensively the present sad state of affairs."

—**Martin Fletcher**, former NBC News Bureau Chief in Tel Aviv and author of *Promised Land: A Novel of Israel*

GHOSTS *of a*
HOLY WAR

GHOSTS *of a*
HOLY WAR

The 1929 Massacre in Palestine That
Ignited the Arab-Israeli Conflict

YARDENA SCHWARTZ

UNION
SQUARE
& CO.

NEW YORK

UNION
SQUARE
& CO.

NEW YORK

Note: Some scenes in this book depict graphic or violent situations that
could trigger emotional distress or discomfort for some readers.

ISBN 978-1-4549-4921-3
ISBN 978-1-4549-4922-0 (e-book)

Library of Congress Control Number: 2024940241

For information about custom editions, special sales, and premium
purchases, please contact specialsales@unionsquareandco.com.

Printed in the United States of America

2 4 6 8 10 9 7 5 3 1

unionsquareandco.com
Interior design by Rich Hazelton and Kevin Ullrich
Picture credits: See page 410

For Shachar, Ayala & Lior

In loving memory of Ken Cohen, 1927–2024

CONTENTS

AUTHOR'S NOTE

October 7 has been called Israel's 9/11, Israel's Pearl Harbor, the deadliest day for the Jewish people since the Holocaust. Yet we need not look beyond the borders of Israel itself—or Palestine, rather—for a massacre of Jews that was hauntingly similar. In 1929, before the State of Israel was born, long before its military occupation of the West Bank began, Palestine was the scene of one of the worst pogroms ever perpetrated outside of Europe.

The massacre of Jews in the Holy Land nearly a century ago was on a scale far smaller than October 7. Yet it transformed the region into what we know today. Hebron, the burial place of Abraham, became ground zero of the world's most enduring conflict. The massacre in Hebron did not just destroy one of the world's most ancient Jewish communities. It set the stage for the Holy War still raging at this time.

Jews had lived in Hebron, their second holiest city, since the days of Abraham. Their pious lives were centered around the Tomb of the Patriarchs and Matriarchs, where the Jewish forefathers and mothers are believed to be buried. The 1929 massacre ended centuries of peaceful coexistence between Jews and Muslims in Hebron. Today that city is the face of the settlement movement, the place where Israeli control over Palestinian life is on fullest display. Hebron has since produced some of the most radical Israelis and Palestinians.

This book was not meant to be about October 7. It was meant to be about the aftershocks of a century-old massacre that continue to reverberate. Those aftershocks culminated in the attacks of October 7.

• • •

My work on this book began five years ago, when I was introduced to a family in Memphis, Tennessee, with an epic tale to tell, of a time and a place lost to history. It was the story of a young American caught in the tidal waves of this conflict, and the complicated Jewish American connection to the Jewish state.

Before I met this family, I had been to Hebron just once. My visit had been so disturbing that I never returned until I began writing this book. My research took me on a journey into Hebron to discover how the cradle of the Jewish people became the deepest wound of this conflict. My goal was to understand why the return of a persecuted people to their native land led to the misery of another people who feel their homeland has been taken from them. Did it need to be this way?

Between 2019 and 2023, I spent hundreds of hours in Hebron, reporting extensively on both sides. During my time there with Israelis and Palestinians, I came to understand why this conflict persists, and why every peace effort has failed.

There is a direct line between 1929 and 2023. The forces that drove Arabs in Hebron to slaughter their Jewish neighbors in 1929 were identical to the forces behind October 7. Just as the riots of 1929 were fueled by passions surrounding Al-Aqsa Mosque, the third holiest site in Islam, so too was Hamas's "Operation Al-Aqsa Flood." On one level, this is a conflict like many others, involving borders and other rational issues. But as the line connecting the 1929 massacre with the Hamas massacre of 2023 makes clear, the religious dimension of this conflict cannot be ignored.

The massacre in Hebron, its impact, and its echoes today, hold the key to understanding how we got here and what needs to change if the people destined to share this land are ever to know peace.

—Yardena Schwartz

INTRODUCTION
The Box in the Attic

On a humid afternoon in the summer of 2009, Suzie Lazarov sat on her living room couch in Memphis, Tennessee, sifting through half a century of memories. Suzie and Paul, her husband of fifty years, would soon be moving to a new house in the leafy suburbs of East Memphis. Before he left for work that morning, Paul had brought down all the dusty boxes from their attic. Scanning the room, Suzie's eyes settled on one mysteriously unfamiliar box.

Important papers do not throw away! wrote someone, she wasn't sure who, in faded black marker on the white box. Suzie carefully peeled off the tape and opened the box, revealing dozens of antiquated handwritten letters, interspersed with typewritten cables, telegrams, black and white photographs, and a diary. All were dated from the mid to late 1920s. As she leafed through the delicate pieces of paper, distant places, names, and dates seemed to float from the yellowed, timeworn pages.

Hebron, Palestine

October 5, 1928

Dear Folks

Rest assured, nothing that I can write or that words can describe can do justice to the beauty of Palestine.

Devotedly, Dave

David Shainberg before his move to Palestine, c. 1925.

The letters, more than sixty of them, each five to ten pages long, were written by Suzie's late uncle, her father Herbert's eldest brother David. Suzie, a 70-year-old grandmother, had never met her uncle Dave. She knew he had moved to British Mandate Palestine in 1928 to study at a renowned yeshiva, and that he had been killed there. Yet she knew little about the massacre that took his life, beyond it being a traumatic subject for her father, his three surviving siblings, and their parents. Growing up in Memphis, that day was rarely discussed. Its memory was simply too painful.

The First Black Sabbath

David Shainberg was 22 years old when he sailed to Palestine in September 1928 and enrolled at the prestigious Hebron Yeshiva. A spiritual seeker and intellectual, David went with dreams of studying Talmud in the Holy Land. In his eloquent letters to his family in Memphis, he described the city's serenity, and the unique comradery between the city's Jewish and Muslim population. One year later, that fragile bubble of peace was violently punctured.

On the morning of August 24, 1929, 3,000 Muslim men armed with swords, axes, and daggers marched through the Jewish Quarter of Hebron. They went from house to house, raping, stabbing, torturing, and in some cases castrating and burning alive their unarmed Jewish victims. The rioters who broke into Jewish homes did not distinguish between men, women, or children. Infants were slaughtered in their mothers' arms. Children watched as their parents were butchered by their neighbors. Women and teenage girls were raped. Elderly rabbis and yeshiva students were mutilated.

Sixty-seven Jewish men, women, and children were murdered, and dozens more wounded. Many of the victims knew their assailants by name. Until that day, the rioters had been their neighbors, landlords, friends.

Among the horrors were heroes: nearly two dozen Muslim men and women risked their own lives to save their Jewish neighbors. Estimates of how many Jews were rescued by Arabs differ from list to list. But at the very least, 250 Jews and their descendants owe their lives to these courageous men and women.

Those who survived were forced to leave Hebron, exiling one of the world's most ancient Jewish communities. For centuries, Muslims and Jews had lived harmoniously in Hebron. This was when that harmony ended, and the reality we know today began.

In Defense of Al-Aqsa

The riots of 1929 were driven by rumors that Jews were planning to conquer Al-Aqsa Mosque. Perched upon a sprawling courtyard on a biblical hilltop in Jerusalem, the mosque sits atop the ruins of the two ancient Jewish temples that were the centerpiece of the Hebrew nation. With the advent of Islam 600 years after the Second Temple's destruction by Roman conquerors, Al-Aqsa was built on the sacred site known to Jews as the Temple Mount. Jerusalem, the holiest city in Judaism, was the capital of the ancient kingdom of Judaea, from which Judaism derives its name. For millennia, Jews around the world have prayed in the direction of the Temple Mount, the single holiest site in Judaism.

In the year that preceded the riots, Haj Amin al-Husseini, the Grand Mufti of Jerusalem, waged a campaign of fear and propaganda to rally the Arabs of Palestine behind him, and to elevate his standing in the wider Muslim world. The Jews of Palestine, claimed the leader of Palestinian Muslims under British rule, sought to conquer Al-Aqsa to rebuild their holy temple. The Grand Mufti's campaign was wildly successful, galvanizing Islamic sentiment against the country's Jewish minority and against rising Jewish immigration from Eastern Europe, where pogroms were raging.

In sermons at Al-Aqsa the morning before the Hebron massacre, Islamic preachers called on the faithful to defend Al-Aqsa with their blood. Armed worshippers flowed from the mosque and down to the Old City, where they attacked Jewish passersby and set fire to Jewish businesses. The riots ricocheted throughout Palestine, killing 133 Jews and wounding 400 more.

The Jews of Hebron paid the heaviest price, suffering more death and brutality than any other community in Palestine. On the eve of the Hebron massacre, there were 800 Jews living among 20,000 Muslims in Hebron. Refusing to believe the many warnings they had received, the city's Jewish leaders rejected offers of protection from the Haganah, the underground Jewish defense force that would later become the Israel Defense Forces (IDF).

Writing of what he witnessed in Hebron in the days after the massacre, the British High Commissioner of Mandatory Palestine, Sir John Chancellor, wrote in his diary, "I do not think history records many worse horrors in the last few hundred years." It was both more deadly and more gruesome than the notorious Kishinev pogrom of 1903, which drove tens of thousands of Eastern European Jews to move to Palestine. Some of those who fled the shtetls of Europe built new lives in Hebron only to have them shattered by a different form of Jew hatred.

Grand Mufti Haj Amin al-Husseini, the father of Palestinian nationalism, would later flee Palestine and ally himself and his cause with Adolf Hitler. Living in a Nazi-financed villa in Berlin throughout World War II, Husseini became Hitler's chief Arab propagandist, and one of the most lavishly paid Nazi accomplices.

The First Sparks of a Holy War

The tensions between Palestine's Arab majority and its Jewish minority had already claimed dozens of lives by 1929. Yet the riots that engulfed Palestine that week marked the conflict's first mass casualty event, turning what had long been a sleepy province of the Ottoman Empire into what remains today a perpetual war zone.

Hebron would never be the same, nor would Palestine or the Jewish people. In many ways, the Hebron massacre is ground zero of this conflict. The hope that these two nations could coexist in peace was extinguished that day, in the sacred city where their ability to coexist had seemed most promising. From that moment on, Muslims and Jews would be engaged in a holy war for the soul of the Holy Land.

The Jewish leaders of Hebron did not believe, or want to believe, that their friends and neighbors would hurt them. After all, they were not militant Zionists, but pious Jews living a quiet existence centered around the Torah. That the massacre happened there, of all places, was a turning point for Zionism and the conflict itself.

In 1929, Zionism was not a mainstream Jewish value. Many Orthodox Jews, including David Shainberg, disdained the burgeoning movement as a secular contamination of Judaism. The return of the Jewish masses to Zion, they believed, could only be realized through God's will, and the arrival of the Messiah. Many secular American Jews also rejected Zionism, fearing it could threaten their fragile place in American society.

This antagonism was challenged by the Hebron massacre, which epitomized the tragedy of the stateless, powerless Jew. Those murdered that day were not Zionists rebuilding the Jewish homeland. They were unarmed women and children, yeshiva students, elderly rabbis, Arabic-speaking Sephardic Jews whose families had lived in Hebron for centuries. Thousands of Jews had returned to their biblical homeland to escape the pogroms of Russia, Ukraine, and Poland. That the pogrom followed them to the city of their forefathers was both devastating and galvanizing.

For centuries, Jews had been treated as unwanted strangers precisely because they lived in exile. European anti-Semites often urged Jews to go back to Palestine. Now they had come home, and the world was seemingly telling them they shouldn't be here either.

The failure of British forces to protect them in 1929 led the Jews of Palestine to unite around Zionism. After the massacre, many of those who had opposed it now agreed that Jews could only be safe in their own country, under the protection of their own army. This was also when many Zionists became radicalized, pursuing a forceful end to British rule and the establishment of an independent Jewish state.

The massacre of 1929 did not just strengthen Zionism. Forty years after the expulsion of Hebron's Jewish community, the settlement movement was born in Hebron. Early settlers envisioned themselves righting a historic wrong—returning an ancient Jewish community to its home. The settlers still see themselves that way.

Letters from Hebron

Until she discovered that box in the attic, Suzie Lazarov and her grown children knew very little about David's time in Hebron. "None of us knew we had these letters," Suzie told me years later. David's parents and siblings had done what their generation often did: they moved on from the trauma of David's death and focused on building their future.

The box from the attic revealed the missing pages not only of David's life, but of a Hebron that has ceased to exist. While David's letters depict a serenely peaceful city nestled in the Judaean Hills, today Hebron is the largest city in the West Bank, a massive urban sprawl whose streets are divided between Israeli and Palestinian territory. Before 1929, Hebron was a symbol of coexistence, the safest place to be a Jew in Palestine. Today, it is the opposite of both. The Old City is patrolled by hundreds of Israeli soldiers, stationed there to protect the settlers, and navigated through checkpoints. A microcosm of the dueling narratives that make peace between Israelis and Palestinians so unattainable, Hebron today represents the dreams of an exiled people to return to their homeland, and the sorrow of a people whose homeland is no longer their own. What is to some the face of Israel's military occupation is to others the face of the Jewish connection to this land and the Palestinian rejection of that history.

From the day he disembarked in Palestine on September 27, 1928, until four days before his death on August 24, 1929, David wrote home to Memphis every week. His eloquent letters paint a vivid portrait of Hebron before the massacre. David walked the alleyways of the Jewish Quarter, with its ancient stone homes arranged like puzzle pieces. He wrote of Jewish holidays and weddings attended by Hebron's Arab leaders and sheikhs, who danced into the night alongside rabbis. He described the Sephardic Jews of Hebron as indistinguishable from their Muslim friends and neighbors. David stood at the center of one of the most pivotal moments in Israel's pre-state history. The events he witnessed and lost his life to brought forth the reality in which Israelis and Palestinians live today.

When Suzie discovered David's letters, her daughter Jill Notowich was captivated by them. Between raising three children and running a handmade jewelry company, Jill had little free time. But over the course of ten years she organized, read, and digitized each one. Jill grew up in a Zionist home and had visited Israel many times, yet she never learned of the massacre until she was an adult. "We just didn't talk about it," she told me the first time I visited her in Memphis. "We're Southern. We like to sweep ugly things under the rug."

After organizing the letters, Jill archived them at her synagogue, Temple Israel, one of the oldest in the American South, founded in 1853. Yet Jill felt this treasure trove of history should not simply gather dust in an archive room in Memphis. She wanted to share David's story. And so, in 2019, Jill found me through a friend and entrusted me with David's letters, his diary, and the telling of this saga.

Truth Seekers

Like David, I too was a young American Jew who returned to the homeland. That, however, is where our similarity ends. David boarded a steamship to Palestine in 1928, when the Jewish state was nothing but a dream, when the Holocaust had not yet destroyed more than one-third of the world's Jewish population. I flew to the State of Israel in 2013 as a 27-year-old Jewish woman raised on the words *Never Again*. David hailed from Memphis, and spoke with a thick Tennessee twang, the way members of his family speak today. I'm from New Jersey, a less exotic home to American Jews. David settled in pastoral Hebron to study ancient Jewish texts. I moved to the liberal bastion of Tel Aviv to practice journalism. David arrived as a religious young man profoundly skeptical of secular Zionism. I came as a secular Jew deeply concerned by the direction in which religious extremists were leading the Jewish state. David and I both came to Hebron seeking truth, albeit a different truth in a vastly different Hebron.

Before I read David's letters, I knew little about the Hebron massacre or the history of Hebron. What I knew was that Hebron today is antithetical to the Hebron David described. The Hebron I knew was the godforsaken place I had visited once in 2011, and never wished to see again.

I was a student at Columbia's Graduate School of Journalism at the time. Led by Professor Ari Goldman, a former *New York Times* religion correspondent, and Adjunct Professor Gershom Gorenberg, author of *The Accidental Empire: Israel and the Birth of the Settlements, 1967–1977*, our Covering Religion class spent ten days reporting from Israel and the West Bank. Each of us covered a story of our choosing. My focus was a grassroots effort to teach Arabic—the language of 20 percent of Israel's population—to Jewish schoolchildren, who were learning only Hebrew and English. The force behind this effort was the Abraham Initiatives*, a Jewish-Arab nonprofit promoting equality in Israeli society, named for the common ancestor of Jews and Arabs.

As the only Jewish student in my Covering Religion class, and the only one to have visited Israel before, I knew more about Hebron than others in our group. Yet nothing had prepared me for what we encountered that day. Our tour was led by a member of Breaking the Silence, an organization founded by Israeli soldiers who had served in Hebron and objected to the injustices they were forced to carry out. They wanted Israelis to know what was being done in the name of security—nightly raids into randomly chosen Palestinian homes, beatings of those who resisted, stifling restrictions of movement on their own streets, and more.

Our tour began just outside Hebron, in the Jewish settlement of Kiryat Arba, at the grave of Jewish terrorist Baruch Goldstein. Just after dawn on February 25, 1994, the Brooklyn-born physician and resident of Kiryat Arba entered the Tomb of the Patriarchs and Matriarchs, the ancient burial site of Abraham and Sarah, Isaac and Rebecca,

---

* Not to be confused with the Abraham Accords.

Jacob and Leah. Sacred to both Jews and Muslims, the imposing stone
complex contains a synagogue and a mosque. As Muslim worshippers bowed their heads to the ground in prayer, Goldstein opened
fire, spraying bullets across the Hall of Isaac. By the time congregants
overtook him and beat him to death, Goldstein had killed 29 men and
boys and wounded more than 100 others.

When visiting a cemetery, it is Jewish custom to place a stone
on the grave of someone beloved or revered as a sign of respect and
mourning. The long gray slab of Goldstein's grave was covered in
stones. "To the holy Baruch Goldstein, who gave his life for the Jewish
people, the Torah, and the Land of Israel," read the words engraved on
his tombstone.

I knew about Goldstein's attack. I did not know he had so many
admirers.

The setting for his grave, in Meir Kahane Park, is itself a glorification of Jewish extremism, a memorial to Goldstein's mentor.
Meir Kahane, the godfather of today's Jewish nationalist movement,
was assassinated in Manhattan in 1990 in one of the earliest cases
of Islamic terrorism on US soil. The gunman, Egyptian American El
Sayyid Nosair, was acquitted following a trial in which his defense
was partly funded by Osama bin Laden. Nosair was later linked to the
1993 World Trade Center bombing.

As we stood around Goldstein's grave, listening to our professors
discuss his and Kahane's actions, a settler from Hebron approached
and listened, then attempted to forcefully remove us from the site.
He called a soldier and threatened to have us escorted out of Hebron
by the military if we didn't leave immediately. Knowing that this man
could easily end our tour, we left and made our way to Hebron.

Hebron is the only city in the West Bank that is populated by both
Israelis and Palestinians. While the notion of Jews and Muslims living
together in such a contentious place may sound like a remarkable sign
of hope, a walk through Hebron's Old City was a good way to extin-
guish that hope. The streets were dotted with memorials to Israelis as

young as 10 months old who had been killed there in terrorist attacks. Young soldiers with M16s slung over their shoulders stood guard at nearly every corner. Others sat behind the glass windows of checkpoints or gazed down from the rooftops of buildings. Lines of barbed wire scratched through every view of what could have been a beautiful landscape of ancient stone homes and terraced hillsides. The streets of the Old City were largely deserted, with Arab storefronts permanently shuttered. Some of the doors of abandoned Arab shops and homes had been spray-painted with blue Stars of David, as if to say, *this is ours now*. Others triumphantly declared "Am Yisrael Chai." *The people of Israel live.*

We walked through the Tomb of the Patriarchs and Matriarchs, the imposing stone edifice built by the Jewish king Herod in the first century BCE. Standing like a fortress atop the cave in which the Jewish forefathers and mothers are believed to be buried, it is one of the world's oldest structures still standing in one piece, still serving the same purpose it served 2,000 years ago. After Goldstein's attack, the holy site was divided into a Jewish side and a Muslim side. From the Jewish side of the tomb, we could hear the Muslim call to prayer, and see Muslim worshippers through the windows of rooms containing cenotaphs of the biblical forefathers and mothers. The cavernous space was humming with worshippers and tour groups, footsteps and blessings. Yet outside, the streets of Hebron were a ghost town.

Parts of Shuhada Street, the main artery of the Old City whose Arabic name means "Martyrs Street," are restricted to Jewish passage only. Jewish settlers, who numbered approximately 800 in this city of more than 250,000 Palestinians, walked with their heads held high, exchanging friendly greetings with the soldiers manning the streets. The few Palestinians we saw on the Israeli side of Hebron walked with their heads down.

Shuhada Street, to be sure, is an anomaly. The only street under Israeli control where Arabs require special permission to walk, it is a street whose Arab history has slowly been erased, as if to avenge the erasure of Jewish history in Hebron under Arab rule. We would later learn that most of Hebron is off-limits to Israelis, as 80 percent of the city is controlled by the Palestinian Authority. The restrictions on Shuhada Street were introduced in 2001, during the Second Intifada, or Palestinian uprising, when deadly terror attacks became a daily fact of life.

Military jeeps rolled by as our guide recounted his IDF service in Hebron. He and his comrades sometimes punished stone-throwing teenage boys by beating them. They conducted regular midnight raids of Palestinian homes, often for no reason other than to remind them who was in control. Every Palestinian was a suspect, treated as a potential terrorist. If a soldier saw a settler harassing a Palestinian, it was not his or her job to interfere. As our guide spoke, I gazed up at what I thought was an abandoned home and glimpsed a pair of tiny hands gripping the iron bars of a window. I locked eyes with a young Palestinian girl, who peered down at me with the look of a caged bird.

That day, a city that should be a monument to Judaism's ancient past, and could embody our shared future, became for me a symbol of Israel's moral unraveling. After moving to Tel Aviv two years later as a freelance journalist in 2013, I stayed away from Hebron. In October 2019, David's letters brought me back on a mission to comprehend how Hebron had come to this.

So began my journey into the heart of the place where the Jewish people at once most deeply belong, and where the consequences of our return home are most harshly felt. My quest to piece together David's life took me through his more than fifty lengthy letters to Memphis, hundreds of documents from the era of British Mandate Palestine, dozens of archival newspaper articles, films, memoirs, testimonies, books, and letters written by survivors of the massacre, and into Hebron itself on dozens of visits to get to know the Israelis and Palestinians who call this tortured city home.

The Jews of Hebron, who cling tightly to the memory of the massacre, are known for harboring some of the most violent elements of the settlement movement. That movement began in 1968, ten months after the Six-Day War, with the goal of reversing the expulsion of Jews from Hebron. Back then, it occupied the fringes of Israeli society. The radical rabbi Meir Kahane, whose anti-Arab ideology was informed by the Hebron massacre, was banned from the Knesset, Israel's parliament, his party outlawed as a terrorist group. By October 7, 2023, one of Kahane's disciples had reached the upper echelons of power. Israel's hardline national security minister, Itamar Ben-Gvir, who lives in Kiryat Arba, is the most prominent Kahanist in Israeli government, but he is not the only one. Palestinians from Hebron are also known for being among the most extreme, with many terrorist attacks emanating from the city. While the more secular Fatah faction technically rules the West Bank, support for the Islamist group Hamas is widespread in Hebron.

The Impact and the Echoes

Most people outside of Israel have either never heard of the 1929 massacre in Hebron or know very little about it. That massacre was the harbinger of the deadliest day for Jews since the Holocaust. The parallels between 1929 and 2023 are haunting, and too dangerous to ignore.

Hamas is the political descendant of the Grand Mufti Amin al-Husseini, the man who sparked this holy war a century ago. Just as the mufti claimed that the Jews of Palestine sought to destroy Al-Aqsa, Hamas perpetuates that claim today. Hamas named its October 7 onslaught Operation Al-Aqsa Flood, presenting itself as the defender of Islam against the Jews, just as the mufti did.

The euphoric celebrations in the West Bank and Gaza on October 7—the images of Palestinians crowding around tortured Israeli hostages in Gaza, cheering Hamas's attack—will not be forgotten in Israel. The perpetrators of the massacre in 1929 were also hailed as heroes. According to Palestinian polls, the majority in the West Bank and Gaza deny that Hamas murdered children, raped women, or killed any innocent civilians. Their supporters on college campuses blamed Israelis for the attack. In 1929, the atrocities in Hebron were also denied by Arabs in Palestine and blamed on the victims themselves.

Just as the Jews who were killed in Hebron in 1929 were not Zionists, the Jews killed in southern Israel on October 7 were not settlers. Many of them, in fact, were peace activists who spent decades building bridges with Palestinians and trying to help civilians in Gaza.

The rejection of a proposal for a two-state solution by every Palestinian leader in history began with the Grand Mufti, who dismissed the first two-state solution in 1937. He did so again in 1947, when the UN voted to partition Palestine into Jewish and Arab states. Palestine could have gained independence for the first time in its history. Instead, Palestine's Arabs and surrounding Arab states declared jihad against the Jews of Palestine. The war that ensued led to the flight and expulsion of more than 700,000 Palestinian refugees.

The mufti's political descendants have rejected every two-state solution they have been offered since. Their dedication to armed struggle has made life for Palestinians ever more hopeless, the prospects for peace ever more distant. It has also allowed Israel to expand the settlement enterprise, which began in Hebron.

The more attacks Israelis suffer, the more wary they become of the prospect of a Palestinian state. A century of Palestinian intransigence has now convinced even left-wing Israelis who oppose Netanyahu and his right-wing government that there truly is no partner for peace. If the massacre of 1929 led to the absolute transformation of the Middle East and laid the ground for the world's most enduring conflict, we can only imagine what the massacre of October 7 will leave in its wake.

This is a book about memory, and the political, religious, and emotional forces sustained by trauma. It is a story of tragedy and triumph, and a nation haunted by grief. Zoom in and this is a story of two nations that so deeply treasure this land, they are willing to die for it. Zoom out and it is the story of how one day can change the trajectory of history. It is the story of how holy places and our connection to them can be weaponized and exploited with the deadly power of disinformation. Rather than serving as the nexus of the shared history of Islam and Judaism, Abraham's burial ground has instead become a focal point of what is, in its essence, a holy war between two peoples who share the same forefather.

PART I

STATELESS

CHAPTER 1

The Floating Palace

SHORTLY BEFORE MIDNIGHT ON SEPTEMBER 12, 1928, DAVID
Shainberg boarded the RMS *Aquitania* at New York Harbor, beginning
his two-week journey at sea to Palestine. As the luxury steamer pulled
out of the port that windy night, David waved good-bye to the dozen
friends and mentors who had gathered at the dock to see him off.[1]

The *Aquitania* sailed out through the mouth of the Hudson River
and into the Atlantic Ocean, passing the Statue of Liberty, the same
monument David's parents gazed upon in awe when they sailed in
the opposite direction four decades earlier from Ukraine to their
version of the Promised Land. Lady Liberty symbolized the new life
that awaited the downtrodden Jews of Eastern Europe. America was
a place where they could practice their religion freely. Twenty-two-
year-old David saw the same statue as a false idol of hope for the
uprooted, wandering Jew.

Rejecting the prevailing ethos of assimilation into American culture, David sought a deeper connection to his roots through a life of
simplicity in his people's ancient homeland. While other young intellectuals were moving to Paris to find themselves, David was moving
to the land of the Bible. His destination was Knesset Israel, also known
as the Hebron Yeshiva, the Holy Land's largest and most prestigious
school of Jewish learning at that time.

Upon reaching Hebron, he would live footsteps from the Tomb
of the Patriarchs and Matriarchs, the 2,000-year-old stone palace,
beneath which lies the cave where Abraham, father of the Israelites,
is believed to be buried. Here, according to Jewish mystical tradition,
Abraham found the resting place of Adam and Eve, the entrance to

the Garden of Eden, and purchased the first plot of land owned by the Jewish people in the Land of Israel. That cave is where Abraham chose to bury his 127-year-old wife, Sarah, and where his sons Isaac and Ishmael buried him. It is through Isaac and Ishmael that the Jewish and Arab people trace their ancestry.

David's friends at the dock were now specks in the distance. He had just moved to New York from Memphis one year earlier, but in that short time had made many friends. All were either Jewish immigrants or sons and daughters of Jewish immigrants. They shared his dream of returning to their homeland, but David was the only one with the audacity to do it. In 1928, young men did not leave their family and move across the world to study ancient Jewish texts. In 1928, Zionism was not yet a prominent force in American Jewish life. The Land of Israel was still relegated to the pages of prayer books, the lyrics of Hebrew songs, the stories of Jewish sages.

David's closest friend in Brooklyn, Henry Chill, was meant to be on the *Aquitania* with him. Instead, Henry watched the steamer disappear into the horizon. He backed out at the last minute, blaming the opposition of his father and vowing to join David in a few months. David's Brooklyn housemate and tutor, Rabbi David Leib Genuth, had also come for the sendoff, along with his childhood friend from Memphis, Louis Engelberg.* Rabbi Georges Bacarat, the man who inspired David's spiritual awakening, was also there to say good-bye. Notably missing at the dock were David's own parents. They were not there to bid farewell to their eldest son, not only because they lived in Memphis, but because they opposed his decision. For recent Jewish immigrants to America, the notion of moving to Palestine was utterly insane. David was meant to finish business school and help run the family business, which his penniless father had started from nothing, and grown into a retail empire. David's parents were Jewish in every sense of the word,

---

* Genuth, who was born in Hungary, went on to become one of the most influential rabbis in Cleveland. Engelberg became the rabbi of Taylor Road Synagogue in Cleveland.

but not nearly as pious as David, who seemed to have taken things a bit too far. While he had mentioned his interest in studying in Hebron, he only notified his parents of his departure after purchasing his ticket to Palestine, in a letter he sent one week before his ship set sail. That letter arrived in Memphis while David was at sea.[2]

Though he yearned for it, David had never needed his father's approval. By now he had already dropped out of business school at Wharton, quit working at his father's store, and moved to Brooklyn to study Torah. After the destruction of the Jewish temples in Jerusalem, and with their exile from Israel, first by the Babylonians and then by the Romans, the Israelites became a wandering people with no country and no king. Flung across the ends of the earth for 2,000 years, they adopted new languages in foreign lands. What bound them together through centuries of dispersion was the Torah. Held by tradition to be the word of God, the Torah is the heart of the Jewish religion, a series of stories that explain Jews' existence and their connection to God, to each other, and to the Land of Israel.

David's father, Sam, a Ukrainian immigrant turned successful Memphis businessman with a growing chain of dry goods stores, could not comprehend David's devotion to ancient texts or his desire to study for spiritual, rather than financial, enrichment. As an unemployed Torah scholar, David could not afford the $260 passage to Palestine—equivalent to $4,750 today—without his father's help. Instead, he secured the support of an influential mentor. David's ticket was paid for by Wolf Gold*, a prominent globe-trotting rabbi who was

---

* Born in Germany in 1889, Wolf Gold descended from at least eight generations of rabbis. Ordained at the age of 17, he moved to the United States at the age of 18 and served as a rabbi in numerous communities, including Scranton, Chicago, San Francisco, and Brooklyn. In 1917 he established Torah Vodaath, a prominent Brooklyn yeshiva. David was likely introduced to Rabbi Gold by his brother, Henry Raphael Gold, who served as a rabbi at Memphis's Baron Hirsch Congregation from 1916 to 1919. Wolf Gold would go on to sign Israel's Declaration of Independence and become an early leader of the Religious Zionist movement.

also at New York Harbor that night to see him off. An early Religious Zionist leader, Gold shuttled between Palestine and the United States, where he raised support and funds for the Land of Israel.[3]

In a letter to his father one week before his departure, David laid on the Jewish guilt:

> Rabbi Wolf Gold is a comparative stranger. He however can perceive the value of the step I am taking, and if you will, of the sacrifice an American young man makes in devoting a few years to the study of our sacred Torah! Even a stranger can appreciate that, yet one's own family, one's own flesh & blood terms the phenomenon as "crazy." . . . Whether I succeed in a materialistic way or not I promise you from the very depths of my soul that you will never have cause to once regret the sacrifice in rearing me to manhood as concerns character and all that the word Jewishness represents.

The Shabbos Goy

Born in Memphis, Tennessee, on May 9, 1906, Aaron David Shainberg was known by friends and family as Dave. Slim and handsome with a thick Southern drawl and deep blue eyes, David was both wise beyond his twenty-two years and beloved by friends for his mischievous smile and wisecracking jokes. David's father, Sam, was born in Ukraine—what was then Tsarist Russia—as Schlome Schonberg in 1882. Fleeing the deadly anti-Semitism of the Russian Empire with his family, he arrived at the port of New York in 1891, then made his way to Memphis, home to a thriving Jewish community. Young Sam became a store clerk and then a department store cash boy, earning $3 a week and saving every cent. In 1904, he married Elizabeth May Lewis. Born Leah Tarschisch in Ukraine in 1878, she had immigrated to the US with her parents and siblings in 1897 and settled in Memphis. Between 1905 and 1911, Elizabeth gave birth to five children. First came Minnie, then David, followed by Nathan, Beatrice, and Herbert.

Shortly before marrying Elizabeth, Sam paid $375 for a half inter-
est in a dry goods store just outside of downtown Memphis. He soon
took over the store and named it Sam Shainberg Dry Goods. Sam,
Elizabeth, and their children lived upstairs. Over the next five decades,
Sam and his sons would turn that single shop into a multi-million-
dollar conglomerate, with thirty-seven Shainberg stores in Tennessee, Arkansas, Mississippi, Louisiana, Alabama, and Kentucky. When
the family unveiled a new shopping center in Memphis in 1954, they
invited a young local singer few Americans had heard of. He was a
friend of the Shainbergs who often served as the Shabbos Goy at their
synagogue, doing the kind of things that Jewish law prohibits on the
Sabbath, like turning the lights on and off. His name was Elvis Presley.[4]

Sam Shainberg served three terms as president of Baron Hirsch
Synagogue, a beacon of Judaism in the South. Established in downtown Memphis in 1862 by Jewish immigrants from Eastern Europe,
the synagogue was named after a Jewish philanthropist who chartered

The Shainberg family in front of the original Shainberg store on South Orleans Street
in Memphis, c. 1913. David is the boy whose face is blurred, fourth from right.

ships to bring persecuted European Jews to America, helping them settle throughout the country. Baron Hirsch is one of the oldest and largest Modern Orthodox congregations in America.[5]

Like most Jews in Memphis, the Shainbergs were not especially observant. They attended services on the high holidays and purchased their meat from the kosher butcher. Yet they drove to synagogue and worked on Shabbat, the busiest day of the week at the Shainberg store, and a day when both driving and working are prohibited by Jewish law. Charming young David was his father's star salesman, destined to carry on his legacy. Then, as a teenager, he became infatuated with Judaism. His inspiration was the Baron Hirsch rabbi, Georges Bacarat, a French Hasid who was educated in Europe and Egypt and adored by young members of the congregation.[6]

After hearing the rabbi's sermon one Saturday in December 1921, David decided that he would no longer work on Shabbat. He quickly went from playing craps at synagogue to becoming one of the rabbi's most dedicated pupils. David's life soon revolved around Baron Hirsch, where he founded a Junior Congregation, and became the youngest member of the synagogue's board of trustees. He managed to convince his father to close his store on Saturdays. Rabbi Bacarat led many of his acolytes to quit working on Shabbat, earning the ire of their merchant fathers, for whom Saturday was not a day of rest but a ticket to the middle class. Sam Shainberg and other leaders of the synagogue would later fire Rabbi Bacarat over this and other perceived transgressions, including his refusal to grant liquor permits to local wine dealers during Prohibition.[7]

After graduating from Memphis Central High School in 1923, David enrolled at Wharton, the business school at the University of Pennsylvania. He made close friends with other Jewish students and walked to synagogue on Shabbat. He excelled in his studies, cheered on Penn at football games, took long walks in Fairmount Park, learned to play the banjo, attended many parties, and went on many dates. After finishing his freshman year, he returned to Memphis in June of

1924, and was persuaded by Rabbi Bacarat not to return to Wharton. Though his father was disappointed, he desperately needed his son's help. For the next two years, David worked for his father by day and studied Torah by night.

From the Torah, David learned, came the world's most fundamental ideas of justice. The notion that every human being is created in the likeness of God, and therefore every life is sacred, first appeared in the Torah. The Golden Rule to treat others as you would like to be treated also emerged from the Torah, as did the concept of social justice. "Justice, justice, you shall pursue," God commands Jews in the Torah. According to the rabbinic sages, "The world endures because of three things: justice, truth, and peace."

David wrote in his diary that during these two years in Memphis, he underwent a spiritual transformation that gave him, for the first time in his life, "peace of mind and tranquility of soul." He came to see Rabbi Bacarat as a messenger of God. The rabbi, in turn, recognized in David a rare talent, and the potential to become a great Jewish leader. He encouraged David to further his studies in New York, at the Rabbi Isaac Elchanan Theological Seminary (RIETS), the rabbinical seminary of Yeshiva University.[8]

In 1927, David moved to Borough Park, Brooklyn, where he immersed himself in study groups with other young intellectuals. He enrolled at New York University, taking classes in English literature, public speaking, and European history. Yet David never felt quite right in New York. Despite his outer shell of dapper suits, Hollywood looks, his penchant for cigars and fedoras, and the calls of young women vying for his attention, David longed for a time gone by. In the pages of his diary, he wrote of trading his calendar of parties, opera, and theater for a more austere setting where he could fully explore his burgeoning spirituality.

Despite David's staunch opposition to the fledgling Zionist movement, he nevertheless followed the Zionist call to return to the Jewish homeland. In one letter to his parents from New York, he

A photo of David in his New York days, c. 1928.

described secular Zionism as a "worthless anti-Jewish cause." In another, he wrote of a Jewish deli that was not kosher enough, "I have seen more clearly than ever here in New York how the Zionists destroy everything Jewish, so open and fearless is this vile movement." Several months later, David revealed his conflicted feelings on the question of Jewish life in the Diaspora, writing, "Our position is never secure in the land of our adoption. We are forever no more than strangers."

David seemed to agree with the fundamental concept of Zionism: that after spending two millennia wandering the world without a home, the Jews needed a place to call their own if they wished to survive. Zionism arose in the late nineteenth century as a response to rising anti-Semitism in Europe. The national liberation movement popularized by the Austro-Hungarian Jewish journalist Theodor Herzl envisioned the return of a long-persecuted people to the ancestral homeland from which they had been exiled: Zion.

David's anti-Zionist stance coexisted with his love for the Land of Israel, and his camaraderie with early Zionist leaders such as Rabbi Wolf Gold. Undeterred by his rejection of the secular Zionist movement, David decided that the only place that could satiate his spiritual thirst was his people's spiritual wellspring.

A Small World After All

In a twelve-page letter to his parents written on the *Aquitania*'s stationary, David documented his journey aboard the luxury ocean liner. Larger and just as opulent as the *Titanic*, the *Aquitania* was, in David's words, a "veritable floating palace." At 900 feet long, 97 feet wide, and 92 feet deep, the *Aquitania* was taller than the Woolworth Building, the world's tallest skyscraper at the time. The ship had a ballroom, garden lounges, a restaurant that served (non-kosher) filet mignon and oysters on the half shell, and a kosher menu overseen by the Chief Rabbi of the British Empire.[9]

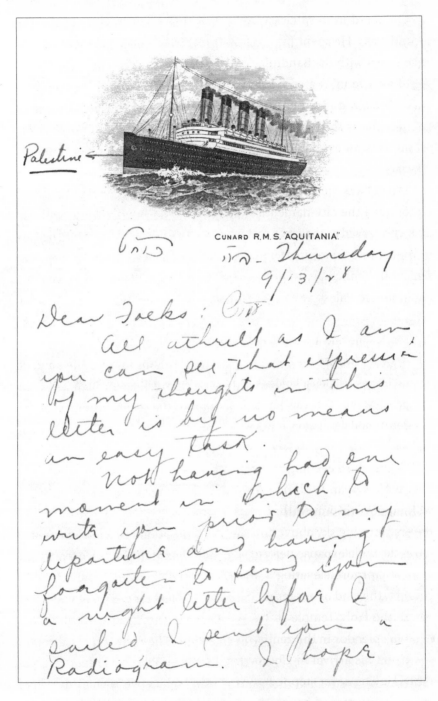

David's letter written at sea aboard the RMS *Aquitania*, September 13, 1928.

On board in third class, David quickly made friends in first and second class. He spent his days on the upper decks, in serendipitous encounters with the handful of other Jewish travelers. "'What a small world we live in' is a common observation," David wrote to his parents. "Seldom do we believe it. I do now. My cabin partner is a Mr. Levine, who is the founder and mayor of the colony Herzliya in Palestine. He's an ex-Tennessean, having resided in Chattanooga some 25 years."

David was referring to Shimon Zev Levine, who in 1924 co-founded the city named after Zionist forefather Theodore Herzl, and who served as the city's mayor. Born in Russia, Levine immigrated to the United States in 1903 following the Kishinev pogrom. Levine settled in Tennessee, where he worked at a car factory. In 1922, he emigrated to Palestine.

> Mr. Levine and I have daily discussions on the Zionist question, since we two are the only ones eating at the Jewish table. He is by no means religious, holds that the Jews are a nationality like other peoples, etc. You can imagine that we have plenty of topics for debate and discussion.

On his third evening at sea, David celebrated Rosh Hashanah, the Jewish New Year. With no synagogue, no service, and no quorum of worshippers to pray with, it was a strange holiday for David. With the shimmering sky above and the glistening sea below, he meditated upon the wide expanse before him, water as far as the eye could see.

"What more elevating a thought than that I am en route to our country, the land of our forefathers," he wrote to his parents. "The land where the Holy Temple stood, where Samuel, Saul, David, Solomon lived in splendor in the zenith of our people's history."

Upon his arrival in Cherbourg, France, David boarded a train to Paris. Having never stepped foot outside the US, every building, every street, every person he saw must have been a revelation. From there he took a train to Milan, marveling at the astounding beauty of the French countryside that rolled past his window. As the sun set over the Swiss frontier, David's train crossed into Switzerland, and beneath a blanket of stars into Italy, where he boarded a train to Venice. There he walked the city's serpentine canals and narrow streets. Arriving in Trieste just before Shabbat on Friday, September 21, David rushed aboard the ship that would take him to Alexandria, Egypt. Yom Kippur, the Day of Atonement, fell on the third night of David's voyage to Egypt. He wrote in his letter that he took advantage of the moonlit Mediterranean night and the endless blue water to reflect on the year behind him. His intention for the next two years was clear: like a Jewish monk, he would devote himself day and night to the study of Talmud. *Who knows*, he may have thought, *perhaps I will become a great rabbi.*

Disembarking in Alexandria, David journeyed to Cairo with seven other passengers, including four Englishmen, a Zionist from New Jersey, an office worker from Jerusalem, and a Jewish Palestinian* lawyer. David spent the night in Cairo and the following day toured the pyramids of Giza on a camel's back. The next day, he sailed to the first modern Hebrew city, home to the radiant white buildings and breezy boulevards that had just been built out of sand dunes by Jewish exiles who gathered from every corner of the earth to realize a 2,000-year-old dream. David was on his way to Tel Aviv.

In a postcard from Cairo to his best friend in Memphis, Israel Kanarek, David described the journey as his own personal exodus. As his rickety boat approached the shores of Palestine, David was blissfully unaware of the holy war that was brewing.

---

* Both Jews and Arabs living in Palestine at the time were considered Palestinian. In his letters David often describes Jewish natives of the land as Palestinians.

CHAPTER 2

The All-Too-Promised Land

On November 2, 1917, as Allied forces advanced into Ottoman-ruled Palestine, British foreign secretary Lord Arthur James Balfour penned a letter at his desk in London to one of the most illustrious Jewish citizens of the United Kingdom. Addressing Walter Rothschild, a former member of Parliament and second baron of the famed Rothschild banking family, the former prime minister of Great Britain wrote, "His Majesty's Government view with favour the establishment in Palestine of a national home for the Jewish people, and will use their best endeavours to facilitate the achievement of this object . . ."

The Balfour Declaration would become one of the most consequential proclamations of the British crown: heralded by one people, reviled by another. In March 1919, after the British conquered Palestine from the Ottoman Empire, President Woodrow Wilson voiced American backing for the decision. "The Allied Nations, with the fullest concurrence of our Government and our people, are agreed that in Palestine shall be laid the foundations of a Jewish commonwealth," Wilson declared.

On July 24, 1922, the League of Nations granted Great Britain the official mandate to govern Palestine on behalf of the international community. The Balfour Declaration was a central pillar of the Mandate for Palestine. While the British committed to establishing a "Jewish national home," the text of the mandate stipulated that "nothing shall be done which may prejudice the civil and religious rights of existing non-Jewish communities in Palestine."[1]

Great Britain's support for the Zionist cause could not have come at a more desperate time for the Jewish people. Between 1918 and

1921, more than 100,000 Jews were murdered in pogroms in Ukraine, Poland, and Russia. While Jews had lived in the Land of Israel since biblical times, that land had been under Muslim rule for more than 1,000 years. As second-class citizens, Jews' religious freedom had been limited, their political aspirations suppressed, and their numbers kept to a minimum by Jewish immigration restrictions. The Balfour Declaration put an end to those restrictions, albeit briefly. With the gates of the United States narrowing to Jewish immigrants due to isolationist quotas—then slammed shut by the Immigration Act of 1924—the Israelites who were scattered throughout the globe began their steady return to their newly open home.

The British would later abandon the Balfour Declaration under Arab pressure, but its impact was quickly felt. When the Mandate began in 1922, Palestine's population was 757,000, including 590,000 Muslims, 73,000 Christians, and 84,000 Jews. By 1928, the Jewish population had nearly doubled to 150,000. Nevertheless, in 1929, the Jewish community of Palestine was a constellation of islands in an Arab sea. Even in Jerusalem, where Jews were a majority, the city felt "as Arab as Cairo or Baghdad," wrote the famed American correspondent Vincent Sheean of his time in Palestine in 1929. The haunting sound of the Islamic call to prayer wafted through every street, piercing the air at sunrise, sunset, and late into the night, Sheean wrote.[2]

To the Arabs of Palestine, the Balfour Declaration was a shocking betrayal. During World War I, when Palestine was ruled by the Ottoman Empire, the British had convinced thousands of Arabs from Palestine, Syria, Transjordan, and Southern Arabia to rebel against their Turkish rulers in exchange for independence. In leaflets dropped by British planes over Palestine, the British army addressed Arab soldiers of the Ottoman army with a plea from Hussein ibn Ali, the King of Hejaz and the Emir of Mecca. In 1916 Hussein proclaimed himself King of the Arabs and entered negotiations with the British for the freedom of all Arab lands ruled by the Ottomans. "The Arab Kingdom has been for a long time in bondage to the Turks, who have killed your brethren, and crucified your men and disported your women and families," read the leaflets. "Come and join us who are labouring for the sake of religion and the freedom of the Arabs."[3]

In a series of letters known as the McMahon-Hussein correspondence, exchanged between King Hussein and British High Commissioner of Egypt Sir Henry McMahon between July 1915 and March 1916, McMahon vowed to recognize Arab independence in return for Hussein's agreement to launch an Arab rebellion against the Ottoman Empire. The revolt began in Medina on June 5, 1916. The ensuing assistance of Arab soldiers was pivotal to the Allied defeat of the Ottoman Empire, with rebel fighters helping British soldiers expel Turkish forces from lands they had ruled for centuries. In Palestine, thousands of Arab fighters deserted their posts in the Turkish army to fight for the Allies, aiding the British in their victory over the Ottoman Empire. It had not been difficult to convince Arabs to turn against the Turks. By the end of Ottoman rule, Arabs in Palestine were dying of hunger and disease. Some parents killed themselves to avoid watching their children starve to death. Others sold their babies for food.

By 1917, Jews and Arabs alike were praying for the British to liberate them from the Turks. When British troops arrived in Jerusalem on December 9, 1917, crowds of Arab and Jewish residents greeted them as heroes.[4]

Arab rebels turned their weapons over to the British with the expectation of gaining independence for a unified Arab state stretching from Syria to Yemen. Instead, they learned of the Balfour Declaration and the secretive Sykes-Picot agreement of 1916, in which France and the United Kingdom carved up former Ottoman territory into British and French control. Sheikh Freih Abu Middein, the Chief Sheikh of Beersheba who recruited hundreds of Bedouin tribesmen to fight alongside the British, would later testify to a British commission, "If we knew that the promise was given to the Jews, we would not have before given any assistance to Great Britain."[5]

The Jews of Palestine quickly laid the groundwork for their future state, building dozens of new towns and socialist agricultural communes, which they called kibbutzim. They developed the infrastructure, industries, banks, welfare organizations, educational, medical, and labor institutions that continue to serve Israeli society today. Between 1920 and 1930, Jews purchased 172,000 acres of land at a cost of nearly £8 million ($39 million). Jewish land ownership nearly doubled, from 160,000 to 300,000 acres. This land was typically acquired from wealthy absentee Arab landowners. The purchase of these lands, often for far more than they were worth, sometimes displaced peasant farmers who subsisted on the land. Some farmers were compensated by the Jews who purchased the land, or given other land on which to live. Others were not.[6]

Among those selling their property were leaders of the Arab nationalist movement, the same men who were vehemently protesting Jewish land purchases and immigration. They included members of the powerful Husseini family, at least eight Arab mayors, and various leaders of the anti-Zionist Arab Higher Committee. One prominent Arab attorney who helped Jews purchase land later went to the British High Commissioner of Palestine demanding a prohibition on exactly these sales. Despite their protests, there was, in fact, more Arab-owned earth for sale than Zionist funds available to buy it.[7]

Much of the land they purchased was infested with malaria-carrying insects or uncultivated, having laid dormant for centuries. Nevertheless, the influx of these Jewish newcomers and their progressive, egalitarian way of life aroused suspicion and fear among the Arab villagers who lived near them—and whose highly traditional, patriarchal way of life could not have been more different from that of their new neighbors. These misgivings would soon be exploited by Arab leaders.[8]

The convergence of two struggles for self-determination was, perhaps, destined to erupt into civil war. For what was to the Jews an ingathering of exiles to their native land and a historic righting of so many wrongs was to the Arabs a colonial enterprise. After Hitler rose to power and European Jewry entered its darkest hour, the British would reverse their commitment to the Zionist cause, placing severe restrictions on Jewish immigration and land purchases to appease Arab fury. Yet the wheels of strife were already in motion.

By the time David Shainberg arrived in Palestine, the friction between Zionism and Arab nationalism was on the verge of erupting into an outpouring of violence, the likes of which the Holy Land had not seen in nearly a millennium. The instigator of that eruption was a young Arab aristocrat who likely would have spent his life in obscurity had it not been for a historic miscalculation by a British Zionist, who plucked him from political exile and made him the first leader of Palestine's Arabs and the father of their nationalist movement.

CHAPTER 3

The Grand Mufti

They called him Faithful.

Born in Jerusalem in 1895* to one of the most prominent Arab families in Palestine, Amin al-Husseini was preordained to a life of luxury. A large and wealthy clan of landowners, the Husseini family traced its lineage to the grandson of the Prophet Muhammad. Under Ottoman rule, the Husseinis produced a long line of Jerusalem mayors and muftis (the chief Islamic official in the Holy Land). Amin's father was Mufti of Jerusalem, as was his father's father.[1]

Amin, the Arabic word for "faithful," was born to his polygamous father's second wife, Zeinab. After attending a Turkish government school in Jerusalem, Amin studied in Cairo under the Islamic scholar Sheikh Rashid Rida, who taught an ultraconservative brand of Islam that advocated the establishment of a global Islamic Caliphate. Amin went on to Al-Azhar, Cairo's preeminent Islamic university, for one year. Failing to complete his studies, he never earned the honorific of Sheikh. At the age of 18, he made a pilgrimage to Mecca, fulfilling the Muslim duty of Hajj. As one of the five pillars of Islam, Hajj is the most significant event a Muslim can experience. From then on, he was known as Haj Amin.[2]

He developed his loathing of Jews from a young age. As a teenager, Amin learned of the Prophet Muhammad's complex relationship with the Jewish tribes of Arabia, descendants of the ancient Israelites who

---

* The mufti's true year of birth is a mystery, as various sources provide varying dates. It has been generally agreed by historians of the mufti that he was born in 1895.

had arrived there after their expulsion from the Kingdom of Judaea. While most Jews in Medina rejected Muhammad as a prophet and did not join his new faith, nearly two dozen Jewish tribes accepted his political leadership and signed a treaty with him. Muhammad married two Jewish women and established close diplomatic and economic relations with the Jewish tribes. One tribe, however, the Banu Qurayza, switched sides, and Muhammad ordered the execution of all its adult men. Hundreds of Jewish men were beheaded, and their women and children enslaved. Gradually, the Jewish presence in Medina declined, and Muhammad expelled the last two remaining tribes from the city. Haj Amin was taught that as the living embodiment of the rejection of Islam, Jews would forever be condemned as infidels.[3]

During his tenure as Mufti of Jerusalem, Haj Amin's father, Tahir, was a fierce early opponent of Zionism, using his power to block Jewish immigration and land purchases in Jerusalem. In 1899, Tahir proposed that "new arrivals be terrorized prior to the expulsion of all foreign Jews established in Palestine since 1891." And yet, he also sold land to Jews in Jerusalem.[4]

Upon Tahir's death in 1908, his eldest son, Kamel, succeeded him. British authorities later anointed him Palestine's first Grand Mufti, a title inspired by Egypt's Grand Mufti. Unlike his father, Kamel pursued cooperation with the Jewish community.[5]

Haj Amin, however, took after his father. After World War I, he returned to Jerusalem, where he joined the emerging Arab nationalist movement. His virulent anti-Jewish speeches outside of mosques and his writing in Arab nationalist journals garnered him a loyal following.[6]

When his half-brother Kamel died in 1921, the all-important post of Grand Mufti was left vacant. Twenty-six-year-old Haj Amin was far from an obvious replacement. Just five months earlier, he had been living in Transjordan, where he had gone into hiding with Bedouin tribes.

"Palestine Is Our Land, the Jews Are Our Dogs"

The annual pilgrimage Nebi Musa was the largest Islamic festival in the region. The annual procession led from Jerusalem to the site in the Judaean Desert where Muslims believe Moses, Nebi Musa in Arabic, is buried. Celebrated since the days of Sultan Saladin, Nebi Musa was the most important Islamic pilgrimage site in Palestine. During Ottoman rule, the Turks deployed thousands of soldiers to maintain order. New to the area, the British did no such thing.[7]

On the morning of April 4, 1920, some 70,000 Muslim men gathered in Jerusalem's Old City, far more than in years past. "We won the country by the sword, we will keep the country by the sword!" they cried, recalling the Muslim conquest of Jerusalem from the Byzantine Empire a millennium earlier. Arab nationalists, including Haj Amin, incited the crowds from balconies. Holding a portrait of Syria's Emir Faisal, Amin proclaimed, "This is your king!"[8]

The declaration of rebellion was clear: Palestine's Arabs would not answer to the British crown. Haj Amin's uncle, Musa Kazim al-Husseini, the mayor of Jerusalem, called on Muslims to "spill their blood" for Palestine. Aref al-Aref, a prominent Arabic writer who would later become mayor of Jerusalem, declared, "Palestine is our land, the Jews are our dogs!" Crowds erupted in cheers, joined by applause from Arab policemen who had been deployed by the British to keep the peace.[9]

Riots swiftly gripped Jerusalem. Arabs beat and stoned Jews in the alleyways of the Old City, ransacked homes and shops in the Jewish Quarter, and set fire to a yeshiva after tearing up its Torah scrolls. Dozens of Jews were attacked over the course of that day and night. Children were beaten, women were raped, and men were killed. Early the next morning, the British withdrew their forces from Jerusalem and sealed off the city, forbidding anyone from entering or leaving. Though they declared martial law later that day and sent in troops to quash the riots, it would take three days to restore order. By then 5 Jews had been killed and 216 wounded. Four Arabs were also killed in

The Nebi Musa procession in Jerusalem's Old City, April 1920.

the riots, including a girl who fell from a window after being struck in the head by a stray bullet.[10]

Muslims heralded the event as a revolt against the Balfour Declaration. The police issued arrest warrants for 200 people, including Haj Amin and his uncle Musa Kazim. Both promptly fled Jerusalem, crossing the Jordan River into Transjordan, where they were sentenced in absentia to ten years in prison for incitement. Thirty-nine Jews were also arrested, including Ze'ev Jabotinsky, a charismatic Zionist leader and journalist from Odessa who cofounded the Jewish Legion of the British army in the first World War. Having organized self-defense units during the pogroms in Russia, Jabotinsky was now training Palestine's Jews in self-defense and firearms.[11] Just weeks before the pilgrimage to Nebi Musa, he had helped to establish the Haganah, the Zionist paramilitary organization. The Haganah, the Hebrew word for "defense," was created to empower Jews to protect themselves from Arab attacks.

On April 4, 1920, Jabotinsky had amassed some 600 young men to aid the Jews under assault in Jerusalem's Old City. British forces kept them outside the city walls. They wouldn't have been of much help, anyway—most of the men, some as young as 13, were armed with sticks. Their training center was a Jerusalem playground, and they stored their weapons at a local library. After finding three rifles, two pistols, and 250 bullets in Jabotinsky's house, the British sentenced him to fifteen years in prison.[12]

Three months later, British prime minister David Lloyd George appointed Sir Herbert Samuel, one of the most prominent British Jews, as first High Commissioner of Palestine. A member of Lloyd George's Liberal party and one of England's most esteemed statesmen, Herbert Samuel was the first Jew to hold a cabinet position. As British home secretary, he had championed women's rights. He was also an ardent supporter of the Zionist dream to establish a Jewish state in the Jewish homeland, and the first British government official to endorse that dream, before Balfour. Now, he was the first Jew to govern the Land of Israel in 2,000 years.[13]

Upon assumption of his duties in July of 1920, Samuel sought to ingratiate himself with Palestine's Arab majority. To demonstrate that he would represent all the country's inhabitants, he ordered the pardoning and release of all Palestinians convicted in the wake of the riots, both Jewish and Arab. Jabotinsky was freed from a medieval prison in Acre, and Haj Amin was permitted to return from hiding in Transjordan. He arrived in Jerusalem in September, and upon the death of his half-brother Kamel five months later, announced his candidacy for the position of Grand Mufti.

There were three other contenders for the job: all of them more qualified, more moderate, and far less anti-Semitic than Haj Amin. His chief rival was nominated by an equally prominent Jerusalem family, the Nashashibis. After the riots of 1920, Haj Amin's uncle Musa had been deposed as mayor of Jerusalem and replaced by Ragheb Bey al-Nashashibi. Mayor Nashashibi actively campaigned against Haj

Amin, who came in fourth—dead last—in the April 1921 elections. Yet according to regulations, it was up to the high commissioner to appoint the new mufti from among the three leading candidates. The Husseini family launched a protest campaign, charging that the Jews had exerted their "sinister" influence against Haj Amin's candidacy. A notice posted in the Old City proclaimed, "Wake up Moslems, the Jews are interfering in the election of the mufti." It went on to warn Arabs that the Nashashibi-backed candidate "would hand over to the Jews the Dome of the Rock and the Aqsa Mosque so that they might pull them down and rebuild the Temple."

The pressure worked. The Nashashibi-backed candidate dropped out of the race, and in a curious failure of his better judgment, Sir Herbert Samuel appointed Haj Amin al-Husseini as Grand Mufti of Jerusalem on May 8, 1921. The position came with a lifetime tenure. Husseini was no stranger to the British. As a 19-year-old officer in the Ottoman army during World War I, he had left his post to recruit 2,000 Arabs to join the revolt against the Turks in Jerusalem.[14]

In 1922, Haj Amin was elected president of the Supreme Muslim Council, a centralized body created by High Commissioner Samuel in 1921 to oversee Palestine's mosques, Sharia courts, and religious schools. Perhaps most importantly, the Supreme Muslim Council oversaw all Waqf property: lands and shrines that were held as charitable trusts, which included the Haram al-Sharif, or Temple Mount, and the Western Wall. The two powerful positions transformed Haj Amin into the indisputable leader of Palestine's Muslims.

The appointment of a man who never completed his religious studies to the highest Islamic calling in the Holy Land drew some controversy. Though Husseini sought to reinvent his biography throughout the years, claiming to be ordained as a Muslim cleric with the requisite knowledge of Sharia law, he had never obtained a degree or taken the necessary study for ordination as a legal scholar.[15]

A slight man with fair skin, blond hair, blue eyes, a trim red beard, and a disarming smile, Haj Amin wore long traditional robes and a white turban wrapped around a red fez. From the beginning of his tenure, he was already emerging as the father of Palestinian-Arab nationalism.[16]

Until the early 1920s, there had been little to no discussion of a Palestinian nation. Haj Amin, like other Muslim leaders in Palestine, championed the ideology of a Greater Syria, in which Palestine would represent Southern Syria. After France defeated Syria's King Faisal in July 1920, putting an end to that idea, Amin and other Arab notables envisioned a new goal: an independent Palestine, centered in Jerusalem.[17]

Palestinian nationalism was born as a direct response to Zionism. Palestine, after all, had never been free or independent. Before the British conquest in 1917, Palestine had been ruled by the Ottomans, who followed the Mamluks, who followed the Ayyubids, who followed the Crusaders, who followed a long list of foreign powers going back to the Romans. And yet, because so many of those ruling factions were Islamic empires, they were not seen by Palestinian Muslims as foreign. The prospect of Palestine becoming home to a large Jewish population, in which Muslims could become a minority, threatened centuries of Muslim hegemony. In the first decade of the British Mandate, Palestine's Jewish population grew by 300,000, giving fuel to those fears.[18]

Keep Your Enemies Close

Douglas Valder Duff, a Royal Navy officer and police constable stationed in Jerusalem during the Grand Mufti's reign, wrote a fascinating memoir detailing his time in Palestine. In it, he described Haj Amin as "both unscrupulous and treacherous" and "among the more picturesque and romantic figures of our modern days." A post–World War II CIA profile of Haj Amin would later note, "Part of his charm lies in his deep Oriental courtesy: he sees a visitor not only to the door but to the gate as well and speeds him on his way with blessings." Yet this soft-spoken, seemingly mild-mannered cleric had a sinister side.

"In spite of his genteel charm," the CIA noted, he "is ruthless toward his opponents."[19]

Haj Amin assured British officials that he would cooperate with them, and that he was the only Arab leader in Palestine who could maintain peace. It was best, the British thought, to keep him close. After all, the Husseini family had filled the position of Jerusalem's Grand Mufti for generations. As a Jew and a Zionist, High Commissioner Samuel had the trust of the country's Jewish population. By supporting Haj Amin, he hoped to win the trust of the Arab population. The decision would come to be regarded as one of Samuel's greatest blunders.[20]

Grand Mufti Haj Amin al-Husseini in Jerusalem, 1937.

CHAPTER 4

Memphis Meets Palestine

DAVID'S BOAT CREPT TOWARD THE ANCIENT PORT OF JAFFA. JUST south of Tel Aviv, the city's silhouette of sandstone towers and minarets welcomed David to a land he had seen only in his dreams. Drifting past wooden fishing boats, he pulled into one of the world's oldest seaports, serving for at least 4,000 years as a gateway to Jerusalem and an ancient center of trade. It was here in the Jaffa port, David may have thought to himself, that the biblical Jonah began his fateful journey into the mouth of a whale.

David disembarked in Jaffa amidst a frenzy of Arab porters who rushed to greet new immigrants and tourists, offering to carry their luggage and transport them by horse and wagon to their destination. Compared to previous years, Jaffa's docks were relatively empty of new arrivals. Palestine was in the throes of an economic crisis. In 1927, more Jews left the country than arrived on its shores. More than half of the 13,000 Jews who arrived in 1926 had left. The year David arrived saw just 2,000 new immigrants.[1]

The day was September 27, 1928, fifteen days since he pulled out of New York Harbor. David sent word to Memphis as quickly as he could, writing a breathless letter to his parents that night. "Eretz Yisrael exceeds my most fantastic visions and dreams," he wrote, referring to the land by its biblical Hebrew name, used by many Jews at the time. "My happiness now that I am at my destination knows no bounds."

He closed his letter with a plea to his parents. "Please I ask you, write me often, at least two or three times a week. Remember I am thousands of miles away and that news from home and from loved ones particularly comes like water to a desert traveler."

David spent his first days in the Holy Land at the Tel Aviv home of Rabbi Wolf Gold, the Religious Zionist who had paid his ticket to Palestine.*2 It was the beginning of Sukkot, the Feast of the Tabernacles, when Jews commemorate their forty-year journey through the desert from Egypt to the Land of Israel. With Rabbi Gold in New York, David celebrated with Gold's wife and children in their home on Kalischer Street, bordering the open-air Carmel Market in the city's Yemenite Quarter. Founded by Jews from Yemen in the late nineteenth century, it was the first neighborhood to be built outside of Jaffa. Like most of Tel Aviv at the time, its streets were made of sand.[3]

Tel Aviv emerged as a small suburb of Jaffa, a predominantly Arab city. Founded in 1909, Tel Aviv was the brainchild of the exiled Jews of Jaffa, who fled harassment and attacks by their Muslim neighbors. Those attacks had culminated in the riots of May 1921, which began in Jaffa and killed 47 Jewish men, women, and children across the country. Those riots led the British to grant municipal independence to Tel Aviv, an all-Jewish city. In 1920, the city's population numbered 10,000. By 1929, it had reached 30,000.[4]

Despite Tel Aviv's reputation as a beacon of secularism, David was enchanted by what he described as "a most modern and magnificently pretty city." Just a decade earlier, these bustling streets, now filled with cafés and shops bearing Hebrew names, had been a vast expanse of swamps and sand dunes. Hebrew, one of the world's oldest living languages, had just been revived by a wave of new immigrants, who sought a common tongue that would unite the Jews who had returned to their homeland from across Europe and the Middle East. The only ancient language to die and be revived centuries later, Hebrew had been spoken by their ancestors in ancient times, but had since been relegated to prayer and religious study.

For all his admiration, David was eager to reach Hebron. But first, he visited the holiest of holy cities, just 30 miles southeast. Perched high on a plateau in the Judaean Hills, surrounded by streams and valleys and dominated by the Mount of Olives, Mount Scopus, and

David Shainberg, shortly after arriving in Palestine, 1928.

the walled Old City, Jerusalem's majesty left David awestruck. As one of three pilgrimage festivals in the Hebrew Bible, the Israelites were commanded to visit the holy temple in Jerusalem during Sukkot, one of three pilgrimage festivals in the Hebrew Bible. David approached the Temple Mount just as a century-long battle over that very site began to take shape.[5]

The Wall

According to Jewish tradition, the Temple Mount is the site of the Foundation Stone, the spiritual junction of Heaven and Earth where God created the world and its first human being, Adam. Mount Moriah, where the First and Second Temples once stood, is the biblical site of the binding of Isaac, and where the Third Temple will be built when the Messiah comes. As the heart of worship in ancient Israel, the temple served as the resting place for the Ark of the Covenant, holding the stone tablets Moses received on Mount Sinai. The innermost sanctum of the temple housed the Holy of Holies, where the divine presence was believed to dwell.

The history of the Jewish people is largely told through the history of the temples that once stood there. The First Temple, built in the tenth century BCE, was sacked by the Babylonians in 586 BCE, sending the Israelites into exile in Babylon, what is today Iraq. After the fall of Babylon to the Persian Empire in 539 BCE, Jews returned to Jerusalem and rebuilt their temple. The Second Temple stood for nearly 600 years until that too was destroyed. After laying siege to Jerusalem in 70 CE, Roman emperor Titus brought Jewish slaves back to Rome to build the Colosseum. That dramatic chapter of history is depicted on the Arch of Titus in Rome.

It was during this time that ancient Israel became Palestine. The Kingdom of Judaea had been the epicenter of the Jewish rebellion against Roman rule. As punishment, the Romans renamed the land Palestina, after the Israelites' biblical enemies, the Philistines.[6]

With the Muslim conquest of Jerusalem 600 years later, Judaism's holiest site became home to Al-Aqsa, the third holiest place in Islam after Mecca and Medina. According to Islamic tradition, this is where the Prophet Muhammad ascended to heaven upon a magical winged steed named Al-Buraq.

The Western Wall is all that remains of the ancient retaining wall surrounding the Temple Mount. The Western Wall, also known as the Wailing Wall, is where Jews have mourned the destruction of ancient Israel and prayed for its redemption for centuries. Dating to the sixth century BCE, the Western Wall is the holiest place in the world where Jews are permitted to pray. With the second Muslim conquest of Jerusalem in the twelfth century CE, the Temple Mount became off-limits to Jews. To this day, only Muslims are permitted to pray there.[7]

Israel in the Exile

Just outside the Temple Mount, David experienced the otherworldly power of the Western Wall, in all its beauty and its sorrow. He placed his hands on its stones, made smooth by centuries of worshippers who had done the same. He may have imagined the generations of Jews before him who had recited the thrice-daily prayer for a return to Zion.[8]

As David touched the wall's colossal stones, dating back 2,000 years to the Jewish king Herod, he was appalled by the site's neglect. The cramped space where Jews were permitted to pray was just 11 feet wide, 100 feet long, and littered with waste from the Arab neighborhood abutting the wall. Residents of the Mughrabi Quarter, named for the North African Muslims who lived there, often cursed, spat, and hurled garbage at Jewish worshippers. Arab residents walked through the narrow passageway with their donkeys, which sometimes relieved themselves beside Jews in prayer. The Western Wall and the Mughrabi Quarter, like the Temple Mount, were property of the Waqf.[9]

"It was enough to break one's heart," David wrote of his first visit to the Wailing Wall. "There, close by the reeking odor of the narrow, dirty streets of the 'old Jerusalem,' a Jew realizes that the glory of G-d has departed from Zion and that Israel is in the exile. And much more so especially at this time."

David arrived in Jerusalem on October 2, 1928, one week after an infamous scandal at the wall.

On September 23, 1928, the eve of Yom Kippur, hundreds gathered there for the holiest day on the Hebrew calendar, when Jews around the world fast, pray, and seek divine forgiveness. As they had done in years past, they brought in a wooden divider to separate men and women, a custom of modesty dating back to the Second Temple period.

This time, Muslim authorities balked. The Grand Mufti and other members of the Supreme Muslim Council appealed to British officials. The Jews, they argued, were overstepping their rights, trying to take control of the Western Wall and, with it, Al-Aqsa. The seemingly

Jewish worshippers at the Western Wall, c. 1910–14.

innocuous cloth-covered wooden frame was merely the Jews' first step in turning the wall into a synagogue, they claimed. In a meeting at the Muslim religious court with Edward Keith-Roach, the British district commissioner of Jerusalem, a group of sheikhs said they would not be responsible for the consequences if the divider was not removed. After leaving the court, which looked out over the Western Wall, Keith-Roach walked down to the wall and approached Rabbi Noah Glasstein, who was overseeing Yom Kippur services. The divider must go, Keith-Roach told him. Glasstein agreed to remove it, but asked if he could wait until after services. The district commissioner approved and carried on with his day.[10]

Patrolling the area that evening, British officer Douglas Duff found that the divider was still standing. If it was still there at 7:00 the next morning, Duff warned Rabbi Glasstein, he would destroy it. Again, Glasstein said he would take care of it. He did not.

Shortly after daybreak on Monday morning, September 24, amidst the Jews' solemn prayers on their most sacred day at the holiest site accessible to them, British officers stormed the Western Wall as if going into battle. Joined by ten armed policemen in steel helmets, Duff was cheered on by crowds of Arabs, many of them holding daggers and sticks. "Kill the Jewish dogs!" they cried. "Islam is endangered. Strike!"[11]

Encountering dozens of poor, elderly Jewish men and women immersed in prayer and weak from fasting, the officers pulled chairs and benches out from beneath those who refused their orders. Worshippers who tried to prevent the screen's removal were beaten by police. When a sergeant tried to destroy the divider, one man wrapped his arms around it, yelling that even if they killed him, he would not let go. Duff and his troops dragged the divider away, along with the man hugging it, and hurled them down a cactus-filled valley.[12]

The use of force against Jewish worshippers on their holiest day at such a sensitive site drew condemnation from Jewish communities around the world. Protests and strikes were held in cities and towns throughout Palestine. In response to their outrage, Keith-Roach echoed the Grand Mufti's false claims. Efforts to convert the Wailing Wall into a synagogue violated the status quo, he told Jewish leaders. Had the divider not been removed, he said, Muslim residents would have stoned Jewish worshippers. According to Duff, police officers who blocked a mob of enraged Muslim men "prevented a general massacre of Jews in those cobbled, sun-drenched narrow streets."[13]

The Jewish community was appalled. They were not trying to turn the Western Wall into a synagogue. Screens had been used to separate men and women at the wall during the High Holy Days for years. Indeed, the very same foldable screen had been placed at the wall during Rosh Hashanah services two weeks earlier, drawing no condemnation. Under Ottoman rule, before the British took over Palestine, Jews had been allowed to pray freely at the Western Wall. Though they often had to pay bribes to Muslim authorities and residents to do so, on High Holy Days, Jews could blow the shofar, the traditional Jewish ram's horn, and set up benches and the ark of the Torah.[14]

From a hotel in Jerusalem's Old City, where he waited to secure his luggage from a customs house before making his way to Hebron, David wrote another dispatch to Memphis.

I tell you it is heart rending! Here in Jerusalem now the feeling runs high. There are near riots almost every day. The Jewish population is putting up a sharp fight and I think the result will be a happy one. At least we pray so!

What had seemed to the British a trivial kerfuffle over an old pile of stones quickly escalated into a battle for Jerusalem's soul. While the majority of the city's residents were Jewish, the same was not true for Palestine as a whole. In 1928, Jews represented just 17 percent of the country's population. A weak minority throughout centuries of Muslim rule, the Jews of Palestine had long accepted their status as second-class subjects.[15]

But the makeup of Jewish Palestine was shifting. Between 1921 and 1928, the country had absorbed tens of thousands of Jewish immigrants from Europe who expected the right to worship freely at the holiest site accessible to them. Arriving with enlightened ideas of religious freedom and emboldened by the British government's support for the Zionist cause, there were increasing calls for the Jews of Palestine to purchase the Western Wall from its Muslim owners. This in turn heightened Muslim fears of a Jewish takeover of Al-Aqsa. Muslims were keenly aware that the Jewish people longed for the coming of the Messiah, when tradition holds the Temple will be rebuilt on the Temple Mount.

To Muslim leaders in Palestine, the wooden divider and the Jews' refusal to remove it were signs of the increasing power Jews were accumulating under British rule.

Guardian of Islam

The Grand Mufti had long faced accusations of corruption and nepotism. One case involved his investing £70,000 from Supreme Muslim Council funds to build a luxurious hotel in Jerusalem's Mamilla Quarter. When his Jewish contractor warned him that workers had found a Muslim burial ground on the site where the hotel was to be built, the mufti tried to keep the discovery a secret. He agreed to lay sewage pipes that would direct the hotel's waste into the cemetery. Adding to his struggle to unite the Arabs of Palestine behind him was the historic feud that placed the Muslims of Palestine in one of two camps. In his memoir, Douglas Duff likened the contest between the powerful Nashashibi and Husseini clans to the Montagues and Capulets, only with more hatred. "Murders, tree-cutting, vine-uprooting, the burning of crops and olive trees in the villages, all most heinous crimes in a land dependent on these things, were carried out in the name of the great feud," wrote Duff.[16]

Perhaps most significantly, after years of lobbying his British patrons, the Grand Mufti had not secured any progress toward Arab independence in Palestine. The incident at the Wailing Wall on Yom Kippur and the Grand Mufti's response to it cemented his role as the irrefutable leader of Palestine's Muslim population. He could now present himself as the country's guardian of Islam.[17]

Following the clashes at the Western Wall, the Palestine Zionist Executive, the liaison between the British government and the Jewish community of Palestine, sent a cable to the League of Nations protesting the affront to Jewish freedom of worship, requesting that ownership of the Western Wall be transferred to the Jews.[18]

The mufti's reaction was swift. On September 29, the Supreme Muslim Council sent its own cable to the British government and the League of Nations, objecting entirely to Jewish access to the site. Such rights endanger Muslim ownership, argued the Grand Mufti. On September 30, he marshaled thousands of Muslims to convene at Al-Aqsa, where sheikhs delivered speeches denouncing the supposed Jewish plot. Crowds proceeded to attack Jewish worshippers at the Western Wall below.[19]

The Grand Mufti recognized a unique opportunity to weaponize Islam. Suppressing Jewish worship at the Western Wall was an effective way to reassert the Muslim domination that had prevailed in Palestine for a millennium. While the vast majority of Palestinian Arabs at the time were illiterate, with only the elites able to read the anti-Zionist editorials published in the Arabic press, they were fervently religious. By emphasizing this imagined threat to the most sacred mosque in Palestine, Haj Amin found a powerful way to galvanize the masses against Zionism, gaining their political support in the process.[20]

In the weeks that followed, the Grand Mufti unleashed a campaign of disinformation, with leaflets and posters accusing the Jews of a plot to destroy Al-Aqsa Mosque. It became known as the Al-Buraq

Campaign, as the Western Wall is known by Muslims as Al-Buraq. According to Islamic tradition, this was where the Prophet Muhammad had tethered his winged steed, Al-Buraq, before ascending on his celestial journey to paradise. The Al-Buraq Campaign included the publication of excerpts of *The Protocols of the Elders of Zion*— an anti-Semitic forgery—as evidence of the Jewish quest for global domination.[21]

The mufti's propaganda was boosted in part by Jewish propaganda. Seemingly oblivious to Muslim fears, some Jewish institutions in Palestine conducted fundraising in the Diaspora by appealing to Jewish memory and longing for the Temple Period. Fundraising appeals and postcards sent to Jewish communities overseas depicted a rebuilt Jewish Temple on the Temple Mount. In some cases, the temple stood beside Al-Aqsa. In others, it replaced it. What to the Jewish community was a harmless display of nostalgia, or an artistic depiction of the traditional prayer for a return to Zion and the rebuilding of the holy temple, was to the Muslim community definitive proof of a Jewish conspiracy.

On October 8, 1928, in a meeting with the Acting High Commissioner of Palestine, Harry Luke, the mufti handed him a memo. "Having realized by bitter experience the unlimited greedy aspirations of the Jews in this respect," he wrote, "Moslems believe that the Jews' aim is to take possession of the Mosque of al-Aqsa gradually on the pretense that it is the Temple, by starting with the Western Wall of this place, which is an inseparable part of the Mosque of Al-Aqsa." The Jews, Haj Amin argued, have no right to worship at the wall. Any historic permission to pray there or to bring religious items, he explained, were merely favors.[22]

To protect Muslim holy sites from this Jewish scheme, the Grand Mufti established the Society for the Defense of Al-Aqsa Mosque, with branches throughout Palestine. He also worked to strengthen Muslim attachment to the Western Wall, and to negate any Jewish right to it. Those efforts were undermined by several realities: Muslims had never prayed at the Western Wall. Their treatment of the area did not reflect that of a holy place. Sewage, garbage, and donkey feces were not normally tolerated at Muslim holy sites. As for the Jewish connection to the Western Wall, Muslim authorities had not only acknowledged but touted the site's Jewish history. Until as late as 1950, the Supreme Muslim Council's own guidebooks, published in English for tourists, portrayed the Temple Mount as one of the oldest sites in the world, whose "identity with the site of Solomon's Temple is beyond dispute." Today, Palestinian leaders claim that no Jewish Temple ever stood there.[23]

The Grand Mufti urged Muslim leaders across Palestine to organize demonstrations in their cities against Jewish efforts to take control of the wall. He sent his associates to spread the word to far-flung tribes and villages. On November 1, 1928, he convened a General Muslim Conference, with attendees from Palestine, Syria, Lebanon, and Transjordan. At the conference, a statement by the mufti's newly established Committee for the Defense of the Holy Buraq was presented as a rallying cry: "Whereas we, the population of the Holy Land, have been entrusted by God with the custody of this House and His Temple, we deem it our duty to submit to all our Muslim brethren in the East and West a statement of the danger which threatens this Mosque owing to the ambitions of the Jews to expropriate it from the hands of Moslems, God forbid."[24]

The Jews of Palestine, in fact, had no plans to destroy the mosque or to rebuild their temple. According to Jewish tradition, the temple will only be rebuilt when the Messiah comes. The Vaad Leumi, or Jewish National Council, which served as the executive institution of the Jewish community under British rule, issued repeated statements declaring that the Jews had no intention or desire to encroach upon Muslim holy sites. They asked the Muslim authorities to respect Jewish rights to pray in peace at the Western Wall, which was not a Muslim holy site.[25]

Meanwhile, Jewish leaders worked on clandestine plans to purchase the wall. As early as 1875, Sir Moses Montefiore, a London banker and philanthropist born to a family of Sephardic Jews in Italy, made the first failed attempt. Baron Edmond de Rothschild, a Jewish banker from France, tried again one decade later. In 1918, soon after the British conquered Jerusalem, Chaim Weizmann, president of the Zionist Organization, made a £70,000 offer to purchase the wall with the help of Jerusalem's then district governor, Ronald Storrs. The sheikhs of the Mughrabi Quarter were interested in the offer, but when Arab leaders objected to the plan, it fell apart. In late 1928, Weizmann again tried to purchase the wall through Storrs, and raised £61,000 to do so. When the new High Commissioner of Palestine, John Chancellor, got wind of Weizmann's plans, he recommended that he hold off until the uproar surrounding the wall died down. Jewish leaders in Palestine also urged the British government to expropriate the wall. Those requests were denied.[26]

The Grand Mufti's own home was just steps from the Wailing Wall. As president of the Supreme Muslim Council, he oversaw all Waqf property. He too was offered large sums to sell the wall to the Jewish community. He of course refused. When High Commissioner Chancellor told the mufti he could sell the decrepit Mughrabi Quarter for an amount of money that could then be used to build more dignified properties for its residents, Haj Amin replied, "It may appear inhuman," but the Muslims reject surrendering any rights that might endanger their exclusive title to Al-Aqsa.[27]

Husseini did everything in his power to restrict Jewish access to the Western Wall. First, he ordered the construction of a 4-foot barrier atop the wall. Its stated purpose was to shield Muslim women from public gaze. On several occasions during construction, bricks fell upon Jewish worshippers below. The mufti then stationed a muezzin atop the wall, who five times a day issued the Muslim call to prayer. Husseini also introduced the zikr, a Sufi Muslim ceremony involving cymbals, gongs, drums, and the chanting of "Allahu Akbar"—God is great—in a garden near the wall. Jewish worshippers seeking to meditate and pray at the wall found the blaring call to prayer, coupled with

A group of Jews stands on a balcony overlooking the Mughrabi Quarter and the Western Wall, with the Dome of the Rock in the distance behind it. c.1920-33.

the sounds of the zikr ceremony, insufferable. They perceived the Arab discovery of the holiness of the area belated and opportunistic. Their complaints to British authorities that the mufti's actions were unacceptable were ignored.[28]

On November 19, 1928, the British issued a policy paper justifying their actions on Yom Kippur, reaffirming Muslim ownership of the wall, and vowing to maintain the status quo. The mufti thanked them for their "impartial" decision.[29]

It would not be the end of the war for the wall, or the efforts to resolve it. On August 29, 1929, six days after the deadliest riots Palestine had ever seen erupted there, Prince Mohammed Ali Pasha, a member of Egypt's ruling dynasty, wrote a letter to High Commissioner Chancellor.

"Having been masters in Palestine for over one thousand years," wrote the Egyptian prince, the Arabs "are fighting for their honor." Apparently unaware of previous Zionist efforts to purchase the wall, Pasha wrote, "The Mohametans may be willing to accept a sum of money which would help them to do good for the community and as the Jews are rich, if this thing is so much desired by them, there seems no reason why they should not pay for it. . . . Let them give £100,000 and I feel sure this would settle the difference."

The prince's letter never made it to Chancellor. It lay hidden in an archive of London's Foreign Office for ninety years. "Surely Ali Pasha never spoke a word of this to anyone in the Muslim world, as he lived peacefully for nearly three more decades," observed Steven E. Zipperstein, the historian who discovered it. "Clearly he did not regard the Western Wall as even a minor Muslim religious site."[30]

CHAPTER 5

City of Abraham

TWENTY MILES SOUTH OF JERUSALEM, THROUGH THE WINDING dirt roads that slithered through the Judaean Hills, up terraced hillsides sprinkled with vineyards and olive groves, David breathed the freshest air he had ever inhaled. At last, he had arrived in Hebron. Nestled between two majestic mountains, it was more beautiful than he had imagined. Hovering 3,000 feet above sea level, the views of biblical Judaea were a panorama of green hills and valleys. Looking out over fig, lemon, and pomegranate trees, David could make out the Judaean Desert and the Dead Sea in the distance.[1]

It was October 4, 1928, and olive harvest season had just begun. Palestinian families were busy plucking the ripe fruits of their ancient trees that dotted the hills of Hebron. Men traversed the dusty streets on mules, carrying burlap sacks overflowing with vibrant green olives. In the vineyards, harvest season had just come to an end. Hebron's market stalls were stacked high with piles of Hebron's famously succulent grapes.

The second holiest city in Judaism, Hebron embodied everything David had yearned for in Memphis and New York: peace. A place untouched by time, where he could lose himself in his studies and live in walking distance to the 4,000-year-old burial place of the patriarchs and matriarchs of the Jewish people.

There were no cars in Hebron. Merchants carried their wares on camels, and men rode by on little donkeys, their feet scraping the ground. Homes made of stone seemed like fragments of biblical days. There was no electricity, and running water was almost unheard of.[2]

Dressed in dapper suits from his father's Memphis shop, David stood out like a Hollywood actor who had strolled onto the wrong set. Walking through town, he could not tell who was an Arab and who was a Jew. Many of the Jewish men in Hebron wore white turbans and flowing robes, which David described as "varying from dirty quilts to expensive window draperies." Arab women, when they ventured outside, were veiled from head to toe, shrouded in what David first mistook for bedsheets. To illustrate the scene to his family in one of his early letters, he wrote, "Imagine walking down Main Street and every direction you turn you see a ghost."

Hebron was light years behind Memphis. "There are no structures made of wood here," he wrote home, "only ancient stones." Residents hauled their water from city wells, some in large tin cans on the backs of donkeys, others in animal skins, which David initially thought were slaughtered animals draped over men's shoulders. Few homes had bathtubs. To bathe, Hebronites filled a basin with water and washed up in the corner of a room. On Fridays, they went to the bathhouse. When it came time for street cleaning, three men strapped water-filled ox skins across their backs and held the open end of the skin while shimmying up and down the streets, sprinkling the thoroughfares with spurts of water that "rival the mighty flow of our kitchen sink."

When David arrived, Jewish life in Hebron consisted of a small, pious community of around 800 Jews who dwelled among some 20,000 Arabs. Living in Memphis and New York City, David had never encountered Mizrahim, Jews who hailed from Islamic lands. The majority of Hebron's Jews were Sephardim. Derived from the Hebrew word for "Spanish," Sephardim were descendants of Jewish refugees who fled the Spanish Inquisition in 1492 and settled in places like Morocco, Iraq, Turkey, Greece, and Egypt before making their way to their homeland. They spoke Hebrew, Arabic, and Ladino, a version of Spanish created by the Jewish exiles to communicate safely while living amid non-Jewish populations. Mizrahi Jews were also Sephardim,

Hebron's Jewish Quarter, c. 1921.

in that both groups maintained similar religious traditions in the Diaspora. As a son of European immigrants, David—like most American Jews—was Ashkenazi. Ashkenazim, whose name comes from the Hebrew term for "German," had vastly different social norms and cultural traditions.[3]

Hebron's Sephardic community had lived there for centuries. In the early nineteenth century, they were joined by Hasidim from Eastern Europe. The Yiddish-speaking Ashkenazim, who traced their roots to Central and Eastern Europe, and the Arabic-speaking Sephardim, led parallel lives. Though they worshipped the same God, recited the same blessings, followed the same dietary laws, and celebrated the same holidays, they attended different synagogues, adhered to different customs, and spoke different languages.

There was a Chief Sephardic Rabbi of Hebron, and a Chief Ashkenazi Rabbi of Hebron. While the Sephardim shared the language, social manners, and dress of their Arab neighbors, the Ashkenazim maintained their Eastern European ways and appearances. The Sephardic men were friends and business partners with their Arab neighbors. Together they drank Turkish coffee, smoked hookah, and played backgammon in one another's homes. Some Arabs turned off the lights for their Jewish neighbors on Shabbat, effectively serving as their Shabbos Goys. Few Ashkenazim spoke Arabic, and so they mainly socialized among themselves. Sephardic boys and girls married other Sephardic boys and girls, and Ashkenazim did the same.[4]

Like David, the highly traditional, religious Jews of Hebron were not Zionists. Most of them opposed the secular movement, which they viewed as a contamination of Judaism. In 1904, when a Zionist group tried to hold a memorial service in Hebron for Theodore Herzl, the recently deceased leader of Zionism, the city's rabbis refused to grant them permission.[5]

For all their differences, the Jews of Hebron were in many ways one. They all lived in Hebron for the same reason: to be close to the Tomb of the Patriarchs and Matriarchs. Their lives all revolved

View of Hebron, c. 1925.

around Torah study, prayer, and the weekly observance of Shabbat. Many relied on *halukkah*, charitable funds donated to the impoverished Jews of the Holy Land by Jewish communities in the Diaspora. The veterans of Jewish Hebron lived in the cramped Jewish Quarter, whose labyrinthine alleys and passageways were lined with stone homes built one on top of another. It was known as the ghetto, the only Jewish Quarter in the Holy Land to bear that name, which originated in Italy. The walled one-acre ghetto had two gates, which were locked at night. The predominantly Sephardic Jewish Quarter was centered around Avraham Avinu (Our Father Abraham) Synagogue, built in 1540 by exiles from Spain. At its peak, the ghetto housed some 1,500 Jews, who had to climb in and over one another's homes to reach their own. In the late nineteenth century, the Jewish community could no longer fit inside the claustrophobic ghetto, and moved outside its walls.[6]

Most of the Ashkenazim lived outside the Jewish Quarter, in homes they rented from Arab landlords. Their rent payments comprised a meaningful portion of the city's economy. Relations between Jewish tenants and their Arab landlords were generally pleasant and friendly.[7]

The Seventh Step

As the physical and spiritual source of Jewish history in the Holy Land, Jews had lived in Hebron and made pilgrimage to the Cave of the Patriarchs since biblical times. In the first century BCE, Herod the Great, the Jewish king of Judaea, erected an imposing stone edifice atop the cave to protect and sanctify it. Still standing in one piece 2,000 years later, the Tomb of the Patriarchs and Matriarchs is the oldest continuously used prayer structure on earth, and one of the most well-preserved remnants of the Roman Empire. More than 40 feet high, 200 feet long, and 100 feet wide, the shrine is made of limestone blocks weighing several tons each. They are the same stones used by Herod's builders for the retaining wall of the Second Temple and Temple Mount, whose Western Wall is all that remains.[8]

David's first visit to the tomb was likely as disappointing as his first visit to the Western Wall. Under Byzantine rule, the Jewish shrine had been transformed into a church. Following the Muslim conquest of Hebron in the seventh century CE, it was renamed the Ibrahimi Mosque. In 1267, the Muslim rulers of Hebron banned non-Muslims from entering the holy site. For the next 700 years, Jews were forbidden from ascending any higher than the seventh step leading up to the shrine. This is where they worshipped, addressing their prayers through a hole in the wall.[9]

When David arrived, just a handful of Jews had been granted the privilege of entering the shrine. One of them was Henry Morgenthau, US ambassador to the Ottoman Empire, who paid a rare visit to the

Holy Land in 1914. Morgenthau arrived in Hebron by carriage from Jerusalem and was greeted by Jewish schoolchildren singing songs of welcome. "This ancient Hebrew burial place of the Patriarchs is today most jealously guarded by the Moslems, who control it, and those of other faiths are not permitted to enter the sacred precincts," read the *New York Times* account of Morgenthau's tour. "Less than a score of persons are today living for whom this rigid rule has been relaxed, and it is several years since any one has been thus favored, as was the small party admitted with the ambassador. . . . While the party was in the mosque a double row of Turkish infantry was drawn across the entrance to keep out the fanatical mob."[10]

Despite the friendly relations between many of the city's Jewish and Arab residents, the Jews of Hebron were treated as an inferior class, subservient to the city's Muslim majority. At times Jews were harassed on the streets with curses or beatings. Arab boys particularly enjoyed pulling the beards of elderly rabbis, and throwing stones at Jewish homes and at Jewish worshippers praying outside the Tomb of the Patriarchs and Matriarchs.

The only Jewish member of Hebron's City Council was Eliezer Dan Slonim, the 29-year-old son of Hebron's Chief Ashkenazi Rabbi Yaakov Yosef Slonim. The Slonims were Hasidic royalty, descendants of a Chabad dynasty who settled in Hebron in the nineteenth century. A native of Hebron, Eliezer Slonim spoke fluent Arabic. As the manager of the Hebron branch of the Anglo-Palestine Bank, he held close ties with the city's Muslim leaders and was the most prominent Jewish member of Hebron society. Local sheiks often gathered at his home to chat, play backgammon, and drink Turkish coffee. Hebron businessmen relied upon Slonim and his bank for loans.[11]

The pride of Hebron's Jewish community was the Hadassah House, a medical center that offered free care to needy Jews and Muslims. The charitable clinic was established in 1893 as Chesed Avraham (Kindness of Abraham), by Rabbi Haim Rahamim Yosef

Outside the entrance to the Tomb of the Patriarchs and Matriarchs, c. 1920.

Franco, a Jew from Greece who traveled the world raising funds for numerous charitable institutions. Until his death in 1901, Rabbi Franco served as Hebron's Chief Sephardic Rabbi, a position later held by his son Meir. The clinic was renamed the Hadassah House after it was taken over by the Hadassah organization, a women's Zionist group founded in New York in 1912 by Henrietta Szold. She would later establish Ihud, the first political party dedicated to coexistence between Jews and Arabs in Palestine.

In addition to the Hadassah House and the Anglo-Palestine Bank, Hebron's Jewish community boasted four synagogues, two guesthouses, two kosher butchers, a baker, a grocer, a ritual bathhouse, and at least two places where, against strict Muslim prohibition, alcohol was sold.[12]

Princes of Palestine

Hebron was also home to the largest and most prestigious yeshiva in all of Palestine, the Slabodka Yeshiva. Also known as Knesset Israel, or the Hebron Yeshiva, this is where David would begin two years of study. For simplicity, I will call it the Hebron Yeshiva. Established in 1925, when the famed Slabodka Yeshiva relocated from Slabodka, Lithuania, to Hebron, it was the first of many European yeshivas to move to Palestine.[13]

Known as the mother of all yeshivas, Slabodka was one of the most preeminent of its time. Founded in 1882 outside of Kovno, Lithuania, Slabodka's graduates established, led, and taught at many of the most renowned yeshivas in the US and Israel. In the summer of 1924, the Lithuanian government issued a decree that rabbinical students of conscription age would be required to serve in the Lithuanian army. Until then, they had been exempted from military service. The yeshiva's leaders quickly decided to move the school to the Holy Land.[14]

It was around this time that many yeshivas in Lithuania and Poland made the same decision, but for different reasons. Facing rising anti-Semitism, deadly pogroms, and severe restrictions on Jewish immigration to the United States, Palestine was the most viable new home in the wake of the Balfour Declaration. Nevertheless, the decision was not easy. Most Eastern European rabbis vehemently opposed Zionism due to its secular, liberal nature. Yeshiva heads feared that the progressive atmosphere in Israel would rub off on their students, leading them to distance themselves from Torah study.[15]

Slabodka was unique. It was led by Rabbi Moshe Mordechai Epstein, one of the leading Talmudists of the twentieth century and an early supporter of the Jewish return to the motherland. Born in 1866, Epstein was one of the first Religious Zionists. He had dreamed of moving to the Land of Israel with his family and the yeshiva since at least 1920, when he received a letter from his cousin, Jerusalem Rabbi Zvi Pesach Frank, urging him to move the yeshiva to *Eretz Yisrael*. Frank, a renowned Torah scholar who would go on to serve three decades as the Chief Rabbi of Jerusalem, believed it was the duty of the great European yeshivas to serve as a counterweight to the secular forces that were beginning to dominate Jewish culture in the Holy Land.[16]

In June 1924, Rabbi Epstein sent his son-in-law, Rabbi Yehezkel Sarna, to scout potential locations. Rabbi Sarna had already ruled out Jerusalem as too well-established a home for Torah study, and Tel Aviv as too secular. The decision was between Hebron and the agricultural settlement of Petah Tikva, which was founded by ultra-Orthodox pioneers from Europe in 1878.

Eliezer Slonim and his father, Yaakov Yosef, Hebron's Chief Ashkenazi rabbi, were pivotal in bringing the yeshiva to Hebron. During Rabbi Sarna's visit to the Holy Land, Hebron and Petah Tikva fought for Sarna's vote. Eliezer, who also dabbled as a writer, lobbied for Hebron in the pages of *Haaretz*, the Hebrew daily published out of Tel Aviv. In a piece titled "Hebron must be saved," Slonim wrote, "To save the Jewish community of Hebron, and with it the entire Yishuv (the Jewish community of Palestine), should be the aspiration of all the land, and anyone who has the moral or material capacity in his hands needs to come to its aid."[17]

Hebron was indeed in need of saving. In 1923, the city's Jewish population had shriveled to 413 souls, down from 1,429 in 1890. Many left during World War I, moving to other parts of Palestine, or in search of a better life in the United States. The arrival of the renowned Slabodka Yeshiva would resuscitate the city's dwindling Jewish community and reinvigorate the city's suffering economy.

During his visit to Hebron, Sarna asked Rabbi Slonim and his son about security. He worried that the city's Jews were heavily outnumbered by Arabs, who he feared might be hostile to Jewish newcomers. Father and son assured Sarna that relations between Jews and Arabs in Hebron were better than anywhere else in Palestine. While violent riots had targeted the Jews of Jerusalem in 1920, and Jaffa in 1921, thanks to Hebron's history of peaceful coexistence, they told him, there were no riots here.[18]

The relative harmony between Jews and Arabs in Hebron was rare in a country largely divided along religious lines. In Hebron, Jews and Arabs celebrated weddings and holidays together. They did business together. Jews traveled between Jerusalem and Hebron in Arab buses, taxis, and horse-drawn carts. The Union Club, an association of Jews and Arabs in Hebron founded in 1920, counted among its members Arab nobles and sheikhs, and Ashkenazi and Sephardic rabbis.[19]

Rabbi Sarna ultimately chose Hebron for its location, climate, and its quiet, spiritual nature, which would allow the students to learn in peace near the resting place of the Jewish patriarchs and matriarchs. Rabbi Epstein enthusiastically approved. Joined by 150 Slabodka students, they moved to Hebron in 1925. During a trip to the United States in 1927, Rabbi Epstein recruited more than two dozen American students to join the ranks in Hebron. David was one of them.[20]

The yeshiva transformed Hebron's Jewish community. By 1929, there were some 200 students. Most of the yeshiva boys hailed from Europe and the United States. In addition to Talmud, the Hebron

Yeshiva emphasized the teaching of Mussar, which stressed ethics and morality, man's duty to humanity, the polishing of one's character, and the cultivation of a positive self-image. The students, ranging from teenagers to married men in their forties, donned sleek suits and ties, fedora hats, and clean-shaven faces—not the long black coats, beards, and side curls that were typical of Orthodox Jews. They looked more like dashing New York businessmen than yeshiva students. They stood out in sleepy, traditional Hebron.[21]

When the yeshiva first opened, there was a large welcome ceremony attended by Hebron's Jewish leaders, British officials, Arab dignitaries, and the city's Arab governor. Yet in the yeshiva's early days, David relayed in a letter to his mother, "There occurred not a little trouble from the Arabs here. Stones were thrown into the institution buildings; students were attacked on the streets. The present state of affairs speaks much for the excellent character of the yeshiva student body [and Rabbi Epstein]," he wrote.

> Friendly relations started in the following manner: A young Arab pelted the rabbi's home with stones, injuring two members of the family and causing considerable damage in broken windows, etc. He was arrested and brought to trial. The Rabbi went before the judge and pleaded that the culprit be set free. This event occurred some three years ago. Ever since then there has been no trouble whatsoever. To the contrary now the Arabs treat the yeshiva students with utmost respect and courtesy.[22]

Unfamiliar with the social and cultural norms of the locals, the yeshiva boys sometimes found themselves in sticky situations. On several occasions, while walking home in the dark, students accidentally wandered into Arab homes or gardens, mistaking them for their own. For the highly conservative Muslims of Hebron, whose women were not to be seen by men unless they were fully veiled, this was a serious violation of privacy. Eliezer Slonim had to bail some yeshiva students out of jail after they mistakenly walked into an Arab house when women were home. And yet, when rumors circulated that the yeshiva might leave Hebron, a delegation of Arab leaders visited the heads of the yeshiva, imploring them to stay. Many of the town's Arabs made their living off the yeshiva, whose students and faculty rented their property and purchased goods from their shops.[23]

A modest stone building rented from an Arab landlord in an open field outside the Jewish Quarter, the yeshiva had no dormitories. It was about a ten-minute walk from the Tomb of the Patriarchs and Matriarchs and the Jewish Quarter. Yeshiva students rented rooms from Jewish residents, most of whom rented their homes from Arab landlords outside the ghetto. David chose the home of Rabbi Betzalel Samarik, a beloved 72-year-old teacher with rosy cheeks and a long white beard whose house was a popular meeting place for yeshiva students. Born in the shtetl of Zitl in what was then the Russian Empire, Samarik was a rabbi in Riga before moving to Hebron in 1924. In addition to teaching Torah at his home, he also taught many of the local children. In a letter to Memphis, David described the rabbi and his wife as an old, refined couple, "true Jewish aristocrats."[24]

In a letter to his friend Israel Kanarek back in Memphis, David wrote, "Yes, I am settled in my new home. Home is a fit name for Hebron, but it is more: it is Paradise itself. It would require your imagination to picture the true 'Gan Eden' [paradise] any more beautiful."

For $40 a month, David rented a well-appointed room with a view of the hills, valleys, and vineyards that surrounded Hebron, and three meals a day cooked by the rabbi's wife. He could have found a much cheaper room, but this was the only available home with running water. His housemates were three other young American students: Moshe Gold, the Brooklyn-born son of Rabbi Wolf Gold; Benjamin Hurwitz, also from New York City; and Tzvi Froiman, who was born in Ontario and raised in Chicago.[25]

At 16, Moshe Gold was one of the youngest yeshiva students in Hebron. Yet he had been attending yeshiva since the age of 6, as one

Avraham Avinu Synagogue, Hebron, 1925.

of the first students at Yeshiva Torah Vodaath, the Brooklyn yeshiva founded by his father. In 1921, at the age of 9, Moshe moved to Palestine with his parents and siblings.[26]

Eighteen-year-old Benny Hurwitz was quiet, generous, and studious. His father, Rabbi Yekutiel Raphael Hurwitz, was a Polish immigrant and silk dyer in Greenpoint, Brooklyn. The family home was on the seashore in Far Rockaway, Queens. After graduating from Rabbi Isaac Elchanan Theological Seminary, where David had also studied during his year in New York, Benny longed to move to Palestine. His parents agreed but only under the condition that his mother and two sisters join him. They moved to Palestine in the summer of 1927, while Benny's father remained in New York to run his business. His mother and sisters lived in Petah Tikva, where they learned Hebrew. Benny enrolled at the Hebron Yeshiva with the goal of becoming a rabbi in America.[27]

Modest, hardworking, and spiritual, 20-year-old Tzvi Froiman aspired to be the head of an American yeshiva. Known as one of the most serious pupils, he was often first to arrive at the yeshiva in the morning, and last to leave at night. Back in Chicago, he wrote articles for local newspapers from the age of 15, critiquing the teaching methods of the day. Younger students who struggled with their studies in Hebron were often sent to learn with Tzvi.[28]

CHAPTER 6

Breathing Holy Air

AFTER SETTLING INTO HIS NEW HOME, DAVID DOVE DEEP INTO HIS studies, learning from sunrise until well past sunset five days a week. His mornings began with a one-hour lesson with Rabbi Samarik, then a short walk to the yeshiva with his housemates. They took their seats in the Beit Midrash, a spacious study hall filled with simple wooden chairs and low wooden podiums with footrests, where they buried their heads in books of Talmud.

David and the 200 other students in the room would sit for hours, studying in groups of two or three, carefully reading, discussing, and debating the words of Judaism's central rabbinic text. Written from right to left in Hebrew and Aramaic, the sixty-three tractates of the Talmud contain the laws of the Jewish people and the comments, questions, arguments, and stories surrounding those laws, contributed by the leading Jewish thinkers of the first millennium CE. The words of sages who lived in distant lands in varying centuries fluttered through the kaleidoscopic pages of the Talmud as if David were witness to an ongoing dialogue that transcended time and space. In one month of learning, students would get through just four pages.[1]

After eight hours at the yeshiva, David would return to his house for a three-hour study session with an older student he paid to tutor him. This was a common side gig for many of the more experienced students, particularly those who had already been ordained as rabbis. On weeknights at 8:00, students returned to the yeshiva for classes in Mussar, followed by evening prayers. From 9:30 to 11:00, a small group of American students learned at David's house with Rabbi Samarik. David also taught himself Hebrew. He and his housemates often stayed up well past midnight discussing and debating what they had learned that day.

After six months of this routine, David had replaced his eyeglasses twice and added eighteen pounds to his slim frame. When he left New York, he weighed 133 pounds. By May 1929, he clocked in at 151.

The Hebron American Society

On Fridays and Saturdays, David and his friends would relax under the shade of Hebron's ancient olive trees, their trunks as wide as haystacks. There were few vacation days, and since most of the students had no family in Palestine, they spent their weekends in Hebron. They quickly became like brothers. When one was sick, friends took turns at his bedside, caring for him.[2]

Of the 200 yeshiva students, 30 were American. They called themselves, David wrote home, "The Hebron American Society." David was the only one with a Southern accent. The others hailed largely from New York, with some from Chicago, Cleveland, Philadelphia, and one teenage student from Seattle. While there were some Palestinian Jews at the yeshiva, most of the students were from Europe. They spoke Yiddish, a language that David and his American friends did not. "If the European boys find it hard to pronounce Memphis, I can break teeth and bite tongues over the name of my 'Rebbi,'" David wrote to his mother. "Mosheh-Chaim 'Zteitcherster,' the nearest thing to a sneeze spelled in letters."[3]

Most of the students were poor, and received little to no support from home. The few who came from well-to-do families, like David and Benny, helped those who couldn't afford their meals, transportation, and other expenses. Every few months, the yeshiva provided a modest stipend for students to pay for their food and accommodations. Yet the yeshiva also struggled financially and was often months behind on these payments. In cases where Arab landlords were unwilling to wait, Eliezer Slonim loaned them the money until the yeshiva could pay them.[4]

David quickly befriended other "American chaps," he wrote to his parents. His closest friend was 23-year-old Bill Berman, "a splendid chap in every sense." Born and raised in Philadelphia, Bill's father was also a clothing salesman, albeit a less successful one than David's father. Yet he managed to scrape together enough money to send two sons to the yeshiva in Hebron. When Bill arrived in 1927, he had already been ordained at the Rabbi Isaac Elchanan Theological Seminary, where he was a top student. Tall and well-built, Bill was adored by students and the heads of the yeshiva, who called him a role model. One of the few American students who spoke fluent Yiddish, he was close friends with the European students as well. Bill was a talented public speaker with infectious good nature, who welcomed and guided new students.[5]

According to the writings of other yeshiva students, David was described as handsome, charming, humble, generous, and thoroughly American. As the only student who came from a relatively secular home, students and teachers were amazed by his passion for learning. They admired him for turning his back on the wealth that awaited him in Memphis to devote himself to Torah in the Land of Israel. David must have basked in that admiration and wished his own family felt the same. With the funds his father sent him in Hebron—often in envelopes containing a check with no letter—David lent money to students in need and refused to let them pay him back. He also created an anonymous charity fund for needy students. No one would discover that David was the one behind it until a year later, when it was too late to thank him.[6]

Once a week, David wrote home to Memphis, often by candle or lamplight, sometimes while smoking a cigar. He penned his letters from his bedroom, gazing out through his window. In one of his first dispatches, he attempted to paint his family a portrait of the "indescribable beauty" of his new home.

> Everything is a golden brown and a very deep green, and even though the sun is quite strong as only the Oriental sun is, you are forced to remove your sunglasses by the sheer natural scenic beauty.

David, far right, with friends outside the yeshiva, c. 1929.

David wrote to his parents on October 15, 1928.

It is now ten days that I entered upon a new life—the life of a Hebron
Yeshiva student. These ten days appear to me now, as I gaze back
upon them reflectively, as so many years. . . . I feel that my past
existence was only a dream, and I have awakened to find the reality
of life more enhanced than the dream.

One month later he wrote to his mother:

I tell you in your wildest flights of imagination you could not picture
Palestine. And to crown your sensations, you are ever aware that you
are treading on holy ground, that you are breathing holy air. This, this
you say over and over again to yourself, is the land given as a divine gift
to our ancestors, this is the land from which religion and civilization
spread to the rest of the world—the light of spirituality, Zion.

He also described the peace and harmony that existed between
local Arabs and the yeshiva. Arab leaders and sheikhs often attended
the yeshiva's celebrations, where they danced alongside rabbis, he wrote.
The yeshiva students would also pay their respects at Arab weddings,
large affairs that were held outdoors, to wish the families mazal tov. Their
joint communal life led some of the students to learn Arabic, including
one whose friend taught him Arabic in exchange for Hebrew lessons.[7]
    Letters from David's mother and siblings arrived about once a
month, sometimes taking nearly two months to get from Memphis to
Hebron. Barely receiving a word from his father, David felt neglected
and homesick. He constantly asked his parents to write more often,
and to send him newspapers from Memphis. News from that part
of the world did not reach Hebron. He especially missed reading the
Memphis Jewish newspaper, the *Hebrew Watchman*, and in particular, "Kany's Kosher Komment," a weekly column written by his best
friend, Israel Kanarek.

Compared to his depressing letters home from New York, which were fraught with a ceaseless search for meaning, David's letters from Hebron were euphoric. As weeks passed, it became increasingly clearer that this was where he was meant to be. "Never in my life has time passed so swiftly," he wrote to his mother in mid-December.

David had finally discovered purpose, and a peace of mind he had struggled to find in the rat race of America. He wished he could transmit the feeling to his family. He wrote home in late December: "If I could but remove a bit of this emotion which at this moment makes my heart beat faster, condense it and mail it home in pills! Here I am in a truly remarkable world—witnessing miracles at every moment."

Love Letters

David received his first weekly letter from Sylvia Chill, his sweetheart in New York, weeks before the first letter from his family, which arrived over a month after he reached Palestine. Though he never mentioned this in the letters that survived in the attic in Memphis, David was planning to marry Sylvia, a fact I discovered through the writings of his surviving classmates, and interviews with Sylvia's nephew, Dan Chill, who owns an art gallery in Tel Aviv.

While David originally planned to spend two years in Palestine, he quickly decided to stay, and convinced Sylvia and her older brother Henry to join him. David had met Sylvia through Henry, his best friend in Brooklyn whose home was a popular meeting point for the group of spiritual intellectuals David kept company with. Henry and Sylvia planned to finish out their school years—Henry in college and Sylvia in high school—then move to Hebron, where Henry would enroll in the yeshiva, and Sylvia would be David's bride. The golden-haired beauty of the Chill family, Sylvia was just 15. Like David, she was both far wiser and more sophisticated than her age would suggest.

As the long Palestinian summer transitioned into winter, Hebron became bone-chillingly cold. The winter of 1929 was especially bitter.

Hebron was covered in a thick white blanket of snow, and the city, perched 3,000 feet above sea level, lacked electric heating. The stone buildings and their stone floors felt even colder than the air outside. In letters home, David asked his mother to send blankets and warm socks. In almost every letter, he also begged his parents to write more frequently. Some of his letters ended with an SOS begging his father to send him a check. At one point, he was over $100 in debt (nearly $2,000 in today's currency), taking out loans to cover previous loans.

Now that he had decided to remain in Palestine, David dropped subtle hints that he wished his parents to join him. He wrote of the many American families who had uprooted themselves from the land of promise to the Promised Land, where they purchased orange groves. The export of citrus, dominated by Palestine's Jewish minority, was now the most profitable enterprise in the country.

"Here a Jew is a native on the land of his forefathers and not a stranger and a tolerated sojourner in foreign lands," David wrote home in late January. Though he was now drinking the "'bitter' cup of a poor man," he wrote, "I assure you I would not exchange these seven weeks for a lifetime of the wealthiest American millionaire. A moment of spiritual life is not to be assessed in the most enormous terms of material wealth."

The Palestinian Spring

The bitter winter did not last long. By late February, spring had arrived in Palestine with all its heralded beauty. "The trees are blossoming, the birds singing, and the weather is a glorious combination of blue skies, a friendly sun and a spring breeze," David reported. "I have been told of the 'Palestinian Spring,' but the reality exceeds their wildest raving. Why Paradise could not be imagined more beautiful."

In late March, David and the rest of Jewish Hebron celebrated Purim, the holiday when Jews commemorate their rescue from annihilation in the Kingdom of Persia in the fifth century BCE. A day of costumes, feasting, dancing, and drinking, David wrote to his brothers in Memphis that they wouldn't have had more fun at their most raucous frat party. The American students led the town's masquerade ball, with David and his "gang" dressing up as sheikhs in silk bathrobes and turbans fashioned from dish towels.

One month later, David celebrated his first Passover in Palestine, a holiday that symbolized his homecoming more than any other. As he prepared for the Seder at Rabbi Samarik's house, he felt overwhelmed by the significance of living in the very land the ancient Israelites had journeyed to, seeking freedom after their enslavement in Egypt. Every year of his life, David had sat down at the Seder table to hear the story of the Exodus, one of the most momentous events in Jewish history. Each Seder closed with the same simple blessing: "Next year in Jerusalem," a wish for the children of Israel to return to their land. Now, for David, that wish had been granted.

CHAPTER 7

A Premonition

AFTER THE SEDER, DAVID EARNED HIS FIRST VACATION IN Palestine. He had by now received several checks from his father, paid off his debts, and could embark on his first road trip through the Holy Land. Joined by his inseparable friend Bill Berman, their first stop was Jerusalem, where they stayed a few nights at the palatial home of the Harbaters, a wealthy New York family whose sons were also studying at the yeshiva.

During their time in Jerusalem, the harassment of Jews at the Western Wall persisted, as it had since Yom Kippur. Rabbi Glasstein was roughed up on an almost weekly basis, and Muslims on the Temple Mount regularly threw stones down at the heads of Jewish worshippers. David may have been aware of this if he was reading the local newspapers or if he had visited the Wailing Wall during his vacation in Jerusalem. If he did, he did not mention that in his letters home. Instead, he detailed his adventures across the Holy Land. One day, he and Bill took a road trip to the south, traversing past herds of grazing goats and caravans of camels. After careening down winding desert roads carved into red rock cliffs that took them 1,400 feet below sea level, they arrived at the lowest point on earth: the Dead Sea.[1]

The following day, Mr. Harbater gave Bill and David a ride to Tel Aviv in his Cadillac. As they drew closer to the Mediterranean coast, they stopped in Rehovot, where Mr. Harbater gave them a tour of his orange grove. Lying on a coastal plain 12 miles south of Tel Aviv, Rehovot was founded in 1890 by Polish agricultural pioneers. When they purchased the 1,500 acres of land from its Arab owner, the area was barren and uncultivated, with no houses or trees. Over the next two decades, the immigrants transformed their wasteland into a thriving agricultural commune, sprinkled with vineyards, citrus groves, and almond orchards. They fought off numerous attacks by Bedouin clans who had previously used that land for grazing. The tensions were settled through financial compensation, with the help of a local sheikh.

By the time David arrived in April 1929, Rehovot had become the powerhouse of the booming citrus industry, boosted by the Rehovot Railway Station, built in 1920 to transport citrus from the town's orchards to the ports of Haifa and Jaffa, where they sailed to Europe.

David and Bill continued their journey to Tel Aviv, where they stayed at the home of Rabbi Gold for the final nights of Passover, an eight-day holiday. During their stay, the city celebrated its twentieth birthday. Tel Aviv was decked out in blue and white flags bearing the Star of David. Tel Aviv Day festivities included a parade of the city's children and founders, a series of speeches by Meir Dizengoff, the city's first mayor, and a jubilee ball.[2]

David wrote to his parents from Tel Aviv that night, "I am all the more in love with the pervasive Jewish atmosphere of the 'all Jewish' city." Having been raised in a country where Jews made up less than 1 percent of the population, in a city where many people had never met a Jew, David traversed its landscape in a constant state of awe. Every street bore a Hebrew name, every shop a Hebrew signpost, and everyone who lived there was Jewish. "Even if there is room for improvement in Judaism in Tel Aviv," David wrote, "one is inspired beyond description to see a city of 40,000 Jews. . . . Can any of you imagine this city?"

David returned to the yeshiva for his spring semester with new energy, eager to get back to his studies. As much as he enjoyed his time touring the country, he wrote, "Torah is a powerful magnet which draws my heart towards Hebron & the Yeshiva."

At the end of May, David celebrated his first Lag B'Omer, which honors the second-century sage Rabbi Shimon Bar Yochai and the day on which he revealed the deepest secrets of Jewish mysticism in the Book of Zohar, the foundational work of Kabbalah. The holiday is also tied to the second-century Bar Kokhba Revolt, a failed Jewish rebellion against the Roman rulers of Judaea. Hebron's Jews joined the brigades of Bar Kokhba, and their city was pillaged by Roman legions. Hadrian, the Roman emperor, sent captured Jewish rebels to Hebron's marketplace, where they were sold as slaves in exchange for barley. In a final blow of humiliation, Hadrian renamed the land of Judaea Palestina, replacing the region's Jewish title with that of the ancient Israelites' enemies, the Philistines. According to the Bible, it was a giant Philistine named Goliath who tested the prowess of a young Israelite named David, who killed Goliath with a slingshot. David was then crowned king of Israel, establishing his kingdom first in Hebron and then in Jerusalem.[3]

Lag B'Omer is marked by communal bonfires to commemorate the fires Jewish rebels lit on mountaintops to spread word of the revolt. David joined the festivities in Hebron, where the city's Sephardim and Ashkenazim gathered for a bonfire outside Avraham Avinu Synagogue. Earlier that week, David received confirmation from British officials in Jerusalem of his long-awaited status as a permanent immigrant. Until then, he had been on a temporary student visa. He was now a citizen of Palestine and was surely celebrating that as well.

In early August, David wrote to his parents that Sylvia Chill was vacationing in the Catskills with her mother for the summer. Exactly one year earlier, when David's parents came to visit him in New York, they spent a week with Sylvia and her parents in the same little Borscht Belt town of Tannersville, in an area known as the Jewish Alps. David extended an invitation to his mother from Sylvia to visit them now. What David didn't mention in his letters was that after her return from the Catskills, Sylvia would be sailing to Palestine. She would arrive in Hebron in October, just before Sukkot. In several of his letters, he asked his father for more money. For what, he explained, he could not yet say. He told his friends in Hebron that soon he would marry Sylvia Chill.

The Wall Is Ours

On August 14, 1929, David and a few of his friends walked to the dirt road leading to Jerusalem and took a taxi bound for the Wailing Wall. It was the afternoon before Tisha B'Av, the Ninth of Av, the most mournful day on the Hebrew calendar, the date that earned the Wailing Wall its name. It was on this day that both the First and Second Temples were destroyed, first by the Babylonians in 586 BCE, then by the Romans in 70 CE, sending the Jews of ancient Israel into their 2,000-year exile. On the Ninth of Av in the year 135 CE, the Roman Empire crushed the Bar Kokhba Revolt.

As the last remnant of the Temple Mount, the Western Wall is the centerpiece of Jewish grieving on the Ninth of Av, a day of mourning and fasting. Shortly after the sun set over Jerusalem that evening, David joined 10,000 Jewish worshippers in the annual pilgrimage to the wall. The few who were lucky to get close enough pressed their hands and faces into the ancient stones. David and the throngs of men and women around him swayed as if in a trance, chanting from the Book of Lamentations. They closed their eyes and recited *Kaddish*, the forlorn prayer of mourning, and *kinot*, sorrowful ancient poems that read like elegies. As their ancestors had done for centuries, they wept over the fall of Jerusalem, and cried out for the redemption of the children of Israel. This year, their grief carried a new layer of pain.[4]

"Jerusalem has been in a state of constant excitement and tension for ten months now, and on Tisha B'Av this tension reached almost the breaking point," David wrote to his father. "A visit to the 'Wailing Wall' brought our national tragedy home to us in the strongest sense."

The tensions between the city's Jews and Muslims over Jewish rights at the Wailing Wall had increased since the incident on Yom Kippur. The Grand Mufti had since initiated various new building projects in the already cramped space, leading Jews to complain that it was the Muslims, not the Jews, who were violating the site's fragile status quo. The British hoped to prevent any clashes, as Jewish mourners would pray at the wall throughout the night and into the next evening. Opposite the masses at the wall stood rows of British police, on foot and horseback, guarding the worshippers.[5]

A week earlier, a Muslim man smoking a cigarette attempted to pass through a group of worshippers at the wall. When one of the men asked him to wait until they had finished their prayers, the smoking man hurled a stone at him. The week before that, two Jewish worshippers were assaulted by Arabs.

The narrow corridor at the wall where Jews prayed had almost never been visited by Muslims until that incident on Yom Kippur in 1928. Sheikh Hasan Abu Sa'ud, a prominent Jerusalem preacher and associate of the Grand Mufti, had since used his sermons to encourage Muslims to visit the wall. Now it was a popular destination for anyone looking to harass Jews.[6]

What most infuriated the Jewish community was the British approval in late July 1929 of the Grand Mufti's construction of a new doorway at the Western Wall, leading directly to the Temple Mount, which was off limits to Jews. The cramped alleyway where Jews were permitted to pray at the Western Wall had since become a busy passageway for Muslims walking to and from Al-Aqsa through the Jewish prayer space. Arab attacks on Jewish worshippers at the wall became ever more frequent.[7]

Soon after construction of the doorway commenced, Joseph Klausner,* a distinguished historian and professor of Hebrew literature at Jerusalem's Hebrew University, established the Pro–Wailing Wall Committee to resolve the growing crisis at the world's holiest site for Jewish prayer. Klausner's historical expertise was the Second Temple Period.[8]

---

* Klausner was the great-uncle of famed Israeli author Amos Oz, depicted in Oz's illustrious autobiography, *A Tale of Love and Darkness* (2002).

Klausner was frustrated by the failure of the Zionist leadership to protect Jewish worship at the wall. Mainstream Jewish leaders tried to quell the influence of Klausner's group. They didn't want to anger the British, whose support they were existentially dependent upon. Hearing of a planned demonstration against the British at the Western Wall, the Zionist Executive tried to have it canceled. Failing to dissuade organizers, the executive published statements in various newspapers, urging calm while they tried to negotiate the issue with British authorities.[9]

Muslim leaders, and Grand Mufti Haj Amin al-Husseini in particular, made no such effort. On Friday, August 2, the mufti's Society for the Defense of Al-Aqsa Mosque held a meeting at Al-Aqsa attended by thousands of Muslims. They made an oath "to defend The Holy Buraq and the Mosque of Aqsa at any moment and with the whole of their might."[10]

In the leadup to the Ninth of Av, Klausner's Pro–Wailing Wall Committee used the pages of *Doar Hayom*, the Hebrew daily edited by Ze'ev Jabotinsky, to rally Palestine's Jews around the cause. "An appeal to the people of Israel in all parts of the world," published on August 12, implored the Jewish people to "Wake up and unite! Do not keep silent or rest in peace until the entire Wall has been restored to us!" The statement called on Jews around the world to form their own branches of the committee and to protest outside British consuls in their countries. "Move heaven and earth at the unspeakable and unprecedented injustice and oppression which tends to rob a live nation of the last of its relics. . . . Those of us who are here will not rest until that relic which has always been ours, which had been sealed with the blood of scores of thousands of our children through two millennia and which has absorbed the tears of Israel for 2,000 years, has been restored to us."[11]

The next day, David returned to the Wailing Wall to pray. Already in a daze from fasting, he watched, mesmerized, as 300 young Jewish men and women marched to the wall, calling for the restoration of the

Western Wall as a Jewish holy site. Carrying the blue-and-white Star of David flag that would become Israel's national flag, they chanted, "The wall is ours," and vowed "to sacrifice all for the Western Wall." After observing two minutes of silence, they sang "Hatikvah"—The Hope—an ode to the 2,000-year-old longing for Jerusalem that would become Israel's national anthem:

> Our hope is not yet lost
> It is two thousand years old
> To be a free people in our land
> The land of Zion and Jerusalem.

Many of the marchers were members of Betar, a paramilitary youth movement founded by Jabotinsky. It drew its name from an ancient fortress in the Judaean Mountains where Jewish rebels seeking an independent Jewish state took their last stand against the Romans. Inhabited since the Iron Age, Betar was the last stronghold of the Bar Kokhba Revolt.[12]

David was awestruck. In an impassioned letter home, he described how it felt to be at the Wailing Wall on the holy day that earned the place its name, at a time when Jews were once again rising up against a foreign occupier and fighting for their freedom.

As we walked along Jerusalem's streets, we could almost imagine the streams of Jewish blood flowing at our feet, the horrible scenes of slaughter. Jewish sages, budding youth, tender babes in their mother's arms, all killed by the barbaric sword of the enemy.

This letter, written on August 20, would be David's last. It would soon become a chilling premonition. Though his words lamented the Jewish blood spilled in Jerusalem 2,000 years earlier, they were a hauntingly accurate description of what was to befall him and the Jewish community of Hebron only four days later.

By the time his letter reached Memphis, David would be gone, his life extinguished in a scene of slaughter much like the one he had depicted. What David witnessed in Jerusalem on August 15 was the drumroll to the end of his life, and the beginning of a century-long holy war. That day, the tensions that had been rising over the Western Wall for close to a year reached a point of no return.

Grand Mufti Haj Amin al-Husseini had seen the march from his own home near the Western Wall. While outwardly furious, inside he likely felt some satisfaction. This display of Jewish nationalism was precisely what he needed to rally the Muslims of Palestine behind him in his battle against Zionism and rival Muslim leaders. For months the Grand Mufti had faced criticism from his political opponents and segments of the Arabic press, with accusations of misappropriated Waqf funds, nepotism, and favoritism in his religious appointments. He was also denounced for seeking to make permanent his position as President of the Supreme Muslim Council. One particularly thorny issue was the mufti's pet project, the Palace Hotel, inaugurated in December 1929. The most luxurious establishment in Jerusalem at the time, Husseini paid for its construction with funds allocated for Muslim religious properties. Baruch Katinka, a prominent engineer and member of the Haganah, was his contractor. Katinka's business partner, Tuviah Dunya, was the brother-in-law of Chaim Weizmann, president of the Zionist Organization. Katinka would later use the Palace Hotel to store Haganah weapons.[13]

The Age of Disinformation

Rumors quickly spread in Muslim circles and the Arabic press: the Jewish youth who marched to the Western Wall on August 15 had attacked Muslim residents, cursed the Prophet Muhammad, and raped Muslim women. None of this was true. Though the demonstration was politically provocative, it had been entirely peaceful. Nevertheless, pro-mufti activists handed out leaflets and posted flyers in towns and villages, spreading those rumors, and calling on Muslims to seek revenge.

"O Arab Nation, the eyes of your brothers in Palestine are upon you," read a flyer signed by the Committee of the Holy Warriors in Palestine. "They awaken your religious feelings and national zealotry to rise up against the enemy who violated the honor of Islam and raped the women and murdered widows and babies."[14]

John Chancellor, High Commissioner of Palestine, had been on leave in London since June, leaving his deputy, Harry Luke, in charge of a country that was careening toward catastrophe. Friday, August 16, was the birthday of the Prophet Muhammad. Husseini's Supreme Muslim Council organized a march to the Wailing Wall "for the defense of Al-Aqsa against the Jews." When Luke got word of the demonstration that morning, he phoned the mufti to report to his house for an urgent meeting. Luke asked Haj Amin to call off the demonstration. With the march planned for that afternoon, the mufti told Luke, it was too late to cancel it, but he could ensure it remained within Waqf property. Luke was satisfied with that response. Perhaps he had forgotten that the Wailing Wall was Waqf property. Luke would later testify that if the British had banned the demonstration, the Arabs "would have killed every Jew they could get hold of," and the British Mandate government "would have been wiped out."[15]

By the time Haj Amin arrived at Al-Aqsa, 2,000 men had already spilled out of the mosque following afternoon prayers. They descended to the Western Wall through the new door the mufti had built for that purpose. Led by the sheikhs of Al-Aqsa, the mob cheered, "Allah is the greatest!" and "Kill the Jews!" Armed with sticks and clubs, they beat a rabbi, tore a Torah scroll, then set fire to Jewish prayer books and to the notes to God that Jews had for generations placed in the crevices of the wall's stones. From there, they passed through the Old City and emerged onto Jaffa Road, where they killed the first Jew they found.[16]

After the mob retreated, Jewish journalist Wolfgang Von Weisl visited the wall and collected the remains of the torn Torah scroll and prayer books. Sir Archer Cust, a senior British official, approached Von Weisl and asked him not to publish any news of the Muslim demonstration "of a character likely to inflame Jewish public opinion." Von Weisl, an Austrian Jew who wrote for numerous German newspapers, disregarded the British officer's request. So did the Hebrew press, which also received warnings from British officials to refrain from publishing "exciting statements about the events of that day." The following day, Muslims returned to the wall to attack worshippers and interrupt Sabbath prayers.[17]

Jerusalem descended into a spiral of mayhem. On Saturday, August 17, a group of Jewish teenagers was playing soccer in a field near Lifta, an Arab village on the outskirts of Jerusalem, when they accidentally kicked their ball into a family's tomato patch. Avraham Mizrachi, a 17-year-old Jewish boy, went to retrieve the ball from an Arab girl. Mizrachi was stabbed by an Arab man. A brawl broke out between the groups, leaving two dozen bruised and bloodied young Arabs and Jews. The Jewish boys proceeded to beat up random Arab residents of the neighborhood, stabbing one young man in retaliation for Mizrachi. Attacks on Jews by Arabs occurred throughout the day in various parts of Jerusalem.[18]

The next four days saw a series of attacks and counterattacks, with Jews roughing up Arabs as they walked through Jerusalem's Jewish Quarters, and Arabs attacking Jews when they entered Arab neighborhoods. The young Arab man who was stabbed by Jews recovered from his wounds. Avraham Mizrachi did not. Following his death on August 20, his funeral the next morning morphed into a protest against the British and the Arabs. Masses of Jews joined the funeral procession, which the police tried to restrict to Jewish areas, hoping to avoid further clashes. The mourners took their time, walking slowly through the city over the course of three hours toward the cemetery. When they tried to break through a line of British officers led by Douglas Duff, the police charged at them with clubs, beating dozens of mourners and wounding nearly thirty of them. Amid the mayhem, Mizrachi's body fell to the ground, uncovered from its shrouds.[19]

The following day, British officials were in a frenzy of meetings, trying to calm the passions raging in Jerusalem's streets. They met with Zionist leaders, who issued appeals to the Jewish community to remain calm and refrain from political demonstrations. They met with Muslim leaders, who promised to tone down the incendiary speeches that were being delivered at mosques.[20]

If those messages were delivered, they made little difference. Around midnight on Wednesday, August 21, a band of 100 Arabs on horseback approached the Jewish neighborhood of Yemin Moshe, a hilltop of cobblestone alleyways and stone homes overlooking the Old City. Police rushed to the area and the would-be attackers retreated. The following day, a group of Jewish worshippers was stoned at the Wailing Wall. A Russian Christian mistaken for a Jew was severely beaten in the Old City. Thirty miles north of Jerusalem, a 70-year-old Jew was stoned and robbed while walking through the city of Nablus.[21]

Rumors were circulating in the Jewish and Arabic press that the mufti had called for masses of Arabs to gather at Al-Aqsa that Friday, August 23, to defend Islam from the Jews. Jewish officials who met with Acting High Commissioner Luke on August 22 asked him if the government would disarm anyone who came to Jerusalem the next day carrying clubs or heavy sticks. Such a step would be dangerous, Luke said, as "it might infuriate people who were carrying sticks without any evil intention." Luke assured them that he had arranged for "calming speeches to be made in the mosques on the following day," and that he had ordered armored vehicles to be sent from Transjordan. Solomon Horowitz, a member of the Palestine Zionist Executive, suggested that Luke hold an emergency meeting between Jewish and Muslim officials to call for a truce.[22]

On Thursday evening, August 22, Luke welcomed three members of the Zionist Organization and three representatives of the Palestine Arab Executive in his Jerusalem home. The goal was to issue a joint proclamation to the country's Arabs and Jews. The hours-long gathering over tea was friendly. Agreements were made on a statement calling for peace. The proclamation, drafted by Zionist Executive member Isaiah Braude, read: "We, the undersigned representatives of the Moslem and Jewish supreme institutions, wish to inform both the Jews and the Moslems that at a joint meeting we came to the conclusion that the present excitement among the Moslems and the Jews is chiefly due to a misunderstanding. We are convinced that by goodwill the misunderstanding can be cleared up. For this reason, we demand that both the Jews and the Moslems should do their utmost to attain peaceful and quiet relations. We all deprecate any acts of violence and appeal to everyone to assist their supreme institutions in the sacred work of obtaining peace between both nations."[23]

When it came time to sign the document, the Arab representatives refused. According to the British account of the meeting, they "would not agree that the time was ripe for the signature of one document by prominent persons of the two races." Before leaving Luke's house around 10:00 that night, the men agreed to reconvene four days later, on August 26. By then it would be too late for too many.[24]

Arab villagers armed with sticks and knives converged on Al-Aqsa that night. The colonial police force was disastrously unprepared. There were 171 British officers in all of Palestine, and no military force to speak of. Of the 1,500 Palestinian policemen, the vast majority were Arabs. Many either joined their brothers in arms or refrained from using force out of fear of becoming targets for vendettas.[25]

The country's head of police, Arthur Mavrogordato, was on vacation in England. The British had six armored cars and no more than six workable airplanes. In Jerusalem, just 72 policemen were stationed across the entire city, and none in the Old City were armed. The Haganah, however, had been preparing for this moment. Commanders of the underground Zionist militia had sensed the inevitability of riots weeks earlier. Throughout that night, armed Haganah men and women patrolled the Jewish neighborhoods of Jerusalem.[26]

Harry Luke requested reinforcements from the British office in Amman in case the situation got out of hand. Over the next three days, 650 colonial soldiers would be sent by air and train from Egypt, along with five of His Majesty's warships, a squadron of the Royal Air Force, three battalions of infantrymen, a company of armored cars, and a detachment of auxiliary troops.[27]

CHAPTER 8

It Won't Happen Here

In early August 1929, 17-year-old Aharon Chaim Cohen stood at a meeting of Haganah fighters in Jerusalem as his officers announced that an attack on Palestinian Jewry was imminent.

"Who is ready to serve as a spy among the Arabs?" a commander asked the group of volunteers. Cohen was the only one who stepped forward. Born in Jerusalem, Cohen was one of the only Mizrahi members of the Haganah. His father was from Iran. His mother's family hailed from Morocco. Cohen was fluent in Arabic, and lived in the mixed Arab-Jewish neighborhood of Musrara. He was told to report to Yitzhak Ben-Zvi, a senior member of the Haganah and the Zionist Executive who would go on to become Israel's second president.

Ben-Zvi instructed Cohen to quit his job at the printing shop where he worked to support his family, and to become a full-time spy. This teenage Palestinian Jew may well have been the first spy for the unborn Jewish state that would come to enlist many like him.

After securing a keffiyeh and abaya, the traditional Arab headdress and robe, Cohen blended in seamlessly. He went by Ibrahim Da'er, taking the surname of a large Muslim clan from Musrara. His first two weeks were spent wandering the streets of Jerusalem's Muslim neighborhoods, perfecting verses from the Quran, practicing Islamic prayer customs, and becoming a familiar presence at Al-Aqsa Mosque. He provided reports to Haganah headquarters, detailing the storage rooms of weapons he discovered at the mosque, the sermons delivered there, and rumors he heard about plans to strike Jewish communities in and around Jerusalem.

The night of August 21, he was stopped by a group of about a dozen armed Arabs just outside the Old City. "Hands up," they ordered him. "What is your name, and what are you doing wandering the streets at this hour?"

"My name is Ibrahim Joz Da'er," Cohen told them. "I've been sick for a few days, and the doctor told me to take long walks at night for fresh air." Still suspicious, the armed men tested him by ordering him to recite the opening prayer of the Quran. He did so calmly and to perfection. "Go home, and don't be seen here again until next week," they told him.

As he walked back to the Old City, realizing that he could have been killed, Cohen fainted. He woke up to the faces of Avraham Ikar, a veteran of the Jewish Legion who was now head of the Haganah's Old City battalion, and Shoshana Gershonovitz, a leading female member of the Haganah who would later establish the women's unit. After finding Cohen unconscious in a dark alleyway, they brought him to the hospital.[1]

On Thursday, August 22, Yosef Hecht, the head of the Haganah, sent Cohen to Hebron with another Haganah member, Saadia Kirschenboim, to assess the city's security needs. Their first stop was the Anglo-Palestine Bank to meet with its manager, Eliezer Dan Slonim, the well-known pillar of Hebron's Jewish community. Cohen asked Slonim to gather the city's Jewish leaders. He had an important message to relay. Slonim agreed and invited various rabbis and elders, including his 49-year-old father, Chief Ashkenazi Rabbi Yaakov Yoseph Slonim, and Meir Franco, the 63-year-old Chief Sephardic Rabbi.

Gathered in the bank, Cohen and Kirschenboim told the men that the Jews of Hebron were in danger of an impending riot. The Haganah wished to send reinforcements to protect them. The young spy presented two options: the Haganah would either send a group of fighters with weapons to safeguard the city's Jews, or they could transfer the Jews from Hebron to Jerusalem until it was safe to return.

The leaders of Hebron's Jewish community were unanimous. "Neither this nor that is necessary," said Eliezer, an imposing figure who stood more than 6 feet tall, with suntanned skin and dark brown eyes. "No harm will come to the Jews of Hebron," he insisted, owing to the warm relations that had prevailed between them and their Arab neighbors. The rabbis echoed Eliezer, assuring Cohen and Kirschenboim they had nothing to fear. The Arabs of Hebron were their friends.[2]

Cohen abruptly left the meeting and walked out of the bank and into a Jewish home nearby, where he changed into his alias, Ibrahim Da'er. Dressed in his abaya and keffiyeh, he went to the market. After walking around for a while and finding nothing out of the ordinary, he entered a busy café and took a seat. Soon after, a man came in and invited four other patrons to the home of Sheikh Taleb Marka, an associate of the Grand Mufti who represented Hebron in the Palestine Arab Executive and led Hebron's Muslim Association.[3] Two of the men returned a few minutes later and summoned another customer at the café to the sheikh's house. Cohen returned to the market, asked someone where Sheikh Marka's house was, and walked in.

Marka, whose black beard was peppered with white hair, was telling the men seated around him about the Jewish plot to conquer Al-Aqsa. Once the Jews of Jerusalem had seized it, Marka explained, the Jews of Hebron planned to conquer Ibrahimi Mosque—the Tomb of the Patriarchs and Matriarchs. "The Jews who live amongst us and nursed from our mothers' milk, it is they who will betray us more than the Moscovites," said Marka, using the derogatory term for Jews who had come to Palestine from Eastern Europe. "It will be a great deed to slaughter them first."[4]

Cohen returned to the Jewish Quarter, changed back into his usual clothes, went to the bank, and told the Jewish leaders who were still gathered there what he had seen and heard. "Please," he begged them, "allow a group of Haganah fighters to come here and protect the Jews of Hebron." Still they insisted there was no need for armed

Jews in Hebron. The Haganah's presence would do more harm than good, they argued. They invited several Arab leaders of Hebron to the bank to make their case. "Even if all the Jews of Palestine are killed, not a hair will fall from the head of a Jew in Hebron," vowed one of the sheikhs.

Eliezer Slonim asked Cohen and Kirschenboim to leave. That day, Cohen met with Ben-Zvi and gave him what he called a "black report" on the situation in Hebron.[5]

Shortly after midnight that night, Eliezer awoke to a knock at his front door. He pulled himself out of bed and opened the door to find a group of unexpected visitors: twelve members of the Haganah and their suitcases. Dressed in civilian clothes, their bags were packed with guns, bullets, and explosives. There would soon be an attack on the Jews of Hebron, the militants told Slonim. They had come—Baruch Katinka, nine young men, and two young women—to defend the community.[6]

Slonim, tired and frustrated, brought the group into his house and proceeded to scold them. "If there was a need for men and weapons, I would request them myself!" he shouted. "There is no need because the Arabs won't raise a hand against us. On the contrary, new faces in Hebron will only provoke them."

Then came another knock at the door. Two Arab policemen entered the house and told the visitors to come to the police station. Ten of them followed, while two managed to stay at Slonim's house with the suitcases of weapons. Arriving at the station, the Haganah fighters were met by the British Chief of Police, Raymond Oswald Cafferata, who was wearing his pajamas.

Born in Liverpool, 32-year-old Cafferata had joined the Palestine Police in 1921. Recruited from the Black and Tans, British reinforcements for the Royal Irish Constabulary who were known for their brutality during the Irish War of Independence, Cafferata had just been assigned to Hebron. Since his arrival on August 2, he had barely scratched the surface of the place and its people. He had met with just a few of the local Arab leaders and hadn't yet gotten to know the city's Jewish community. The only Englishman stationed in Hebron, Cafferata commanded a paltry force of 33 constables, nearly half of them elderly or in poor shape. All but one of the policemen were Arabs.[7]

"Who are you and what are you doing here?" Cafferata asked the group of Haganah men and women at the station. They had come for a hike, they told him. It was a pitiful cover story considering they had arrived well after dark and tensions in the country were worse than they had ever been. Like Slonim, Cafferata was out of patience. Now was no time for hiking, he lectured them. "Go back to Jerusalem at once," he commanded. And so they went, leaving Hebron's Jews to defend themselves with nothing more than their prayers. Slonim was the only Jew in Hebron with a gun. On Friday morning, he told the two Haganah men who had stayed at his house with their suitcases to drive back to Jerusalem as well.[8]

This had not been the Haganah's first foray into Hebron. Back in 1928, Haganah commander Yaakov Pat had paid a visit to the Hebron Yeshiva. He met with a group of students and asked them what they would do if Arab riots broke out in Hebron.

"Without a doubt we would defend ourselves," they told him.

"How would you do that if you don't have the necessary training?" he asked.

"With the help of God," they said.[9]

The Safest Place for Jews in Palestine

The Jewish community of Hebron did not need the Haganah to tell them they were in danger. Whispers of what was to come were seemingly everywhere. They just didn't want to believe they were true.[10]

One week earlier, on Friday, August 16, Rabbi Franco heard from Arab friends that the imam at Ibrahimi Mosque had proclaimed in his sermon that the Jews wished to conquer it. On Thursday morning, after meeting with Cohen and Kirschenboim, Rabbi Franco was in the shop of an Arab friend who told him of a letter that had arrived from the mufti, calling on Muslims to go to Jerusalem to defend Islam from the Jews. Another customer overheard them and said that a letter from the mufti had also come to his village, urging Muslims there to "rise up against the Jews." Franco dismissed it all as rumors. Earlier that week, David Gozlan, a Jewish shoemaker in Hebron, was at the home of an Arab friend when Sheikh Taleb Marka paid a visit, and told the men gathered there to support the mufti's calls for revenge.[11]

On Thursday afternoon, Shifra Ben-Gerson and her neighbor Tzvia Chodosh were doing their Sabbath shopping at the market just outside Hebron's Jewish Quarter. As they approached a fruit stall, Shifra, who understood Arabic, paused, overhearing a disturbing conversation between the Arab shopkeeper and two friends. "This Saturday every one of us will have a Jewish woman," said one of the men. "They will have their Sabbath, but we will have the pleasure," the shopkeeper laughed. The women rushed home to tell their husbands, who went to the bank to ask Eliezer Slonim what they should do. When they arrived, the bank manager was in the middle of a business meeting with a group of sheikhs. Tzvia's husband, Rabbi Meir Chodosh, told Slonim what the women had overheard. "Nonsense!" Slonim replied. "Such a thing will never happen here. We live in peace among the Arabs. They won't let anyone harm us." Slonim turned to the sheikhs gathered around his desk and relayed in Arabic what Chodosh had just told him. The men looked insulted. "Heaven forbid!" said one of the sheikhs. "On our heads, such a thing will not take place in Hebron."[12]

Despite the many warnings, the Jewish leaders of Hebron were not afraid. The riots of 1920 and 1921 had both spared Hebron. Then too, rumors had swirled through town that the Arabs of Hebron would attack the city's Jews.[13]

What might happen *there* will not happen *here*, the Jewish leaders of Hebron assured themselves. This, they insisted, was the safest place for Jews in Palestine. David, meanwhile, was not so sure. In Sylvia's weekly letters to David, she often asked him if he needed anything from New York. In his final letter to Sylvia, he told her the Jews of Hebron needed guns.[14]

David's housemate, Benny Hurwitz, shared his concerns in his last letter to his father in Queens, dated August 21. "How terrible are the happenings that occur daily in Jerusalem, our Holy City in our Holy Land," he wrote. "There are attacks on the Jews, the government ignores them . . . and the world is quiet. Is this why we have returned to rebuild our desolate land?" Sensing that the violence had not reached its peak, he wondered, "Who knows what today will breed?"[15]

The diary David kept in Hebron, and any letters he might have written after August 20, were lost in the riots. Yet I imagine that David awoke on Friday morning, August 23, looking forward to his favorite day of the week: *Shabbat Hamalka*, the Sabbath Queen. The day of rest would begin at sunset that evening, ending with the appearance of three stars in the sky on Saturday night. Rising from his bed, David might have looked out his bay window to savor the panorama spread before him. The smell of freshly baked challah, the scent of Shabbat, might have drifted into David's room. As he did most every day, he likely dressed in his finest: a suit and tie, Oxford shoes, and a fedora.

While David prepared for a day of study, Khaled, the Arab apprentice of the Jewish carpenters Jacob and Daniel Mizrahi, was in the brothers' workshop, delivering a warning. "The Arabs in the streets are armed," Khaled told them. "They are preparing an attack in order to kill you." Jacob and Daniel went straight to Rabbi Franco, who went to the Anglo-Palestine Bank to consult with Eliezer Slonim and his father. Only now did the men understand that their people truly were in danger. They decided to seek help from Hebron's district governor, Abdullah Kardous, an Arab Christian who served the British government.[16]

Around 10:00 on Friday morning, chief rabbis Franco and Slonim met with Kardous and told him what they had heard. "The Arabs are preparing to attack the Jews," Rabbi Franco told Kardous. "As far as we know, the number of police here is very limited," said Rabbi Slonim.

Kardous tried to calm the shaken rabbis. "I have just been in the market to smell out the situation and I find that there is no danger," he told them. "Rest assured, the British government knows what to do."

"Well, what will you do if they really do attack? What forces have you to save us with?" asked Rabbi Franco.

"The British government always sends six soldiers where only two are needed, and we have many men wearing civilian clothes going among the crowd," said Kardous. "When there will be a need, they will take action."

To prove they could trust him, Kardous told the rabbis that during the riots of 1921, when he was the governor of Jericho, he armed the one Jewish man who lived there with a rifle to defend himself. This put the rabbis at ease. Kardous instructed the men to go back to their people and assure them that all was well. The rabbis obeyed.[17]

Meanwhile in Jerusalem earlier that morning, thousands of Muslims had streamed into the Old City from surrounding villages. Heading to Al-Aqsa for Friday prayers, many were armed with sticks, clubs, and daggers. On one side of the city, police were disarming the villagers, leading to complaints from Muslim leaders. Around 9:00 a.m., Major Alan Saunders, deputy inspector general of the Palestine Police, canceled the order to disarm. Taking the weapons of some and not others, he argued, could cause unrest. Plus, he reasoned, the police force was too understaffed to disarm everyone, and there was nothing stopping people from rearming once inside the Old City.[18]

By late morning, more than 10,000 men had convened outside Al-Aqsa. Jewish shop owners closed their doors early and headed home. Shortly after 10:00 a.m., Saunders visited the Grand Mufti's house outside the Western Wall, and asked him why so many of the villagers arriving in Jerusalem were armed. Given the demonstrations and attacks that had taken place throughout the previous week, the mufti explained, many feared they might need to defend themselves from Jewish attacks. Muslims would not attack anyone unless they were provoked, Haj Amin assured Saunders.[19]

During noon prayers at Al-Aqsa, the mufti followed through on his promises to try to calm the explosive atmosphere. When he arrived, worshippers in the courtyard greeted him ecstatically. "The Sword of Religion, al-Haj Amin!" they cheered. Standing on a platform, the mufti told his disappointed audience to return to their towns and villages after Friday prayers. He instructed the sheikhs of the mosque to call for peace and calm in their sermons. At first, they listened. But worshippers urged the crowds to pay no mind to the lies they felt their leaders were feeding them. Just one week earlier, the same sheikhs had led the violent Muslim march on the Western Wall.[20]

One imam, Sheikh Saad el Din, then mounted the podium and told the crowd what they really wanted to hear. With a sword in his hand, he proclaimed, "If we give an inch to the Jews in regard to their demands at the Wailing Wall, they will ask for the Mosque of Aqsa; if we give them the Mosque of al-Aqsa they will demand the Dome of the Rock; if we give them the Dome of the Rock they will demand the whole of Palestine, and having gained the whole of Palestine they will proceed to turn us Arabs out of our country. I ask you now to take the oath of God the Great to swear by your right hand that you will not hesitate to act when called upon to do so, and that you will, if need be, fight for the Faith and the Holy Places to the death."

The barefoot congregants, seated on the floor in row upon row, raised their hands to the sky and swore to shed their last drop of blood in the name of Allah. "Then go," the imam instructed them, "pounce upon your enemies and kill that you in doing so may obtain Paradise."[21]

When the mufti emerged from the mosque with throngs of worshippers, shots rang out from the crowd surrounding him, as men fired their rifles into the skies. "The country is our country, and the Jews are our dogs," they chanted. Thousands poured down from the Temple Mount, pressed through the narrow streets of the Old City, and spilled out of the Damascus and Jaffa Gates, killing 2 Jewish

Jews fleeing the riots in Jerusalem, 1929.

passersby before making their way to Jaffa Road. They set fire to Jewish shops, attacked Jewish pedestrians, and looted Jewish homes. Waving swords, daggers, clubs, and rifles, mobs cried out in rhythmic roars, "The religion of Muhammad came with the sword!"[22]

Mounted British police tried to push back the rioters, but they were overpowered by the crowds, who spread to every Jewish Quarter of Jerusalem. Many Arab policemen joined the riots. When a mob gathered outside the office of Acting High Commissioner Harry Luke, he called the Grand Mufti, demanding that he calm his people. Haj Amin came and spoke to the crowd, but his presence excited them even more.[23]

Police fired their first shots around 2:00 p.m., some two hours after the riots erupted, and only after they began to target British policemen. Until then, the attacks had focused exclusively on Jews. Had they shot into the crowd, British officials reasoned, the mobs would have turned their anger on the beleaguered, outnumbered police force.[24]

That afternoon, Harry Luke called up reinforcements from Amman, telegraphed Malta to send warships, and wired the Colonial Office in London to send battalions of British troops. In some Jewish neighborhoods, Haganah squads managed to repel bands of rioters using pistols and hand grenades. "The government here is losing control of the situation," the US consul general in Jerusalem cabled the secretary of state.[25]

CHAPTER 9

Prelude to a Massacre

FRIDAY PRAYERS AT IBRAHIMI MOSQUE HAD JUST ENDED WHEN THE streets of Hebron swelled with hundreds of men. Many were holding daggers, clubs, and wooden sticks. Outside the mosque, sheikhs delivered speeches to growing crowds. "The Jews have killed a thousand Arabs in Jerusalem," declared one of the mosque's preachers, Mahmud Sultan. "The Jews have taken the Wailing Wall and Al-Aqsa, and if you wait longer the Jews will also take the Patriarchs' Tomb."[1]

In truth, the Jews had conquered nothing, and no one was being killed by the thousands. The Jews of Jerusalem had been attacked by Muslims. By day's end, 9 would be dead, and at least 100 wounded. Three Arabs would also be killed by responding British policemen and Jewish defense units working to quell the riots. But the truth had become irrelevant.[2]

Just outside his home in the Jewish Quarter, Chief Sephardic Rabbi Meir Franco saw Sheikh Taleb Marka addressing dozens of armed men. "God and Muhammad are calling upon you to avenge the blood of your brethren that has been shed in Jerusalem," announced the sheikh. Marching down the street, he led the crowd in a chant. "Slaughter the Jews!" he shouted, and the men behind him repeated.

Down the road near the Hadassah clinic, Yehuda Leib Schneerson, whose family owned the Eshel Avraham guesthouse, was tending to the needs of the more than 30 out-of-town Jewish guests who were staying there that Shabbat. Some of them had rented rooms for an entire month. With its mountaintop climate, cool breezes, and quiet surroundings, Hebron was a popular vacation destination for those who wished to escape the blistering heat and humidity that made other parts of Palestine unbearable in August. Around 2:00 p.m., Schneerson heard a sound that was foreign to Hebron. He looked out the window to see a man on a motorcycle arriving on the road that leads to Jerusalem. A motorcycle was a strange sight in a place where traveling by horse and donkey was still more common than driving by car. The motorcycle came to a stop beside a large crowd of men who gathered around him. Schneerson, a descendant of the Chabad dynasty whose family had been in Hebron since the 1800s, understood Arabic. "The blood of thousands of Muslims is being shed by Jews in the streets of Jerusalem," announced the man on the motorcycle before he sped off. "The responsibility devolves on you to avenge yourselves on the Jews."[3]

About an hour later, from his window on the top floor of a house that faced Jerusalem, an American yeshiva student named Dov Cohen saw a procession of cars streaming into Hebron. The mere presence of dozens of cars in Hebron seemed an aberration to the 17-year-old from Seattle. But even more alarming was what was inside them. Overflowing from the doors and windows and sitting on the car roofs, raging men shouted to anyone they passed about Jews killing Arabs in Jerusalem, and calling for revenge.

Cohen watched as a massive crowd gathered around the cars as two of his fellow yeshiva students walked by. Joseph Axelrod was on his way to the doctor when he and his friend Benjamin Sokolovsky stopped to see what the commotion was about. Sokolovsky recognized two prominent sheikhs at the head of the crowd reading aloud from a letter. Suddenly a man in the crowd spotted Sokolovsky and Axelrod. "Here's a Jew!" he screamed. Within seconds, they were being pelted with stones.

Sokolovsky ran home as fast as his legs could carry him. Axelrod, who was stabbed in the back, his hand broken by a rock, scrambled back to his house. While his friends dressed his wounds, their Arab neighbor rushed to get Dr. Zvi Kitayin, a physician from the Hadassah clinic. Kitayin, escorted by a policeman, already knew that something was wrong in Hebron. That morning at the clinic, an Arab patient named Bakri had told a nurse that he would gouge her eyes out that day. Kitayin chased him out of the building, after which another Arab man came in and apologized on his behalf. Kitayin forgave him, and Bakri returned for his medicine.[4]

While Kitayin treated Axelrod's wounds, Raymond Cafferata was walking from the police station to the post office, where he came upon a crowd of 300 to 400 armed men. Sheikh Marka was at their center, delivering a speech in Arabic. When the police chief approached, the crowd dispersed in various directions. One group marched toward the yeshiva, hurling stones at Jewish homes as they passed. Panicked Jewish families scrambled inside, locked their doors, and closed their windows. The shattering of glass and the cries of women and children echoed through the streets. David was at the yeshiva when he heard the mayhem erupt. He rushed home with his housemates and locked the doors.[5]

Rabbi Slonim peered out his window in disbelief as Arabs rushed out of their homes, joining the crowds as they shattered the windows of Jewish houses. Ignoring the pleas of his five children, the rabbi rushed outside, thinking he could calm the raging men. Among them were some he knew well: the greengrocer Said, and various Muslim preachers, teachers, and merchants. Certain that they would hear him out, Slonim begged them in Arabic to calm down and speak with him. No one was listening. Overwhelmed, the rabbi cried and beat himself in the head with his hands. The mob responded by pelting him with stones, then marched toward the yeshiva. Waving his hands in the air, Slonim followed them, hoping to prevent an attack on the students. Police Chief Cafferata, riding a horse alongside four mounted Arab policemen, suddenly appeared.

To the rabbi's shock, rather than stop the rioters, they blocked him from passing and ordered him to go home. As Slonim begged Cafferata for help, a group of Arabs surrounded the rabbi, beating him with sticks. Slonim tried to defend himself with his walking cane while police pushed him home with their horses. From his window, he saw his son Eliezer heading toward the yeshiva. Thinking he would have better luck with his son, Rabbi Slonim ran out again. He was immediately surrounded by a group of Arabs who hit him in the head, back, and arms, all in the presence of Cafferata, who did nothing to stop them, but ordered the rabbi to go home.

From his window, David's best friend, Bill Berman, who lived in the house opposite Slonim's, was stunned to see the crowd beating the rabbi while the police stood by, shouting at him. Berman ran out of his house and tried to rescue the rabbi, but he too was struck with sticks and stones. Rabbi Slonim turned to Cafferata in desperation. "Why don't you stop the rabble from beating us instead of driving us home?"

Ignoring his question, Cafferata repeated his command to go inside. Berman's American landlord, Fanny Sokolover, ran out to her balcony to see what was going on. "Why, this is the Chief Rabbi of Hebron!" she cried out to Cafferata, pleading with him to help Slonim.

"You go inside," Cafferata shouted back at her, raising his police baton in the air, adding, "You Jews are to blame for all of this."

"Yallah, yallah!" the policemen shouted in Arabic, dispersing the rioters, and forcing Rabbi Slonim into his house.

A large pack of men marched toward the yeshiva, about five minutes up the road on the outskirts of Hebron. Another group surrounded the home of Rabbi Moshe Grodzinsky, who lived next door to the Sokolovers with his wife and children. Rioters smashed the windows, hurled stones at the family inside, and tried to break open the doors. The rabbi's children ran to the rooftop, screaming for help. Eliezer Slonim, joined by a few mounted policemen, managed to disperse the rioters. Eliezer then tried to go to the yeshiva, but he too was turned around by the police and ordered to go home. Too afraid to stay inside, Grodzinsky's wife and children went home with Eliezer. Rabbi Grodzinsky refused to leave. Fanny Sokolover, her husband, Ephraim, Bill Berman, and the other yeshiva students who rented rooms from the Sokolovers, also joined Eliezer. With his stature in the city and his friendships with so many of the city's Arab leaders, his house was believed to be the safest in Hebron.[6]

On the other side of town, the yeshiva's stone walls were empty, save for one dedicated pupil. Shmuel Halevy Rosenholtz was already dressed in his Sabbath best. Immersed in his reading, the 24-year-old was unaware of the chaos outside. Like the yeshiva itself, Rosenholtz had moved from Lithuania to Hebron several years earlier. As the rioters approached the entryway, clubs and swords in hand, the yeshiva's Yemenite keeper, Zecharia Ben Meshail, searched for a hiding place. He jumped into a cistern just in time to notice four policemen near the yeshiva. They did nothing to prevent what followed.[7]

Sitting in the yeshiva's main room, visible from the open entrance, Rosenholtz rocked back and forth as he silently studied the wisdom of the Talmud. As his fingers traced the ancient Hebrew letters on the page, a rain of stones shocked him out of his reverie. Blood flowed from his head, trickling onto the pages of his holy book. Dazed, he stood from his seat and ran for the yeshiva doors, directly into the mob. Rosenholtz had just crumpled to the ground in a pool of blood at the threshold of the yeshiva when two mounted policemen arrived. As the crowd retreated, Ben Meshail, still in his hiding place, recognized the man leading the rioters as Abdullah Yaqoub, a teacher at a local Muslim school. In Yaqoub's hand was Rosenholtz's bloodied hat. He raised it in the air with pride, shouting to his followers, "It's a pity we only found one today, but tomorrow we will continue the slaughter!" The men behind him cheered as the moon emerged in the fading summer sky.[8]

Just that morning, Rosenholtz had written a letter to his parents, telling them that if they hear anything about riots erupting in Palestine, they need not worry. In Hebron, he wrote, "There will be peace and quiet."[9]

When Eliezer Slonim finally arrived at the yeshiva, he found Ben Meshail bent over Rosenholtz, pouring water over his head. Thinking Rosenholtz was still alive, Eliezer ran to the home of Dr. Kitayin.

When they returned to the yeshiva, joined by two officials from the British government health office, it was clear that Rosenholtz was dead. Lying at the entrance of the yeshiva, face down on the blood-soaked earth, they lifted his body and rested it on a long study table, usually reserved for examining Jewish texts. Fuming, Eliezer set off for District Governor Kardous's house, while policemen walked Dr. Kitayin home. As he entered his house, Kitayin dodged stones hurled at him by a passing group of Arab teenagers. He would later learn that on his way home from the yeshiva, a man had attempted to stab him. He was held back by the government health officials.[10]

Arriving at Kardous's house, Eliezer demanded that he take charge of the situation. A yeshiva student has been killed, he told him. Another has been stabbed in the back. The windows of nearly every Jewish home have been shattered.

Kardous repeated his advice from that morning, as if nothing had changed. "Stay in your homes and don't go outside," he told Eliezer. "This way you won't get hurt." Kardous instructed Eliezer to warn the rest of the city's Jews to do the same.

As Sabbath settled over Hebron, the city was quiet. The narrow streets of the Jewish Quarter were empty, as families huddled in their darkened homes, waiting for the fragile silence to break.

Now they understood the warnings, but it was too late. Hebron would not be the haven they thought it was.

Having no other choice but to trust Kardous and Cafferata, Eliezer went from house to Jewish house, joined by the city's lone Jewish policeman, Chanoch Brozinsky, and Feivel Epstein, son of the head of the yeshiva, Rabbi Epstein. None of them were armed. Brozinsky's rifle had been confiscated that day, presumably because Cafferata feared he might shoot the rioters. The 32 other policemen on Cafferata's force were Arabs. Their guns had not been taken. Slonim, the only other Jew with a gun in Hebron, had never used it before. As Jewish families sat around their Shabbat tables, Slonim, Brozinsky, and Epstein knocked on doors and warned those inside to stay there. They repeated the promises of Kardous and Cafferata, who had vowed to be responsible for their lives so long as they remained indoors.[11]

David, his housemates, Rabbi Samarik, and his wife, Feige, gathered in the main room of their house to welcome Shabbat with the other Jewish families who shared their multistory home near the yeshiva: the baker, Noah Immerman; his wife, Rissa; and their four children; and the mechanic, Shlomo Unger; his wife, Nehama; and their two children. The windows of the house had been shattered by rioters that afternoon. After the women lit the Shabbat candles, everyone took their seats around the dinner table. The rabbi had just blessed the wine when there was a knock on the door. It was Eliezer Slonim, who came to tell them to stay inside that night, and not to step foot outside in the morning.[12]

Around 9:00 p.m., Raymond Cafferata received a visit from the leaders of Dura, an Arab village just south of Hebron. A car had come to Dura from Hebron, they told him, with a driver who reported that Arabs were being slaughtered by Jews in Jerusalem and Hebron. The mufti wanted them to go out and fight and would fine those who refused, they told Cafferata. "All is quiet," the police chief assured the men, insisting it would stay that way so long as they remained in their village. Before they left, the village heads promised Cafferata they would do all they could to keep their people calm.[13]

After they left, Cafferata phoned police headquarters in Jerusalem and asked for additional men. No one could be spared, he was told. He tried Jaffa, but there too the district police superintendent told him there were no men to send. Next, he called the Gaza station, and was finally promised help "as soon as it was available."[14]

The night passed quietly in Hebron, the silence broken only by the shuffle of horses' hooves as mounted policemen patrolled the streets, and by the occasional Jewish family slowly making their way to what they thought would be the safest place in town: the home of Eliezer Slonim.

CHAPTER 10

Black Sabbath

As the sun rose on August 24, 1929, 70 men, women, and children rose from a sleepless night in the spacious home of Eliezer Slonim. It was early Saturday morning, a time when Eliezer; his wife, Hannah; their 5-year-old son, Aaron; and 11-month-old son, Shlomo, would normally be sleeping. But this Sabbath was no day of rest. The windows of every Jewish home, save for their own, had by now been shattered by stones.

A few of Eliezer's Arab friends knocked at the door, offering to bring his family to a safe house. "I'm staying here, together with my brothers who have gathered in my home," he told them. "Whatever happens to them will happen to me." His friends sat on the steps outside his front door, keeping watch. The doors and windows were locked and barred. Inside, men gathered their prayer books and wrapped their black-and-white prayer shawls around their shoulders. Eliezer looked around at the women and children, elderly rabbis, and young yeshiva students who had taken refuge in his home throughout the night. His wife's parents and younger sister were there too. They had come to stay for Shabbat on Thursday. Eliezer wanted to believe that they would be safe, but he was no longer certain. Leaving his friends to guard his house, he walked to the home of another friend, Issa Arfa, his landlord's brother, and asked him to accompany him for safety.

They picked up Eliezer's father, followed by the Eshel Avraham guesthouse manager, Yehuda Leib Schneerson, and finally Rabbi Franco. Weighing their options, they decided to meet with District Governor Kardous and Police Chief Cafferata. Their offices were just a few minutes' walk down the road, but they would need Arfa's protection. The streets were already filling with men holding clubs and daggers. They eyed the Jewish men and their Arab escort suspiciously as they passed. Rabbi Franco was struck in the head by a stone just before they reached the police station, around 7:30 in the morning. Cafferata, who had slept in the station Friday night, emerged exasperated.

"What do you want?" he asked, incredulously. "I sent an order that all Jews should be in their houses. What are you wandering about for?"

"This order gives the Arabs a chance to attack us," said Eliezer. "It shows the government has no force with which to protect us."

"That is not your business," Cafferata responded.

"You know what happened last night," implored Rabbi Franco. "We demand you protect us."

"Enough! Go home!" Cafferata shouted. "If you go out I am not responsible, but if you stay in your houses I am responsible."

"We are afraid," Eliezer pleaded.

"Go along," Cafferata insisted. "There's nothing to fear."

He sent them home with Brożinsky, the unarmed Jewish policeman.

Walking back to Eliezer's house, the streets had grown busier. Cars were arriving from Jerusalem, and villagers were pouring in from the hills and valleys surrounding Hebron. Arfa became fidgety. Suddenly he stopped and exchanged whispers with a passing friend. Arfa turned to Eliezer and told him that Hebron's Muslim Council was willing to make a deal. "If you hand over the foreigners among you, your lives will be saved," he said. Eliezer stared back at his friend, pondering his reply. Then, looking Arfa directly in the eyes, Eliezer responded calmly. "We Jews are one people," he said. "There are no foreigners among us."

By 8:00 a.m., the streets of Hebron were filled with some 3,000 Arab men from Hebron and neighboring villages, armed with swords, daggers, hatchets, butcher's knives, iron bars, and wooden sticks. Rioters marched through the streets calling on Arab residents still inside their homes to join them. Many in the crowd waved their swords in the air, chanting, "Slaughter the Jews!"

At the head of a large mob not far from the police station stood Sheikh Taleb Marka, his son, and other sheikhs and schoolteachers. "In the name of Mufti Haj Amin al-Husseini, we inform you that the day has come to annihilate all the Jews, young and old, and to take their women and property," they announced to enthusiastic cheers from the crowd, which broke off into groups. Some headed for the Jewish Quarter. Others marched in the direction of the yeshiva, on the outskirts of Hebron. Those watching from their shattered windows saw nearly a dozen police officers on the streets, making no attempt to stop them. Some spotted policemen among the rioters.[1]

Minutes later, hundreds of men surrounded the home of the Abushdid family, where the Gozlan family had also gathered. They had roots in Algeria and Morocco, and had lived in Hebron for generations. Fifty-five-year-old Eliahu Abushdid owned a grocery store. His 25-year-old son, Yitzhak, was a tailor.

As the mob approached the house, family members ran out to their long balcony facing the road. Still dressed in their pajamas, they called out to policemen and men they knew in the crowd. "Help us!" they screamed. When rioters entered the house, slashing at them with their swords, Eliahu and Yitzhak recognized many of the raging men. From the balcony, Eliahu's wife, Venesia, spotted Issa Shawish El Gorgi, a policeman she knew, walking past the house. "Help us!" she begged him. "If I come up there I will slaughter you myself," El Gorgi shouted back.[2]

"Have mercy on us," pleaded Yitzhak, the tailor who had made clothes for some of them. "Aren't you our friends?"

Yitzhak was strangled with a rope, and swords pierced Eliahu's body. Venesia screamed in agony. "We are natives!" she cried out to the rioters. "Why are you doing this to us?"

One of them grabbed her by the arm. "Curse your religion!" he said as he beat her with his sword. Venesia's 22-year-old daughter,

Shoshana, ran to her mother, clutching her baby boy in her arms. Stabbed and beaten, Shoshana fainted. Her 9-month-old son was taken from her arms, his head smashed against the wall.[3]

As her husband, Yaakov, and her daughter, Victoria, were stabbed by rioters inside the house, Sultana Gozlan sobbed on the balcony. The Abushdids' balcony collapsed under the weight of the attackers and their victims.

Next door lived Meir and Sarah Castel, another Arabic-speaking native family of Hebron. Sixty-nine-year-old Meir was a revered Torah scholar and rabbi, beloved by the city's Jews and Arabs alike. His Arab friends referred to him by his *kunya*, the Arabic name given to mothers and fathers in honor of their firstborn. Rabbi Castel was Abu Yussef, the father of Yosef. Abdullah Bashir was one of those friends. "As soon as I heard about disturbances in Hebron I feared for you and came," Bashir told the Castels on Friday afternoon. Bashir's teenage son had slept at their house on Friday night to protect them. He left shortly after sunrise on Saturday morning, and his father returned. "Collect your valuables, your gold, silver and jewelry, and any bank notes, and give them to me for safekeeping," Bashir told the elderly couple. Sarah gathered all their money and jewelry and handed it to Bashir, who stationed himself on the rooftop with his brother and two cousins. "We will protect you," Bashir assured the Castels, who hid in their bedroom.

Hundreds of rioters amassed outside the house with axes, swords, hatchets, and iron rods.

"Slay them, slay them!" the crowd screamed to the men on the rooftop. "Your brothers in Jerusalem have been killed!"

Realizing that Bashir was guarding the Jewish family inside, one of the rioters declared, "Slay Abdullah Bashir and those who are with him!"

Stones rained over the men on the roof.

Fearing for their lives, Bashir's brother and cousins descended. Just outside the house stood Ali Mustafa Bitar, a policeman they knew. Unarmed, Bitar was trying, with little success, to disperse the mob. Bashir's cousin asked Bitar to go in and rescue Bashir. Bitar went up to the roof, brought Bashir down, and left the house. Seeing Bashir walk out, still carrying all the valuables she had given him, Sarah cried out to him, "Why are you doing this to us?" He left without a word.

Sarah locked the front door behind Bashir, ran back to the bedroom, and closed the door behind her. Atta al-Zeer, a resident of Hebron who was at the head of the mob, broke through the front door with an axe. Dozens of men poured inside. Sarah and Rabbi Castel held each other tight. The door opened, and the mob lunged at them with their daggers. "I will give you all of our possessions, but please give us our lives," begged the rabbi. "We will take your lives and your possessions," said one of the men, who raised his sword over Castel. He and others stabbed the rabbi and his wife. When Sarah fainted, the rioters presumed she was dead. They looted the house, set the beds and pillows aflame, and left. Waking to the smell of smoke, Sarah's eyes darted around the room in search of her husband. She found his body crushed beneath a wardrobe. Rabbi Castel was castrated, a fate that would befall several other elderly rabbis and young yeshiva students.[4]

Down the street, smoke billowed from the Hadassah clinic. Flames licked the stone walls of the building where Hebron's Arabs had received free medical care from the city's Jewish community. Rioters ransacked the rooms, destroying the charitable institution and ensuring that wounded victims would not be treated there. Next to the clinic lived Ben-Zion Gershon, the 73-year-old one-legged pharmacist who had worked there more than forty years. Born in Turkey, Gershon had lost his leg a few years earlier when he went to help a patient and fell down the stairs. His broken leg was amputated to avoid blood poisoning.

Hearing the mob approach, Gershon was sure his family would be spared. He was mistaken. He and his wife, Zehava, cried as men raped their daughter Esther, a 22-year-old seamstress, before murdering her. Gershon's nose and fingers were severed before he was stabbed to death, along with Zehava. Their five younger children were beaten with sticks and left, orphaned, weeping beside the bodies of their mother, father, and eldest sister.[5]

Sixteen-year-old Zmira Mani watched in horror from the window of her family's fourth-floor apartment. Men marched down the street below, singing and waving their swords as if celebrating some gruesome holiday. Some held sacks filled with the spoils of looted houses over their shoulders, while their wives ran out of their homes to take the loot inside. Boys as young as 8 followed their fathers, watched the rampage, and assisted in the plunder.

As the mob approached their building, Zmira and her parents could only wait, knowing they were next. They could not fathom how they could lose their lives at the hands of their own neighbors after their family's history in Hebron. Zmira's grandfather, Rabbi Eliahu Mani, had come from Baghdad in 1848. An esteemed Torah scholar who wrote a dozen books on Jewish spirituality, Mani had served as Hebron's Chief Rabbi and helped establish the Hadassah clinic to serve the city's poor.

Through the doors, windows, and balconies of the houses near their own, Zmira's parents had seen women and girls raped in front of their husbands and fathers before they were killed. Fearing this would be their daughter's fate, they told Zmira to jump to her death from the balcony if the rioters reached their home. Hearing the cries of women and children rising from the floors below their apartment, Zmira began to climb onto the balcony. As she prepared to jump, there was a knock at the door. "Do not be afraid," whispered the voice on the other side. Zmira's father peeked through a crack in the door. It was their Arab neighbor, Abu-Eid Zeitun. He held a wooden stick, and a sword hung from his belt. Zeitun's brother and son stood behind him. As she prepared to throw herself from the balcony, Zmira was pulled back inside. Her parents grabbed her hands and told her to come with them. The family followed Zeitun down the back staircase of the building. Zeitun, his brother, and his son held up their swords, ready to defend the Mani family. As she walked down the stairs trembling, Zeitun took Zmira's hand in his. "It will be all right," he assured her.

Zeitun brought Zmira and her parents to his house, hiding them in a cellar. He closed the door and left. Soon he returned with other Jews to hide, then more. In all, about two dozen people huddled in his cellar that morning. Zeitun's brother handed them a bag of clean

The Hebron riots on August 24, 1929.

clothes and blankets. Sitting beside Zmira was a bereft woman named Simcha Levi. Zeitun had found her crying on the street. Levi had run from her house because she couldn't bear to watch her 17-year-old daughter being raped. Bleeding and weeping, Simcha buried her head in her hands, crying out for the daughter she couldn't save.[6]

More than a dozen people had taken shelter in the home of Rabbi Moshe Goldshmidt, a 31-year-old Chabad Hasid. Before the mob reached their house, everyone except the rabbi, his wife, and three young children had jumped from the second floor of the house into the closed yard behind it, which was owned by the Goldshmidts' Arab landlord. He took them into his home and all survived. Two dozen rioters stormed in and proceeded to torture Rabbi Goldshmidt. When his 5-year-old daughter tried to pull the men from her father, she was struck in the head with an axe. His wife, Mina, was stabbed in the stomach. Lying in a pool of blood, she played dead. Her children hid beneath a bed, and when the men left, local women looted the house.[7]

Swaying back and forth in their prayer shawls, the men inside Eliezer Slonim's house grew quiet. Yeshiva students dragged furniture to the doors. Men and women peeked out the windows. Their guards, Eliezer's friends, were gone. Stones shattered the windows, and men pounded at the front door with axes. The walls of the house rattled. For fifteen minutes the men inside held the doors like stone pillars, keeping the mob at bay.[8]

Suddenly there was gunfire, accompanied by an anguished cry. A bullet had shot through the door and into the face of the yeshiva secretary, Zalman Ben Gershon Wilensky. Another bullet tore through the stomach of Yisrael Mordechai Kaplan, a student from Lithuania. Those who had not lost their power to speak recited their final words, a prayer. *Shema Yisrael, Hear O Israel, the Lord is our God, the Lord is One.*

Rioters burst through the door. Eliezer, the only one with a gun, aimed his pistol at the men who stormed inside. Before he could fire, he was struck over the head with an iron rod. The gun fell from his hand and onto the floor. As he was slashed with swords, Eliezer cried out in Arabic. His last word was *khalil*. Friend.

Issa Arfa, the man who had escorted him through the streets that morning, was now inside his home. Among the dozens of rioters inside his home were others Eliezer had considered friends, and men he had helped during his years as the bank manager.[9]

The 70 people who had taken shelter in the Slonim house hid in the bedrooms and bathrooms, in kitchen cupboards, and beneath dead bodies. Fanny Sokolover and her husband, Ephraim, barricaded themselves inside the master bedroom with 25 others. Men pushed their weight against the door to keep out the mob. The Sokolovers lay on the ground. Fanny placed cushions over their heads and bodies. Peeking through, she saw a man enter the room with an axe, swinging. The first body to fall on top of hers was 17-year-old Jacob Wexler, a student from Chicago. Seven more bodies fell on top of Fanny and Ephraim. Soaked in the blood of others, the rioters presumed they were dead.

Like most who had taken shelter at Slonim's house, Yehoshua Leib Grodzinsky arrived on Friday night, along with his mother and brother. Grodzinsky's father, a rabbi, had refused to leave their home. Grodzinsky ran to a side room and found his mother at a window screaming for help. A crowd of Arabs stood outside the window, laughing at her. Grodzinsky grabbed his mother and hid her behind a large bookcase. A young woman, a little boy, and a yeshiva student were also in the room, paralyzed by fear. He pushed them behind the bookcase, then crouched behind it with them.

The slaughter inside the Slonim house went on for thirty minutes that passed like hours. One survivor recalled witnessing "greater horrors than Dante in hell."[10]

When the mob decided that everyone in the house was dead, they took everything of value they could find, and left for the next house. They had slain 22 men, women, and children in the home of their friend Eliezer.[11]

Slowly, quietly, people emerged from behind and below furniture, and from side rooms undiscovered by the attackers.[12]

The survivors went to work quickly, pouring water on the wounds of the injured, tearing their clothes and using them as bandages and tourniquets. After squeezing himself out from behind the bookcase, Grodzinsky's stomach turned when he saw the bodies at his feet. In every direction lay butchered corpses. He took a few steps, straining to walk around the bodies. Some were nearly unrecognizable. His younger brother, Yaakov, had also sought refuge at the Slonim house. Grodzinsky scanned the rooms to find him.[13]

Near the entrance to the house lay the dead bodies of Eliezer Dan Slonim; his wife, Hannah; and their 5-year-old son, Aaron. Hannah's dress was raised, and her underwear torn. Fanny Sokolover approached Hannah's body and saw that her arms were still cradling her infant son, Shlomo. Barely a year old, he had been stabbed in the forehead, and the fingers of his right hand were severed. Sokolover realized that Shlomo was still breathing. Lifting him from Hannah's arms, she gave him first aid, saving his life.[14]

In a heap of bodies next to Hannah's was that of her father, Rabbi Avraham Yaakov Orlinsky. His shoulders were still draped in his prayer shawl, his arms wrapped around his wife, Yentel. On another side of the room lay Shimon Cohen, a 27-year-old yeshiva student from Iran. Next to him was David's best friend, Bill Berman. In another pile was Rabbi Aharon Leib Gutlevski and his son-in-law, Rabbi Bezalel Lazarovsky. Beside them lay Bezalel's wounded 5-year-old daughter, Devorah. She would later die of her wounds.[15]

In a side room, Grodzinsky finally found his 23-year-old brother, Yaakov. His head had been struck with an axe and there was a large bruise on his forehead, likely from a rock. But Yaakov was breathing. Grodzinsky poured water on his head and helped him stand up. While Yaakov waited, too weak to move, Grodzinsky continued to search for survivors. In a side room, he came upon the lifeless body of his brother's 27-year-old wife, Leah. Her dress was pushed up to her waist, and her underwear was ripped apart. Yaakov and Leah had just gotten married four months earlier. Through the window, Grodzinsky noticed police officers outside the house. "Send doctors!" he called out. Many people in the house could still be saved, he told them. "Soon," said one of the policemen. By the time police ferried the injured from Eliezer Slonim's house to the police station half an hour later, Grodzinsky's brother, Yaakov, had died of his wounds. Later that day, Grodzinsky discovered that his father, Rabbi Moshe Grodzinsky, had been tortured and murdered in the home he refused to leave.[16]

Eliezer's home was at the entrance to the city. Up the hill, near the ancient Jewish cemetery, was the home of his father, Rabbi Yaakov Yosef Slonim. Separated by an empty field, Eliezer's 8-year-old sister, Rivka, could only see the front steps of her brother's house. She watched as feathers fluttered over the stairs. At first, Rivka thought it was snow. As if they had studied the pogroms of Eastern Europe, after cutting people to pieces in their homes, rioters tore apart pillows and blankets, covering the carnage in feathers.

Rivka's mother had died in childbirth, leaving Rabbi Slonim to raise his six children on his own. Earlier that morning, he had run outside to seek help from policemen, but was surrounded by rioters. Struck in the head by a thick rope with a heavy knot, he nearly lost consciousness. His 14-year-old daughter, Malka, dragged her wounded father home.

Now the rabbi, his children, and a dozen other Jews who had taken shelter in his home prayed for a miracle. "Slaughter the Jews!" they heard men cheering outside. "Palestine is ours and the Jews are our dogs!"

Slonim's landlord, Abdul Shaker Amer, was known by his kunya, Abu Shaker, father of Shaker. His wife was Umm Shaker. "Go get your father!" Umm Shaker told her son. "They're killing our Jews." It was grape harvesting season, and Shaker's father was in the vineyard. Shaker ran, and minutes later, his father appeared on a white horse. Abu Shaker dismounted and sat on the front steps of Rabbi Slonim's house. "I just wanted you to know that I'm here," he said with a knock on the door. "I won't let them touch you. Don't open the door. Close all the windows and shutters. May God be with you."

The family was grateful, but not so reassured. Abu Shaker was at least 70 years old. They waited in silence as he reported what he saw. "The bastards are killing Jews, and no one is there to help," he said, his voice choking. "The police are accompanying the murderers to the homes of the Jews and waiting outside while they commit acts of murder, and then accompanying them onwards."

Malka would never forget the sound of the mob approaching, with "howls of murder." Rabbi Slonim stood and prayed. Others joined him, preparing themselves for death as they whispered their final blessings. Suddenly they heard Abu Shaker's booming voice. "Get away from here!" he commanded. "You will not kill here." The men pushed him, but he resisted. Despite his age, Abu Shaker had a mighty build. He threw himself at the entrance to the house. "Only over my dead body will you go through here," he shouted.

One of the rioters drew his knife and held it over Abu Shaker's leg. "I will kill you, traitor!"

"Kill me! Kill me!" Abu Shaker dared him. "The rabbi's family is inside, and they're my family too."

Abu Shaker held a special place in his heart for Rabbi Slonim. His son Shaker had once fallen sick with a burning fever. "He won't last the night," doctors told his parents. Rabbi Slonim, their holy man of a tenant, was more optimistic. He sat at the boy's bedside all night, praying for his recovery. By morning, his fever relented, and Shaker recovered. Umm Shaker and Abu Shaker never forgot Rabbi Slonim's kindness. They credited him with saving their son's life.

"Kill me!" shouted Abu Shaker. "I will not move." The knife sliced through Abu Shaker's leg. As his blood flowed, he continued. "Cut me. I won't budge." There was a moment of silence as the rioters consulted one another. The men, women, and children inside the house, hearts pounding, listened closely. And then, a miracle. The crowd walked away. Malka and her father tried to bring Abu Shaker into the house to thank him and treat his wounds, but he refused. "Maybe others will come," he said. "My job is not yet over."[17]

Landlords and Neighbors

Four yeshiva students rented rooms in the home of Liebe Segal and her husband. On Friday night, their Arab landlord, Shaker Halawani, who lived on the ground floor, had tea at the Segal home with several of his brothers, who also lived downstairs. Halawani, the one-eyed proprietor of the house, promised to protect them if there was any trouble the next day. He explained that the riots were the result of Jewish prayer at the Western Wall. Jews were using their money to drive the Muslims out of the country, he told them. Yet he assured the Segals that on Saturday they would close the iron doors of the house, and no one would be able to enter.

Now, as a mob of 50 men approached her house, 26-year-old Segal saw her one-eyed landlord leading them. Rioters poured inside, swinging axes and swords. Among them were two of the men who lived downstairs. Two of the yeshiva boys were stabbed, while another was stoned to death. Liebe Segal huddled in a corner, clutching her 2-year-old son, Menachem, tightly to her chest. Her husband stood guard beside her. One of the attackers approached her with an axe in his hand. "Kill me, but please spare my son," she begged. Segal recognized him as the man who lit the city's streetlamps. He raised his axe and brought it down on her son's head. After losing consciousness, she awoke to the sound of someone walking through the house, asking, "Who is alive?" She thought it was some kind of horrific dream. In her arms was her dead baby, and beside her lay her dead husband. Suddenly Segal felt her own throbbing pain and realized that three of the fingers on her right hand had been severed. Her head pounded from a wound that penetrated to her skull. Suddenly Halawani entered the room. "May I have some water?" she asked him. "There is no water," he told her. "Soon you will all be dead, so give me all the money you have." Segal was too numb to respond. Halawani grabbed a gold watch from the dresser and left.[18]

In the house of Rabbi Samarik, David was doing what he must have believed was the only thing he could do as the sounds of slaughter flowed into the house from every direction. Together with the rabbi and his housemates, Benjamin Hurwitz and Tzvi Froiman, David prayed. Their other housemate, Moshe Gold, had left the house the night before. Around midnight on Friday, after silence had taken hold of the streets, Moshe insisted he check on the head of their yeshiva, Rabbi Moshe Mordechai Epstein. David, Benjamin, and Tzvi thought Moshe had lost his mind. The silence outside was only temporary, they told him. He wouldn't be safe out there; they begged him to stay at the house. Moshe left to be with the revered rabbi. He was the only housemate who survived.

At first, the furniture David and his housemates propped up against the heavy front door kept the mob out, until they discovered that they could tear the shutters off the windows. Rioters dragged 73-year-old Rabbi Samarik outside, beating and stabbing him to death. Inside, David, Benjamin, and Tzvi tried to fight off their attackers. Outnumbered, they were overtaken with swords, knives, and clubs. Rabbi Samarik's wife, Feige, was the only survivor. When the atrocities in Hebron were later denied by Arab leadership and the Arabic press, some of the bodies were exhumed as proof. Hurwitz had been castrated, his face and skull smashed. David's body was not exhumed.[19]

After tearing apart the Samarik house, the mob descended to the lower floor of the house. Shlomo Unger, a 26-year-old mechanic from Poland, was there with his 22-year-old wife, Nehama, and their young children. Unger's Arab employer had promised he would protect his family. He was nowhere to be found. Shlomo and Nehama were killed with axes. Their 2-year-old son, Baruch, and 2-month-old daughter, Shoshana, were later found crying beside them. Baruch was trying to wake them up.[20]

When the Target Shifted

The home of the Heichel family, a grand white building that housed many yeshiva students, was surrounded. Just when the mob had nearly broken down the front door, Police Chief Cafferata approached on horseback, joined by five other mounted policemen. At first, the crowd backed away. Two of the Heichel boys, Dov and Lieb, who had been standing against the door to fend off the attack, opened it and ran to the police officers, begging them to protect the people inside. Seventeen-year-old Dov was quickly surrounded by rioters who stabbed him with daggers as he tried to fight them off with his fists. He fell at the feet of the police officers' horses. Dov's 20-year-old brother, Lieb, hugged Cafferata's horse, dangling from its neck as he begged for help. Rioters beat Lieb with clubs and stabbed him with knives.

After killing the brothers, the rioters turned their attention to Cafferata. "We need to kill him too!" shouted a man in the crowd, as others hurled stones at the British police commander. Realizing his own life was in danger, he fired his revolver into the air, and the mob scattered. Cafferata instructed the other policemen to retrieve their guns from the station. Until now, all of them, save for Cafferata, had carried only clubs. The reinforcements he had been promised from Gaza had not arrived.[21]

The rampage in Hebron ended minutes after police opened fire. Nine rioters were shot dead, most of them by Cafferata. Many others were injured, including an Arab police constable from Jaffa whom Cafferata recognized. Cafferata found him standing, dagger in hand, over the bloodied body of a young woman. Seeing Cafferata aiming his rifle at him, the policeman ran toward another room, shouting, "Sir, I am a policeman!" Cafferata followed him into the room and shot him. Cafferata would later testify before a British commission of inquiry to seeing another Arab "in the act of cutting off a child's head with a sword. He had already hit him and was having another cut, but on seeing me he tried to aim the stroke at me but missed." Cafferata shot him in the groin.[22]

With the streets cleared, District Governor Kardous, groups of policemen, and a government doctor went from house to house gathering Jews and driving them to the police station. Survivors looked like the walking dead. The air was so filled with smoke, feathers, and the smell of death that it was difficult to breathe. Remnants of looted homes were strewn across the streets. Hebron's synagogues were burned and ransacked, and their Torah scrolls, many of them centuries old, destroyed. Torn pages of prayer books fluttered through the streets. Yeshiva students used doors that had been ripped from their hinges as stretchers to carry the wounded. They took care not to step on the holy books that littered the roads.

All told, 59 Jewish men, women, and children had been slaughtered. Dozens more were injured, and hundreds left traumatized for life. Eight more men, women, and children would succumb to their wounds in the days and weeks that followed, bringing the death toll in Hebron to 67, including 12 women and 3 children under the age of 5. Of the dead, 24 were, like David, yeshiva students.

CHAPTER 11

Mourner's Kaddish

THE HEBRON POLICE STATION LOOKED AND SMELLED LIKE A slaughterhouse. On the first floor of the three-story building sat hundreds of Jewish survivors covered in blood: their own, and that of the dead bodies that had shielded them from death. One floor below their victims were the Arab suspects. Cafferata had ordered his men to round up any Arab with blood on his hands or clothing.

Close to 500 Jews were held in three otherwise empty rooms. Against the walls and in the corners sat disheveled men, women, and children. The cries of their friends and loved ones still rang in their ears. Even if they closed their eyes to tune out the world, the horror they had witnessed played in their minds. Widows sat like stones, their somber faces breaking every few minutes to let out an agonizing cry. Children walked around the rooms, holding hands, and offering people help. Yeshiva students who saw their friends butchered wept. There was no need to tear their clothing in mourning. They were already torn.[1]

The police station was in the Romano House, a sprawling stone building with dozens of rooms, built in 1879 by Haim Yisrael Romano, a Jew from Istanbul who established the first center for Jewish life outside the ghetto. During World War I, it was confiscated by the Ottoman authorities for military use. When the British conquered Palestine from the Ottomans in 1917, they turned it into a police headquarters, courthouse, and prison.

When Rabbi Franco saw District Governor Abdullah Kardous enter the building, he asked him, through tears, "Where was your promise that you are responsible for us?"

"The attack was sudden and I couldn't know," Kardous replied.

"Where were the police in civilian clothes who you said would act when needed?" Franco pressed him.

Kardous was silent.[2]

Cries mingled with whispers as people began to ask each other what had befallen their friends and neighbors. No one knew what had transpired outside their own homes and hiding places. Now they discovered who they had lost, and how they had spent their final moments.[3]

Amid tales of horror were tales of heroism. While most survivors lived by feigning death or by hiding behind and beneath furniture and in undiscovered rooms, many others were saved by their courageous Arab friends, neighbors, and landlords. Estimates differ from list to list, but at least 250 Jews were rescued by their Arab neighbors. While roughly 3,000 men participated in the massacre, some two dozen Arab families risked their lives to save at least half the Jews in Hebron.

When rioters arrived at the home of Rabbi Moshe Mesh, the Jews inside were already on the roof. The mob began to climb up to the roof when the rabbi's Arab neighbor, Shaker El Kawasmeh, signaled to the Jews to jump onto his roof. All 7 survived.

Thirty people, including Yehuda Leib Schneerson and Dr. Zvi Kitayin, were saved by their Arab landlord, whose home shared a courtyard with the Eshel Avraham guesthouse. Haj Issa El-Kurdieh hid everyone in his cellar and stood guard outside with his wife, Umm Mahmoud.[4]

A few minutes later, rioters arrived. "Where are the Jews?" they asked.

"They're all gone!" said Umm Mahmoud.

All who hid in Kurdieh's house lived.[5]

After being taken to the police station with the rest of the survivors, including his wife and two children, Dr. Kitayin was summoned to the government health office to treat the dozens of wounded, along with Dr. Daniel Elkana, another Hadassah physician. Many of the injured required surgery at a proper hospital. Yet the roads to Jerusalem were too dangerous. The riots had swept through towns and villages across Palestine. Kitayin and Elkana had not witnessed the destruction of Hebron. Both had been saved by their Arab neighbors. As they treated the wounded, they listened to tales of unimaginable cruelty.

One young girl told of her sister who was stripped naked and rescued from rape by death, after begging her attackers to kill her. A British surgeon told one of his patients that in four years of digging tunnels in World War I, he had never seen atrocities on this scale.

Dr. Lieb Levit, a government surgeon, was treating Liebe Segal when suddenly she pointed at a young Arab man who was also being treated for his wounds. "Here is the man who killed my husband and my son!" Segal screamed. Levit asked his colleagues who the man was. He worked for the city as a lamplighter. When he reported this to Hebron's chief government doctor, Abdul-El, he was told, "This is not a court of justice."

The doctors treated the wounded throughout the night. On Sunday morning, the survivors awoke with a mission to give the fallen a proper Jewish burial. The British officials permitted just 10 Jewish men to attend. They had initially ordered even fewer participants, but 10 was the minimum required for a minyan, the quorum of men stipulated by Jewish law.[6]

Whistle While You Work

From the police station, the British sent 20 Arab prisoners to dig a mass grave for the victims. Some still had blood on their hands and clothes from partaking in the massacre a day earlier. That afternoon, government officials collected the dead bodies from the government health office. They laid them in a field and summoned a group of Jews to identify each one.[7]

As the sun set over the city of their forefathers, hundreds of survivors who were gathered at the police station ascended to the roof. At least their eyes could be part of the funeral procession for their parents, children, sisters, brothers, grandparents, friends, and spiritual leaders. They watched as a row of 10 men, heads bent in mourning, began their journey up the hill to the ancient Jewish cemetery, which sits atop the peak of Hebron and shares the land with ancient olive trees. On the rooftop, they raised their hands to the sky and uttered the same words they summoned on the cusp of death the previous day. "Shema Yisrael!" they cried out, voices cracking.

The mourners walked up the dirt road to the cemetery, carrying the bodies of the fallen. There they met a new kind of horror. The grave diggers were singing and clapping. "We have killed, and we have buried," they sang in Arabic. A few Jewish men approached the district governor in protest. Singing invigorates their work, Kardous explained. After insisting that the police make the singing stop, their request was granted.[8]

The setting sun cast a dark shadow over the cemetery. Glimmers of light peeked through the tree branches. Over the course of the

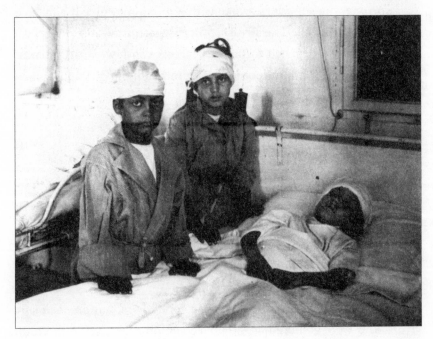

Wounded Jewish boys in Hebron, August/September, 1929.

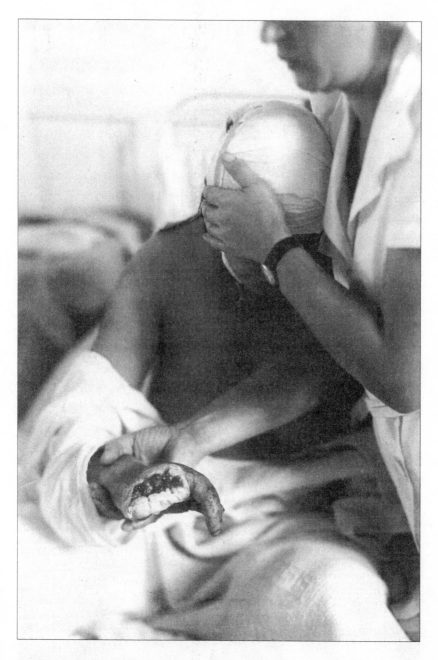

Liebe Segal, whose husband and infant son were killed, and whose fingers were severed by rioters, August/September 1929.

Shlomo Slonim, recovering with his aunt, August/September 1929.

night, under the light of the moon, mourners delicately rested each body in the shallow mass grave, one by one, side by side, in five rows.

The yeshiva students at the cemetery took one last look at their friend from Memphis. Only after his death did the leaders of the yeshiva divulge to the students that it was David who established and financed the yeshiva's charity fund for the less fortunate students. Many of those who came from Europe were poor, and relied on the fund for tutors, clothing, and trips outside Hebron. In letters to Memphis, David often asked his father to send money for new suits and eyeglasses. Sometimes he didn't even give a reason. As it turned out, he was donating much of what his father sent.

With the last victim laid to rest, mourners lifted the shovels of the grave diggers and covered the bodies in soil. It had taken them all night. As the sun rose on Monday morning, they filled the mass grave with the last shovels of dirt. A trembling voice choked back tears and began.

Yitgadal v'yitkadash sh'mei raba....

Standing at the edge of the grave, they looked to the heavens and wept as they recited the chilling words of the Mourner's Kaddish, the ancient Aramaic prayer for the dead, each syllable echoing in the wind.

> May He establish His kingdom in your lifetime and during your days, and within the life of the entire House of Israel, speedily and soon.... May He create peace for us and for all of Israel. And let us say, Amen.[9]

CHAPTER 12

The List

BEDOUINS FROM DESERT TRIBES AND ARAB MILITIAS FROM Transjordan and Syria joined the Arabs of Jerusalem, Jaffa, and Haifa in continued assaults on Jews throughout Palestine. The riots reached nearly every Jewish community. In some parts of the country, the *New York Times* reported, "Assemblages of Arabs in fanatical mood have grown to mobs of 15,000 to 20,000 strong."

The British government, despite all signs of an impending attack on Palestine's Jewish population, had been caught by surprise. Until Saturday, August 24, 1929, Palestine's military force was nonexistent, its skeletal police force worthy of a calm British isle. The colonial army in Palestine was born that day, when the Royal Army responded by air, land, and sea, calling in reinforcements from across the empire to quell the chaos.

More than 4,000 British troops streamed into the country. Eighteen warships, 100 warplanes, tanks, artillery, and infantry battalions were summoned to Palestine. Armored cars arrived from Baghdad, warships sailed from Malta, and infantrymen arrived from Cairo, South Wales, Transjordan, and Great Britain.[1]

"There is not one corner of the land where Jews are to be found, from Dan to Beersheba, which had been left unmolested," wrote a reporter for the *New York Times*. In towns across Palestine, homes were turned to ashes, and people were burned alive. Kibbutzim were destroyed and evacuated. Convoys carrying their residents were brought to Jerusalem and Tel Aviv under the protection of armored cars and troops. "Occasionally," read a report in the *London Times*, "when a convoy is passing through a village, a Jew will run like a hunted animal from his hiding place to the protection of the armored cars."[2]

In Jerusalem and other towns with a mixed population, Christian homes were marked with a blue cross, which told rioters to avoid them. While armed Jewish residents of some towns and cities were able to defend themselves from attack, British authorities were disarming Jewish defense teams and arresting members of the Haganah. Meanwhile, Arabs continued to receive arms and ammunition from Transjordan.[3]

In Hebron, hundreds of men, women, and children remained on the police station floor. They had been given almost no food or water. When Arab merchants came with pita and grapes, the hungry survivors had to pay for them.[4]

Only on Monday, August 26, two days after the massacre, was the road leading from Hebron to Jerusalem deemed safe enough to drive the wounded to a proper hospital. Sixty injured men, women, and children were taken in a convoy of armored cars, joined by hundreds of other women and children, to Nathan Strauss Hospital in Jerusalem. Like the vanquished Jewish clinic in Hebron, the hospital was operated by Hadassah.

As they left Hebron, they breathed in the air, still charred with destruction, and stole final glimpses of the ruins of their beloved city, which most of them would never see again. In that moment, it dawned on them that they were now refugees.

The news from Hebron arrived in the United States that day.

"12 AMERICANS KILLED BY ARABS IN HEBRON AS BRITISH TROOPS REACH JERUSALEM—ARMED MOSLEMS THREATEN NEW ATTACK," read the headline on the front page of the *New York Times*. The riots in Palestine occupied the front page of most American newspapers for close to a week.

David's father, Sam Shainberg, was in New York on business. He'd been worried all weekend, as the headlines from Palestine dominated newsstands.

"47 DEAD IN JERUSALEM RIOT—ATTACKS BY ARABS SPREAD," read the front page of the *Times* a day earlier, on August 25. Upon seeing that news, Sam had cabled Hebron, seeking confirmation that his son was alive. In addition to censoring the Hebrew press in Palestine, the British had severed communication lines across the country. Sam's cable went unanswered.

Newspaper reports named only a few of the slain Americans. David was not one of them. Sam cabled his wife and children in Memphis:

SAW CONGRESSMAN WHO HAS COMPLETE LIST OF
KILLED AND WOUNDED
DAVES NAME NOT THERE

—DAD...

On Monday afternoon in lower Manhattan, a solemn procession of 35,000 Jews marched down Broadway to 44 Whitehall Street, headquarters of the British Consulate General in New York City. Walking peacefully beside rabbis and yeshiva students were Jewish artists, intellectuals, young women with babies in their arms, and elderly Yemenite Jews. Jewish veterans of the Great War who fought alongside the British in Palestine joined the demonstration. It took up twelve city blocks. Two men tapped their way over the pavement on crutches. Both had lost a leg fighting under Field Marshal Edmund Allenby in Palestine.

Led by Elias Ginsburg, a former member of the Jewish Legion in Palestine, and Commander Julius Berg, of the Jewish War Veterans of the United States of America, the masses of mourners stopped when they reached Whitehall. The choir of the Cantors Association of America recited El Maleh Rachamim, a prayer for the soul of the dead. Elias Ginsburg then stood before the microphone and read the resolution they were delivering to the British Consul, Sir Harry Armstrong:

England, which solemnly assumed and accepted from the League of Nations the duties and obligations of the Mandate for Palestine, the chief of which was and is "to place the country under such political, administrative and economic conditions as will secure the establishment of the Jewish National Home," has flagrantly ignored and violated these duties and obligations from the very beginning and has, instead, maintained in Palestine an administration which has shown persistent hostility to the Jews and neglected even to accord them the elementary protection of a civilized government. The present massacre of the innocent Jews of Palestine is and was the inevitable consequence.[5]

The American Jewish community was beginning to understand what many in Palestine already knew. For all its power and its promises, the British Empire could not protect the Jews of Palestine.

On Hawthorne Avenue in Memphis, David's mother could neither eat nor sleep. Elizabeth had not heard from her son in two weeks. David's last letter to his family would only arrive days later.

"The last one we got," Elizabeth told a reporter for the *Memphis Press-Scimitar,* "my boy was so happy because he was progressing so well in school."

Surrounded by her four other children, Elizabeth waited with hope and dread for news from Hebron. Sam was making his way back from New York. Newspapers in Memphis reported reasons for optimism. David's name had not been on the US consulate's list of Americans killed in "clashes" between Arabs and Jews in Palestine. A report in one paper, the *Commercial Appeal,* titled, "Memphis Boy Safe in Rioting Zone," falsely described the school where David was learning as "the scene of severe fighting between Arabs and Jews." Mischaracterizations of the attack on the Jewish community, presented as "clashes between" the Jews and Arabs of Palestine, were common. Still other reports on the "fighting" in Hebron noted that the "Hebrew" victims had been killed not by guns, but by axes, knives, clubs, and swords by "Moslem mobs." Even the Sephardic Jews who lived along-side the Arabs since the time of the Spanish exile were not spared, noted a United Press dispatch.[6]

News of David arrived on Tuesday, in a newspaper on the Shainberg doorstep. The American consulate in Jerusalem had released a complete list of the riots' American victims. Among the dead was a David *Shunberg* of Memphis, Tennessee.

At first came a sigh of relief. There must have been another David from Memphis in Hebron, David's siblings assured their mother. But Elizabeth knew there was no Shunberg family in Memphis. Seeing the names of David's housemates on the list, Elizabeth collapsed. It would take days for her to gather the strength to move.[7]

From that day forward, the Shainberg family would never be the same. David's adoring younger brothers, Herbert and Nathan, lost their faith in God. After all, they thought, if God could not protect a soul like David's, what sort of God is he?

Nevertheless, Herbert and Nathan would go on to establish the Memphis Jewish Community Center two decades later. They remained committed to their fellow children of Israel, their heritage, and their history.

Dozens of condolence letters arrived at the Shainberg house from around the world. In Memphis newspapers and in prominent Jewish publications, David was remembered as a hero. The *Jewish Forum*, a monthly literary magazine published in New York, carried an entire page dedicated to David. "A Hero of Hebron" appeared alongside the poetry of the prominent female Zionist thinker Jessie Sampter, and the writings of the Chief Rabbi of Ireland Isaac Herzog, and literary historian Meyer Waxman.[8]

"The history of the Jews is written in blood and punctuated with tears," said Hardwig Peres, a leader of Memphis's Jewish community, at a gathering of mourning for David on September 1. The memorial was also a rally of indignation by local non-Jewish officials. Addressing the crowd at the Baron Hirsch Synagogue, County Judge David William DeHaven said David's death "focused the attention of all of us on the problem of reviving the Jewish homeland for the Jews."[9]

Next to its front-page dedication to David on August 30, the *Hebrew Watchman* published an anguished outcry by the paper's editor. Titled "Great Britain We Charge You: An Open Protest," the letter proclaimed: "We have heard the cries of pain of the Jewish wounded in the hospitals of the Holy Land. The final echoes of Sh'ma Yisrael of the dying Yeshiva students still resounds in our ears—and even as we write these lines, some Jew is doubtless meeting his death." Just below his letter was a report from Tel Aviv: 1 Jew killed and 13 injured in an attack by Muslims. "Great Britain, we charge you," the letter continued. "You must account for the Jewish dead, for they

Jewish refugees from Hebron in Jerusalem, 1929.

were under your protection—the protection which they should have received under the terms of the Balfour Declaration."

On the same page was a letter written by Bernard Segal, a rabbinical student in New York who had known David. "No Kishinev Pogrom or Romanian massacre robbed Dave from us," observed Segal. "It was a war—the first war for Jewish liberty in the past two thousand years."

It was, in a sense, the first war between Israelis and Palestinians, though neither side would call themselves by these terms for at least another two decades.

CHAPTER 13

Red Tuesday

On August 27, the last remaining Hebron refugees were loaded into cars, driven to Jerusalem, and told never to return. Many lost all their belongings. The Hebron Yeshiva relocated to Jerusalem, where it remains. For the first time in nine centuries, the City of Abraham was a city without Jews. Hebron was, as many European cities would become in the decades to follow, *Judenrein*.[1]

With armored cars at the front and back, the last convoy of Hebron's refugees arrived in Jerusalem to the staccato of machine gun fire. The 6:00 p.m. curfew had set in, and British troops were still fending off Arab attacks on Jewish neighborhoods throughout the city.

"The Moslem Arabs seem to take particular delight in destroying Jewish religious institutions," read a front-page report in the *New York Times* that day. A bomb had been thrown into the Chayei Olam Rabbinical College in Jerusalem. The Rabbinical College of Etz Chaim was in flames, along with Jewish homes. Over the weekend, three synagogues in the Old City had been burned to the ground, and 18 Jews had been killed. Of these, 16 were buried in a single grave on the Mount of Olives, near the grave of Eliezer Ben Yehuda, the man who had pioneered the revival of Hebrew as a spoken language. On Monday, two more synagogues were set aflame, destroying ancient Torah scrolls that were more than 1,000 years old.[2]

Jews had been evacuated from the Old City and other Jewish quarters, taking shelter in the American consulate and heavily guarded hotels. Nearly every Jewish neighborhood in Jerusalem had been plundered, and many Jewish homes destroyed. Among the newly homeless were some prominent Jerusalemites, including

Joseph Klausner, founder of the Pro–Wailing Wall Committee that spearheaded the August 15 march to the Wailing Wall.

Jerusalem's humanitarian situation was dire. Food was scarce, and with work stopped for days, people who were previously earning a few shillings a day, living hand to mouth, were now penniless.[3]

Gaza, home to an ancient Jewish settlement mentioned in the Talmud, also came under attack. Gaza's Jewish community of some 50 families was relocated to Tel Aviv by train. Like the Jews of Hebron, the British instructed them not to return. Across the country, low-flying aircraft drove off Arab looters who had taken over Jewish homes and villages.[4]

Aboard one of the warships that pulled into the Jaffa port on August 27 was the leading British official in Palestine, High Commissioner John Chancellor, who had been on vacation in England for the last month. General William Dobbie, who had signed the ceasefire telegram that ended World War I and was now commander of the Cairo Brigade, arrived by air to help restore order. Still on his way back to Palestine was Arthur Mavrogordato, commander of the Palestine Police. Coincidentally, the day of High Commissioner Chancellor's return to Palestine, the British Colonial Office issued a strange proclamation: "The situation is reported well in hand," it read. "All is quiet in Jerusalem and Jaffa."[5]

Scandals of Jewish Propaganda

On August 29, another massacre was carried out in Safed, the ancient hilltop city that gave birth to Kabbalah, Jewish mysticism. Much like in Hebron, many of the Jewish victims hailed from the Islamic world. Yitzhak Mammon, who lived with an Arab family, was the first casualty. After being stabbed and trampled to death, his lifeless body was mistaken for that of an Arab. Seeking revenge, Arabs from Safed and the valley below ran through the Jewish Quarter with axes and bludgeons. In their rampage, 18 Jewish men, women, and children were killed and 80 others were wounded. Survivors and eyewitnesses described brutality akin to what was seen in Hebron. Bodies were mutilated. Inside an orphanage, rioters smashed children's heads.[6]

The massacre in Safed was considered the final act of the riots. By the end of that bloody week, 133 Jews had been killed and nearly 400 injured across the country. More than half of the casualties were in Hebron, where the attacks were the most savage, and the population most defenseless.

On September 1, High Commissioner Chancellor issued his first proclamation since the outbreak of the riots on August 23. By then British forces had mostly quelled the riots, killing at least 116 Arabs and wounding hundreds more.

"I have learned with horror of the atrocious acts committed by bodies of ruthless and bloodthirsty evildoers, of savage murders perpetrated upon defenseless members of the Jewish population regardless of age or sex, accompanied as at Hebron, by acts of unspeakable savagery," read the proclamation, published in Arabic, English, and Hebrew, and plastered in city squares.

In response, Muslim leaders and the Arabic press worked to redefine what had transpired and who was responsible. According to a New York Times report, Muslims throughout Palestine were claiming that Jews had initiated the riots in Jerusalem by tossing hand grenades at Muslim worshippers emerging from Friday prayers. There was no proof to support that claim, which contradicted every eyewitness report of what had occurred in Jerusalem that morning.[7]

The Arab Executive issued a series of denials and fabrications. The first was a telegram sent to the High Commissioner and posted throughout the land. "Palestine Arabs read with astonishment and regret your Excellency's Proclamation," the statement began. It went on to insist, against all evidence and eyewitness testimony, that "there were no mutilations among Jewish casualties," that "Arabs were mutilated by Jews," and that "Jewish mobs" had murdered women and children. The "troubles in Palestine," the leaders of the Arab Executive went on, "are directly caused by British Zionist Policy, which aimed at annihilating the Arab Nation in its country in favor of reviving a nonexistent Jewish Nation."[8]

Another declaration by the leaders of the Arab Executive carried the title "SCANDALS OF JEWISH PROPAGANDA." Under the headline "No Atrocities," the highest Arab organizing body in Palestine declared, "Actual facts do not substantiate the High Commissioner's statement" regarding "acts of unspeakable savagery." The proclamation ended with these words: "Jewish propaganda in these disturbances was built on falsehoods to deceive public opinion, collect more money and reflect on the dignity and honor of the Arabs."[9]

In a parody of the Arab leadership's denials, the *Times of London* reported, "The Arabs will soon be saying the Jews of Hebron killed one another."

Three weeks later, they did. One of Palestine's Arabic newspapers reported that the Jews of Hebron were murdered by Hebron Yeshiva students to evoke sympathy from American Jews. The statement was attributed to Paul Knabenshue, the US Consul General in Jerusalem. Knabenshue promptly denied ever uttering such an absurdity.[10]

In an appeal to the Muslim world, Palestine's Chief Rabbi proclaimed as libel the accusations that had appeared in Arabic newspapers. Rabbi Abraham Isaac Kook expressed "the hope that notwithstanding the present bloody events, the traditional friendship between Arabs and Jews who are united by race and monotheistic faith, will finally prevail."[11]

That appeal, like others, was ignored. On September 4, the Grand Mufti sent a letter to the High Commissioner, protesting the facts that had emerged from Safed. In his letter, he claimed the city's Jews had instigated the attacks by opening fire on unarmed Arabs. Since Arabs had been killed in the riots, Jews should also be arrested, he argued. His argument that Jews had initiated the attack was quickly proven false.

And, while two Arabs had indeed died in the riots, both were killed by a British police commander.[12]

That same day, the High Commissioner declared the formation of a commission of inquiry to investigate the causes of the riots. The Palestine Commission on the Disturbances of August 1929 were commonly known as the Shaw Commission, named for the commission's chairman, Sir Walter Shaw. The commission would be overseen by three members of British Parliament, one from each of the three political parties.[13]

The Jewish National Council delivered a scathing letter to the High Commissioner, signed by Palestine's Chief Rabbi, explaining that the cause was quite clear to anyone with eyes and ears in Palestine. "There has been conducted in the country a systematic propaganda, both secret and open, for an attack on Jews who are engaged in work of peace and reconstruction. In 1921 they spread within the Moslem masses fears and apprehensions as to their land, their property and their women-folk. Realizing that on religious grounds they would find it easier to incite the Moslem masses, the instigators have now chosen the Wailing Wall as a starting point." This incitement, they continued, was carried out under the watchful eyes of a powerful government that could have stopped it, and should have understood the consequences of allowing it to fester. The government's culpability was at its worst in Hebron, "a butchery without equal in the history of the country since the destruction of the Temple, and one which could have been promptly suppressed by a few shots fired in the air."[14]

The exiled Jewish leaders of Hebron appealed to High Commissioner Chancellor to meet with them, and to visit Hebron to see the aftermath of the massacre himself. In an eleven-page letter written to Chancellor on September 5, the newly formed Committee of Hebron Refugees detailed the atrocities they had witnessed, and the abject failures of the police. They described how the Heichel brothers were killed in the presence of Police Chief Cafferata. They recounted how, when the leaders of the Slabodka Yeshiva first visited Hebron, they had met with the British governor of Hebron, who assured them they would be protected. One-third of the casualties in Hebron were yeshiva students. Had it not been for the heroic Arabs who risked their lives to hide them, they wrote, "Not one Jewish soul would have survived in Hebron."[15]

On September 22, the Zionist Executive published in newspapers throughout Palestine a letter thanking the courageous men and women who saved at least half of Hebron's survivors. "The only redeeming feature in this terrible story is the action of certain of the Arabs who, sometimes at the risk of their lives, sought to protect Jews who had been living among them against the future of the mob incited to acts of barbarity by the deliberately false statements which had been circulated among them by their leaders. To those Arabs of Hebron, who thus sought to live up to the traditions of Arab hospitality, the Executive takes this opportunity of expressing their appreciation."[16]

While the Colonial Office in London published proclamations that the "situation" was "well in hand" in Palestine, and officials assured doubtful journalists that "order had been restored," High Commissioner Chancellor sent a report to London that painted a darker picture. "The latent deep-seated hatred of the Arabs for the Jews has now come to the surface in all parts of the country," he reported. "Threats of renewed attacks upon the Jews are being freely made and are only being prevented by the visible presence of considerable military force."[17]

On October 8, Chancellor visited Hebron to see the homes where Jews had been murdered. "The horror of it is beyond words," he wrote in his diary. Fifteen days after the massacre, the floors, walls, and bedding were still stained with blood. "I do not think history records many worse horrors in the last few hundred years," he wrote.[18]

Journalists who visited Hebron in the weeks after the attack found that Hebron was commercially dead. In the once lively bazaar, merchants' stalls were heaped high with unsold fruit and vegetables, not only because the Jewish residents had been evacuated, but Jews in

Jerusalem and other nearby towns refused to purchase merchandise from the city where the greatest massacre had taken place. At the Tomb of the Patriarchs and Matriarchs, wrote foreign correspondent Pierre van Paassen, "Arabs are burning innumerable lamps before the tombs of the Hebrew Patriarchs in order to calm the phantoms who are restlessly bewailing the shedding of innocent blood. Many superstitious Moslems, it was explained by a sheik, are still afraid to enter the sanctuary."

God Help Palestine

In the weeks after Chancellor's return from London, the British rounded up thousands of Arabs and hundreds of Jews, mainly Haganah fighters who had defended Jewish communities during the riots. Most of the Arabs were soon released or acquitted. Seven hundred were put on trial for inciting or participating in the attacks. One hundred Jews were tried on charges of murder. Some had repelled attacks on Jewish communities. Others had waged acts of revenge.[19]

In the trials of suspects from Hebron, witnesses testified before British judges in white wigs, and the Arab neighbors who they had seen kill their family members. The city's Arab policemen and District Governor Kardous testified almost exclusively in defense of the accused. After hearing the testimony of one policeman, the judge advised him to go back to his former occupation of selling vegetables. After another, the judge declared, "If the police is created just to defend the accused, God help Palestine." The Arab officers in Hebron who stood by as crimes were committed before them were never held accountable. None were removed from their posts.[20]

On September 24, the Hebron court heard the testimony of two orphaned children, 13-year-old Judith Reizman and her 12-year-old brother. The almond-eyed, olive-skinned, Palestinian-born siblings had witnessed the murder of their father, uncle, and grandmother. Asked by the judge if she could identify any of the prisoners who were brought into the court, Judith calmly walked up to Ibrahim Abd El-Aziz, a Hebron merchant and the family's next-door neighbor. "Ibrahim was nearest my father with a knife uplifted when the mob overtook my father," Judith told the judge, her voice barely a whisper. Speaking to Ibrahim, who hung his head in shame, she asked him softly, "Ibrahim, how could you?"[21]

On October 16, Sheikh Taleb Marka stood trial in Jerusalem. A member of the Supreme Muslim Council, Marka was considered a close confidant of the Grand Mufti. Mazal Mizrahi, a Sephardic woman whose father and brother were killed, testified in Arabic to having seen the sheikh at the head of the mob gathered outside her home. Marka had urged the crowd, she said, to slay the Jews inside "in the name of the Prophet and the mufti," and to "take their women and do anything with them you like." She held no grudge against Muslims, Mizrahi insisted. Both she and her husband had been saved by a Muslim friend.[22]

The Commission

From its arrival in Palestine on October 24, until its return to England on December 29, the Shaw Commission held hundreds of hours of hearings in Jerusalem. The commission heard testimony from 140 witnesses, including British officers, the Grand Mufti, leaders of the Arab Executive and the Zionist Executive, and survivors of the massacre in Hebron. The findings of the Shaw Commission and the evidence heard provide the most detailed account of the riots of 1929.[23]

In his hearing on November 7, Cafferata testified that Hebron's Jewish population was not Zionist, and had lived in peace among the Arab majority until August 23. No land or labor, he said, had been expropriated by Hebron Jews at the expense of the Arab population. He confirmed that many Arab notables had led the crowds of rioters, and that other than himself and one Jewish constable, all other officials in Hebron were Arabs. Cafferata characterized the assault as sporadic, fueled by rumors that Jews had killed Arabs in Jerusalem. Had the Jews listened to his orders to remain indoors, Cafferata insisted, he could have maintained order. He confirmed that police first fired at the crowd only around 10:00 a.m., and that the police, being Arabs themselves, were reluctant to shoot. None of them actually hit anyone, he said, as they seem to have fired at the ground or in the air.[24]

In England, Cafferata became a minor celebrity, hailed in the papers as the "Hero of Hebron" who "single-handedly stood up against 20,000 people and saved Jewish children." He received the King's Police Medal for Gallantry and a promotion to police superintendent of Tel Aviv-Jaffa. Among the Jews of Palestine, Cafferata was loathed for what many believed was a deliberate failure to protect Jewish lives. He would later elude several assassination attempts by underground Jewish militias.[25]

Meanwhile, attacks on Jews persisted throughout Palestine. In late September in Jerusalem, an elderly refugee from the massacre in Safed was stabbed to death on his way home from a wedding. In November, a Jewish woman was killed while walking home with a friend who was also nearly stabbed to death. That same week in Nazareth, a Jewish man was stoned on his way to work. In some cities, Jews stopped going out after dark. *Haaretz* declared, "In no country in the world is Jewish life and property so unprotected as now in Palestine."[26]

The denial of Jewish freedom of worship, led by the Grand Mufti, also persisted. On November 14, the mufti's Society for the Defense of Al-Aqsa Mosque held a meeting in Jerusalem in which a letter was written to Palestine's Chief Rabbi. The letter, purporting to represent the views of 1,000 Arabs from Palestine, Transjordan, and Syria, vowed that no organized Jewish worship would be permitted at the Western Wall, "a purely Moslem religious site." If the Jews disobey, the letter warned, "We swear by God to carry our demands into force and place all responsibility which might ensue thereof upon the government. For the sake of peace and public security we deem it a duty

to communicate this to you so that you may take steps to prevent the
Jews from encroaching upon and passing beyond the limits granted
by the Moslems."[27]

The Shaw Commission saved its star witness for the end of its hearings, waiting until December to bring in the mufti. They had already
heard from a long list of Jewish leaders who blamed him for the riots,
and from British officials who claimed they had done everything
within their limited resources to prevent even more carnage.

Over three days of testimony, Haj Amin al-Husseini rejected the
charge that he had orchestrated the riots, while repeating the false
assertions that drove his Al-Buraq campaign, which instigated the
riots. The Grand Mufti began by insisting that the Western Wall was
not the Wailing Wall holy to the Jewish people, but the Western Wall
of the Mosque of Omar, known as Al-Buraq. Jews, he falsely claimed,
had only been praying at the Western Wall for one hundred years at
most. To bolster his claims that the Jews wished to conquer Al-Aqsa,
the mufti referred to *The Protocols of the Elders of Zion*, published in
Arabic under the title "The Jewish Conspiracy against the Nations."

Excerpts had been published throughout 1928 in *Al-Jamia
al-Arabiya*, a nationalist newspaper that was closely associated with
the Supreme Muslim Council, and edited by a member of the Husseini family. *The Protocols* had been exposed as an anti-Semitic fraud
in 1921. The mufti and his British lawyer, W. H. Stoker, did not believe
it was fabricated. Stoker, the former colonial judge representing the
Palestine Arab Executive, assured the commission, "Certain people
who did not like the book being published said it was a forgery."[28]

If Haj Amin truly believed there was a global campaign of Jewish
domination, it was a great feat of mental acrobatics. Had Jews indeed
controlled the world or sought to, they were doing quite a terrible
job of it. While there was no shortage of Arab kings and Arab lands
throughout the Middle East, there were no Jewish kings or Jewish

lands, no country in the world with a Jewish leader or a Jewish majority, and a long list of countries with impoverished, persecuted Jewish
communities.

The mufti's account of what took place on Friday, August 23, differed wildly from the accounts of British officials who were present.
Amid the massive crowds of Arabs in Jerusalem that day, the mufti
did not see anyone carrying clubs, knives, or sticks, merely some
innocent walking canes. The crowds of Muslims who poured into
Jerusalem from neighboring villages that morning, he claimed, had
been beaten by Jews as they walked through the city's Jewish Quarters
on their way to Al-Aqsa. Those gathered inside the mosque "were in a
peaceful and quiet frame of mind," he told the commission. Haj Amin
claimed, against all evidence, that the riots were initiated by Jews who
fired revolvers and threw bombs at worshippers. He then confirmed a
statement he had made to a Reuters reporter, blaming "Jewish ambition and greed," for provoking the Arabs, "in order to gain the support
of the whole world."[29]

The letter signed by the mufti, urging Muslims to fight the Jews
that Sabbath, found in Hebron and many other cities, was a forgery, he
claimed. He had never seen it before. In response to questions regarding
any culpability he had, the mufti's stance was consistent: the Jews were
the only party responsible. The riots were not premeditated or pre-
planned by him or the Arabs, but by the Jews themselves, he claimed.[30]

The mufti blamed Arab anger on the Balfour Declaration, which
he described as an "unjust and unnatural policy." Pressed numerous
times to explain how the Balfour Declaration had negatively impacted
the Arab population, the mufti evaded the question. Finally, asked a
fifth time in a different way, he expressed the fear that Palestine will
become "home for another nation which will come from various parts
of the world," and introduce too many immigrants to the country.
"Many of them have social principles inconsistent with the circumstances and conditions prevailing in this holy land."[31]

What the mufti refused to concede was that Jewish immigration and development had brought great economic benefits to Palestinian Arabs. The editor of the *Filastin*, a prominent Arabic newspaper in Palestine, would later tell the *New York Times*, "Any Arab would openly admit in private how much plenty and progress the Jews have brought him and his country in the course of their building up a national home."[32]

The mufti was asked to confirm a declaration presented at the Muslim conference he oversaw in November 1928. First, it called on the government to "immediately and perpetually" prevent Jews from praying at the Western Wall. It then warned of the consequences if Jews were to pray there, which would compel Muslims "to defend at any cost this Holy Moslem place." Finally, the declaration stated that the government would be held responsible for "any measures which the Moslems may adopt for the purpose of defending the Holy Buraq themselves" if the government failed to prevent an "intrusion on the part of the Jews." He confirmed the declaration was accurate.

Under cross-examination, Sir Boyd Merriman, counsel for the Jewish Agency, read aloud to the mufti one of the many statements published by Palestine's Jewish leaders insisting that their desire was merely to pray freely at the Western Wall, and that there was no desire or intent to encroach upon Al-Aqsa. The mufti confirmed he was aware of these reassurances. He was also aware that the British Mandate, in addition to affirming the right of the Jews to reestablish their homeland, also pledged to uphold the rights of Muslims and guaranteed the immunity of sacred Muslim shrines. He then repeated his belief that Jews have no right to pray at the Western Wall. Their ambition, he testified, was to gradually "expropriate the Mosque of Aqsa."[33]

In hindsight, this claim is even more absurd today than it was then. Al-Aqsa Mosque is now within Israeli territory. Thousands of Muslims pray there nearly every day, and hundreds of thousands every year. Though a limited number of Jews are permitted to visit the Temple Mount during restricted hours, they are forbidden from praying there. Had the Jews truly wished to take over Al-Aqsa, rebuild their temple, or prevent Muslims from praying there, they could have done so long ago. They have not.

In his final hearing before the commission, the mufti was asked why the Western Wall had suddenly become known as the Holy Buraq, and why protecting it had become his passion. Largely evading the question, Haj Amin claimed the wall had been referred to as Al-Buraq since at least the nineteenth century. Merriman then referred the commission to previous criticism of the mufti in the Arabic press, and allegations that explained his exploitation of the Western Wall to distract from such criticism. The mufti nodded. "I agree that what you have said appears in the paper."[34]

While the riots succeeded in ending much of the criticism he had sustained, and united support behind him, Haj Amin continued to attract accusations of corruption. The Supreme Muslim Council went on to raise funds for Arab families impacted by the riots. Needy families never received those funds, which had instead lined the pockets of the council's leaders.[35]

After claiming that the British had favored the Jews and had not involved Arab leadership in governance of the country, the mufti was faced with some facts during his final day of testimony. For years the British had tried to involve the Arabs in governing bodies that made decisions for the country, noted the counsel for the British government, Kenelm Preedy. The most recent example was the effort to create an Arab Agency, much like the Jewish Agency, which oversaw the various institutions of the Jewish population. The Arabs, led by the mufti, had spurned those efforts.[36]

Since the Mandate began, the British had appealed to the Arab leadership to engage in the kind of nation-building that the Jewish community was advancing. In March 1925, Lord Balfour visited Palestine for the first time, where he visited Arab and Jewish villages and took part in the inauguration of Jerusalem's Hebrew University. Ignoring requests to meet with Balfour during his historic visit, the

Palestine Arab Executive held a general strike, draping its offices in black and ordering all Arab shops to close. Arab opinion was divided on the wisdom of the strike, with some in the Arabic press suggesting that instead of futile protests, the leaders of Palestine's Arab population could focus their efforts on more productive pursuits, such as establishing an Arab University in Jerusalem. Sheikhs from across Palestine ignored the mufti's strike, attending Balfour's dedication ceremony at Hebrew University on April 1, where he called on Arab leaders to build the country's Arab institutions. "This gathering marks a great epoch in the history of a people who made this little land of Palestine the center of great religions," declared Balfour. Dressed in a red cloak, he delivered his speech atop Mount Scopus, the golden Dome of the Rock gleaming in the distance behind him.

> From where you are sitting you can see the very spot where the children of Israel first entered the Promised Land, and that it was from this very hill that the Roman destroyers of Jerusalem conducted their siege which brought to an end that great chapter in the life of the Jewish people. Could there be a more historic spot?

Balfour ended his speech with an overture to Arab leaders.

> I hope the Arabs will remember that in the darkest days of the dark ages, when Western civilization appeared almost extinct and smothered under barbaric influences, it was the Jews and Arabs together who gave the first sparks of light which illuminated that gloomy period. If, in the tenth century, for example [as in Cordoba], the Jews and Arabs could work together for the illumination of Europe, cannot Jews and Arabs work now in cooperation with Europe and make this not merely a Palestinian university, but a Palestinian university from which all sections of the population of Palestine may draw intellectual and spiritual advantage?[37]

The first chancellor of Hebrew University was Rabbi Judah Leon Magnes. An early leader of Reform Judaism who dedicated his life to Jewish-Arab cooperation, Magnes envisioned the university as an ideal place to foster such cooperation. Magnes rejected the Zionist vision of a Jewish state in Palestine. He championed the ideal of a Jewish cultural center in a binational state of Palestine, where Jews and Arabs would share equal rights. Magnes played an integral role in building Palestine's first peace movement, Brit Shalom, the Covenant of Peace. Brit Shalom, and the hope of a binational state, disintegrated in the aftermath of the riots of 1929, with several of its leaders acknowledging that its goals were no longer realistic.

"Do you realize that the fact that the Arabs would not co-operate with the Government may be one of the causes why the Arabs have not succeeded in getting some of the things they think they were entitled to?" asked the British counsel. "In a sense, yes," replied the Grand Mufti. "Then, Your Eminence," Preedy concluded, "I will have it at that."[38]

Closing out his testimony, Haj Amin likened himself to Jesus Christ. "It would not be surprising that such a charge would be proffered against me," he said, referring to the charges of incitement levied against him. "The same happened 1,920 years ago, when Jesus Christ Himself was charged and was sentenced, when the Jews were then under the Mandate of the Romans."[39]

On December 24, Sir Boyd Merriman delivered his closing remarks on behalf of the Jewish Agency. In months of hearings, Arab representatives and their lawyers had worked to instill the idea that the riots were fueled by Arab disenfranchisement caused by the Balfour Declaration. If there is true grievance in connection with land, argued Merriman, "why was it that from end to end of this land," during the riots in August, "there was no seething mob crying, 'Give us back our land, our land is being taken from us.' The cry was 'Our holy places are being attacked, our brothers are being murdered in defense of the holy places.'" If the riots were truly about disenfranchisement, he asked the commission, how can you explain what happened in Hebron and Safed, where there were no issues with land or labor. "The answer is that it was incitement not in connection with land. . . . The incitement comes from the top for political reasons."[40]

Noble Heroes of Palestine

In March 1930, the Shaw Commission issued its conclusions. The commission's report delivered a crushing blow to Palestine's Jewish population. While it described the riots as "from the beginning an attack by Arabs on Jews," in which "a general massacre of the Jewish community at Hebron was narrowly averted," the Shaw Commission placed much of the blame on the Jewish community.[41]

The immediate cause of the riots, the report concluded, was the peaceful Jewish demonstration at the Western Wall on August 15, "without which in our opinion disturbances either would not have occurred or would have been little more than a local riot." The fundamental force behind the riots, the report explained, was "the Arab feeling of animosity and hostility toward the Jews consequent upon the disappointment of their political and national aspirations and fear for their economic future." While Jewish enterprise and immigration "have conferred material benefits upon Palestine in which the Arab people share," the report found, the sale of large tracts of land to Jews had led to the eviction of peasant farmers who often had no alternative land on which to subsist. "The Arabs have come to see in Jewish immigration not only a menace to their livelihood but a possible overlord of the future." To ease the tensions in the Holy Land, the commission recommended that the government limit Jewish immigration and Jewish land purchases.[42]

In another blow to Palestine's Jewish community, Haj Amin al-Husseini was cleared of culpability. He retained his all-powerful positions of Grand Mufti and President of the Supreme Muslim Council.

While the violence was influenced by "propaganda among the less-educated Arab people of a character calculated to incite them," the Shaw Commission determined that the British-appointed mufti had neither deliberately incited the masses nor planned the riots.

Yet the report warned, in language that could have been written today: "To the Arab and Moslem leaders there falls a duty which is unmistakably clear. They should make it known to all their followers and to all their co-religionists that, both collectively and as individuals, they are opposed to disorder and to violence ... without cooperation in a spirit of mutual tolerance, there is little hope that the aspirations of either people can be realized."[43]

In a "Note of Reservations" published with the report's conclusions, Sir Henry Snell, one of three British Members of Parliament who oversaw the commission, dissented from much of his colleagues' conclusions. Snell, a socialist politician of the Labour Party who would go on to be party leader, disagreed chiefly with the recommendation to restrict Jewish immigration and land purchases. What is required in Palestine, he concluded, is not a change in policy so much as "a change of mind on the part of the Arab population, who have been encouraged to believe that they have suffered a great wrong and that the immigrant Jew constitutes a permanent menace to their livelihood." These fears are not only exaggerated, he wrote, but wrong. "The Arab people stand to gain rather than to lose from Jewish enterprise."[44]

Snell pointed to reports that found the country to be both underpopulated and undercultivated. The government, he argued, was wrongly and dangerously encouraging the idea that Jewish immigration threatened the economic future of Palestine's Arabs. Jewish development of Palestine, he noted, had increased Palestinian prosperity, raised the standard of living for Arab workers, and "laid the foundations on which may be based the future progress of the two communities and their development into one State." The riots, he believed, were caused by fears and animosities which "Moslem and

Arab leaders awakened and fostered for political needs." The mufti, Snell argued, should be held accountable for his campaign of incitement. "I believe that desire to secure the support of a united Moslem people provided the Mufti with all the motive that he required," Snell wrote. The Muslim innovations at the Western Wall, he argued, "were dictated less by the needs of the Moslem religion and the rights of property than by the studied desire to provoke and wound the religious susceptibilities of the Jewish people."[45]

The 183-page Report of the Shaw Commission ended with Snell's closing arguments. Written nearly one hundred years ago, his words are a damning account of the century-long failure to heed them.

Snell ended with the humble recommendation that "a few men of both races" should meet and establish grassroots movements toward racial cooperation to establish interracial justice and goodwill. "Out of their efforts would grow a reserve of understanding," he proposed, "to unite Arab and Jew in the task of building up a happy and prosperous land."[46]

By the time the Shaw Commission delivered its findings, the trials of those who had participated in the riots had also reached their verdicts. Out of 700 Arabs who stood trial, 55 were convicted of murder and 25 were sentenced to death. Under pressure from Arab leaders, High Commissioner Chancellor commuted all but three of those sentences to light prison terms. Sheikh Taleb Marka, who was tried on charges of incitement to murder, received a two-year jail sentence. He served one month. Atta al-Zeer, Mohammed Jamjoum, and Fuad Hijazi were sentenced to hang.[47]

Of the 160 Jewish suspects who were tried, 2 were found guilty of murder.[48] Naftali Rubenshtein, a 23-year-old Jew from Poland who served as a British police officer until 1929, when he joined the Haganah, was sentenced to three years in prison. After hearing of the massacre in Hebron, he and other Haganah fighters had waged an attack on an unsuspecting group of Arab workers. He was jailed in Acre Prison, alongside the three Arabs who were sentenced to hang.

Rubenshtein was released after thirty months, resettling in the coastal village of Rishpon with the help of the Jewish Agency.[49]

Atta al-Zeer of Hebron was sentenced to death twice. In one trial the court ruled that he had wielded an axe at the head of the mob that broke into the home of Rabbi Castel, where Castel was stabbed to death and castrated. In another case, al-Zeer was convicted of attacking the Kapiluto home, where he murdered a yeshiva student, and stabbed Eliahu Kapiluto, who died of his wounds a year later. Al-Zeer, who worked in his family business as a butcher and skinner, was known for his strength and his temper. He stood more than 6 feet tall, had two wives, and had once lifted a camel. Denying his involvement in the attack, al-Zeer claimed to have been in his vineyards the day of the massacre. The court found the testimony of Eliahu Kapiluto's wife to be more reliable. Mrs. Kapiluto testified that when the mob entered their house, she and her husband ran to the backyard, where Al-Zeer followed them. She turned to him, held him with both her hands, and pleaded with him not to kill them. He threw her to the floor and ran after her husband, stabbing him.[50]

Mohammed Jamjoum was sentenced to death for the murder of four people in the Abushdid house: Eliahu and his son Yitzhak, Yaakov Gozlan and his son Moshe.[51] Fuad Hijazi of Safed was found guilty of killing members of the Afriyat family. "He hated the Jews because they had killed the prophets, and because they had come to Palestine to expel its inhabitants," wrote Ahmad al-Alami in *Thawrat al-Buraq* (The Buraq Revolt), published in 2000.[52]

When Atta al-Zeer, Mohammed Jamjoum, and Fuad Hijazi were sentenced to hang, Arab leaders in Palestine lobbied the British to reconsider. Even Jewish leaders campaigned for lighter sentences, fearing the executions would cause more violence against the Jewish community. Albert Einstein, a self-described Zionist who had helped establish Hebrew University, wrote a letter to the high commissioner urging him to pardon the men, to "help achieve the peace between Jews and Arabs that we strive for."[53]

On June 2, 1930, High Commissioner Chancellor announced his final decision: al-Zeer, Jamjoum, and Hijazi would hang. The Palestinian press condemned the decision, depicting the attacks in Hebron and Safed as acts of self-defense. Crowds gathered in cities throughout Palestine to protest, glorifying the men as martyrs. Palestinian poet Ibrahim Tuqan honored "their bodies in the soil of their homeland, their souls in paradise," in what would become one of his most famous poems, "Red Tuesday."

On Tuesday, June 17, 1930, a day cemented in Palestinian memory as Red Tuesday, Al-Zeer, Jamjoum, and Hijazi were brought to the gallows at Acre Prison, an Ottoman-era citadel built on the ruins of a twelfth-century Crusader fortress. Arab leaders in Palestine soon designated June 17 as Martyr's Day. It is still honored annually.[54]

According to Palestinian writer Yasmeen el Khoudary, these three men are today considered "noble heroes of Palestine" and "three of the most important martyrs in the history of the Palestinian struggle." "From Akko Prison," written by another Palestinian poet in 1930, remains one of the most popular Palestinian anthems. Penned by the nationalist writer Nuh Ibrahim, the song commemorates "Three men and three verdicts; The accusation: love of Palestine; The ruling judgement: execution."[55]

On June 17, 2020, Balad, an Arab party in Israel's parliament, commemorated the ninetieth anniversary of their execution, describing the men as "heroes and martyrs" whose memory is "engraved in the hearts of the Palestinian people on the long road to national liberation." On the anniversary of their execution in June 2022, the Palestinian Authority's official newspaper published an article dedicated to the martyrs. Quoting from a letter written before their execution, the article in *Al-Hayat al-Jadida* read, "We have willingly sacrificed our souls and skulls so they will be foundations for building our nation's independence and freedom, so that the nation will continue to be united and carrying out jihad in order to remove the enemies from Palestine."

The martyrs of Red Tuesday are also glorified in official Palestinian textbooks. "Long live the souls who sacrifice for their own homeland," reads a poem that is used to teach advanced Arabic to children in eleventh grade. "The greatest reward is the death of a martyr," the lesson continues. In the Israeli curriculum, the 1929 Hebron massacre is first taught in the ninth grade. The lesson includes stories of the courageous Arab families who protected their Jewish neighbors from the riots.[56]

CHAPTER 14

Revolution

IF ARAB LEADERS HAD HOPED TO WEAKEN THE THREAT OF ZIONISM, the riots of 1929 had the opposite effect, accelerating the very process they wished to forestall. The trauma of the Hebron massacre and the British response to it was a rallying cry for Zionism, uniting Jews in Palestine around what had until then been a divisive cause. Prior to August 23, 1929, Zionism enjoyed little support from Orthodox Jews, who believed the reestablishment of the Jewish state to be God's realm alone, not a task of mortals.

Until then, many Arabic-speaking Jews in Palestine had viewed the secular Zionist movement with skepticism. In some respects, they had more in common with their Arab neighbors than with the new immigrants from Europe. Now they understood that despite their shared language, culture, and dress, the Arabs of Palestine nevertheless viewed them as the enemy. The Hebron massacre proved to the Jews of Palestine that they could not depend on a foreign country or its police force to protect them. If they wished to live peacefully in their homeland, they understood, they would need their own state and army. The Hebron massacre, in this sense, served as a unifying force for the evolution of Zionism.

Most of the Jews who were massacred in Hebron, Safed, Jerusalem's Old City, and other parts of Palestine were either Arabic-speaking Sephardic Jews or pious Orthodox Jews who rejected Zionism. That these people paid the heaviest price during the riots was a bitter awakening for their communities. After all, massacres of defenseless Jews were only committed in parts of the country where no Hebrew defense forces were present. Where they were deployed, they succeeded in repelling Arab attacks. That was enough to prove that only a Jewish army could save the Jews of Palestine.[1]

In his testimony before the Shaw Commission, Hebron's Chief Sephardic Rabbi Meir Franco was asked if he considered himself a Zionist. His response one year earlier would have likely been in the negative. But on December 23, 1929, he told the Shaw Commission, "We are all Zionists. In our services, in our prayers, three times a day we mention the name of Zion and we hope for the rebuilding of Zion."[2]

In August 1929, the Haganah was almost exclusively an Ashkenazi militia. The riots changed that dynamic, leading a growing number of Sephardic Jews to join the Zionist militias, including the Haganah, and later its breakaway, the more radical Irgun, also known as Etzel.[3]

Shevah Yekutieli, a Haganah commander in 1929, would testify decades later on this dramatic transformation of the community's relationship with Zionism. "The Sephardim did not mix with the Ashkenazim. The European boys with their shorts were alien to them," said Yekutieli, who was responsible for the Haganah's armory in Haifa in 1929. "They always charged that we brought them trouble. Because they lived well with the Arabs." The Arab attacks on Jewish communities had forced them to choose a side. Though many still felt alienated by the secular Zionist movement, they were more alienated by the emerging Arab nationalist movement. "Beginning in 1929, the Sephardim began joining the Haganah," he said. That was when "the Arabs began to do with the Sephardim what they did with us."[4]

The Covenant of Tough Guys

The report of the Shaw Commission was soon followed by the Passfield White Paper, which dealt an even heavier blow to Zionist aspirations. Issued in October 1930 by Colonial Secretary Lord Passfield, the White Paper sought to redress British policy in Palestine. Contradicting the language of the British Mandate, the Passfield White Paper clarified that the development of a Jewish National Home in

Palestine was not, in fact, central to the mandate. It introduced strict quotas on Jewish immigration and severely limited Jewish land purchases, calling for plots of land to be sold only to landless Arabs who had lost the land they lived on when it was sold by Arab landowners to Jews, who then employed Jews alone to work that land. The White Paper criticized that labor policy, promoted by the Jewish Agency, describing it as severely damaging to the economic development of the Arab population. There was no criticism of, or calls for, the Arab landowners who made millions of dollars from these sales, to compensate or otherwise help their own countrymen.

The Shaw Report and the Passfield White Paper were the most disastrous spate of decisions the Zionist movement had encountered. Yet this blow to Zionist aspirations, combined with the deep wound of the Hebron massacre, led to a hastening of the Zionist mission.

For the Jewish community, the immigration restrictions that followed the massacre of Jews in the Holy Land was the epitome of victim-blaming. This was the moment when many Zionists became militaristic in their efforts to establish a Jewish state. The seeds of the Jewish rebellion against the British that ultimately ended the British Mandate were planted here, in the aftermath of the Hebron massacre.[5]

For years the Zionist movement had been divided between the socialist, left-wing Labor party, led by David Ben-Gurion, and the more nationalist, right-wing Revisionist party, led by Ze'ev Jabotinsky. While the Labor Zionists toed the line of the British, supporting cooperation with the Arabs, the Revisionists called for the use of force, if necessary, to establish a Jewish majority state. Leaders of the World Zionist Organization, chiefly its leader Chaim Weizmann, considered that stance too provocative, and rejected pressure from Jabotinsky. After the riots, the Revisionists, once deemed too extreme, now made the more pacifist Labor Zionists seem naïve. Writers and intellectuals previously associated with Labor Zionism, such as Uri Zvi Greenberg, flocked to the Revisionist camp. In the 1929 elections for the 16th Zionist Congress, held weeks before the riots, the Revisionist party had won 7 percent of the votes. In the 1931 elections, the Revisionists won 21 percent.[6]

In the aftermath of the riots, the Revisionists established several clandestine organizations. The first was Brit Habiryonim, the "Covenant of Tough Guys." Founded in October 1930, the group drew inspiration both from Fascist Italy and from the ancient Jewish Sicarii insurgents. In the years that preceded the Roman destruction of Jerusalem in 70 CE, this group of Jewish zealots tried to expel the Roman occupiers of Judaea. Named for the *sicae*, small daggers, they concealed in their cloaks, the Sicarii would draw these daggers at large gatherings, attacking Romans and their sympathizers before disappearing into the crowd. Though the Sicarii are regarded as the earliest model of cloak-and-dagger assassination units, the Covenant of Tough Guys refrained from violence. Cofounded by three writers, including Uri Zvi Greenberg, they mostly staged acts of civil disobedience, including protests against British arrests and deportations of Jewish refugees to Europe, removing Nazi flags from German consulates in Palestine, and blowing the shofar at the Western Wall.

Revisionist Zionists also established a clandestine militia in protest of what they perceived as the Haganah's failure to adequately protect the Yishuv.

The Haganah had been established in 1920 to protect Jewish communities from Arab attacks. Until 1929, it was a decentralized group of poorly armed and barely trained local Jewish defense units who guarded Jewish towns, farms, and neighborhoods. The riots transformed the Haganah into a larger, more capable army, encompassing nearly every Jewish town and city, in which young men and women were trained in the use of arms. Amidst this transformation of the Haganah arose a quiet rebellion from within. Commanders were frustrated by the organization's official policy of restraint, which required members to merely defend Jews from attacks. Counterattacks were forbidden. In April 1931, this group of disillusioned members broke away and formed the Irgun, also known by its Hebrew acronym, Etzel, which stood for the National Military Organization. Abandoning the Haganah's exclusively defensive approach, the Irgun embraced offense and deterrence to counter Arab attacks and British inaction. A decade after its founding, the Irgun and its own breakaway group, Lehi, would come to be regarded as terrorist organizations by the British, the US, and the Jewish Agency.

While the Revisionists grew more extreme, the Labor Zionists, who constituted the mainstream Zionist movement and its leadership, remained dedicated to a peaceful resolution with the Arabs, and to the British promise of a Jewish home in Palestine. On April 8, 1933, Haim Arlosoroff, a socialist Zionist at the Jewish Agency, organized a historic reconciliation meeting at the King David Hotel in Jerusalem, where Zionist leader Chaim Weizmann met with Emir Abdullah, the Arab ruler of Transjordan. The meeting represented the first time Zionist and Arab leaders had publicly gathered to discuss efforts toward cooperation and peaceful coexistence. Palestinian Arab leaders, particularly the mufti, were furious. Both Abdullah and Arlosoroff were later assassinated. Abdullah was killed by an associate of the mufti, while Arlosoroff's assassin remains unknown.

Meanwhile, the refugees of Hebron carried out their own clandestine operation. By June 1931, 96 Jews had returned to live in Hebron—against the orders of the British government, the Jewish Agency, and the Zionist Executive, which viewed the mostly Sephardic, elderly, religious community as too vulnerable to another attack. Upon their return, the refugees discovered that their homes in the Jewish ghetto had been destroyed. The ancient Jewish cemetery, where the victims of the massacre were buried, was desecrated. Nevertheless, they remained, renting homes from Arab landlords.[7]

The Arab president of Hebron's Chamber of Commerce, who favored the Jewish return to the city, told a Zionist official, "The Jews have a claim to be natives of this city no less than we do." Arab business leaders in Hebron had bemoaned the exodus of Jews as the primary factor behind the city's economic collapse after the riots.[8]

The return of this small fraction of Hebron's Jewish community would not last long.

White Paper, Black Letter

However painful the sting of the Passfield White Paper, it wore off quickly. Winston Churchill and other prominent Englishmen penned open letters of protest, highlighting the dissonance between harsh restrictions on Jewish immigration and land purchases, and the British Mandate's commitment to the establishment of the Jewish National Home. Chaim Weizmann's Zionist Organization applied pressure through important channels, leading British Prime Minister Ramsay MacDonald to reverse course.

In a fashion that was typical of Britain's zigzagging Palestine policies, Prime Minister MacDonald sent a letter to Weizmann that essentially annulled the Passfield White Paper. "The obligation to facilitate Jewish immigration," read the February 1931 letter, "can be fulfilled without prejudice to the rights and position of other sections of the population of Palestine."[9]

Arabs in Palestine referred to it as the Black Letter. The promise of equal treatment of Arabs was inconsequential to Arab leaders. What troubled them was the empowerment of a population it had only tolerated so long as it remained a weak minority. For some 1,000 years, Palestine had been a Muslim-majority country ruled by other Muslim countries. They were not prepared to become a minority in a land of Jews.[10]

In the ensuing years, Jewish immigration to Palestine surged, and the tensions of 1929 festered. Between 1932 and 1936, the Jewish population doubled to 400,000, representing nearly one-third of the country's population. With the growth of the Haganah and the Irgun, the Jewish population was no longer defenseless.[11]

Palestinian Arabs had reached the conclusion that the British had no intention of granting them independence. They were beginning to understand that the only way to evict both the British and the Jews was with force against both. Egypt had declared independence from the British Empire in 1922. Iraq had won independence in 1932. In early 1936, Syrians waged a strike that led to negotiations over France's withdrawal from the country. Meanwhile in Palestine, the British were reasserting their commitment to the Zionist cause.

In March 1936, British lawmakers in the House of Commons debated a proposal by the new High Commissioner, Sir Arthur Grenfell Wauchope, to establish a legislative council that would grant Palestine's Arab majority a greater say in the country's administration. Lawmakers from the left to the right were unanimous in their opposition. Save for two conservatives who favored the proposal, members of parliament viewed the council as a threat to the British Mandate's fundamental purpose: the establishment of the Jewish National Home. Lawmakers voiced their support for the moral justice of Zionism and Jewish self-determination, the establishment of the world's first Jewish majority state, to serve as a refuge for the world's most persecuted nation. The earth was brimming with Muslim states and Christian states. The time had come for a state for the Jews in their native land. Zionism had already led hundreds of thousands to flee oppression and pogroms for the one country where their religion did not make them an outcast. Against the backdrop of Hitler's anti-Jewish policies and the near-ban on Jewish immigration in the United States, Winston Churchill warned against trapping Germany's 500,000 Jews in a land where they were "subjected to most horrible, cold, scientific persecution . . . surely the House of Commons will not allow the one door which is open, the one door which allows some relief, some escape from these conditions, to be summarily closed."

The high commissioner's proposal failed in the House of Commons and the House of Lords. One member of parliament observed that he had never witnessed a debate with such unanimous agreement across the political spectrum.[12]

The following month, a new Arab uprising erupted. What began as a spontaneous attack on Jews by followers of a radical sheikh would soon become the greatest rebellion against British rule the Middle East had ever seen.

The Al-Qassam Brigade

On April 15, 1936, Israel Hazan, a 70-year-old new immigrant from Greece, left his home in Florentine, a scrappy neighborhood of Tel Aviv inhabited mainly by Jewish immigrants from his hometown of Thessaloniki. Hazan worked in the poultry business, buying chickens from Arab farmers, and selling them in the market in Florentine. That morning, he and his neighbor Zvi Dannenberg, a young member of the Haganah, filled a truck with empty chicken coops and set out to visit several Arab villages near Nablus. After filling their coops, they began their journey back to Tel Aviv. The sun had set over the hills of Nablus when they reached a roadblock of Arab gunmen, their faces covered with keffiyehs. The armed men were ordering Arab passersby to hand over their cash for the sake of jihad. The men planned to purchase arms to avenge the death of Izz ad-Din al-Qassam.[13]

Al-Qassam, a radical Muslim preacher from Syria, had fought in the rebellion against the French in his homeland. After the French condemned him to death, Qassam fled south to Palestine, settling in the northern city of Haifa, whose mixed Arab-Jewish population would soon become majority Jewish. The Grand Mufti appointed him imam of a new mosque built by his Supreme Muslim Council. Qassam, who preached jihad against the Jews and the British, often with a gun or a sword in his hand, garnered a devout following. His base was the largely illiterate and growing class of former tenant farmers, and Haifa's discontented class of railway and construction workers. The charismatic preacher with a long white beard was a different kind of leader. Unlike the mufti, who lived in a palatial home and rarely spent time with the peasants and working class, Qassam lived and taught among them. In 1931, inspired by the riots of 1929, Qassam established an armed group of guerilla fighters. Known as the Black Hand, the group waged a series of deadly attacks over the next four years, terrorizing Jewish farms and kibbutzim, and destroying British-constructed railways and telephone lines. New recruits pledged their allegiance to Qassam with a pistol or dagger beside their Quran, which they carried everywhere. Qassam provided military training to pious peasants and men who had been released from prison in the wake of the 1929 riots.[14]

Frustrated by the inaction of Palestine's Muslim leaders, in early November 1935, 52-year-old Qassam and two dozen of his disciples sold their possessions to purchase arms, and took to the rugged hills of Mount Carmel. Outside a cave in the Gilboa mountains, they ambushed a group of police officers, killing the Jewish sergeant, and allowing his fellow Arab officers to escape. A two-week manhunt ended with Qassam and his fighters surrounded by British police in a forest outside of Jenin. Resisting calls to surrender, Qassam waged a fierce four-hour battle that concluded with his death. Already a hero to many Arabs, the preacher-turned-warrior was now a legend.

David Ben-Gurion, the leader of the Jewish Agency and chairman of the Zionist Executive, instantly grasped the significance of Qassam's death. This was not just another Arab rioter killed by the British, or an Arab leader interested in power but unwilling to put his own life on the line. This was a man driven by his devotion to the Quran, a man willing to die for what he and his followers considered Islamic land. "This is the first time the Arabs have seen that a man could be found ready to give his life for an idea," he observed in December 1935. There would now be "dozens, hundreds, if not thousands like him."[15] Ben-Gurion had apparently seen into the future: Hamas's military wing is named after al-Qassam.

When Israel Hazan and Zvi Dannenberg drove through those Arab villages in April 1936, they were likely unaware of plans by Qassam's followers to avenge his death by waging the jihad he had preached.

When their truck pulled up to the roadblock, masked gunmen told them to turn off their headlights and give them their cash. When another car passed with a Jewish driver and a German passenger, the Jewish driver was told to get into Hazan and Dannenberg's truck. More Arab cars passed. Their drivers handed over their contributions to the cause, and went on their way. When the gunmen turned back to the Jews in the truck, demanding more money, they told them they had none left. Hazan begged the men to have mercy. All three were shot.

Hazan was the first fatality in what would come to be known as the Great Arab Revolt. Hazan's wife and son, who had remained in Greece, would later be sent to the gas chambers in Auschwitz. It was a fate that befell 95 percent of Thessaloniki's Jews.[16]

The Cheesemaker

The night after Hazan was killed, two young Jewish men dressed in khaki shorts strode into a banana plantation. They knocked on the door of a worker's hut, and opened fire on the fruit picker who opened it. Hassan Abu Rass and his housemate, Salim al-Masri, were the revolt's first Arab casualties.

The coming days saw violent Arab attacks on Jews in Jaffa, where mobs chased down Jews with metal pipes, knives, stones, and bricks. A Jewish electrician who had spent his morning repairing the wiring at an Arab café was knocked off his ladder and stabbed in the back. A 77-year-old rabbi from Afghanistan was stabbed to death in his home. Two days of bloodshed in Jaffa left 16 Jews dead, and 5 Arabs killed by police.[17]

Anticipating another massacre, British authorities evacuated the Jews from Hebron to Jerusalem one last time. After their exodus, just one Jewish family remained. An eighth-generation native of Hebron, Yaakov Ezra's ancestors had arrived after their expulsion from Spain. They were descendants of the famed Spanish poet and philosopher Moses Ibn Ezra, and one of the most distinguished biblical commentators of the Middle Ages, Abraham Ibn Ezra. When the Ezra family fled Spain in 1492, they brought with them several ancient Torah scrolls dating to the eleventh century. Yaakov managed to rescue one of them from the Avraham Avinu synagogue in 1929.

A cheesemaker since childhood, working as his father's apprentice, Yaakov owned a Hebron dairy business with an Arab friend. His son Yosef worked with them. At home, the Ezras spoke Ladino, the Judeo-Spanish language of Sephardic Jews, but they were also fluent in Arabic, and were friends with their Arab neighbors. Under vows of protection from those friends, Yaakov and Yosef stayed in Hebron during the week, locking themselves in their dairy shop at night, and returned to their family home in Jerusalem every Friday for Shabbat.

They too would be expelled one decade later, when the battle between Palestine's Jews and Arabs erupted into civil war.[18]

CHAPTER 15

The First Two-State Solution

THE FIRST SHOTS OF THE GREAT ARAB REVOLT HAD BEEN FIRED BY the brigades of Qassam's followers. But the rebellion was quickly co-opted by Grand Mufti Haj Amin al-Husseini, who organized, armed, and financed the insurgency. The sacred Al-Aqsa compound became a base of operations where weapons were stored, meetings were held, and wanted suspects were granted sanctuary.

Using the Supreme Muslim Council's religious judges to channel weapons to rebels, the mufti received assistance from a new ally: Benito Mussolini. Having made a quiet alliance with Britain's Fascist foe, the mufti received £88,000 from the Italian dictator between September 1936 and September 1937. The elaborate scheme, involving code names and covert meetings in Rome, Geneva, and Lake Lucerne, amounted to nearly $10 million in today's currency.[1]

The mufti's love affair with Fascism began three years earlier. On March 31, 1933, two months after Hitler was sworn in as chancellor of Germany, Haj Amin met with Heinrich Wolff, Germany's consul general in Jerusalem. "Today the mufti told me that Muslims inside and outside of Palestine greet the new regime in Germany, and hope for the spread of Fascist and anti-democratic state authority to other lands," Wolff cabled Berlin. The mufti was eager to promote the Nazis' anti-Jewish efforts, Wolff informed his colleagues.

Germany held its first boycott of Jewish-owned shops the next day. One week later, German Jews were banned from holding positions in government, schools, and universities. They were then barred from working as accountants, doctors, lawyers, and musicians. One month later, Germany ordered the burning of all books by Jewish authors.

In late April 1933, Consul General Wolff met again with the mufti. This time he was joined by other Arab notables. Claiming to speak for all Muslims in Palestine, they declared their admiration for the Nazi regime, and their approval of Hitler's anti-Jewish policies. They had one request: that the Reich do everything in its power to prevent the half million Jews in Germany from reaching Palestine.

The Arab and German representatives may have desired similar ends, but at that point in time, their means of reaching those ends were diametrically opposed. After all, the primary driver of Jewish immigration to Palestine at that time was the Nazi regime's anti-Jewish policies. In October 1933, Wolff warned Berlin, "The Arabs will begin to assign guilt to Germany for their unhappiness when they say that it is the Reich government that sends the Jews to this land."

Soon enough, the Nazis' means would shift, and fewer Jews would have the chance to reach that land.[2]

The effect of Nazi propaganda in the Arab world was already being felt. In 1934, more than 100,000 Jews lived in Algeria, a Muslim-majority country of more than 6.5 million people that was then ruled by France. The Nazi regime had worked to deepen divisions in the French colony through a historically reliable strategy that transcended continents: resentment and suspicion of the country's Jewish minority.

When a drunk Jewish soldier walked into a mosque in Constantine, Algeria's third-largest city, in August 1934, deadly riots engulfed the Jewish Quarter. Newspaper accounts detailed the mutilation of women, the slaughter of children, and families locked inside their homes and burned to death. The scenes in Algeria bore a haunting resemblance to those in Hebron in 1929.[3]

Palestine's Jewish Question

After Mussolini's Fascist army invaded Ethiopia in 1935, and Germany was well on its way to resolving its Jewish question, many Arabs hoped the march of Fascism would reach Palestine and help resolve their own.

"The Middle East is awaiting this opportunity and is doing what it can to hasten its arrival," read the pro-mufti newspaper *Al-Difa* on September 30, 1935. "War is the only means whereby the Arabs could achieve their national aspirations and put an end to the Zionist threat."[4]

On April 20, 1936, five days after the murder of Israel Hazan by a band of Qassam's followers, Arab leaders in Nablus announced the formation of an Arab National Committee, and called for a general strike by Arab workers. After similar committees were organized by other Arab leaders hailing from prominent families in Arab towns and cities, the mufti felt his dominance threatened. Scrambling to place himself at the forefront of what began as a grassroots revolution, he negotiated an alliance with the Qassam group. On April 25, he established the Arab Higher Committee, a nationwide leadership council that united the rival Arab clans, declaring himself chairman. The committee announced a nationwide strike of workers and businesses that would end only when the British government agreed to halt Jewish immigration and land purchases entirely, and establish a system of governance led by the Arab majority. High Commissioner Wauchope tried to negotiate with Husseini, but the talks proved futile. The mufti threatened Britain with the "revenge of God" if Jewish immigration was not frozen.

The strike paralyzed the Arab population and its economy. Arab businesses and agriculture ground to a halt. With teachers on strike, Arab schools across the country closed their doors. Arab men of all strata were instructed to wear the traditional keffiyeh of the working class and peasantry. Arab women, including Christians, were forced to cover their faces with veils, or their entire bodies with burkas. Along with the strike came violent demonstrations in cities across the country, where Jews were assaulted and stoned.[5]

There was a new sense of unity among Palestine's Arabs, with all the normally sparring factions backing the strike. Those who dared not to paid the price.

When one Jerusalem shop kept its doors open, the owner had sewage dumped on his head. A bomb was planted at the home of Hassan Shukri, the Arab mayor of Haifa who expressed sympathy for local Jews who had been forced to flee their homes. Shukri, who had supported the Balfour Declaration and praised the benefits of Jewish immigration and development on the Arabs of Palestine, survived. Others were not as fortunate. A Muslim police officer was assassinated for pursuing Qassam's disciples. The head of Haifa's national committee was killed for his alleged willingness to work with Jews, as was the acting mayor of Hebron.[6]

Jewish and British casualties of the rebellion mounted quickly. In June, attacks by Arabs killed 9 Jews. A group of British soldiers was slain while swimming in the Sea of Galilee. Jewish farmers found 75,000 of their trees uprooted, and 50 of their cows slaughtered. In August, Lewis Bellig, a Jewish professor of Arabic literature, was murdered at his desk at Hebrew University. According to Bellig's obituary in the *Palestine Post,* the manuscript he had been preparing, a "Concordance of Ancient Arabic Literature," was splattered with blood. Bellig, the obituary read, "probably did more for Arabic culture and advancement than any of the present Arab leaders."[7]

Six months into the strike, the death toll had reached 28 Britons, 80 Jews, and at least 200 Arabs. Another casualty, the Arab economy, was becoming a liability for the mufti. Farmers begged the Arab Higher Committee to allow them to return to their harvests. To save face, the mufti turned to neighboring Arab monarchies to call for a pause in the rebellion. A joint plea, drafted by the mufti's AHC, was released by the rulers of Saudi Arabia, Iraq, and Transjordan, calling for the Arabs of Palestine to end the carnage and cooperate with the British. The strike ended on October 12, 1936. Yet this was merely the first phase of the Great Arab Revolt.[8]

Chief Villain of the Peace

With the incessant attacks behind them, at least for now, the British Mandate government took to a favorite pastime: a Royal Commission of Inquiry. The Peel Commission, named for its chairman, Lord Peel, was sent to Palestine to determine the causes of the violence and a plan for the future. The mufti boycotted the Peel Commission even before it arrived, declaring that no Arab would participate in the inquiry so long as Jewish immigration continued. Though the Colonial Secretary sought to appease Arab sentiment by approving just one-fifth of the immigration quota the Jewish Agency had requested—1,800 people over six months—the mufti refused to cooperate and threatened the life of any Arab who did.

Over the course of two months, the Peel Commission held hundreds of hours of secret hearings on the future of Palestine, featuring a cast of leading British and Jewish officials, including Winston Churchill, David Ben-Gurion, Herbert Samuel, John Chancellor, Chaim Weizmann, and other lesser-known figures. The hearings, held behind closed doors, were conducted at the Palace Hotel. The aptly named palatial establishment had been financed by the mufti's Supreme Muslim Council and built by Weizmann's brother-in-law, Haganah commander Baruch Katinka.

Arriving at the hotel, the six men appointed to the commission received letters from the mufti welcoming them to "this holy Arab land." He apologized for not being able to participate in their commission, but Britain's efforts to "Judaize" a "purely Arab country" had left him no choice.[9]

The Six Million in 1936

Weizmann, who appeared before the commission five times, began his testimony with an urgent plea to allow more Jews to enter Palestine before it was too late. In words that are chilling in retrospect, he explained that there were now in Europe "six million people pent up in places where they are not wanted, and for whom the world is divided into places where they cannot live, and places into which they may not enter."[10]

The United States had for more than a decade closed its doors to Jews fleeing persecution in Europe. In Stalin's Russia, Judaism was effectively outlawed. The Jews needed a home. That home, Weizmann told the commissioners, was in the Jewish homeland. The Muslims had vast kingdoms in Egypt, Iraq, Saudi Arabia, Transjordan, and Syria, on top of at least a dozen other states where Muslims were a majority, represented by a Muslim head of state.

Could the Jews not have one small sliver of land to call their own in this world?

"The underlying cause is that we exist," Weizmann argued. "The only question you have to answer is—have we a right to exist? If you answer that question positively, everything else flows from it."[11]

Revisionist leader Ze'ev Jabotinsky had been banned by the British from entering Palestine in 1930 after he delivered the harshest public condemnations of the British in the aftermath of the riots. Jabotinsky was interviewed by the commission in London. Echoing Weizmann, Jabotinsky told the commission that the source of Jewish oppression was being "everywhere a minority, nowhere a majority," writes Oren Kessler in *Palestine 1936.* Jabotinsky cautioned the commissioners that time was of the essence. "We have got to save millions, many millions," he warned.

Yet he differed from Weizmann in his solution to that stateless-ness. Weizmann had told the commission that the Jews did not need a majority Jewish state. He proposed a governing system with equal representation for Arabs and Jews. Jabotinsky, however, insisted the Jews needed nothing less than a sovereign Jewish state with a Jewish majority. That state would be inhabited by Arabs as well, he explained, but the creation of a Jewish state should not necessitate war.

"The Arabs of Palestine will necessarily become a minority," said Jabotinsky. "What I do deny is that is a hardship. That is not a hardship on any race, any nation, possessing so many national states now and so many more national states in the future. One fraction, one branch of that race, and not a big one, will have to live in someone else's state."[12] Living in other peoples' lands was something Jews were long accustomed to. Perhaps it was time for other people to live in a Jewish state.

A Clean Cut

The Peel Commission was the first time the British raised the idea of dividing Palestine in two. This was, in essence, the first official proposal of a two-state solution. British officials envisioned the Jewish state forging ties with neighboring Arab states "who will be badly in need of their initiative and money."

In hearings with Jewish officials, the two-state solution was welcomed. Weizmann had in fact been quietly considering such a plan for several years.[13]

After hearing from 80 witnesses, half of them British, half of them Jewish, the Peel Commission prepared to sail back to London. Owing to the mufti's boycott, they had not heard from a single Arab during their two months in Palestine. From the outset, Arab leaders warned that this boycott would lead to a report that favored the Zionists. The mufti, pleased to see how powerful and feared he had become, did not seem to care. According to British police reports, Haj Amin created an atmosphere where any Arab who even approached the commission's members was risking their life.

Days before the commission returned to London, pressure from Arab kings convinced the mufti to change course. He agreed to testify, and would allow Arabs he personally approved to do so as well. Lord Peel agreed to stay another week to hear from Arab witnesses.

Haj Amin appeared before the commission in mid-January. Speaking through an interpreter, as he did not speak English, his testimony was brief and unambiguous. The Balfour Declaration, the British Mandate, the project of creating a Jewish National Home, were all illegitimate, he said. Palestine was and would always be Arab land. He called for the British to ban Jewish land purchases and immigration, and to cancel the Mandate. He repeated his claims that the Jews were a danger to Muslim holy sites. The Western Wall, he insisted, was a "purely Muslim place," to which the Jews had no connection or claim. Their goal, he explained, was to rebuild the Jewish Temple on the ruins of Al-Aqsa.

Without broaching the idea of partitioning Palestine, the commission asked the mufti what he proposed should be done with the 400,000 Jews now living there.

"We must leave all this to the future," he demurred.

Asked if they could remain in Palestine, the mufti replied simply, "No."[14]

In the eyes of many British officials, the mufti's fate had been sealed. Even before the commission arrived, British officials were already tired of him. In a cable sent to Colonial Secretary William Ormsby-Gore late that summer, High Commissioner Wauchope had stated, "The mufti is no real leader." Ormsby-Gore agreed. "I believe him to be not only bitterly anti-Jewish but also anti-British and a rascal."[15]

The British were a bit late to this appraisal. It was the British, after all, who had elevated the mufti to his all-powerful position following his incitement of riots in Jerusalem in 1920. Then, after a commission of inquiry that made clear his responsibility for inciting the riots of 1929, the British inexplicably decided to keep him in that powerful position.

Now, Ormsby-Gore suggested that Haj Amin be deported. The mufti was the "chief villain of the peace," he wrote to the foreign secretary, "and the Seychelles are being got ready to welcome him and a few friends." The islands of the Seychelles, then a British colony, would soon house several deported Arab leaders.[16]

In his testimony before the commission, former high commissioner Chancellor said, "It was a great mistake that the mufti should have been given the enormous powers he now enjoys. . . . I think a change of air to the Seychelles would not be a bad thing."

Though he disapproved of the mufti, Chancellor unwittingly revealed that he had fallen for Haj Amin's propaganda during his years in Palestine. Discussing the ongoing battle over the Western Wall, Chancellor grumbled that the Jews have still "never admitted that the Wailing Wall is a Moslem holy place."[17]

On July 7, 1937, the 400-page Peel Report was published. Declaring that the League of Nations Mandate for Palestine was doomed, it recommended a "clean cut" of the land in two.

"Half a loaf is better than no bread," the report read, quoting an English proverb. "Partition means that neither will get all it wants. It means that the Arabs must acquiesce in the exclusion from their sovereignty of a piece of territory, long occupied and once ruled by them. It means that the Jews must be content with less than the Land of Israel they once ruled and have hoped to rule again. But it seems to us possible that on reflection both parties will come to realize that the drawbacks of Partition are outweighed by its advantages. For, if it offers neither party all it wants, if offers each what it wants most, namely freedom and security."

The Arabs of Palestine, the report went on, would be free from their fears "of being 'swamped' by the Jews." With the protection of their holy places guaranteed by the League of Nations, the proposal "removes all anxiety" over Muslim sites. The Jews, meanwhile, would achieve the primary objective of Zionism—a Jewish nation, planted in Palestine, giving its nationals the same status in the world as other nations give theirs. They will cease at last to live a "minority life."[18]

◆◆◆

The report ended with an appeal to Arab leaders to recognize that there is no prospect for peace in any other policy. The authors told of an unnamed Arab representative with whom they had met, who expressed "his sympathy with the fate of the Jews in Europe."

"There is no decent-minded person," he told them, "who would not want to do everything humanly possible to relieve the distress of those persons," so long as that relief was "not at the cost of inflicting a corresponding distress on another people."

"Considering what the possibility of finding a refuge in Palestine means to many thousands of suffering Jews, we cannot believe that the 'distress' occasioned by Partition, great as it would be, is more than Arab generosity can bear," wrote the commissioners. "If the Arabs at some sacrifice could help to solve that problem, they would earn the gratitude not of the Jews alone but of all the Western World."[19]

For the Arabs of Palestine, who viewed the entire country as their own, the loss of any part of the land represented a great sacrifice. Of all the two-state solutions that would come in its wake, the Peel proposal was the most favorable to the Arabs: 80 percent of Palestine would have been allotted to Arab Palestine. The two independent states would be separated by a buffer zone, stretching from Jaffa to Jerusalem, which would remain under British authority.[20]

Though the Jewish state would encompass just 20 percent of what was already a tiny piece of land, the Zionist leadership, including Ben-Gurion and Weizmann, welcomed the plan as an extraordinary breakthrough. Though they decried its small size and disagreed with its specific borders, they recognized this proposal of an independent Jewish state as a prize with which they could work to negotiate a better framework in the future.

Ben-Gurion described it as a "political conquest and historic chance we have not had since our country was destroyed . . . an opportunity of which we never dreamed, and couldn't dare dream except in our wildest imaginings."[21]

Less moderate figures in the Zionist movement opposed the plan, but with Ben-Gurion and Weizmann behind it, the opposition was overpowered. At the 20th Zionist Congress in Zurich in August 1937, forty years after Theodor Herzl's First Zionist Congress in Basel, the partition plan was the central debate. Urging delegates to support the plan, Weizmann delivered a message to the Arabs.

"There is an Arab nation with a glorious past. To that nation we have stretched out our hand and do so even now—but on one condition." They must recognize, Weizmann declared, "that we have the right to build our home in the Land of Israel, harming no one, helping all. When they acknowledge this, we shall reach common ground."

With just over half of delegates opposing the plan, Weizmann and Ben-Gurion concluded the conference with a compromise. The World Zionist Organization would neither reject nor accept the proposal. Instead, they authorized continued negotiations with the British over the partition of Palestine into a Jewish and Arab state.

At first, an array of Arab leaders supported the partition plan, including the mayors of Jerusalem, Jaffa, Haifa, Jenin, and Nablus; Transjordan's ruler Emir Abdullah; the president of Lebanon; leaders of Syria's nationalist movement; and Musa Alami, a close associate of the mufti and fellow nationalist who had been the go-between for Mussolini's funding of the mufti's rebellion.

All this support vanished when the mufti rejected the plan and deemed any Arab who supported it a traitor who risked assassination.

The mufti's position—that there was to be no Jewish state on Muslim land—became the position of all Arab leaders. The Jews, he said, are "a minority of intruders, who before the war had no great standing in this country and whose political connections therewith had been severed for almost 2,000 years." Palestine, he insisted, will remain an Arab land.[22]

Haj Amin's stance has defined Palestinian identity, politics, and armed struggle ever since.

A century of resistance has not only chipped away at the amount of land allotted to a future independent Arab state in historic Palestine, but also at the reserves of Jewish faith in the Palestinian desire or ability to live side by side in peace.

One month after the Zionist Congress gathered in Zurich to debate partition, the mufti organized a summit at a hilltop village near Damascus, attended by 400 Arab leaders representing nearly every Arab country. Here there was no disagreement. It was "the duty of Arabs and Muslims everywhere to fight as one man" against partition and the creation of a Jewish state, the delegates agreed. The summit concluded with a prayer for Allah to grant victory to their jihad.

Days later, 100 of the conference's participants gathered in a medieval marketplace in Damascus to plan the revival of the revolt that had been on hold for nearly a year. The campaign of terror would begin anew. It would be characterized not only by deadly attacks on Jewish civilians and British officials, but against any Arab deemed a collaborator with the British or the Jews.[23]

CHAPTER 16

The Mufti and the Führer

THE FIRST TIME THE BRITISH TRIED TO ARREST THE MUFTI WAS
one week after the publication of the Peel Report. On July 17, 1937,
police arrived at the offices of the Arab Higher Committee, but Husseini had been tipped off. He slipped out a back door and took refuge in a place he suspected no British official would dare detain him:
beneath the golden Dome of the Rock, atop the Temple Mount.

As his relationship with the British unraveled, the mufti was
already making contingency plans. One day before his escape from
arrest, he held his first meeting with Germany's new consul-general in
Jerusalem, Walter Dohle. Requesting closer ties with the Nazi regime,
Husseini told Dohle he would send a confidential agent to Berlin to
forge those ties.[1]

He would continue to direct the Great Arab Revolt from his sanctuary on the Temple Mount for the next three months, until the rebellion crossed a line and the British decided they had finally had enough
of the Grand Mufti.[2]

It was a Sunday morning in late September 1937. Lewis Yelland
Andrews, the District Governor of the Galilee, planned to begin his
birthday with prayers at the Anglican Christ Church in Nazareth, the
childhood home of Jesus Christ. Andrews read the Bible daily, and
knew the Holy Land better than most British officials. Early in the
revolt, when British forces sought to destroy a building that was suspected of housing rebels and arms, it was Andrews who prevented its
demolition. The domed building just outside of Bethlehem was the

tomb of Rachel, the biblical wife of Jacob and mother of Joseph and Benjamin, two of the twelve tribes of Israel.

As he walked into church that morning, Andrews was assassinated on the front steps by a group of Arab insurgents wearing keffiyehs. While two dozen colonial soldiers and policemen had been killed in the mufti's rebellion, Andrews was the first senior government official to die. No evidence tied Haj Amin directly to the assassination, but the British didn't need any. Ormsby-Gore was convinced that the mufti was not just a "black hearted villain," but the primary source of violence in Palestine, and the greatest obstacle to peace.[3]

On September 30, the British deposed the mufti as leader of the Supreme Muslim Council, declared his Arab Higher Committee illegal, and issued arrest warrants for its members. Five of them were placed on a ship bound for the Seychelles. The mufti, ensconced within the Al-Aqsa compound, protected by armed Nubian guards, hatched an escape plan. Two weeks after he was stripped of his titles, he disguised himself as a Bedouin and descended from the walled Temple Mount by rope. Under cover of predawn darkness, he slipped into a Palestine police car and was spirited away to Jaffa, where he boarded a steamer to Lebanon.

Despite his demotion from the Supreme Muslim Council and his escape from Palestine, the British had no legal means with which to remove Haj Amin from his lifetime post as Grand Mufti. He would retain the title until his death.

Under the surveillance of French colonial authorities, the mufti moved into a villa north of Beirut, where he continued to pull the levers of the revolt and the Arab nationalist movement in Palestine.[4]

As the British worked to implement their partition plan through yet another commission, this one called Woodhead, the mufti led another boycott, ordering rebel fighters to kill any Arab who cooperated with the commission. The only Arab leader courageous enough to ignore the mufti's threats was the ruler of Transjordan, Emir Abdullah. Branded a traitor in Palestine's Arabic press, Abdullah responded by telling one critic, "The Arabs are as prodigal in selling their land as they are useless in wailing and weeping."[5]

One Rebellion Leads to Another

The Great Arab Revolt that began in April 1936 continued until August 1939. By the time the British managed to quell it, 500 Jews and 250 British forces had been killed by insurgents. But, as in nearly every uprising the Arabs of Palestine have waged since, it was they who paid the heaviest price. More than 20,000 were wounded and as many as 8,000 killed. Some 2,000 homes were demolished, and more than 100 Arabs were executed by the British. While most Arab casualties of the rebellion were felled by British bullets, at least 1,500 were killed by their fellow Arabs, mainly the mufti's assassins. In the final months of the revolt, Haj Amin was ordering not just the death of collaborators and political opponents, but anyone suspected of opposing him, including members of his own family.[6]

The British ended the revolt with the help of Jewish defense squads, who were—for the first time in the Mandate's history—armed and trained by the British to aid in counter-terror operations. When the Great Arab Revolt ended, so too did British support for the Haganah, and for Zionism itself.

While the Arabs paid a heavy toll in lives lost, they also gained a historic victory: the end of the British commitment to the Balfour Declaration, announced in the 1939 White Paper.

As war with the Axis powers loomed, the British could no longer afford to risk the wrath of the Muslim world and its leaders, all for the sake of aiding a stateless people in their quest for self-determination.

And so, in 1939, after Hitler threatened "the annihilation of the Jewish race in Europe," the British decided to sever their commitment to Zionism and seek favor with the Arabs. Since Hitler's rise to power, Jewish immigration to Palestine had increased dramatically. With more than 136,000 Jews arriving between 1933 and 1936, the

British concluded that Arab anger could be alleviated through a new immigration policy.[7]

Abandoning the partition plan and its vision of independent Jewish and Arab states, the White Paper called for the prohibition of Jewish land purchases in all but 5 percent of Palestine. Against the backdrop of Nazi persecution, the White Paper capped Jewish immigration to Palestine at 75,000 people over the next five years, a steep decline from the previous two decades, during which 300,000 Jews had arrived on Palestine's shores. Once those five years had ended, future Jewish immigration would be determined by Palestine's Arab majority, which would likely ban Jewish immigration altogether.

Issued in May 1939, the White Paper proclaimed, "His Majesty's Government therefore now declare unequivocally that it is not part of their policy that Palestine should become a Jewish state."[8] It was effectively a death sentence for hundreds of thousands of European Jews.

If the abandonment of the Balfour Declaration had been the goal of Palestine's Arab population, few were celebrating. The Great Arab Revolt had crippled the Arab economy and the fabric of Arab society. One in every five Muslim men had been arrested in the British crackdown on the rebellion. More than 40,000 people had fled the country, mainly those with money and political power. Fields and crops had dried up, half of all cargo that had once gone to the Arab port in Jaffa was now arriving at the new Jewish port in Tel Aviv, and the Arab boycott of Jewish businesses had reduced Arab wages. With most of their political and spiritual leaders detained, deported, or dead, the Arab population was left defeated and hopelessly divided.[9]

The White Paper marked the end of the British-Zionist alliance. Though they had suffered a devastating blow, the Jews of Palestine were in many ways stronger than they had ever been. They were, for the most part, united behind their leader, David Ben-Gurion, and had spent the last decade building up their educational, medical, financial, and agricultural institutions and infrastructure.

By the time the White Paper was published, Palestine's Jewish population had swelled to 450,000—one-third of the population—up from 84,000 in 1922. Jewish landholdings had more than doubled since the mandate began, amounting to one-seventh of the cultivable land in Palestine. The 30-year-old town of Tel Aviv had developed into an all-Jewish city of 150,000 residents. The ancient Hebrew language had been revived, and was now widespread.[10]

Having gained tactical experience waging reprisal attacks against Arabs during the Great Arab Revolt, the Haganah and the Irgun had both become fiercer and more organized fighting forces.[11]

The Freedom Fighters of Israel

On August 26, 1939, the Irgun assassinated Ralph Cairns, a Scottish police officer who was vilified among Irgun members for his alleged torture of the group's members. As commander of the Jewish Section of the Palestine Police's Criminal Investigation Department, Cairns had been pursuing Irgun commander Avraham Stern, when he was killed by a remote-controlled landmine in Jerusalem.

The first assassination of a British official by Jewish militants was widely condemned by Zionist leaders, the Jewish press, and the Jewish Diaspora, but the Irgun was undeterred.

On August 31, Irgun commanders met in an apartment in Tel Aviv to discuss plans to declare insurrection against Palestine's British authorites. British forces raided the apartment, arresting Stern and other commanders.

World War II broke out the next day. In an instant, the World Zionist Organization, the Haganah, and the Irgun set their qualms with the British aside and pledged their allegiance to a far more pressing cause: the Allied fight against the Nazis.

The Irgun declared a ceasefire to allow the British to fight "the Hebrew's greatest enemy in the world—German Nazism." The Irgun turned its focus to facilitating illegal immigration of Jewish refugees from Europe, and sent its fighters to assist Allied forces in the Middle East.

A more radical segment of the organization—led by Avraham Stern—disagreed with that truce. Britain, Stern believed, was the more urgent enemy. As the obstacle to Jewish independence in Palestine, Stern held the British to be a legitimate target despite the war.

The debate within the Irgun raged until the sudden death of the organization's figurehead, Jabotinsky, in August 1940. The dissenting members of the Irgun formed a new group. Its name was Lehi, the Freedom Fighters of Israel, also known as the Stern Gang. Led by Avraham Stern, Lehi's insurgents would prove to be one of the most lethal rebel forces in Palestine, and a pariah of the mainstream Jewish leadership.

On the Run

The Great Arab Revolt had brought the Arabs of Palestine their first victory under British rule. The 1939 White Paper had delivered nearly everything they had called for: negating the Balfour Declaration, it promised heavily restricted Jewish immigration and land sales, majority rule for the Arabs, and full independence within a decade.

Officials at the League of Nations—the precursor to the United Nations—opposed the White Paper because the new policy conflicted with Britain's responsibilities under its mandate.

Despite its overwhelmingly pro-Arab orientation, Arab leadership in Palestine rejected the White Paper. The mufti insisted on a total ban on Jewish immigration and land purchases.[12]

Haj Amin was still pulling the puppet strings in Palestine, and remained a wanted man, whose cunning escape from Jerusalem would not be his last. In 1939, he fled Lebanon dressed as a veiled Arab woman, taking refuge in Iraq, where he remained for two years.

Living in Baghdad, then home to some 100,000 Jews, he joined a pro-Nazi group led by Rashid Ali al-Kaylani. Together they led a rebellion against Iraq's British-backed regime, staging a failed military coup in April 1941. Two months later, after the Farhud pogrom killed at least 180 Jews and wounded 1,000 more,* the mufti and Kaylani fled British forces. They made their way to Iran, which was soon occupied by the British. From there, Haj Amin sought refuge in Mussolini's Italy. His stay there would be brief.[13]

A Preeminently Sly Old Fox

On November 7, 1941, the mufti reached Berlin. Three weeks later, after declaring jihad against the Allied powers, he met with Adolf Hitler at the headquarters of the Third Reich. The official German record of their 90-minute meeting on November 28, 1941, at the Reich Chancellery in Berlin, is painstaking in its detail.

Haj Amin began by thanking the Nazi leader for his sympathy for the Arab cause. You are "admired by the entire Arab world," he told the Führer. Some Arabic newspapers had likened Hitler to the Prophet Muhammad. When Nazi forces defeated France in 1940, there were celebrations in the streets of Damascus. "No more Monsieur, no more Mister, Allah's in Heaven and Hitler's on earth," crowds chanted. Arabic was one of the first foreign languages into which *Mein Kampf* had been translated, in 1934.[15]

"The Arabs were Germany's natural friends because they had the same enemies," the Grand Mufti told Hitler. "The English, the Jews and the Communists." The Arabs, he vowed, "stood ready to participate in the war, not only negatively by the commission of acts of

---

* The Farhud was one of the deadliest pogroms in the Middle East. According to historian Edwin Black, some of the victims were decapitated. Jewish babies were sliced in half and thrown into the Tigris River. Girls were raped in front of their parents.[14]

sabotage and the instigation of revolutions, but also positively by the formation of an Arab Legion."[16]

In lending the support of the Arab world, the mufti sought Hitler's support for the creation of an independent Arab state in Palestine, and the removal of the proposed Jewish homeland. While he received full backing for the extermination of Jews in Palestine, the time was not ripe for German-backed state-building, Hitler told his guest.

Germany was waging an "uncompromising war against the Jews," said the Führer. Naturally, that entailed "active opposition to the Jewish national home in Palestine, which was nothing other than a center, in the form of a state, for the exercise of destructive influence by Jewish interests." Haj Amin could rest assured that the Nazis would do their utmost to prevent more Jews from reaching Palestine, said Hitler. Germany was "resolved, step by step, to ask one European nation after the other to solve its Jewish problem, and at the proper time to direct a similar appeal to non-European nations as well."

Hitler then delivered a solemn vow, instructing Haj Amin to "lock it in the uttermost depths of his heart." First, Hitler would carry on his battle for "the total destruction of the Judeo-Communist empire in Europe." After conquering Europe, Germany would "give the Arab world the assurance that its hour of liberation had arrived." Germany's goal would then be "the destruction of the Jewish element residing in the Arab sphere under the protection of British power." The mufti, Hitler promised, would be "the most authoritative spokesman for the Arab world."[17]

Hitler was impressed with the mufti, whom he described after their meeting as a "preeminently sly old fox." Not one to favor the Semitic race, Hitler attributed Haj Amin's "quite exceptional wisdom" to the likelihood of Aryan genes. The blue-eyed mufti, Hitler speculated, was "a man with more than one Aryan among his ancestors."

The Führer designated the Grand Mufti as "an honorary Aryan," envisioning his most trusted Muslim ally as a potential Aryan ruler of a future Nazi-controlled Middle East.[18]

Haj Amin al-Husseini meets with Adolf Hitler in Berlin, 1941.

The Führer of the Arab World

The mufti faithfully fulfilled his promises to Hitler. Over the next four years, he was a fixture of the Nazi propaganda machine. Under the supervision of Joseph Goebbels's Ministry of Propaganda, the mufti's newly created Arab Bureau prepared and transmitted Arabic broadcasts across the Muslim world. He was also the Nazis' leading recruiter of Muslim fighters, leading tens of thousands to join Hitler's Waffen-SS and auxiliary units.

Haj Amin was generously compensated for his contribution to the Nazi cause. He was furnished with a lakeside mansion in Berlin as his office and residence, a full staff of servants, and a chauffeured Mercedes. As director of the Nazis' Arab Bureau, he had a staff of 20 to 30 men, and a salary of more than 50,000 reichsmarks per month. The base salary of a German field marshal, by comparison, was 26,500 marks per year. Though records offer differing figures, the mufti was arguably one of the most lavishly paid men on the Nazi payroll. In addition to his monthly salary, he received, on average, 80,000 marks for his monthly living costs and operational expenses. Given his penchant for fine food and luxury, the Nazis also procured him a second private residence on one of Berlin's most fashionable streets and suites in two of the city's most glamorous hotels. Haj Amin's generous budget enabled him to entertain the many other pro-Nazi Arab leaders living in or visiting Germany. During World War II, Berlin became home to the largest number of Muslim leaders outside the Middle East.[19]

In Germany, the Grand Mufti was portrayed as the spiritual leader of Islam. Much like his German inspiration, Haj Amin was a uniquely charismatic and hypnotic speaker. His audiences hailed him as "the führer of the Arab world." He was a valuable asset to the Nazi cause, raising support and collaboration among Muslim populations within Axis-controlled countries, and inspiring violence and rebellion in Allied-controlled regions where Axis powers hoped to take control. One of his most substantial contributions to the Nazi war effort was his recruitment of Muslim volunteers from Bosnia and Albania, who participated in the murder of Jews in Croatia and Hungary.[20]

Haj Amin's radio broadcasts from Berlin were much like Nazi broadcasts, only imbued with Islamism. "The divine anger and the curse that the Quran mentions with references to the Jews is because of this unique character of the Jews," he declared on November 2, 1943. "They cannot mix with any other nation, but live as parasites among the nations, suck their blood, embezzle their property, corrupt their morals, and yet demand the same rights that the native inhabitants enjoy." In a broadcast on March 1, 1944, the mufti implored Muslims, "Kill the Jews wherever you find them. This pleases God, history, and religion."[21]

The mufti earned the great appreciation of Heinrich Himmler, a chief architect of the Final Solution, with whom he corresponded often. On November 2, 1943, amidst the mass extermination of Jews in Nazi death camps, Himmler sent Haj Amin a letter of praise and gratitude. "The common recognition of the enemy and the joint struggle against it is what creates the firm foundation between Germany and freedom-seeking Muslims around the world," wrote Himmler. The telegram ended with "warm wishes for your continued struggle until the great victory."[22]

It was from Himmler that Haj Amin learned, in the summer of 1943, that the Nazis had already exterminated 3 million Jews. In contrast to the widespread denial of the Holocaust in parts of the Muslim world today, the mufti was both aware of and pleased with the Final Solution. In November of 1943, Husseini declared that Germany had "recognized the Jews for what they are and resolved to find a definitive solution for the Jewish danger that will eliminate the scourge that Jews represent in the world."[23]

The mufti's influence was not limited to Germany or the Muslim world. According to his memoir, Husseini lobbied the leaders of Hungary, Italy, Romania, Turkey, and Bulgaria, urging them to prevent Jews in their countries from fleeing to Palestine. In the summer of 1943, after receiving reports that 4,000 Jewish children, accompanied by 500 adults, had reached Palestine, Haj Amin asked the German foreign minister to prevent such cases in the future. In the summer of 1944, hearing that Hungary had approved the release of 900 Jewish children and 100 adults, the mufti wrote the Hungarian foreign minister of "the necessity of preventing the Jews from leaving your country for Palestine." By now he knew precisely what was being done to Jews in concentration camps. Nevertheless, he urged Hungary to send Jews "to other countries where they would find themselves under active control, for example, in Poland." That is, in the death camps.[24]

Grand Mufti Haj Amin al-Husseini delivers the Nazi salute to Bosnian recruits
in the Waffen-SS, November 1943.

Nazis at Jerusalem's Doorstep

In late 1942, World War II seemed destined to engulf Palestine. After
seizing a British fortress in Libya in June, German Field Marshal
Erwin Rommel set his sights on the strategic Suez Canal and the vast
oil fields of the Middle East. "Those fighting Jewry can always rely
on the sympathy of the Arab population," wrote the General Staff of
the German army in a pamphlet to prepare troops for the invasion of
Palestine. The mufti's moment had arrived. Just as Hitler had promised in 1941, he could now "unleash the Arab action that he has
secretly prepared."[25]

He came so close.

In October 1942, British forces routed Rommel's army in Egypt, halting the German advance into Palestine and sparing the Jews of the Holy Land the fate of European Jewry. Rommel's Afrika Korps returned to Tunisia, where their campaign had begun, and where the SS had established a network of labor camps. In six months of German occupation, more than 2,500 Tunisian Jews were killed.[26]

Hitler's support for the Arab cause in Palestine never reached the levels Haj Amin had expected. The mufti's requests for the Germans to bomb Jewish targets in Tel Aviv and Jerusalem were rejected. When he succeeded in convincing the Nazis to create a Palestinian unit of the Waffen-SS, its first disastrous operation became its last.[27]

Operation Atlas involved three Germans and two Palestinian Arabs recruited and personally briefed by the mufti. They were tasked with perpetrating what would have been the deadliest attack on the only all-Jewish city in Palestine. The plan, masterminded by the mufti, was to poison the water system of Tel Aviv. The Arab members of the unit were Abdul Latif and Hassan Salama. Latif, a native of Jerusalem, had been sent into exile for his involvement in the Great Arab Revolt. Salama had been a rebel leader in Nablus during the revolt.

On October 6, 1944, the five men leaped from a German airplane into the skies over Jericho, parachuting into the Jordan Valley. Arabs in the area who witnessed the men falling from the sky informed the British police, who launched a search operation. Armed with explosives, £5,000, radio equipment, dynamite, and submachine guns, the operatives dropped some of their equipment as they fell. Their scattered evidence was quickly discovered. On October 16, three of the men were found in the caves of Wadi Qelt, near Jericho, with maps of Tel Aviv, weapons, gold coins, radios, and canisters of white powder. Taken to a lab, the flour-like substance was determined to be arsenious oxide. According to Fayiz Bey Idrissi, the Arab district police commander involved in the case, "Each container held enough poison to kill 25,000 people, and there were at least ten containers."

According to files in British archives detailed by journalist Ronen Bergman in his book *Rise and Kill First*, the captured assailants confessed to their British interrogators that their aim "was to inflict maximum damage on the common enemies of the Palestinians and the Nazis—Jews, British, and Americans." Salama, who was injured during his parachute drop, managed to evade the police. He went into hiding before emerging once again as a leader of Palestinian rebels. Three decades later, his son, Ali Hassan Salameh, would carry out a massacre of Israeli athletes at the 1972 Munich Olympics.[28]

Ironies of History

The Nazi persecution of European Jews accelerated the very process the mufti had rallied against for two decades. Between 1937 and 1947, an estimated 250,000 Jews fled Europe for the Jewish homeland. The continued displacement of Holocaust survivors after the war and their determination to reach their ancestral home helped persuade the UN to propose a two-state solution in Palestine.[29]

With the collapse of the Nazi regime in 1945, the mufti was on the run again—not from the British, but from prosecution for war crimes. In July 1945, the United Nations placed Haj Amin on its official list of Nazi war criminals. Yugoslavia sought to indict him for his role in recruiting 20,000 Muslim SS volunteers. Fleeing to Switzerland, he was caught by Swiss authorities and turned over to the French, who placed him under house arrest in a villa outside of Paris. The British, seeking to have him extradited, were rebuffed by the French, who sought to appease the Arab states.

And then, once again, the mufti escaped. With the help of various Arab leaders, including ambassadors and ministers from Syria, Lebanon, Algeria, and Morocco, he flew to Syria. From there, he traveled through Aleppo and Beirut to reach Alexandria, Egypt.[30]

Appeasement and Protégés

Despite his collaboration with the Nazis, Haj Amin al-Husseini remained the undisputed leader of Palestinian Arabs. The Arab Higher Committee, made illegal a decade earlier, was reincarnated in Palestine by the mufti's cousin Jamal al-Husseini. Pleading before British officials that Palestine's Arabs were "deprived of their chief leader, the Grand Mufti, for whom they cannot accept any substitute," Jamal succeeded in having Haj Amin reinstated as president of the AHC, with British approval, in 1946.

From his base in Cairo, the mufti continued to spread anti-Jewish propaganda throughout the Muslim world and harvested the next generation of Palestinian leaders.[31] It was soon after Haj Amin's arrival in Cairo in 1946 that he became the mentor of his young cousin, a charismatic and ambitious 17-year-old named Mohammed Abdel-Raouf Arafat Al Qudwa al-Husseini. Born in Cairo in 1929 to the daughter of the mufti's cousin, he was better known as Yasser Arafat. The mufti's leading protégé would come to inherit his mentor's throne as leader of the Palestinian people, groomed by the mufti as his successor.[32]

If the mufti felt remorse for his work with the Nazis, or his efforts to keep Jews from fleeing extermination in Europe, he never showed it. In his memoir, he wrote, "I asked Hitler for an explicit undertaking to allow us to solve the Jewish problem in a manner befitting our national and racial aspirations and according to the scientific methods innovated by Germany in the handling of its Jews."[33]

The Grand Mufti's Nazi past has not undercut the reverence that other Palestinian leaders felt for him. One decade after the mufti's death in Beirut in 1974, Yasser Arafat proclaimed his "immense pride" in being the mufti's disciple. As chairman of the Palestine Liberation Organization, Arafat said he was "continuing the path" the mufti had paved. In 2002, Arafat hailed "our hero al-Husseini" as a "symbol of withstanding world pressure, having remained an Arab leader in spite of demands to have him replaced because of his Nazi ties."

In 2013, in an address on Palestinian Authority TV honoring the forty-eighth anniversary of his Fatah movement's first terror attack against Israelis, Palestinian president Mahmoud Abbas declared, "We must remember the pioneers," first among them, "the Grand Mufti of Palestine, Hajj Muhammad Amin al-Husseini." In 2019, Mahmoud al-Habbash, the PA's Supreme Shariah Court Judge and an advisor to President Abbas, posted a memorial to the mufti on Facebook, writing, "Our leaders are our role models."[34]

Though the Grand Mufti was on the Nazi payroll and well aware of the Final Solution, his political descendants deny the very facts of the Holocaust. "We believe the number of 6 million is exaggerated," a new Grand Mufti of Jerusalem, appointed by Arafat, told the *New York Times* in 2000. Israel, he said on another occasion, "is trying to make a new Holocaust of the Palestinian people." Asked how, the mufti argued that taking land is equivalent to genocide. "Besides," he added, "Hitler didn't kill the Jews. That's why we still have Jews today!"[35]

Hamas has long compared Jews to Nazis, and denied the facts of the Holocaust. The Palestinian Authority has done the same. In his doctoral dissertation in 1982, Mahmoud Abbas accused the Zionists of collaborating in the Holocaust, murdering Jews to speed their emigration to Palestine. In a study he published two years later, he argued that the gas chambers were not actually "for murdering people."

As recently as August 2023, President Abbas delivered a speech in which he argued that the Nazis did not kill Jews "because they were Jews," but because of their "social role." Hitler "fought the Jews because they were dealing with usury and money. In his view, they were engaged in sabotage, and this is why he hated them."[36]

CHAPTER 17

Army of the Holy War

As one war ended, another was just beginning.

The liberation of Nazi Europe should have brought a new dawn for Jewish life and freedom. Yet while millions of Europeans displaced by the war returned to their homes, the Jews had no home to return to. An estimated 250,000 languished in displaced persons camps, many of them established in former concentration camps and Nazi barracks. Those who returned to their towns were often beaten, sometimes killed. An infamous case was in Kielce, a Polish town home to 24,000 Jews in 1939. In 1946, 42 Jews who had recently returned were killed and 50 injured. A mob of townspeople had heard a rumor that Jews had killed Polish children for their blood.

Others didn't wait to be killed.

Shlomo Cohen was born in Greece in 1920. After being liberated from the Bergen-Belsen concentration camp by the British army, he returned to his hometown of Thessaloniki to see if any of his family members had survived. The Jewish homes in the city were gone. In their place were pits where locals had dug, searching for gold and other valuables. "I met one Greek whom I had known before the war," Cohen said in testimony before he boarded an illegal ship to Palestine. "He asked me: 'Why did the Germans leave you alive? Why didn't they turn you into soap?' After hearing that, I understood that there was no longer place for me here."[1]

Most survivors never considered going back to the places they no longer called home. They preferred the arduous, illegal journey to their homeland, aboard ships procured by the Haganah. As those ships arrived, Jews in Palestine watched in disbelief as Jewish refugees were turned away by British forces. Thousands were sent to British internment camps that had been established to house them.

Throughout World War II, the British maintained the stifling immigration restrictions that the 1939 White Paper had introduced. While Jewish immigration was capped at 18,000 people per year, there was no restriction on Arab immigration.[2]

In August 1946, the British established more detention camps on the Mediterranean island of Cyprus, where they would hold more than 50,000 Jewish refugees. The prisoners, most of them Holocaust survivors, were once again surrounded by barbed wire and watch towers.[3]

The New Jews

Around noon on July 22, 1946, an ominous call reached the switchboard of Jerusalem's King David Hotel, an imposing landmark of sand-colored stone overlooking the Old City.

"Tell everyone to leave the hotel," a woman told the operator. "It is going to be blown up in a few minutes."

The warning was ignored, and fifteen minutes later, the ground in Jerusalem shook with the tremors of nearly 800 pounds of explosives. Plumes of smoke rose from the six-story building. Aside from providing the poshest lodging in town, the King David was also the British Mandate government's administrative and military headquarters. The entire southwest corner of the hotel, where the British offices were housed, came crashing down. Dozens were missing in the ruins as stretchers carried out the dead and wounded. Dazed men and women, their faces covered in blood and white dust, staggered out of the hotel. It took rescuers three days to sift through the rubble and reach a final accounting of the dead.

The destruction was astounding. Ninety-one men and women were killed inside the hotel, on the street, and in nearby buildings. Of the casualties, most of them government employees, 41 were Arab, 28 were British, and 17 were Jewish. Nearly half of all government staff in the building had been killed.[4]

There was little mystery as to who had perpetrated the attack. Moments before the switchboard operator received her warning, a group of Jewish militants dressed as Arab hotel workers had been spotted emerging from the hotel's basement café, where they had planted milk cans laden with explosives. The Irgun took responsibility for the bombing the next day, in a statement that blamed the "British tyrants themselves" for the carnage they had caused.[5]

The Irgun, under orders of its leader, Menachem Begin, had committed the deadliest act of terror in British Mandate history. The Zionist rebellion against the British, suspended while the British fought their common enemy, began anew. It was the beginning of the end of the British Mandate in Palestine.[6]

The bombing of the King David was immediately condemned by Palestine's Jewish press and the country's Zionist leadership, including the Jewish National Council and the Jewish Agency, which called on the Jewish community to "rise up against these abominable outrages."[7] Ben-Gurion, head of the Jewish Agency and de facto leader of Palestine's Jewish community, declared the Irgun "the enemy of the Jewish people."[8]

The Irgun and Lehi undergrounds doubled down on their violent quest to evict the British from Palestine. The King David was their deadliest attack, but it was not their first or their last.

When Zionist militias declared a ceasefire against the British at the outset of World War II, thousands of Irgun fighters enlisted in the British military. But the Irgun ended its ceasefire before the war's end, announcing its decision on posters plastered across the country. The British are refusing to carry out rescue missions or ease immigration restrictions, "despite the betrayal of the Arabs and the loyalty of the Jews; despite the mass enlisting to the British Army; despite the ceasefire and the quiet in The Land of Israel; despite the massacre of masses

of the Jewish people in Europe . . . millions more are in danger of erad-
ication. And The Land of Israel is closed off and quarantined because
the British rule it."

The ceasefire was over, the Irgun proclaimed, and the war with the
British for "our people's last hope" would now begin.[9]

Between 1944 and 1948, the Irgun and Lehi perpetrated a wave of
ambushes and assassinations, including several failed attempts on the
life of Raymond Cafferata, the British police chief in Hebron during
the riots of 1929.[10]

The Haganah, the mainstream Zionist militia that was essentially
the military arm of the Zionist leadership, opposed the violent tactics
of the Irgun and Lehi. The Haganah focused its rebellion on facilitating illegal immigration. Between 1945 and 1948, some 70,000 illegal Jewish immigrants arrived in Palestine on ships that sailed from
Europe. Most were Holocaust survivors whose families had been
obliterated. With the help of the Haganah, they were spirited away
from DP camps in Germany, Austria, and Italy and brought to Palestine aboard escape ships from ports in France, Italy, and the Balkans.[11]

More than half of those ships were intercepted. In some cases,
survivors drowned. In others, British forces clashed with passengers
who resisted capture, killing Jewish refugees on board. It was a public relations disaster for the British, encapsulated by one particularly
egregious incident.

The ship named *Exodus 1947* began in 1928 as an American
steamship named *President Warfield*. Originally carrying passengers and freight across the Chesapeake Bay, the ship was deployed in
the 1944 invasion of Normandy, then sold as scrap metal for $8,000
before it was purchased by the Haganah. On July 18, 1947, the ship
named *Exodus* was surrounded by a fleet of Royal Navy destroyers
off the coast of Palestine. On board were 4,515 Jewish refugees who
had boarded in France with no legal permit to enter Palestine. Of
them, 655 were children, many of them orphans. Fifty Royal Marines

boarded the *Exodus* armed with guns, clubs, and tear gas. When Haganah members and Holocaust survivors on board resisted, the British opened fire, killing 2 passengers. Another died of a fractured skull from being clubbed. The Royal Navy forced the ship to anchor in Haifa, where soldiers boarded the ship. After forcibly removing the refugees, they were sent back to DP camps in Germany. While the *Exodus* is the most famous of all these incidents, there were dozens of lesser-known cases like it.[12]

Partition

As fighting between Jews and Arabs intensified, acts of anti-British terror by both sides led the British to consider various exit strategies to bring independence to a land ruled by foreign powers for millennia. British rule over two hostile populations in Palestine, in open rebellion against one another and their occupier, had to end.

Since 1936, the British government had engaged in desperate attempts to resolve the conflict, holding meetings between Jewish and Arab leaders, sending commissions of inquiry to Palestine, and issuing a flurry of white papers to assess every possible solution. The London Conference, held in February 1939, exemplified these attempts. The British initiated the conference to negotiate a compromise between Palestine's Arabs and Jews. The Arab delegates agreed to attend on one condition: they would not meet directly with the Jewish delegates. After holding separate meetings with both sides, the conference ended in failure one month later.[13]

In September 1947, with all options considered and discarded, an exasperated Great Britain voted to leave Palestine, handing its future to the newly established United Nations. On November 29, 1947, the UN General Assembly voted to partition Mandatory Palestine into two states. The Partition Plan envisioned that with the end of British rule in Palestine, the land would be divided between a Jewish state and an Arab state. The area surrounding Jerusalem would be under international control overseen by the UN.

The UN Partition Plan was a historic opportunity, not only for the Jews, but also for the Arabs. This would be the first time in history that the Palestinian people would have self-rule. The Jewish state would be the first in 2,000 years. The Arab State of Palestine proposed in 1947 was larger than any proposed since then. But in 1947, Palestinian Arabs opposed partition, and viewed the plan as a grave injustice. Palestine, at the time, was home to more than 1.2 million Arabs and 625,000 Jews. The Jewish State of Israel and the Arab State of Palestine were to be roughly the same size, though much of the land allotted to the Jewish state was desert.

Though many Zionists felt the plan ceded too much of historic Israel to the Arab nation, which already had many countries of its own, and left the vulnerable Jewish state with frontiers that were virtually indefensible, the majority of Jews of Palestine and their leaders embraced the UN Partition Plan.

The Arabs of Palestine, and the Arab world at large, vehemently rejected it.

When the vote was announced, the Zionists in the packed General Assembly Hall in Flushing Meadows, Queens, erupted in cries of joy. The public lobby, filled to capacity with an overflow crowd of at least 1,000 people, was overcome with hugs, kisses, and tears of relief.

Abba Hillel Silver, chairman of the Jewish Agency's American branch, expressed his people's gratitude and hopes for the future. "The Jewish people will forever be grateful" to the nations that contributed to "this noble decision to re-establish the Jewish state and restore the Jewish people to its rightful place in the family of nations," he said. "The Jewish people will strive to build the Jewish state in Palestine in the spirit of its heroic spiritual leaders of the past, whose teaching made that country the Holy Land of mankind."

Silver turned to the Arabs of Palestine, whose leadership had boycotted the vote. "We extend a hand of genuine friendship to the new

Arab state which is to be established in Palestine," he said. "In this historic hour we call upon the Arab people of Palestine and all neighboring Arab countries to join with us in an era of peaceful and fruitful collaboration."

Even before the vote was counted, all the Arab delegates had stormed out of the building, warning that, in their eyes, the United Nations was dead. "Murdered," fumed Syria's prime minister, Fares al-Khoury. Before entering their limousines, the Arab representatives announced that they would have nothing to do with partition. The bloodshed to come, they warned, would be on the hands of those who had supported the plan. All ten Arab member states at the UN voted against partition, joined by Cuba, Greece, and India. The US and the Soviet Union, whose leaders disagreed on nearly everything, were among the plan's staunchest supporters. Thirty-three nations voted for partition, while ten, including the United Kingdom, abstained.[14]

It is an exercise in lost hopes and dreams to imagine what could have been, had Arab leaders agreed to share the land of Abraham with the children of Abraham. It would not be the last time Arab leaders rejected a proposal for an independent state of Palestine.

"A Purely Arab Nation"

The day after the vote, the last remaining Jews in Hebron—the dairy farmer Yaakov Ezra and his son Yosef—were warned by their Arab friends and neighbors that war was coming. They quickly packed up their belongings and left for Jerusalem. Vanquished in 1929, the ancient Jewish community of Hebron had now vanished entirely.[15]

The second holiest city in Judaism, with a four-millennia history of Jewish life, would not see a Jewish soul for the next two decades.

By the time the Ezra family left, the blood Arab leaders had threatened at the United Nations was already flowing. The very next day, 7 Jews were murdered in three separate killing sprees. The mufti's Arab Higher Committee called for a renewed national strike, urging

Muslims to take to the streets after Friday prayers. That night Hussein Khalidi, the committee's acting chairman in Palestine, told the *New York Times*, "The Arabs will wage a holy war if an attempt is made to enforce the partition plan." Khalidi, the former mayor of Jerusalem who was deported to the Seychelles during the Great Arab Revolt, was permitted by the British to return to Palestine in 1943. (Hussein Khalidi's nephew is the well-known Palestinian American author and Columbia University historian Rashid Khalidi.) Partition, Khalidi warned, was a "Zionist scheme," and a "declaration of war against Arab countries" that would "lead to a crusade against the Jews."[16]

Two days later, Jewish quarters of Jerusalem were in flames. In scenes reminiscent of August 1929, hundreds of Arabs marched out of the walled Old City, smashing and looting Jewish shops and stabbing innocent Jewish passersby. Deadly riots once again gripped Palestine, as Jewish civilians were killed in attacks across the country. Under orders not to interfere, British troops stood by and watched. The Haganah became the unofficial defense force of the besieged Jewish communities. In pitched battles with mobs on the seam between Jaffa and Tel Aviv, 7 Jews and 5 Arabs were killed. Stressing that its forces were only on defense now, the Haganah issued an ultimatum: Should these "bloody outrages continue, we shall be obliged to take drastic measures against the rioters and those responsible for them." Khalidi, of the Arab Higher Committee, rejected any blame. Irresponsible elements, he told the *Times*, had taken matters into their own hands. The riots claimed the lives of 62 Jews and 32 Arabs. In response, the Irgun launched a wave of reprisal attacks and bombings that killed 78 Arabs.[17]

At violent protests in Egypt, Syria, and Lebanon following the UN vote, demonstrators called for Palestine to remain a "purely Arab nation." Egypt's prime minister vowed that his country would take all measures necessary to ensure it would be. Teachers at Egypt's Al-Azhar University called for Muslims to wage a holy war. Hundreds of students rallied in Cairo, chanting, "The Jews are the dogs of the world." Egypt was then home to at least 75,000 Jews. Many would soon flee to Palestine. As of December 2022, there were reportedly only 3 Jews living in Egypt.[18]

The Partition Plan led the Arab world to declare war against the unborn Jewish state. From his base in Cairo, the mufti's Arab Higher Committee declared jihad in Palestine. He established Jaysh al-Jihad al-Muqaddas, the Holy War Army, to lead that jihad, and appointed Abdul Qadir al-Husseini and Hasan Salama to command it. Abdul Qadir was the mufti's cousin, the son of former Jerusalem mayor Musa Kazim al-Husseini. Salama was a former member of the Arab commando unit in Hitler's Waffen-SS, who had parachuted into Palestine in 1944 as part of the mufti's failed Operation Atlas.[19]

In Cairo, 18-year-old Yasser Arafat procured weapons to be smuggled to the Holy War Army. He would join the jihad in Palestine one year later, fighting not with the Holy War Army, but with the Muslim Brotherhood. Established in Egypt in 1928, the Brotherhood advocated rule by Sharia law and the return of the Islamic caliphate. The group's founder, Hassan al-Banna, had been in close contact with the mufti since 1927. He established a military wing to enter the war in Palestine.[20]

On December 11, 1947, the British government announced that it would withdraw from Palestine on May 15, 1948. Outnumbered by the Arabs within and the sea of Arab countries without, the future of the Jewish state was bleak. Two years after World War II ended, civil war in Palestine had begun. Yosef Ezra, fresh out of Hebron at the age of 16, joined the Irgun.

In Damascus, the Arab Liberation Army was established by the Arab League, which recruited its own troops to invade Palestine. The first assault came on January 9, 1948, when a force of 1,000 armed men crossed Syria's southern border into Palestine, attacking two kibbutzim in the northern Galilee.[21]

CHAPTER 18

Between Independence and Catastrophe

STANDING BEFORE 250 GUESTS AT THE TEL AVIV MUSEUM OF ART on May 14, 1948, David Ben-Gurion cleared his throat. Above him hung a portrait of Theodor Herzl, flanked by two blue-and-white Star of David flags. Until now it was the flag of a nation without a country.

"We hereby proclaim the establishment of the Jewish state in Eretz Yisrael, to be called Israel," Ben-Gurion announced to thunderous applause.[1]

The squat, white-haired leader of the new Jewish state read aloud from Israel's Declaration of Independence. "We appeal to the Arab inhabitants of the State of Israel to preserve peace and participate in the upbuilding of the state on the basis of full and equal citizenship and due representation in all its provisional and permanent institutions." As Arab armies gathered on Israel's borders, he continued, "We extend our hand to all neighboring states and their peoples in an offer of peace and good neighborliness."[2]

There were few dry eyes in the room. Among those present was Rabbi Wolf Gold. Ben-Gurion signed the document, followed by 25 of the 37 members of the provisional state council, including Rabbi Gold.

The remaining members of the provisional government were trapped in Jerusalem, which had been under siege since February. The Holy War Army, under the command of Abdul Qadir al-Husseini, had blockaded the roads leading from Jerusalem to Tel Aviv, preventing food, water, and other essentials from reaching the Jewish population of Jerusalem, and ambushing Jewish vehicles that sought to aid them.

On May 14, the Arab Legion, the British-backed army of Jordan, joined that siege.[3]

The Parade

As the clock struck midnight, the British Mandate expired, and the State of Israel was born. Minutes later, a ship carrying the first new immigrants arrived at Haifa port: 200 Jewish women and children, all of them refugees, huddled on a dark sidewalk near the dock, waiting for welfare services.[4]

At dawn, Egyptian war planes bombed Tel Aviv. That morning, the armies of Egypt, Jordan, Iraq, Lebanon, and Syria invaded from the east, north, and south. Egyptian generals said it would be "a parade without any risks." Tel Aviv, they estimated, would be conquered within two weeks.[5]

The Haganah, now serving as Israel's military, had no air force to speak of, no tanks, no artillery, no anti-tank or anti-aircraft weapons, no heavy machine guns, and no armored vehicles.[6] The newly established Israel Defense Forces scraped together members of the Haganah, Irgun, Lehi, and men and women who had recently arrived on immigrant ships from European DP camps. Some were recruited off the boat. The Israeli military had no air force, no tanks, no anti-tank or anti-aircraft weapons, no heavy machine guns, and no armored vehicles. In May 1948, Israel seemed doomed to a very swift and violent end.

By May 1949, that calculus had been reversed. Israel had not only routed the armies of five Arab states, but captured 5,000 square kilometers beyond the territory the UN had allocated to it.

For all its achievements, however, the war had been devastating. More than 6,000 Israeli soldiers and civilians, 1 of every 100 Jews in Palestine before the war began, had been killed. Estimates of Palestinian fatalities vary widely, but between 3,000 and 13,000 Palestinian combatants and civilians were killed. Entire Arab towns and villages had been expelled. In some cases, Jewish refugees arriving in Israel moved into abandoned Arab homes.[7]

The Nakba

The war that began in 1947 and ended with various armistice agreements in 1949 has different names depending upon which nation one asks. To Israelis and Jews of the Diaspora, it was Israel's War of Independence. To Palestinians and to most Muslims, it was the *Nakba*, the catastrophe. While the war marked a triumphant end to 2,000 years of statelessness for the Jewish people, it ushered in a new era of statelessness for the Palestinian people.

The war led to the exile of roughly 700,000 Palestinians, about half of the country's Arab population. Some, particularly the wealthy, fled during the civil war that preceded Israel's establishment, before the invasion of neighboring Arab armies. By May 3, 1948, all members of the Arab Higher Committee had left Palestine for other Arab countries, leaving their people to live through the war they initiated. For Palestinian civilians, it was a mix of flight and expulsion. Many left to escape the fighting, which saw massacres of civilians perpetrated by Jewish and Arab militias. The slaughter of more than 100 villagers by Irgun and Lehi fighters in the Arab village of Deir Yassin in April 1948 sparked a panicked exodus of Palestinians from other villages who feared a similar fate. Many who fled expected to return when the war was over, following what was sure to be Israel's swift destruction.[8]

The Other Occupations

Israel was not the only one to gain from the war. Egypt took control of Gaza, a twenty-five-mile-long narrow strip of land lined with white sandy beaches on the Mediterranean coast of Israel's southwest border with Egypt. The Jordanian army captured East Jerusalem and the West Bank, named for its location on the western edge of the Jordan River. Israelis know the territory by its biblical name, Judaea and Samaria.

Under Jordanian occupation, the Jewish population of East Jerusalem was expelled and the Western Wall became inaccessible to Jewish worshippers. Jerusalem's ancient Jewish Quarter was obliterated, with all but two of its fifty-eight synagogues destroyed. Jewish fighters were taken as prisoners of war and paraded through Hebron. The Jewish cemetery on the Mount of Olives, used continuously for 2,000 years, was desecrated by Jordanian authorities and Palestinian residents. Much like Arabs in Jordanian territory were forbidden from entering Israel, Israelis were forbidden from entering East Jerusalem and the West Bank.[9]

In 1950, Jordan annexed the West Bank, and Jewish history in Hebron was slowly, definitively, erased. The ruins of Avraham Avinu Synagogue, built in 1540 by exiles of the Spanish Inquisition and destroyed by rioters in the massacre of 1929, was transformed into an animal pen. The Jewish Quarter that circled the synagogue was replaced by a wholesale market, public toilets, and a garbage dump. The ancient Jewish cemetery, where victims of the massacre were buried alongside rabbinic sages, became a vegetable garden. Tombstones, added to the mass grave of the massacre's victims half a year after their burial, were taken by locals and used as bricks in their homes and gardens.[10]

Most Palestinian refugees settled in Syria, Lebanon, Egyptian-controlled Gaza, or the Jordanian-controlled West Bank. Palestinians were denied citizenship in each of these countries—the same countries whose invasion of Israel led to the Palestinians' expulsion. Most were relegated to refugee camps.[11]

In Gaza, Palestinian refugees established the All-Palestine Government, unanimously electing the mufti as president. Like the Arab Higher Committee, the All-Palestine Government consisted largely of Husseini's family members and loyalists. The mufti's cousin Jamal, who was vice-chairman of the AHC, was named foreign secretary of the All-Palestine Government.

After annexing the West Bank, Jordan viewed the mufti as a threat, and banned his government from operating there. Even in Gaza, the new entity proved so useless it was dissolved in 1953. Husseini, once again, relocated to Lebanon, where he continued to lead the Palestinian resistance.[12]

The Forever Refugees

To this day, many of the Palestinians in Gaza, Syria, Jordan, and Lebanon live in densely populated refugee camps, relying heavily upon UNRWA, the United Nations Relief and Works Agency for Palestine Refugees in the Near East, established in 1949. All of these countries have denied Palestinians citizenship and the rights that come with it. In Lebanon, Palestinians are barred from accessing social services, and cannot legally own property or hold an array of high-paying jobs. In Egypt, Palestinians are neither citizens nor recognized refugees. A marginalized community, they are denied access to free education and health care, and the right to work in any trade they wish. In Jordan, Lebanon, Syria, and Egypt, Palestinians, including those born in these countries, are neither eligible to vote nor hold public office.[13]

Unlike other refugee populations, Palestinian refugees pass their refugee status to their children, grandchildren, and great-grandchildren. Today, the original refugees and their offspring number nearly 6 million people.

The Nakba and the hope of returning to Palestine form the basis of Palestinian identity. Many still hold the keys to the homes their parents, grandparents, and great-grandparents fled. Most of those homes no longer exist. In the wake of 1948, many of the Arab villages that were destroyed in the war became Israeli towns with Hebrew names.

Originally designed to be temporary, UNRWA is now one of the largest UN bodies. With an annual budget of $1.6 billion, UNRWA employs some 30,000 people, nearly all of them Palestinians. Almost all of the 6 million Palestinians served by UNRWA are descendants of the original refugees.

The United Nations High Commissioner for Refugees, UNHCR, oversees all the world's other refugees. Though it provides aid to more than 59 million refugees around the world, it employs 18,000 people on an annual budget of $10 million.[14]

Nearly 60 percent of UNRWA's budget is allocated to education programs, which claim to teach Palestinian children values of peace, tolerance, and nonviolent conflict resolution. Yet according to numerous studies of the UNRWA curriculum, the agency is grossly failing that mission.

UNRWA textbooks depict Jews as enemies of Islam, glorify so-called martyrs who have died while committing terrorist attacks against civilians, and promote jihad for the liberation of historic Palestine. UNRWA maps of the region do not include the state of Israel, which is labeled as Palestine. Throughout the UNRWA curriculum, Israel is referred to as "the Zionist Occupation."[15]

CHAPTER 19

Ingathering of the Exiles

THERE IS A WORD IN THE HEBREW LANGUAGE FOR THE ACT OF immigrating to the Land of Israel: *Aliyah*. Ascent. One does not merely move to Israel, but ascends from the world of the ordinary to the land of the sacred. The term is believed to derive from the ancient tradition of making pilgrimage to the holy temple in Jerusalem, which stood 2,500 feet above sea level. Two years after Israel's establishment, Aliyah was enshrined into law. The Law of Return allows any Jew in the world, and their spouse, to acquire Israeli citizenship upon moving to Israel.

Under Ottoman and British rule, there were different names for the waves of Aliyah that brought the scattered children of Israel back to their homeland. The tidal wave that followed the birth of the Jewish state was called Kibbutz Galuyot, the Ingathering of the Exiles. In its first three years, Israel's Jewish population rose from 650,000 to more than 1.3 million. The year 1949 saw the greatest influx in the country's history. Roughly 250,000 made the journey that year, mostly from DP camps in Europe and British internment camps. When Israel declared independence, some 30,000 Jewish prisoners were still being held in Cyprus.[1]

Many of the new immigrants also hailed from Muslim countries that were violently purging their Jewish communities. Iraq, home to 150,000 Jews at the time of Israel's birth, made Zionism a capital offense punishable by imprisonment. Iraqi Jews were forbidden from engaging in banking and foreign currency transactions, dismissed from civil service, and had millions of dollars in assets and property seized by the government. Nearly 130,000 Iraqi Jews have moved to

Israel since 1948. As of 2021, there were only 4 known Jews living in Iraq. In Tunisia, home to 100,000 Jews in 1948, violent attacks and repressive government decrees that followed the birth of Israel led most of them to flee. Fewer than 1,000 Jews remain in Tunisia today. In Syria, where some 30,000 Jews lived in 1947, deadly riots were followed by repressive government policies, ranging from freezing Jewish assets, paving over the ancient Jewish cemetery in Damascus, and banning Jews from purchasing property, working in banks, and holding government positions. Similarly oppressive measures were taken in Egypt, Yemen, Algeria, and Libya, spurring a mass migration of Jews from the Arab world. Within the first two decades of Israel's establishment, around 850,000 Jews arrived from Muslim lands. Today, Jews with roots in Muslim countries constitute more than half of Israel's population.[2]

At the dawn of Zionism in the late nineteenth century, less than 1 percent of the world's Jewish population lived in the Land of Israel. Since 1948, more than 3.4 million Jews have made Aliyah. With 46 percent of the world's Jewish population as of 2023, Israel is home to more Jews than any other country.[3]

PART II
HOMELAND

CHAPTER 20

The First Settler

MALKA SLONIM STOOD BEFORE THE TOWERING TOMB OF THE
Patriarchs and Matriarchs on a hot, sunny day in June 1967. It was
her first time in Hebron since August 1929, when half her family was
murdered, and she and the rest of Hebron's Jews were evacuated from
the city of her birth. She was just 14 years old then. Now she was 52.

Malka took one step. Then another. At the seventh step, she
stopped. She tried, but could not bring her feet to move. As a young
girl, she had visited this monument to the Jewish forefathers and
mothers dozens of times. But she had never dared to cross the seventh step. The anxious crowd squirming behind her wondered what
was wrong with this unmoving woman, who was keeping them from
going inside the place few living Jews had ever been. "Why are you
standing there?" they asked. "Get moving!" Malka stepped forward,
in shock.[1]

Since the year 1267, when Muslim rulers forbade Jews from entering the site constructed by a Jewish king more than 1,000 years earlier, Jews could only pray outside the shrine. Now worshippers of any
religion could pray inside these walls, sacred to Muslims, Christians,
and Jews. For the first time in 700 years, Jews could pass beyond the
seventh step.

Just days before Malka's visit, Israel had been on the precipice of
destruction. In early June 1967, the armies of Egypt, Jordan, and Syria
amassed along the 9-mile-wide borders of the Jewish state, threatening
to put an end to their common enemy. Egyptian president Gamal

Abdel Nasser ordered UN peacekeeping forces to leave the border, and they obliged.

Still recovering from the Holocaust and the labor pains that followed the birth of a nation of refugees, Israelis braced themselves for what seemed to be certain annihilation.[2]

Then, on June 5, that destiny was reversed when Israel launched a preemptive strike. In just six days, Israel achieved a stunning victory. Its 19-year-old military had not only defeated the armies of Egypt, Jordan, and Syria, but more than tripled the country's size. By June 10, Israel had seized control of Gaza and the Sinai from Egypt, and the Golan Heights from Syria, which had used the mountainous region to terrorize civilians in northern Israel. Most significantly, Israel captured East Jerusalem and the West Bank from Jordan, bringing the biblical heartland of the Jewish people under its control for the first time in 2,000 years.

As Israeli tanks approached Hebron, Palestinian fighters laid down their weapons. Hebronites waved white linens of surrender from their windows and balconies. Fearing the Israelis would show little mercy for the people of Hebron for what they had done in 1929, many prepared for a blood bath of revenge. Men took their wives and daughters to the Hebron hills, hiding them in caves. Families who saved Jews in 1929 retrieved the letters of gratitude they had received from Hebron's Jewish leaders, showing them to the approaching Israeli troops.[3]

There was no revenge in Hebron. The IDF took the city without bloodshed, and Mayor Ali Jaabari surrendered Hebron. He recognized one of the soldiers, a reservist named Yosef Ezra, whose father had owned and operated Hebron's dairy factory before he and Yosef left in 1947.

As a peace offering, Israeli Defense Minister Moshe Dayan left control of the Ibrahimi Mosque—the Tomb of the Patriarchs and Matriarchs—in the hands of the Islamic Waqf. He did the same for the Temple Mount, the holiest site in Judaism, delivering these olive branches in the hope of avoiding a holy war with the Muslim world.[4]

Both sites are still administered by the Islamic Waqf, which prohibits Jews from praying on the Temple Mount and opposes Jewish visits to the site. When Jews go there, they are portrayed in the Arabic media as "storming" Al-Aqsa.

Beneath the Cauliflower

In the spring of 1968, a tall, lanky, little-known rabbi named Moshe Levinger arrived in Hebron with one of the city's elders, Avraham Franco. Born in Hebron in 1894, Franco had been a leader of Hebron's Sephardic community before it was extinguished in 1929. Both his father and grandfather served as the city's Chief Sephardic Rabbi. His father, Meir, survived the massacre, living just long enough to testify before the Shaw Commission in December of 1929. He died less than a year later, never having recovered from the shock of witnessing the violent destruction of his community, and the mutilated bodies of his closest friends, Rabbis Chanoch Hasson and Meir Castel. He was buried alongside them in Hebron.

Rabbi Levinger followed Franco to the ancient Jewish cemetery, nestled on a hilltop, shaded by olive groves. They entered the neglected burial grounds, walking past grazing sheep and vegetables planted over the graves. "Here is the plot of the martyrs of 1929," said Franco, pointing at the vegetable garden. "At the end, under that cauliflower, my father is buried."[5]

In the days and weeks that followed the war, thousands of Israelis streamed into Hebron to visit the holy city and to pray at the Tomb of the Patriarchs and Matriarchs for the first time. Aside from the Jewish prisoners of war who were paraded through Hebron's streets in 1948, Jews had not stepped foot in the City of Abraham since 1947. Hebron's exiled Jews and their descendants trickled in to see what remained of their homes and synagogues, and the Arab families who had protected them.[6]

Some of the refugees, like Avraham Franco and Yosef Ezra, sought to reclaim their property, showing Israeli officials the deeds to their family's land. The government and the military refused. *It's too soon,* they were told. *The situation is too volatile.*[7]

The State of Israel was now the custodian of Jewish property in Hebron, and Jews were forbidden from living there. Hebron was, after all, the largest Palestinian city in the West Bank.

The Jewish state had not merely absorbed land in its victory against three Arab armies. On that land lived more than 1 million Palestinians. Just days before they were the adversary, living under Egyptian and Jordanian rule, and hoping for Israel's destruction if not actively fighting for it. Now they resided within Israel's new borders.[8]

While Israel annexed East Jerusalem, it stopped short of annexing the Golan Heights, the Gaza Strip, and the West Bank. Instead, military control was declared until a lasting resolution could be reached with Syria, Egypt, and Jordan. Israeli leaders believed the capture of these territories could pave the way for a historic treaty. Israel, they envisioned, would withdraw its forces from conquered lands in exchange for peace and security. Shortly after the war, Foreign Minister Abba Eban declared that "everything is negotiable." Moshe Dayan echoed that sentiment, telling the BBC, "We're waiting for a phone call from the Arabs."[9]

The Arab states responded with the Khartoum Resolution, announced at the Arab League Summit on September 1, 1967. "The main principles by which the Arab States abide," read the defiant resolution, is "no peace with Israel, no recognition of Israel, no negotiations with Israel." So began Israel's military occupation.

Passover at the Park Hotel

In 1967, the decision to revive the ancient Jewish Quarter of Jerusalem was accepted by Jewish Israelis as self-evident. Jerusalem had

been a majority Jewish city before 1948. Hebron was more complicated. Even before their violent expulsion in 1929, Hebron's Jewish
population had numbered just 800 people among more than 20,000
Arabs. Now the city was home to 50,000 Arabs and not a single Jew.[10]

In October of 1967, Rabbi Yehezkel Sarna, the leader of the
Hebron Yeshiva, which had relocated to Jerusalem in 1929, asked the
Defense Ministry if the yeshiva could return to Hebron. His request
was denied. Defending his decision before the Knesset, Defense Minister Dayan told lawmakers it didn't seem to him the best idea to
send 30 yeshiva students to live among 50,000 Arabs. "They are cer-
tainly not paratroopers," he quipped. "With all respect for the Hebron
Yeshiva, this is not the tip of the hammer with which you enter the
West Bank."[11]

Refusing to give up so soon, Avraham Franco and another Hebron
descendant, Yoel Hasson, sent a letter to Prime Minister Levi Eshkol
in January 1968. The letter, written by their lawyers, requested the
government's renewal of Hebron's Jewish community, the repatria-
tion of all Jewish property in Hebron, and the restoration of the city's
ancient Jewish cemetery. The response to their letter came from General Shlomo Gazit of the IDF, who had been tapped by Dayan to lead
the army's new Unit for the Coordination of Operations in the Territories (COGAT). The government had not yet decided the future
of Hebron or Jewish property there, wrote Gazit. That decision, he
explained, was part of a wider discussion of the rights of Jewish residents of Israel to return to their property in the West Bank, and like-
wise, for Arab residents of the West Bank to return to their property
in Israel. "The prevailing policy on this matter," Gazit wrote, "is to see
this as one of the issues that will be resolved in the overall settlement
of the Israeli-Arab conflict."[12]

Avraham Franco was determined to find a way. That way was
Moshe Levinger.

Born in Jerusalem in 1935 to parents who fled Germany two years
earlier, Levinger was then the rabbi of Nehalim, a small agricultural

village in central Israel. He had studied at the Mercaz Harav Yeshiva in Jerusalem, a bastion of Religious Zionism whose leader, Rabbi Zvi Yehuda Kook, believed that Israel's military victory in 1967 was the fulfillment of a messianic vision. Like Rabbi Kook, Levinger believed the return of the Jewish people to their biblical land was the work of God.[13]

The duty of the Jewish people now, as Levinger saw it, was to fulfill the mission God had bestowed upon them: to bring the people of Judaea back to the land of Judaea. There was one gaping flaw in that plan: the modern territory of Judaea and Samaria was not just home to more biblical sites than any other part of ancient Israel. It was also home to the greatest population of Arabs under Israeli military control.[14]

By the time he took that walk through the graveyard-turned-vegetable garden, Levinger had already helped to establish the first Jewish settlement in the occupied West Bank.

Kfar Etzion was another Jewish community uprooted by a massacre. Founded in 1927, Kfar Etzion was a farming village established by a group of Jewish families from Jerusalem. Most of them were originally from Yemen. During the riots of 1929, they fled the village, and their homes were destroyed. After additional land was purchased from local Arabs in the 1930s and 1940s, the original farm grew into a large bloc of kibbutzim, agricultural communities based on a socialist framework, known as the Etzion Bloc.[15]

On May 13, 1948, one day before Israel declared independence, Palestinian fighters and Jordanian forces killed 127 Jewish men and women who were defending Kfar Etzion, and razed the village to the ground. One of the fallen was Shalom Ezra, the 19-year-old brother of Yosef Ezra. For Israelis, the loss of the Etzion Bloc and the death of its defenders was one of the most devastating battles of the war. The date on the Hebrew calendar on which Kfar Etzion fell became Israel's Memorial Day. To this day it is commemorated the day before Israel's Independence Day.

In September 1967, Hanan Porat, a fellow student at Mercaz Harav who was evacuated from Kfar Etzion as a young boy, reestablished the kibbutz with the help of Moshe Levinger.[16]

From the time Hebron came under Israeli control, Rabbi Levinger had been infatuated with the vision of reviving the city's Jewish Quarter. This was the birthplace of Jewish existence, first lost to the Romans, then longed after for thousands of years by Jews scattered across the globe, and now redeemed by a Jewish army from an occupying power, Jordan, in a defensive war for Israel's survival. If Jews should be able to live anywhere in the Land of Israel, be it Haifa or Tel Aviv, surely they should be able to live in Hebron. All of this seemed obvious to Levinger and to many other Israelis.

But when he requested permission to rehabilitate former Jewish property in Hebron, he too was dismissed by the government and the military. After months of rejections and empty promises from various Israeli officials, the rabbi's Bronx-born wife, Miriam, urged him to do it himself. "The government won't send you there," Miriam told her husband. "Go settle, and things will work out." And so Levinger took an approach that would become a hallmark of the settlement movement. As Miriam Levinger would later recall, it was one of their supporters in the government, Transportation Minister Yigal Allon, who suggested it. "Allon told my husband that when it came to settling the Land of Israel, first you establish facts on the ground and then you inform the authorities."[17]

Avraham Franco held the deeds to various properties owned by Hebron's Sephardic community. One of them was the Hadassah House. After leaving the cemetery, he and Levinger walked past the former charitable clinic. There Franco promised Levinger, "When you settle Hebron, this building will be yours."

Three weeks later, Moshe and Miriam Levinger loaded their 4 young children and their refrigerator, washing machine, and suitcases containing enough clothing to last two weeks, into a truck. Several hours later, after picking up other young families and yeshiva students along the way, they pulled up to Hebron's Park Hotel. A group of women was already hard at work koshering the hotel's kitchen. Mezuzahs had been placed in the doorways of the hotel rooms. Miriam Levinger joined the women in the kitchen, rushing to prepare the festive meal in time for the Passover Seder, which would begin in just two hours.[18]

Their Seder would not only celebrate the Exodus from Egypt, but the return to Hebron.

Rabbi Levinger had rented the entire two-story hotel through the end of Passover. Yet his plan was to stay until the government acquiesced to his wishes. So long as Hebron remained a city without Jews, he and his entourage refused to leave. Levinger had paid for their stay in full, telling the hotel's Muslim owner, Fahed Qawasmeh, that the reservation was for a large group of Swiss tourists. Whether Levinger knew this or not is unclear, but members of the Qawasmeh clan had saved dozens of Jews during the massacre of 1929.

Hours before the Seder, Levinger met with Hebron's military governor, asking him how the group should protect itself. Taking the newspaper in front of him, the governor wrote in its margins a note to the chief of police: "Give this man two Uzis, and four rifles."

The Passover Seder was held in the hotel's ornate dining room, furnished with plush leather couches and walls adorned with Quranic verses. Among the 60 participants were liberal intellectuals from Tel Aviv, including the novelist and Labor Zionist Moshe Shamir. Leading the Seder was Rabbi Haim Drukman, one of the spiritual leaders of Religious Zionism. A decade later, he would become a member of Israeli Parliament, advocating for Jewish settlement throughout biblical Israel.

After drinking the mandatory four cups of wine that are integral to the celebration of freedom at the Seder, the blissful group emerged from the hotel to dance and sing beneath the light of a full moon. To Levinger's pleasant surprise, they were joined by soldiers as they danced to the words of Jeremiah's prophecy, "And your children shall return to their borders."[19]

In the ensuing weeks, hundreds of Israelis from across the country and the political spectrum thronged to Hebron to show their support for the young pioneers. Levinger and his followers envisioned themselves as a new vanguard of idealistic Zionists, settling the Land of Israel precisely as the early pioneers had done.

That Passover in Hebron, Rabbi Levinger laid the seeds of the movement that would go on to plant half a million Jews in the West Bank. Here Levinger was crowned the father of Israel's newly born settlement movement.

A Decision to Not Decide

Mayor Jaabari issued an open letter to Prime Minister Eshkol and Defense Minister Dayan, demanding that the settlers leave immediately. The people of Hebron don't want Jews living here, Jaabari told a reporter for the *New York Times*. Jews could return to their homes in Hebron someday he said, when Palestinians could return to the homes they had left in Israel in 1948.[20]

David Ben-Gurion, since retired to his farm in the Negev Desert, sent a letter to Levinger at the Park Hotel, urging him not to give up. "Hebron is still awaiting redemption, and there is no redemption without extensive Jewish settlement," wrote Israel's founding father. In his introduction to *Sefer Hevron* (The Book of Hebron), published in 1970 by members of the city's exiled Jewish community, Ben-Gurion wrote: "We will make a great and awful mistake if we fail to settle Hebron, neighbor and predecessor of Jerusalem, with a large Jewish settlement, constantly growing and expanding, very soon."

At first, Prime Minister Eshkol denounced the would-be settlers. Then, after six weeks of indecision, he approved a plan to establish a yeshiva in Hebron. In the meantime, 7 families and 15 yeshiva students were permitted to live in the city's sprawling military headquarters. Each family, no matter how large, was given one room. "I think they figured that after a while we all would pack up our bags and return to our homes," recalled Miriam Levinger. During their three years in the compound, the settlers bombarded the government with requests to rebuild Hebron's Jewish Quarter or to repopulate the Jewish-owned buildings that stood abandoned. Their requests were denied or ignored.[21]

The government was walking on a tightwire. Israel had made clear its intent to retain control of territories it captured during the war until the Arab states from which it had captured them agreed to live in peace. Israel was also trying to avoid actions that would validate Arab charges that it was effectively annexing those territories.

Eshkol's Labor government was under pressure from all sides, not just from settlers. Yigal Allon, a minister from Eshkol's own party, had lent his support to Levinger's group. Menachem Begin, the former Irgun leader who was now a government minister and leader of the rival Herut party, was calling for the permanent retention of lands captured in 1967. There were ten small settlements in the territories at the time. All of them were paramilitary outposts established on unpopulated land. This would be the first purely civilian settlement, and the first in an urban center of Arab life.[22]

Ben-Gurion aside, members of Israel's liberal vanguard were not as pleased with the reports from Hebron. There was already a sense of unease among some intellectuals at the control Israel now had over Palestinian lives. "Even unavoidable occupation is a corrupting occupation," wrote famed Israeli writer Amos Oz in 1967. The sight of Hebron flooded with Jewish visitors and soldiers "provoked vigorous debate in government circles over the fruits of victory, the rights of conquest, the claims of history, and possibilities for peaceful coexistence," wrote historian Jerold Auerbach. The presence of Levinger and his followers in Hebron created a split in Israel's cabinet. "The conflict of loyalties was agonizing," reported the *New York Times*. "By heritage, the Jews felt they belonged in Hebron as much as anyone belonged anywhere; in law and politics, they knew theirs was a dangerous and provocative move."[23]

The settlers smelled hypocrisy. After all, the only difference between them and the secular Zionist pioneers so admired by mainstream Israeli society was that now, the pioneers were Religious Zionists wearing kippot. In their eyes, they were the very embodiment of Zionism. Though the political movement was established by secular Jews, Zionism was, in its essence, a deeply spiritual concept: fulfilling the 2,000-year-old Jewish longing for a return to Zion. What made Religious Zionists less worthy, less moral, than the early Zionists who decades before them built agricultural settlements amidst the Arab villages of Palestine? How was Hebron, the very source of the Jewish connection to this land, any less deserving of Jewish revival than the nearly 200 Jewish towns built on confiscated Arab land and deserted Arab villages during and after Israel's War of Independence? If Jews should be permitted to live anywhere, they argued, how could they not be permitted to live in Hebron?[24]

The Never-Ending Cycle

The week Levinger arrived at the Park Hotel, an Israeli policeman was killed while patrolling the city's market. In October, during the weeklong holiday of Sukkot, hundreds of Jewish pilgrims came to pray at the Tomb of the Patriarchs and Matriarchs. On one especially crowded day, a 17-year-old from Hebron tossed a grenade into a crowd gathered at the shrine, wounding 47 people, including foreign tourists, young children, and an infant. Mayor Jaabari denounced the attack, calling it an assault on Arabs and Jews alike. One month later, another explosive was hurled by a Palestinian outside the tomb, injuring 3 Arab children, an elderly Arab man, and a Jewish man and his son.[25]

Israel responded to these attacks with the force of a nation that had firmly taken its place in the Middle East. Soldiers would now be

stationed outside the tomb and on the roofs surrounding it, to better protect worshippers and tourists. Demonstrating that the Jews of
Israel in 1968 were not the Jews of Palestine in 1929, the IDF demolished the notorious seventh step of the outdoor stairwell, where the
October attack had emanated from.[26]

In what quickly became an unwritten rule of Israel's haphazard
settlement enterprise, the Israeli government's response to the terror
attacks in Hebron was to authorize the establishment of a new Jewish
settlement. In 1969, the Labor-led government proposed the creation
of a Jewish town next to Hebron. Kiryat Arba, one of Hebron's biblical names, would be perched on a hill overlooking Hebron, half a
mile from the Tomb of the Patriarchs and Matriarchs. The Knesset
approved the resolution in 1970. Deputy Prime Minister Yigal Allon
proclaimed to his fellow lawmakers, "We must not acquiesce in making Hebron 'Judenrein' of our own volition because of a murderous
pogrom in August 1929."[27]

This series of events between 1967 and 1970 would become a pattern. First, pressure on the government by settlers is first met by government refusal. Then, attacks by Palestinians place further pressure
on the government to stand strong and not submit to terror, lest it
be seen as legitimate and effective. The government then approves
settlement construction or expansion. The military forces necessary
to protect the settlers further entrenches the occupation, placing
additional restrictions on Palestinian freedom of movement. Tension
leads to violent interactions between Israeli troops, frustrated Palestinians, and settlers. It is a cycle that continues to this day.

Brooklyn Moves to Hebron

The West Bank was still referred to as "Israeli-occupied Jordan" when
the first apartment building rose from a rocky hillside in September 1971. Moshe and a perpetually pregnant Miriam Levinger were
among the first residents of Kiryat Arba. Miriam had given birth to 2

more children in Hebron's military compound. "After 42 Years, Jews Are Part of Hebron," read the headline in the *New York Times*. "The Arab city," the story read, "will have a resident Jewish community for the first time since an Arab massacre of the Jews here in 1929."

Rabbi Levinger was not satisfied. His goal remained the revival of the ancient Jewish presence in Hebron's Old City, not a barren hill with a distant view of it. He and his followers accepted Kiryat Arba as a temporary compromise. It was the best they would get for now.

Moshe Dayan, who had by now accepted the facts on the ground, did not see Kiryat Arba as an obstacle to peace. When a treaty was reached, he said, Jews could live under Arab rule just as Arabs were living under Israeli rule. "We Jews have always lived together in this land with other nations," Miriam Levinger told the *New York Times*. "I see no reason why we can't live with the Arabs peacefully in Hebron."[28]

With forty apartment blocks made of Jerusalem stone arranged in clusters, Kiryat Arba was, at that time, the largest settlement in the West Bank. It quickly became a hub for Jewish radicals. The most well-known resident extremist was the Brooklyn-born Rabbi Meir Kahane, founder of the Jewish Defense League. The JDL began innocently enough in 1968 with the goal of protecting Jewish Americans from violent anti-Semitic attacks, and campaigning for the freedom of Soviet Jewry. After a series of bombings targeting Soviet institutions in the US, the JDL earned the status of a terrorist organization.[29]

In 1971, Kahane moved to Israel, settling in Kiryat Arba. Soon after his arrival, he established Kach, a political party that called to evict Arabs from the Land of Israel. Kahane drew very little support at the time. His party won a single seat in Israeli Parliament in 1984, after which it was banned under a new law that prevented parties that encouraged racism from appearing on the ballot.

Since Kahane's assassination in 1990 (see page 10), his dogma has spread, and his masses of followers have grown. Perhaps the most infamous of his disciples was Baruch Goldstein, the Brooklyn-born Jewish doctor who also lived in Kiryat Arba. Goldstein perpetrated the 1994 massacre at the Tomb of the Patriarchs and Matriarchs, killing 29 Muslim worshippers during the holy month of Ramadan. Today Kiryat Arba is home to another acolyte of Kahane who until recently had a framed portrait of Goldstein on his living room wall: Israel's National Security Minister, Itamar Ben-Gvir.[30]

Jacob's Ladder

On March 26, 1979, Israel signed its first peace agreement, a historic treaty with Egypt, one of its staunchest foes. While most Israelis celebrated this monumental achievement, the settlement movement felt betrayed. Menachem Begin, the former opposition leader and founder of the right-wing Likud party, had championed the settlement cause and ended the left-wing Labor party's monopoly over Israeli politics. Begin, known for his thick horn-rimmed glasses and a wide gap between his two front teeth, was now Israel's sixth prime minister. Three decades after ordering the attack on the King David Hotel to hasten Israel's independence, Begin had agreed to amputate a piece of Israel. More than 2,500 Israelis would be evacuated from their homes in the Sinai desert. Most Israelis saw this as a small price to pay for what Israel received. In return for the Sinai, captured by Israel in 1967, Egypt became the first Arab state to recognize Israel's right to exist and announce an end to its war with the Jewish state. Gaza, a far more populated piece of land that Egypt did not want to rule, was retained by Israel. Begin and Egyptian president Anwar Sadat were awarded the Nobel Peace Prize in 1978. Three years later, Sadat was assassinated by members of Egypt's Islamic jihad.

Half a century after the Hebron massacre and a dozen years since Israel had won the West Bank, Hebron remained a city without Jews. Since moving to Kiryat Arba, Levinger had established Gush Emunim, the Bloc of the Faithful, an organization of like-minded activists committed to settling lands captured in 1967. The Bloc of the Faithful interpreted the peace treaty as a call for bolder measures. Days after it was signed, Levinger and his comrades gathered in Kiryat Arba for an urgent meeting. Hebron, they feared, could be the next biblical land Israel severed in return for what, they predicted, would bring no real peace. If there is a Jewish community in Hebron, they agreed, it would be far more difficult for Israel to sacrifice Judaism's second holiest city in a future treaty.

There was another reason for their desperation. Since establishing Kiryat Arba on the outskirts of Hebron, the government had refused their requests to expand beyond the initial 250 housing units, which filled up immediately. Israel's Supreme Court had frozen building permits, owing to the contested nature of the West Bank. "People who wanted to move to Kiryat Arba couldn't," recalled Yehudit Katsover, a prominent activist from Kiryat Arba. "It was decided that the time had come, and that if the government wasn't ready, we would make it ready."[31]

With the memory of 1929 as their guide and Miriam Levinger as their leader, a group of women carried out a mission that would forever alter the face of Hebron.

It was around 3:00 in the morning in late April 1979 when Miriam Levinger climbed onto a truck with her 10 young children. Driving slowly down the dark road to Hebron, they stopped to pick up more women and children, including Yehudit Katsover and her 3 children. After passing the Arab market that had once been Hebron's Jewish Quarter, the truck stopped behind the abandoned Hadassah House. Out of the truck came 10 women, 35 children, dozens of mattresses, a refrigerator, portable stoves, fuel, water, sacks of potatoes, and sweets for the kids. With the help of a few men from the Bloc of the Faithful, the women and children climbed up a ladder and entered the decrepit building through a second-story window. Built in 1893 by Rabbi Haim Yosef Franco, the grandfather of Avraham Franco (see pages 66–67), the Hadassah House was a lingering symbol of the 1929 massacre. During the riots, Arabs had destroyed the clinic and tortured the pharmacist and his family.[32]

"Going inside the abandoned building felt like landing on the moon," Katsover recalled. The floors were covered in dirt and dust, and the air was rancid from years of neglect. And yet, the first thing the women and children did was celebrate. Hearing Hebrew voices singing, a soldier stationed on a rooftop nearby came to inspect. Mystified by what he found, he asked the women and children, "How did you get here?" To which a 4-year-old girl replied, "Our forefather Jacob built us a ladder and we climbed in."[33]

The women planned to stay as long as they needed to. "Hebron will no longer be *Judenrein*," Miriam Levinger declared in a press conference announcing their arrival, in a nod to her family members who perished in Auschwitz. Branding themselves "The Women of the Hadassah House," the group released a statement published in Israeli newspapers, explaining that they were evicting no one by moving into the empty building. "Our heart's desire was and still is: Jewish settlement in Hebron—without dispossessing a single Arab," they stated, referring to the many other empty properties once owned by Jews. Their statement ended with a warning. "If we are removed by force, we will return again and again!"

By taking over this structure steeped in tragic memories, they hoped to force the government's hand. The military, they predicted, would not have the heart to forcibly evict dozens of Jewish women and children from such a place.[34]

Their hunch was right. Prime Minister Begin, who was at Camp David negotiating Israel's withdrawal from the Sinai, demanded that they leave the building at once, calling their operation illegal. Yet, he said, he would not use military force against women and children.[35]

This was not the first effort to reclaim the Hadassah House. Rabbi Kahane and his followers had tried to take over the symbolic building several times in 1978. Yeshiva students from Kiryat Arba had done the same in 1976. In every case, Israeli soldiers had swiftly removed the men. Some were arrested and fined.

The settlers insisted that since the building had been owned by Jews, and Avraham Franco had given Rabbi Levinger the deeds to all property owned by the Sephardic community in Hebron, it was their right to live there.[36]

The government tried to pressure the squatters to leave voluntarily by making life there unbearable. Soldiers surrounded the building, effectively placing it under siege. No one was permitted to enter the building, and anyone who left could not return. School for the children was out of the question, as were visitors. Katsover, a teacher, became the Hadassah House schoolteacher. At first, the military forbade the delivery of food and water. Rabbi Levinger reminded Begin that during the Yom Kippur War in October 1973, when the Israeli military surrounded the vanquished Egyptian Third Army, Israel allowed the enemy soldiers to receive food, water, and medicine. Begin relented, and visitors were permitted to bring supplies to the Hadassah House, delivered through a window using a system of ropes, buckets, and pulleys.[37]

The first people to deliver food to the women and children were Arab families who lived nearby. One family, whose windows were just feet away from one of the few windows of the Hadassah House, positioned their television to be closer to the window so that the Jewish women and children inside could watch with them. Not all Arabs welcomed their presence. Fahed Qawasmeh, the owner of the Park Hotel who was now mayor of Hebron, demanded they leave at once.[38]

While Prime Minister Begin publicly opposed the takeover, branding the women "invaders" who were "arrogant and neurotic," other members of his government did not hide their support. On their third day, the women received a visit from Ariel Sharon, then minister of agriculture. Speaking to them from outside the building, he said, "Jews have the right to live anywhere in Judaea and Samaria." Before he left, he placed a mezuzah on the building's doorway.[39]

The conditions in their new home were medieval. Before days of cleaning, the floors of the empty building were covered in garbage, cockroaches, and rats the size of cats. For a bathroom, the women hung a blanket around a garbage pail they emptied every few hours. There was no running water, but one woman was permitted to retrieve water, carried in a jug from outside. For bathing, they filled baby baths with water, using cups to bathe themselves and their children. "We didn't feel the hardship," recalled Katsover. "The meaning of what we were doing there overpowered everything else."

Husbands of the women began a weekly tradition. After welcoming the Sabbath with prayers at the Tomb of the Patriarchs and Matriarchs on Friday nights, they walked up the street to the Hadassah House, a quarter of a mile away. Gathered outside, as their wives and children looked out from the windows, they sang Shabbat songs and said Kiddush, the blessing that sanctifies the Sabbath. The tradition quickly attracted more residents of Kiryat Arba, mainly yeshiva students and their friends from across the country, who came to express solidarity with the women's cause.

Pressure mounted on the government. From the left came demands for the settlers to be evacuated. From the right came calls for the renewal of Hebron's Jewish community, and the righting of a historic wrong.[40]

Nine months into their stay, the government remained divided over Hebron's fate. Military officials warned of the difficulties and dangers of protecting a small group of Jewish settlers in the heart of a population of 60,000 Arabs. Then, on January 31, 1980, Yehoshua Saloma, a 23-year-old yeshiva student from Kiryat Arba, was walking through Hebron's market, buying fruit for Shabbat, when he was shot by Palestinian gunmen. At Saloma's funeral, attended by more than 2,000 mourners, Rabbi Levinger stood beside his grave and demanded that the government respond by taking back "all our stolen places and all the places where Jews were killed." Less than two months later, the Israeli government authorized the establishment of a small Jewish school in Hebron, the first to exist there since 1929. The Hadassah House would be its home.[41]

At a rally following the government's announcement, Mayor Qawasmeh declared to a crowd of Muslim religious leaders outside the Tomb of the Patriarchs and Matriarchs, "We have no choice but to put force against force. The Zionist empire will fall." Alluding to calls for his deportation over previous inciteful rhetoric, Qawasmeh said, "I find it easier to be deported from my homeland than to accept the settlement of Jews in Hebron." Sheikh Rajab Bayud Al-Tamimi, a Sharia judge in Hebron, called for a holy war to return "not only Hebron and Al-Aksa, but also Jaffa, Haifa and Acre" to Muslim rule. "The Jews have to know this land has masters and is entirely Muslim," said the sheikh.[42]

Tensions in Hebron intensified. Less than two weeks later, in a midnight raid, Palestinian militants infiltrated Misgav Am, a kibbutz in northern Israel near the Lebanese border. After entering the kibbutz's sleeping quarters for children, the militants took a group of babies and toddlers hostage, killing a 2-year-old and 2 adults. After the hostages were rescued, Arab students in Hebron held demonstrations praising the attack. "We are going to do to you what they did in Misgav Am," they chanted.[43]

CHAPTER 21

Revenge of Renewal

SHORTLY AFTER THE SUN WENT DOWN ON MAY 2, 1980, TAYSEER Abu Sneineh set out from a cave hideout on the outskirts of Hebron with three Palestinian comrades. Armed with assault rifles, hand grenades, and improvised explosive devices, they took their positions at a building across the street from the Hadassah House. Their eyes were locked on the 50 or so young men and women who had just emerged from prayers at the Tomb of the Patriarchs and Matriarchs. It was Friday night, and the Jewish worshippers were on their way to visit the women and children who were still squatting in the Hadassah House, more than a year after their predawn operation.

The presence of this predictably large crowd was precisely why Abu Sneineh's group had chosen this place and time for its attack. A 28-year-old math teacher, Abu Sneineh was also, like his comrades, a member of Yasser Arafat's Fatah resistance group, the leading faction of the Palestine Liberation Organization (PLO). They had received their instructions from Abu Jihad, one of Arafat's closest confidants and a fellow cofounder of Fatah. One of them had undergone training in guerilla warfare in Lebanon, another in the Soviet Union.[1]

Even before the death of the mufti in 1974, Arafat had claimed his mantle as leader of the Palestinian people and its resistance against the Jewish state. The mufti's most promising disciple was elected PLO chairman in 1969. Founded in Egypt in 1964, the PLO's stated goal was armed struggle for the establishment of an Arab state in historic Palestine, from the Jordan River to the Mediterranean Sea—a state that would replace Israel. According to the PLO, Zionists had invented the history of the Jewish presence in the land as a pretext for occupying Palestine. "Claims of historical or religious ties of Jews with Palestine are incompatible with the facts of history," read the organization's charter.[2]

As chairman of the PLO, Arafat continued the mufti's legacy. One year after Arafat became its chairman, the PLO recruited two former Nazi officials. One was a former leader of the Gestapo's Jewish affairs section. The other was an SS officer at the Mauthausen concentration camp. A Belgian neo-Nazi recruited volunteers for the PLO. Fatah, the Quranic word for conquest, is the reverse acronym for Harakat al-Tahrir al-Falistiniya, the Palestinian Liberation Movement. Spelled forward, the acronym reads "Hataf," which translates to "death."[3]

Fatah and the PLO were already known for committing horrific acts of terror in Israel. On May 14, 1974, Palestinian militants infiltrated the northern Israeli town of Ma'alot, murdering a couple and their 4-year-old son at their home before taking 115 Israelis hostage. Nearly all the hostages were schoolchildren. What became known as the Ma'alot Massacre ended on May 15 with the murder of 31 Israeli civilians, 22 of them children. In 1978, the Coastal Road Massacre, planned by Abu Jihad and carried out by Fatah militants, killed 38 Israeli civilians, including 13 children, in the hijacking of a bus on an Israeli highway.

Until May 2, 1980, the West Bank had never seen a large-scale act of terror.

As the crowd of worshippers approached the Hadassah House, with Moshe Levinger leading the way, Abu Sneineh stood in a darkened doorway clutching a submachine gun. The other gunmen peered down from the roof, holding hand grenades and Kalashnikovs. They waited for the whole group to arrive for maximum impact.

As Rabbi Levinger opened the gate outside the Hadassah House, women appeared in the windows above, holding their sons and daughters in their arms. "Shabbat Shalom," they called to the men and women below, just seconds before crackling explosions ripped through the air. After showering the crowd with bullets, grenades and homemade bombs, the militants ran for cover in the nearby Muslim cemetery, then retreated to their cave.

Six young Jewish men were killed in the attack, and 20 young men and women were seriously wounded. Five of the dead were yeshiva students. The sixth was a 32-year-old American veteran of the Vietnam War. Born a Christian in Virginia, James Eli Mahon Jr. had lost a thumb in Vietnam, then joined a biker gang in Washington, where he was known as Crazy Jim. After the Yom Kippur War, he moved to Kiryat Arba, converted to Judaism, and gave himself a Hebrew name, Eli HaZe'ev (Eli the Wolf). An avowed Jewish nationalist and follower of Meir Kahane, he had served jail time in Israel for breaking into Palestinian homes in Hebron and beating up residents. HaZe'ev was the only one who was armed that night, as it was Shabbat. He was struck by eight bullets in the back as he reached for his M16.[4]

The impact of the ambush at the Hadassah House reached far beyond those killed and wounded. Arafat and the PLO claimed immediate responsibility, hailing the attack as a "new phase" in the armed struggle against Israel. The objective was "to destroy the Israeli settlement thesis," Arafat declared. "Our people will never allow the Israelis to settle on Palestinian soil."[5]

The attack had precisely the opposite effect, further entrenching the settlement enterprise and the forces that drove it. As it had before and as it has since, Palestinian terrorism pushed the goal of a Palestinian state even farther into the distance. By feeding into the claims of Jewish extremists who stated there could be no coexistence with the Palestinians, the attack hardened the opinions of more moderate Israelis and strengthened the resolve of the Israeli government to respond forcefully in the hopes of deterring future attacks.

According to reports in the *New York Times* and other outlets, the attack was aimed at scuttling ongoing peace negotiations between Israel and Egypt. While the Camp David Accords had already been signed, talks were underway in Tel Aviv to grant autonomy to Pales-

tinians living in the West Bank and Gaza. By hardening Israel's negotiating stance, the *Times* reported, the attack could "torpedo the Camp
David accords of September 1978, which the PLO and most of the
Arab world have rejected as legitimizing perpetual Israeli occupation
of the West Bank and Gaza."[6]

In the immediate aftermath of the attack, the IDF demolished a
row of Arab shops adjacent to the ambush, turning half a block into
rubble. Hebron mayor Fahed Qawasmeh; the mayor of nearby Halhul,
Muhammad Milhem; and the chief judge of Hebron's Islamic court,
Sheikh Rajab Al-Tamimi, were accused of making inciting speeches in
the weeks leading up to the attack. All three were deported to Lebanon.

Milhem had been a central figure in the National Guidance Committee, a militant Palestinian leadership council that had recently
been established to coordinate opposition to the talks on Palestinian
autonomy. Settlers in Kiryat Arba had been pushing the government
to act against the committee and its members. Now the government
was listening.[7]

The United States was appalled by the men's deportation, not only
because it violated international law, but complicated the US-backed
peace negotiations. Many Israelis echoed that criticism, lamenting
the deportations as counterproductive to Israel's interests. Though
the PLO and many Arab officials, including the two mayors, had boycotted peace talks, American officials had high hopes for both men.
Qawasmeh and Milhem were considered relative moderates. Qawasmeh had been Hebron's first elected mayor—prior to Israeli rule over
the territory, municipal elections had not been held. Qawasmeh had
met with Israeli government figures and members of Israel's peace
movement during his tenure. Unlike other PLO figures, such as Arafat, Qawasmeh's vision for an independent Palestine did not involve
the elimination of Israel. A Palestinian state, he believed, could exist
alongside Israel. He opposed the negotiations because the autonomy
being discussed would be within territory still occupied by Israel,

and because they were between Israel and Egypt. Palestine's future, Qawasmeh believed, could only be negotiated by the PLO. The PLO, however, opposed a two-state solution.

"There's really no one left to whom we can talk," lamented an American official.[8]

Resistance at All Costs

While the US was disappointed by the shadow cast over peace talks, Arafat was thrilled. Greeting the deported men with a hero's welcome at PLO headquarters in Beirut, a young, plump, beaming Arafat held a press conference with the mayors. The attack in Hebron was a justifiable act of "resistance by those who are under occupation," said Arafat, dressed in his signature Fidel Castro–style hat and khaki shirt.

In Kiryat Arba, troops were deployed to prevent vigilante attacks by settlers seeking revenge. When a group of men tried to make their way to Hebron, soldiers fired into the air. Another group managed to get around the soldiers, smashing windows of Arab homes and cars before they were sent home. Arab teenagers stood along streets across the West Bank, hurling stones at cars with Israeli plates and shattering windshields.[9]

Deporting the mayors was not sufficient for the Bloc of the Faithful. Hundreds of settlers protested outside Prime Minister Begin's residence in Jerusalem, demanding the resignation of Defense Minister Ezer Weizman. He had been too lenient, they insisted. He resigned three weeks later.[10]

In what remains a staple of this conflict, what was meant to deliver a blow to Jewish settlement served instead to expand it. The Israeli government responded to the act of terror with an act of Religious Zionism: the revival of the Jewish community that was violently expelled in 1929. "There should be no impediment to Jews living in Hebron, or anywhere in the Land of Israel," read the government decision.

Permission was granted not only for Jewish families to live in the Hadassah House, but in three additional abandoned buildings adjacent to it: the Schneerson House, the Castel House, and the Hasson House, all named for the Jewish families who owned them before they were expelled or killed in 1929. The government also approved the rehabilitation of the Avraham Avinu Synagogue.[11]

The most brazen attack against settlers did more to revive Hebron's Jewish community than any settler tactic had. Reviving Hebron's Jewish Quarter, albeit on a small scale, was one of the greatest victories the settlement movement had achieved. The dogmatic settlers of Hebron, and their taste for provocation, became the face of the settlement movement.

The renewal of Hebron's Jewish Quarter did not end with the attack on the Hadassah House, nor did it end what remains the bedrock of the West Bank settlement enterprise: Palestinian attacks continue to generate further settlement construction and expansion.

In 1981, after a Jewish man was stabbed in Hebron, Israel seized the Romano House and granted settlers permission to establish the first yeshiva in Hebron since 1929. Ever since the Jordanian occupation, the Romano House had been an Arab girls' school. But its history was more complicated. Established by a Jew from Istanbul named Haim Yisrael Romano, it was built in 1879 as an alternative to the crowded Jewish Quarter. Ottoman authorities took over the palatial building during World War I, and when the British conquered Palestine, the Romano House became the Hebron headquarters of the British police. This was where the Jewish survivors had been taken on August 24, 1929.[12]

The Shavei Hebron Yeshiva, whose name means "the Returnees to Hebron," opened its doors in 1982. In July 1983, the yeshiva was attacked with Molotov cocktails. One week later, one of its founding students, a 19-year-old American citizen named Aharon Gross, was standing in the Arab market waiting for a ride, when three men jumped from a passing car, stabbed him in the stomach, and slit his throat. Mistaking Gross for a wounded Arab, local Palestinians rushed him to a Hebron hospital. When doctors there noticed his ritual Jewish fringes, they refused to treat him. By the time he arrived at an Israeli hospital, his heart was still beating, but he was beyond saving.[13]

Gross's murder led the Israeli government to approve new Jewish settlement in Hebron. Speaking in the Knesset a week after Gross's death, Defense Minister Moshe Arens said it was intolerable "that the sight of a Jew should make the blood of local Arabs boil."[14]

Just before he was killed, Gross had joined Rabbi Moshe Levinger in a one-man strike he was holding in a tent in front of an IDF building, protesting the lack of security for Hebron's Jews. While relations between Arabs and Jews in Hebron were often inconsequential—Jews shopped in the Arab market and had their hair cut by Arab barbers, while Arabs purchased their liquor in Kiryat Arba (forbidden by Islam, there were no liquor stores in Hebron)—there was also open hostility. Some settlers intimidated and threatened Palestinians. Some Palestinians threw explosives at Jewish homes, stoned Jewish cars, and looted synagogues. Complaining that Israeli soldiers often stood by and failed to intervene, at times settlers took matters into their own hands. One night, after a grenade was hurled at a passing Israeli car, settlers from Kiryat Arba burned an empty Arab bus.

In the aftermath of the ambush at the Hadassah House, Rabbi Levinger gave his blessing for the creation of a secret cell within the Bloc of the Faithful. The Jewish Underground, modeled after the anti-British underground Lehi, carried out a wave of attacks to avenge the murders of Israelis. The first attack came on June 2, 1980—the one-month memorial for those who were murdered at the Hadassah House—with a series of car bombings that crippled two Palestinian mayors. In July 1983, in retaliation for the killing of Aharon Gross, members of the group opened fire on students outside the Islamic College of Hebron, and tossed a grenade through a window. Three students were killed, and more than two dozen wounded. The assailants were three settlers from Hebron, including Rabbi Levinger's son-in-law. "Whoever did this has sanctified God's name," said Levinger, praising the attack.[15]

The following year, the Jewish Underground was eradicated as it attempted to carry out what would have been the worst act of Jewish terrorism since the days of the Irgun. Their arrest revealed an even more destructive plan that was so provocative it could have set off a global war between Israel and the entire Muslim world.

On April 27, 1984, Jewish Underground operatives planted powerful explosives beneath five buses serving Palestinians in East Jerusalem. Agents of the Shin Bet, Israel's internal security service, intercepted the bombs before they exploded, and carried out a sweeping arrest operation, detaining dozens of the group's suspected members.[16]

Capping off a two-year effort to dismantle the group, the Shin Bet's interrogations revealed a far more sinister plan. A rogue cell of the Jewish Underground was plotting to blow up the Dome of the Rock. In the days after that shocking discovery, police arrested dozens more suspected members. Many were residents of Kiryat Arba and Hebron. The most prominent among them was Rabbi Moshe Levinger. Suspected of providing his rabbinical blessing for the Jewish terrorists, he was released several days later without charge. By late May, 27 members of the Jewish Underground had been indicted on charges of terrorism.[17]

The yearlong trial that followed deeply divided Israeli society. While some viewed members of the underground as heroic figures who had acted in the face of deadly Arab attacks, many others saw them and the settlement movement as messianic extremists who were hijacking Israel's future, making the country's already precarious position in the Middle East even more so. According to polls, half of Israelis wished for the trials to end, and for anyone convicted to receive an immediate pardon. Calls for their release swelled after Israel agreed, in May 1985, to free more than 1,000 Palestinians imprisoned for committing acts of terror, including murder. They were released in exchange for 3 Israeli prisoners of war held by the Popular Front for the Liberation of Palestine, a radical militant group whose members had committed some of the deadliest attacks against Israeli civilians.

Demonstrators on both sides of the debate took to the streets for weeks. In Jerusalem, supporters of the defendants called for the government to end the trials and pardon the accused. In Tel Aviv, protests organized by the anti-settlement group Peace Now demanded that the trials continue, and that anyone convicted serve their sentence in full.[18]

In July of 1985, 3 members of the Jewish Underground were convicted of murder and sentenced to life in prison. Twelve others, convicted of various crimes against Arabs, received sentences of three to ten years. Rabbi Levinger's son-in-law, Uzi Sharbaf, received a life sentence for his role in the 1980 car bombings that crippled the mayors, and the 1983 attack on Hebron's Islamic College. Menachem Livni, the commander of an IDF reserve battalion of combat engineers who cofounded the Jewish Underground and was a student of Rabbi Levinger in Hebron, was also sentenced to life. Livni had built many of the group's bombs, and masterminded both the attack on the Hebron college and the Jerusalem bus-bombing plot. Yehuda Etzion, who conspired to blow up the Dome of the Rock, was sentenced to ten years.[19]

Unrepentant, Etzion shouted after his sentencing, "The Temple Mount will be ours one day!"

Others displayed a similar lack of remorse. Speaking outside the courtroom where he was convicted of planting a bomb that crippled the mayor of Ramallah in June 1980, 37-year-old Yitzhak Novik told Israeli radio: "Looking back, it's been proven that what I set out to do was successful in that for two years after what I did, there were almost no grave terrorist incidents in the West Bank."[20]

The relatively light sentences handed down to most of the Jewish Underground members illuminated the vast gulf that separated Jewish and Arab suspects facing the Israeli justice system. Of the original 27 Jews indicted on terrorism charges in 1984, 10 signed plea deals with sentences ranging from eleven months to ten years. The punishment for Palestinians convicted of lesser crimes was often far harsher. That same year, 5 Palestinians in Gaza received sentences of nine months to thirteen years for merely belonging to a terrorist organization. None had ever carried out an attack.

Even the defense lawyers for the Jewish Underground members noted the imbalance. One of them told Israeli radio, "It seems that all the judges took into account the special situation in which the inhabitants of Judaea and Samaria found themselves security-wise, and they took into account that what they did was in reaction to murder and Arab terror."[21]

Appeals for amnesty poured in as soon as the sentences were read. Likud leader Yitzhak Shamir, the former prime minister then serving as foreign minister, called the convicted murderers "basically good boys" who had been led astray. Shamir, who in his own youth had been one of the leaders of Lehi—the original Jewish Underground— vowed to fight for their amnesty. Ironically, it was Shamir who had ordered their arrest when he was prime minister. At the time, a lawmaker from his own party appealed to Shamir for a general pardon. "Anything is possible," Shamir had responded then.

Amnesty

Less than two years after they were sentenced to life in prison, Israel's president, Chaim Herzog, commuted the life sentences of the 3 convicted Jewish terrorists to twenty-four years each. By then 17 other convicts had already been released due to sentence reductions and parole.

Hailed as heroes in ultranationalist circles, several former members of the underground remain at the forefront of the settlement movement today. Yehuda Etzion, the man who plotted to blow up the Dome of the Rock, now leads a group of activists dedicated to changing the status quo on the Temple Mount to allow Jewish prayer. Uzi Sharbaf, the son-in-law of Rabbi Levinger, was released on parole after serving just seven years in prison. Today he is one of the spiritual leaders of the movement among far-right Israelis to resettle Gaza.[22]

The discovery of the Jewish Underground's shocking plans led to the demise of the Bloc of the Faithful. Yet the settlement movement became forever tainted by its radical influence. The embrace of violent, vengeful tactics among extreme elements of the settlement movement persists, as does their general lack of accountability.[23]

In September 1988, Moshe Levinger's car was stoned by Arabs, leaving his windshield shattered and his son injured. He got out of his car and opened fire in the street, killing the Palestinian owner of a shoe store. "I did not have the privilege of killing that Arab," Levinger told reporters in Hebron, referring to the man who had stoned his car. "Not that I may not have wanted to kill him or that he did not deserve to die, but I did not have the privilege of killing that Arab." He was sentenced to five months in prison for negligent homicide. He served ninety-two days.[24]

It is a pattern of impunity that continues today. According to a study conducted by the Israeli human rights group Yesh Din, which analyzed police investigations into violence committed by Israelis against Palestinians in the West Bank between 2005 and 2023, 94 percent of cases it reviewed were closed without an indictment.[25]

CHAPTER 22

The Mayor

THE SUN WAS SHINING ON THE TOMB OF THE PATRIARCHS AND Matriarchs when a veiled Palestinian woman holding a kitchen knife rushed at a young Israeli soldier standing guard outside the shrine. His fellow troops opened fire, and Israeli medics evacuated the woman to a Jerusalem hospital in critical condition.

Soldiers had cleared the scene of the attack by the time I set out for Hebron that morning. It was a routine they were accustomed to. So began my first visit to the City of Abraham since my first disturbing visit eight years earlier.

It was October 30, 2019, and the road leading into Hebron looked much like the road leading into any town in Israel. The bulletproof public bus turned off the highway and into Kiryat Arba, passing a gas station, a bank, a kebab shop, and a convenience store. The traffic circles were planted with pink flowers, and the streets were lined with shrubs. But as we turned a corner down the road to Hebron, the view from my window no longer resembled an Israeli town. The flowers lining the streets were replaced by garbage, discarded furniture, and hulking concrete buildings that housed a disproportionate number of auto body shops. The road connecting Kiryat Arba to Hebron is known as Worshippers Way, as it leads directly to the Tomb of the Patriarchs and Matriarchs. The street, like all of Hebron, save for the Jewish Quarter, is overseen by the city's Palestinian municipality and its Palestinian mayor.

Barefoot Palestinian children played on the side of the road, throwing rocks into the street and at each other. The winding road was lined with bricks, as if someday someone planned to fix it. Drawing closer to the tomb, the road grew narrower, the buildings more ancient. Abandoned stone homes crumbled into the streets. Signs on buildings and fences bore images and quotes from the city's rabbis past and present, including Moshe Levinger.

The Hebron Protocols

The city where the first Jew made his covenant with God looked like the most godforsaken place I had ever seen. Hebron did not resemble any Israeli town because, technically, this is not Israel. Kiryat Arba and Hebron live in the murky legal waters of Occupied Territories, or the term Israel prefers, Disputed Territories.

Hebron is deeply sacred to both Jews and Muslims, for whom Abraham, or Ibrahim, is revered as a precursor to the Prophet Muhammad. Through his son Isaac, Abraham is the patriarch of the Jewish people, and through his son Ishmael, the patriarch of the Arab people. The root of Hebron's Hebrew name, Hevron, and its Arabic name, Al-Khalil, both mean "friend." The city is named after Abraham, referred to as the friend of God in both the Hebrew Bible and the Quran. According to the Bible, as King David's first capital, Hebron was the original center of the biblical Kingdom of Israel.

Hebron's seemingly irreconcilable political divisions are codified in its geography. Ever since Benjamin Netanyahu signed the 1997 Hebron Protocols in his first term as prime minister, withdrawing from most of the city in peace negotiations with Yasser Arafat, Hebron has been divided. The Palestinian Authority controls 80 percent of the city. Known as H1, it is home to most of Hebron's nearly 300,000 residents. H2, the remaining 20 percent of Hebron that is controlled by Israel, is a small, depressing zone of ancient, decrepit stone buildings and largely deserted streets.

Though H2 contains the Tomb of the Patriarchs and Matriarchs, Hebron's Old City, and the Jewish enclaves, it is otherwise devoid of the usual signs of urban life. There are no supermarkets, restaurants, or gas stations in H2. Meanwhile H1 is a bustling Arab city that reflects its status as the economic hub of Palestinian life on the West Bank. Israelis are forbidden from entering Palestinian-controlled H1. The movement of Palestinians within H2 is heavily restricted by soldiers and checkpoints. Though Israel controls 20 percent of Hebron, its 800 Jewish residents can access only 3 percent of the city. The other 34,000 residents of H2 are Palestinian. If they wish to shop, fill up their gas, or go out to eat, Palestinians in H2 must cross the checkpoint to H1. Jewish residents go to Kiryat Arba.

On an expansive stone courtyard surrounded by ancient olive trees and towering date palms, I gazed up at one of the most historic sites between the Jordan River and the Mediterranean Sea. The Tomb of the Patriarchs and Matriarchs stands like a holy watchtower over the bones of the mothers and fathers of the Jewish people. Yet seemingly everywhere I looked, any beauty I saw was interlaced with barbed wire fences, soldiers, checkpoints, or guard posts. Hebron's holiness had been marred by decades of conflict, its serenity sacrificed for security. The dissonance between the spirituality of the shrine and the physical degradation all around it felt tragic.

After passing through a metal detector, I walked up a long staircase of smooth Jerusalem stone and into the fortress of worship. As I stepped inside, I noticed someone familiar leaving. It took me a moment to realize that it was my husband's elderly uncle Saadia. Born in Yemen, Saadia emigrated to Israel as a young boy with his parents, siblings, and the rest of Yemen's Jewish inhabitants. He now lived in the desert city of Beersheba, where my husband grew up. He had taken three different buses to get to Hebron that morning. I was surprised to learn that he made this journey once a month. *Why?* I asked him. "Because it's important that we never forget our roots," Saadia told me in his soft, gravelly voice. "This is the birthplace of our nation. The people of Israel, it all began here."

He grabbed my wrist as if sharing a secret. "I am a Cohen," he said with a warm smile. Cohens are the descendants of Jerusalem's ancient priestly class. They trace their lineage to Zadok, who founded the priesthood of Jerusalem when King Solomon built the First Temple in the tenth century BCE. Through Zadok, Cohens are direct descendants of Aaron, who was appointed the first Jewish priest by his brother, Moses. My maternal grandfather was also a Cohen, and so I know that Jewish law forbids this priestly class from coming in close contact with a grave, or being under the same roof as a dead body. "We are allowed here because the graves are three stories down from where we are standing," Saadia whispered, pointing at the sand-colored stones beneath our feet. And with that, he went to catch his first bus home.

I stepped inside and walked slowly. Women dressed in long skirts prayed quietly in hallways and alcoves, within or just outside the six rooms containing the cenotaphs of Abraham, Isaac and Jacob, Sarah, Rebecca, and Leah. I walked through the cavernous rooms of the tomb, lit by chandeliers, candelabras, and sunlight shining through arched windows. The stone walls were adorned with colorful tiles, Islamic stenciling, and golden calligraphy, reminiscent of the great mosques of the Ottoman Empire, with vaulted ceilings painted in rich tones of blue, green, and gold. At the end of the main hallway, I came to the Hall of Isaac. The most ornate of all the rooms, it is reserved for Muslim prayer. Several Jewish men were praying just outside its doors. Jews are allowed inside the Hall of Isaac ten times a year, on the holiest days in the Jewish calendar, when the entire shrine is closed to Muslims. On the ten holiest days of the Islamic calendar, the shrine is open only to Muslims, and Jews are forbidden from entering. I stood there for a few minutes, trying to feel something, but I couldn't. Any sense of spirituality or historic resonance was overwhelmed by the aura of conflict that enveloped the space. Every time I have visited the Western Wall in Jerusalem, the feeling of sacred spirituality was so present it was almost chilling. Each time I have touched the stones of the Western Wall, I wept. It pained me that I felt none of that in the Tomb of the Patriarchs and Matriarchs.

Descending from the tomb, I walked up the main road of Old Hebron. Like the city itself, that road has two names. In Hebrew, the road that leads to and from the tomb is King David Street. It is better known by its Arabic name, Shuhada Street, which means "Martyrs Street." Only Israeli pedestrians and cars, tourists, and Palestinians with permission are permitted on Martyrs Street. The Arab storefronts that once made this the central hub of urban life in Hebron have long been shuttered. Hundreds of shops in Hebron were closed by military order in 1994, after the violent riots that followed Baruch Goldstein's massacre. Others were forced to close during the Second Intifada, or Palestinian uprising, which between 2000 and 2005 made suicide bombings and other deadly attacks a near-daily part of life in Israel and the West Bank.

The Tomb of the Patriarchs and Matriarchs, 2019.

Al-Khalil

At the end of Shuhada Street I reached a checkpoint, one of two dozen that dot the city.[1] I was standing in Israeli Hebron. On the other side was Palestinian Al-Khalil. I crossed that checkpoint for the first time to meet with the mayor of Hebron, a man who embodies the dueling narratives that define this conflict, and how little has changed over the course of a century.

Tayseer Abu Sneineh sat at his polished wooden desk beneath a framed portrait of Palestinian president Mahmoud Abbas. The air in his office in Hebron's city hall was thick with stale cigarette smoke. It was December 2019, and Israel's then defense minister, Naftali Bennett, had just announced a new neighborhood in Hebron that would double the number of Jewish residents in the city. The mayor's office invited a group of foreign correspondents to hear his response.

We were served thick Arabic coffee and sweet sage tea. "In the name of Allah, I would like to welcome you all," the mayor said in Arabic, pausing for his translator to relay his words. "This is a very dangerous decision," he continued. "This is a terrorist act against the Palestinian people."

Abu Sneineh, a pudgy man with a bulbous nose and thin black hair combed over the top of his half-bald head, was dressed in a black suit and a striped tie. He hunched forward in his black leather armchair. "It is well known that the Jewish community is raised on extremism in this area. We are against violence. We want to live in peace."

In a room of over a dozen foreign journalists based in Israel, I was the only one aware of the mayor's role in the terror attack that led to the renewal of Hebron's Jewish Quarter. Tayseer Abu Sneineh, the math teacher and Fatah member who murdered Jewish worshippers at the Hadassah House on May 2, 1980 (see pages 242–44), had since become mayor of Hebron.

Four months after his attack, Israel arrested Abu Sneineh and his three accomplices. Sentenced to life in prison, they were all soon released in prisoner exchanges between Israel and the PLO. Abu Sneineh was 1 of 4,700 Palestinian prisoners freed in 1983 in exchange for 6 Israeli soldiers who were taken hostage in 1982 by Fatah militants at an IDF outpost in Lebanon. After being deported to Algeria, Abu Sneineh was permitted to return to the West Bank, along with other exiled PLO members, as part of the Oslo Accords, a set of agreements between Israel and the Palestinians, first signed in 1993.[2]

Welcomed home as a warrior of Palestinian resistance, Abu Sneineh was appointed head of the Hebron Waqf, the Muslim authority that oversees the city's mosques. Three decades later, his prestige had not faded. In 2016, Fatah—led by Arafat's successor, Palestinian president Mahmoud Abbas—selected Abu Sneineh as the party's candidate in Hebron's municipal elections. Fatah hailed Abu Sneineh as a hero, calling his attack "one of the most important battles and acts of bravery of the Fatah movement." On May 14, 2017, following a campaign in which he embraced his role in the terrorist attack, Abu Sneineh was duly elected. He was reelected in 2022.[3]

Hebron is "well known for being the economic capital of Palestine," the mayor told the journalists gathered in his office. The city's population now stands at more than 300,000, up from 215,000 in 2016, he said. The establishment of this new Jewish neighborhood, he warned, "will lead to the expulsion of the Palestinian people" and the "Judaization of the entire area." There had already been a forced "mass expulsion" of Palestinians from H2, the side of Hebron controlled by Israel, the mayor claimed, inaccurately. When the Hebron Protocol was signed in 1997, there were 35,000 Palestinians living in H2. That figure has since fallen to 34,000. The size of the Jewish population of Hebron has remained stagnant for more than a decade, at around 800, the same as it was in 1929. That includes the 300 students who live at Shavei Hebron Yeshiva.[4]

Echoing the rumors that swirled in 1929 of the impending Jewish conquest of Al-Aqsa Mosque, Abu Sneineh warned that the expansion of Hebron's Jewish community was merely another step in Israel's effort "to control all of the Ibrahimi Mosque." The proposed residential building, encompassing seventy apartment units, is planned to rise from the site of a shuttered fruit and vegetable market on an unpopulated acre of land in the Old City. In the five years since it was first announced, however, the plan has remained a plan alone. The building project faces a torrent of legal challenges, including from the mayor and Israeli organizations such as Peace Now.

The House of Peace

Like nearly every inch of Hebron, the land upon which the new Jewish neighborhood would be built has a tangled history—though it all comes back to 1929. Until 1994, it was a bustling Arab market on Martyrs Street. After Goldstein's deadly attack, which was followed by violent Palestinian riots, the market was closed by the Israeli military. Before it became an Arab market, however, it was Jewish property. Purchased in 1807 by Rabbi Haim Bajayo, a leader of Hebron's Sephardic community, the neighborhood was a center of Jewish life until 1929, when Arab residents took over those Jewish homes. Under Jordanian rule from 1948 to 1967, the area was taken under state custodianship and turned into a market.

Building new neighborhoods is one of the only ways settlers can circumvent the formidable obstacles to Jews purchasing property in Hebron. Under Palestinian law, selling property to Jews is a crime punishable by death. In the few cases where settlers have managed to purchase property, the transactions were contested in Israeli courts. One example is the curiously named House of Peace, whose story is a fitting metaphor for Hebron itself. Originally named the Rajabi House, after the Palestinian businessman who purchased the land, construction on the building began in 1995. It was almost complete when, on the evening of March 19, 2007, some 200 settlers entered the empty four-story apartment building, singing and dancing. They renamed it the House of Peace. That night, in a statement celebrating the purchase of the first

Jewish property on the strategic road linking Kiryat Arba to Hebron, the Jewish Community of Hebron announced, "This building will provide homes for dozens, if not hundreds of Israelis waiting to live in Hebron. . . . It is our hope that this will truly be a place of peace, and that our new neighbors will finally accept that Jews have returned home."

Their neighbors were not pleased. Rajabi denied selling the building and insisted the settlers were illegal trespassers. That week, Jordan and the Palestinian Authority arrested 2 Palestinians suspected of selling the building to Jews.[5]

At first, soldiers were stationed at the building to protect the settlers, but in 2008, the IDF forcibly evicted them, since they had not received authorization from the defense ministry to move in. From there, the House of Peace entered nearly a decade of contention, ping-ponging between differing court rulings. In 2014 it was proven that the Jewish community had legally purchased the building for $700,000 through a Jewish-American businessman whose family had survived the 1929 massacre. Israel's Supreme Court ruled that the settlers could return to the building.

The sordid case of the House of Peace is representative of all Jewish property in Hebron, whether purchased from Palestinians or newly built with government approval. Here, it is never as simple as buying a home or building one.[6]

I asked Abu Sneineh if he opposes Jews living in Hebron. "We are not against Jewish existence as Palestinians, who lived in Hebron before, as Palestinians," he responded. In other words, he would countenance a return to the conditions that existed prior to Israel's establishment, when Jews and Arabs living under British and Ottoman rule were all Palestinian. When I asked him about the massacre of Palestinian Jews in 1929, he insisted the attack was perpetrated by the British authorities, not by the Arabs of Hebron.

I later returned to interview the mayor, and asked him about his own terrorist attack. He argued that it was carried out not on a crowd of Jewish civilians returning from prayer at the Tomb of the Patriarchs and Matriarchs, but against a group of armed extremists and soldiers. This claim is contradicted by all news reporting of the incident: one settler was armed, but most of the group was not. All the victims were civilians.

Abu Sneineh refuted any Jewish connection to any part of the Holy Land. "This claim that the Jewish religion springs from here and it comes from Palestine, I will tell you this is absolutely not true," the mayor insisted. "There is no holy place in Palestine which is linked with the Jewish religion through history," he added, calling all archeological evidence to the contrary "Zionist propaganda." Why, then, have Jews around the world prayed in the direction of Jerusalem for more than 2,000 years? Abu Sneineh did not reply.

"What about the Tomb of the Patriarchs and Matriarchs?" I asked the mayor, curious how he viewed the history of Abraham's burial place. "The Ibrahimi Mosque is a Muslim holy site," he replied. "There are Jewish religious people who still refuse to visit the Ibrahimi Mosque and only go to the seventh step." The stone enclosure surrounding the cave in which the first Jew is believed to be buried was in fact built by a Jewish king centuries before Islam was born. I reminded Abu Sneineh that for 700 years, the Jews of Palestine were forbidden by Muslim officials from entering the shrine, and forced to pray outside. Preposterous, the mayor replied. "Palestinians have never prevented any party from visiting their holy places."

To prove his claim that Jews have no historical connection to the site, the mayor referred me to the 2017 UNESCO designation of Hebron's Old City as a Palestinian World Heritage Site. That designation, which includes the tomb, was slammed by Israel for ignoring the area's Jewish history. Abu Sneineh was heavily involved in the campaign that led to the UNESCO decision. "This occupation, Israel, has been built on a false narrative," Abu Sneineh told me. "The world is now waking up to the Palestinian narrative."[7]

Mayor Abu Sneineh is not the only former terrorist to be revered in Hebron. While the Israeli government clamped down on Jewish extremists in the wake of Baruch Goldstein's attack and criminalized the Kahanist Kach movement he followed, many settlers in Hebron describe Goldstein as a hero. His gravesite in Kiryat Arba remains a shrine to hardcore settlers.

Revisionist History

Leaving the mayor's office, I walked through H1, the side of Hebron controlled by the Palestinian Authority. I expected it to look much like H2, the side controlled by Israel. Instead, I encountered a lively Arab city humming with people, restaurants, shopping centers, open-air markets, taxis, and honking cars. Young men and women sat in cafés sipping espresso, smoking cigarettes, working on their laptops. I could stay in one of several hotels here, something I could not do on the Jewish side, where there are no hotels, shopping centers, or cafés. There was more life on one block of the Palestinian side of Hebron than there was on the entire Israeli side. Some streets were spray-painted with swastikas. A new gate at the Polytechnic University in Hebron was dedicated to Abu Iyad, the Palestinian mastermind of the 1972 massacre at the Munich Olympics, which killed 11 Israeli athletes.

Although the mayor's revisionist history stunned me at the time, I came to understand that such views are mainstream. In a separate conversation with Abu Sneineh's spokesman, he repeated the same canards about the British carrying out the 1929 massacre and about the Jewish people having no history in "Israel"—his air quotes. After we left, and I expressed my shock at how he could believe the Jewish people have no roots in this land, my Arabic translator, Manar, a young woman from Ramallah, said that most Palestinians share this view. To test that theory, she suggested I ask people on the street. Together we approached two young men sitting on a bench outside the Hebron municipality, drinking coffee.

Ahmad Muhtaseb, 21, and Bara'a Bilhem, 23, were both accounting students at nearby Hebron University. Neither had ever heard of the

1929 Hebron massacre. Both insisted that Jewish history in this land was a fabrication. "The Jews have no connection here," said Muhtaseb.

"What about the Tomb of the Patriarchs and Matriarchs?" I asked.

"They think it's theirs, but they have no connection to Ibrahim and Sarah's burial place. The Jews are known to be the killers of the prophets," said Muhtaseb, in an apparent reference to Jesus, who is revered in Islam as a Muslim prophet.

"Are these views common among your friends and family?" I asked.

"A true Muslim would give only the answer I just gave," replied Muhtaseb. "Otherwise, they've been Westernized."

Bilhem agreed with his friend. "Jews have no roots here."

I found it difficult to digest the fact that millions of people who share this land not only believe that Jews have no roots in Israel, but that Israeli history is a lie. Judaism, at its heart, is grounded in the Jewish people's connection to the Land of Israel. Was Judaism a lie?

I asked Manar to help me understand how so many Palestinians could outright deny Jewish history and identity. "This is what Palestinian children are taught, in school and at home," she explained. That fleeting comment would lead me on a months-long investigation for *Foreign Policy*, researching Palestinian textbooks, and visiting a Palestinian school in East Jerusalem. The school, like many in the West Bank and Gaza, was operated by UNRWA, the UN body tasked with aiding Palestinian refugees.

Manar was right. Not only were Palestinian children being taught that Israel has no right to exist, in schools operated by the United Nations, they were, unthinkably, being taught to aspire to martyrdom and jihad. I found this in the curriculum, in textbooks, and in painful conversations with schoolchildren.

"We are taught that martyrs go to a very high level of heaven," a fifth-grader told me and Manar outside her UNRWA school in East Jerusalem in 2021. She told us that her class had learned about Dalal

al-Mughrabi, a perpetrator of the Coastal Road Massacre, in which
38 Israeli civilians were killed, including 13 children. "They taught us
that she is a hero," said the young girl with big brown eyes. When we
asked what she had been taught about peace, she replied, "We haven't
learned about peace. This is for older students."

We asked an older girl nearby the same question. She was in the
seventh grade. "We learn that the Jews stole our land, and that we
need to keep fighting until Palestine is ours," she said.

The Palestinian government has codified this glorification of
martyrdom into law. According to an official incentive program that
the US and Israel have tried for years to end, the families of Palestinians who are killed while carrying out attacks against Israelis are auto-
matically entitled to payments from the Palestinian Authority. The
families of terrorists who survive their attacks also receive payments.
The heavier the sentence—meaning, the deadlier their attack—the
more financial assistance they receive. Israeli and American officials
refer to this as the "Pay to Slay" program. The Palestinian Authority calls it the Martyrs Fund. Palestinians have long argued that the
fund is necessary to counteract the actions of Israel, which regularly
demolishes the homes of Palestinian assailants.

Modern Muftis

Jamil Abu Sneineh stood barefoot in the Hall of Isaac and pointed
out the five bullet holes in the marble walls. "This is where the imam
was standing the morning of February 25, 1994, leading dawn prayers
on the fifteenth day of Ramadan," he said, pointing toward the green
metal door through which Baruch Goldstein entered this room named
for the son of Abraham.

"The same imam still leads prayers here today," said Jamil, the former director of the Hebron Waqf. To our left was a covered hole in the
ground, beneath which, according to Jewish legend, lies the entrance
to the Garden of Eden.

"There are three doors to the caves below us," Jamil said as he looked down at the maroon floor. "One of them is under these carpets, where the worshippers were praying when they were killed."

I arrived at Hebron's Ibrahimi Mosque that chilly morning in December 2019 to learn more about the Muslim side of the Tomb of the Patriarchs and Matriarchs. Upon entering the mosque, I was given a hooded full-body covering. "All women who enter the mosque must cover their hair and body for reasons of modesty," said a man stationed at the entrance.

Jamil greeted me with a smile that wrinkled the skin around his brown eyes. That smile remained a permanent fixture of his tan, still-youthful face. From 2009 to 2016, 66-year-old Jamil oversaw all of Hebron's mosques. Before that, he spent fifteen years in Israeli prison. "Fourteen years, six months, and seven days," he corrected himself. His face, framed by a trim white beard, glowed as he recalled planting a bomb in Hebron the night of November 28, 1984. Then 26, Jamil placed the explosive device on a street called Al-Salam, which in Arabic means "peace." "They found it before it detonated," he said with a glimmer of pride in his eyes.

As we walked through the mosque, I overheard lies and half-truths delivered by the site's official tour guides. "Jews have taken over the entire building," one man told his European tour group, despite the fact that more than half the building is reserved for Muslims. The same guide falsely described Hebron's Jewish community as having all come from America—in fact less than 10 percent are American. Nearby, another guide falsely told his group that there were no Jews living in Hebron until the twentieth century. When an American tourist asked her guide about the ancient Jewish connection to the tomb, her guide responded, "This is propaganda, so the Israelis could take control of the mosque."

Outside the Hall of Isaac, Jamil introduced me to Sheikh Hefzi Yassin Abu Sneineh, the 59-year-old manager of Ibrahimi Mosque, who has been an imam there for more than two decades. When I asked Jamil and the sheikh if they are related to one another and the mayor of Hebron, they both laughed. As one of the largest clans, there are nearly 40,000 Abu Sneinehs in Hebron, they said. In fact, an entire neighborhood of Hebron is named Abu Sneineh. "In the end we're all Abu Sneineh," joked Jamil. Other parts of Hebron are named after other large families, such as the Jaabari clan, also numbering some 40,000 people.

We sat down in Hefzi's office, a cavernous stone room with massive green doors that are locked shut. This had been the main entrance to the mosque before Goldstein's massacre. I asked Jamil and Hefzi about life in Hebron. They both continued the thread of mistruths I had overheard from the tour guides. Goldstein's attack, Hefzi insisted, was not an individual act, but an orchestrated plan by the Israeli government to take over the Ibrahimi Mosque. "From 1967 to 1994, nobody from the occupation was allowed inside," said Hefzi, substituting the word *occupation* for *Israel*. "There were some times when there were problems with Jews coming here," he continued, "but for the occupation to really set their foot inside, they needed Goldstein's massacre."

This was factually incorrect. "Israelis prayed inside the Tomb of the Patriarchs and Matriarchs before the site was divided in 1994," I told him. "This is not only a mosque, after all. It's also a Jewish holy site."

"This place is a Muslim holy site," Hefzi said passionately. The hand resting on his desk turned into a clenched fist. "It has never been documented or told that Abraham was Jewish. Jews have no right to be here."

"Muslims don't go and pray in synagogues and churches," added Jamil. "That's why religious Jews never went inside the mosque. They only went as far as the seventh step."

Hefzi nodded in agreement, explaining, "The Jews believe that if they go past the seventh step, they will bring ruin upon the world." Only settlers pray inside, he insisted. "Real Jews only pray outside." Why religious Jews would pray there at all if it were not a Jewish holy site did not occur to them. They were somehow unaware that hundreds and sometimes thousands of religious Jews pray inside on holidays.

The Islamic officials likened this mistaken Jewish connection to the Tomb of the Patriarchs and Matriarchs to the fictitious connection to the holiest site in Judaism. "It's the same at Al-Aqsa," said Jamil. "They claim that Solomon's Temple was there, but it was never there."

The denial of the existence of the Jewish temples in Jerusalem is today a common refrain among Palestinians. It was not always so. The Grand Mufti's Supreme Muslim Council not only acknowledged that the First Temple once stood on the Haram al-Sharif, the Islamic name for the Temple Mount, but touted that history. *A Brief Guide to al-Haram al-Sharif*—a tourist guide published in 1950, one year before the Jordanians dismantled the Supreme Muslim Council— stated, "The site is one of the oldest in the world. . . Its identity with the site of Solomon's Temple is beyond dispute."[8]

The Hebron Waqf officials are not outliers. Their outlook reflects that of the current mufti of Jerusalem, Mohammad Hussein, who carries the torch of Grand Mufti Haj Amin al-Husseini.

Appointed by Palestinian president Mahmoud Abbas in 2006, Hussein is the chief cleric of Al-Aqsa Mosque, equivalent to the post of Israel's Chief Rabbi. In interviews with journalists, he has expressed his support for suicide bombings, "as long as it plays a role in the resistance."[9] In his sermons, he has invoked the Islamic hadith, or saying attributed to the Prophet Muhammad, which reads: "The Hour will not come until you fight the Jews. The Jews will hide behind stones or trees. Then the stones or trees will call: Oh Muslim, servant of Allah, there is a Jew behind me, come and kill him."[10]

Hussein's predecessor, Sheikh Ekrima Said Sabri, told journalist Jeffrey Goldberg that Jews were a manifestation of Satan. Sabri remains an imam at Al-Aqsa, where he often praises terrorist attacks on Israeli civilians. In a visit to the family of a gunman who was killed while carrying out an attack in 2022, he encouraged other young Palestinians to join the "family of martyrs," a status that is "sublime and divine, and to be aspired to."[11]

During my time in Hebron, I came to understand that the widespread rejection of Jewish history was not a fringe opinion, nor did it emanate from Palestinian leaders alone. This theory of Israelis as foreign occupiers with no history in this land was being endorsed by some of the most respected international institutions. One example was the UNESCO decision, in which the Tomb of the Patriarchs and Matriarchs was designated as a Palestinian heritage site with no mention of its Jewish history. Another is the Al-Khalil Old Town Museum on the Palestinian side of Hebron. Dedicated to telling the city's history, and funded by UNESCO and the government of Sweden, the museum makes no mention of the Jewish people. Though it begins its telling of Hebron's history in the year 4500 BCE and ends in the present day, the first mention of Israel is in the year 1967. Israel is only referred to in the context of "occupation forces" and "colonial settlements." The Hadassah House, which was built by the Jewish community in 1893, is described as an Ottoman building that was occupied by illegal settlers. A similar description is provided for the Romano House.

As I walked down a tree-lined path not far from the museum, I stopped to read a weathered plaque, written in English and Arabic, describing the city's history. "Hebron/al-Khalil is one of the oldest continuously inhabited cities in the world, with a history spanning over six millennia," it began. The sign went on to list all the empires and people that inhabited Hebron throughout time. All were mentioned except the Jewish people, until the timeline reached 1967. "In 1948, the Mandate was lifted and the city was administered by Jordan until it fell in the hands of the Israeli Occupation Army, in 1967, which promptly sought to build settlements in and around the city to Judaize it and alter its identity."

As I heard those claims repeated by Palestinians in Hebron, I kept returning to the same questions in my mind. Why would the

Palestinian people ever agree to share this land with a people who they believe have no legitimate connection to it? How could there ever be peace if this post-truth indoctrination continues?

In recent years, the erasure of Jewish history in the Holy Land has grown so pervasive that it is now common to claim that Jesus was Palestinian, as Democratic congresswoman Alexandria Ocasio-Cortez did during Christmas 2023.[12]

Jesus, the Jewish shepherd, was from Judaea. Palestine did not yet exist. It was only in the second century after Christ that Judaea was renamed by the Romans. Explaining this phenomenon of misplaced identity in *The Atlantic*, Peter Wehner wrote, "To acknowledge that both Jews and Palestinians are indigenous to the land between the Jordan River and the Mediterranean Sea is to shatter the widespread narrative that Israel is a 'settler-colonial state.'" As Pulitzer Prize–winning historian Barbara Tuchman once noted, Israel is in fact "the only nation in the world that is governing itself in the same territory, under the same name, and with the same religion and same language as it did 3,000 years ago."[13]

The goal of the Romans in renaming the land Palestina was much like the goal of Palestinian leaders today: to sever the bond between the Jewish people and the Land of Israel. And yet, the centrality of the land to the Jewish people was never broken. While efforts to erase the Jewish connection to this land have failed, they have succeeded in perpetuating a conflict that could have otherwise been resolved. The notion that only the Arab inhabitants of Palestine have a legitimate claim to this land fuels the popular opinion that Jews do not deserve a country of their own on any part of their ancestral homeland. That in turn has fueled the rejection by Palestinian leaders of every two-state solution since the beginning of this conflict.

CHAPTER 23

Heirs to the Mufti

THERE IS A TEACHING IN JUDAISM THAT HAS DEFINED THE STATE OF Israel since its founding. *Pikuach nefesh.* The saving of a soul. According to this principle of Jewish law, the preservation of human life overrules nearly every commandment of Judaism. This national reverence for life above all has been one of Israel's greatest strengths—and weaknesses. Knowing how far it is willing to go to save a life, Israel's enemies have learned to exploit it.

Two years after Israel released Tayseer Abu Sneineh and nearly 5,000 other Palestinian prisoners in exchange for 6 captured Israeli soldiers, another skewed prisoner swap led to the rise of Israel's greatest foe.

On May 20, 1985, Israel released more than 1,000 Palestinian prisoners in exchange for 3 Israeli soldiers who were captured in Lebanon and held by the Popular Front for the Liberation of Palestine. Many of the prisoners had either planned or perpetrated deadly attacks that killed dozens of Israeli civilians. The release of these prisoners would haunt the country for decades to come. Among them was Sheikh Ahmed Yassin, a leader of the Muslim Brotherhood in Gaza.[1]

Born in 1929 in al-Jura, an Arab city near Ashkelon that was depopulated during the war of 1948, Yassin's family fled to Gaza. Before he was sentenced to fifteen years in prison in 1984 for stockpiling weapons in the mosque he had built in a slum in southern Gaza, Yassin was an influential imam. He preached the Islamist perspective that, by virtue of its existence, Israel was an affront to Islam. Palestine, he proselytized, was "the property of Muslims until the day of judgment." No ruler had the right to relinquish any part of it. After his release from prison in 1985, the sheikh's eminence and influence grew.

By the time the First Intifada erupted in protest of twenty years of military occupation in the West Bank and Gaza, Yassin was the most prominent religious figure in Gaza, if not all of Palestine. When that uprising began in December 1987, Yassin established a new paramilitary wing of the Palestinian Muslim Brotherhood. Its name was the Islamic Resistance Movement, or Harakat al-Muqawama al-Islamiya—best known by its acronym, Hamas. Until that point, the major Palestinian resistance groups had been secular. Hamas was unabashedly Islamist. Given the highly religious, conservative nature of Palestinian society in Gaza, it quickly attracted a large and loyal following.[2]

The Butcher of Khan Yunis

Hamas's founding charter, unveiled in August 1988, declared the group's mission to establish "an Islamic state throughout Palestine." Hamas called for the destruction of Israel as essential to the liberation of Palestine and the establishment of a theocratic state based on Sharia, Islamic law. Israel's destruction, the charter explained, required relentless jihad. "Our struggle against the Jews is very great and very serious," it declared. The official slogan of the organization was: "Allah is its target, the Prophet is its model, the Quran its constitution: Jihad is its path and death for the sake of Allah is the loftiest of its wishes."[3]

Just as the Grand Mufti used *The Protocols of the Elders of Zion* in his own campaign of incitement, Hamas's founding covenant is laden with references to the fabricated text. According to Hamas, "The Zionist plan is limitless. After Palestine, the Zionists aspire to expand from the Nile to the Euphrates. When they will have digested the region they overtook, they will aspire to further expansion, and so on. Their plan is embodied in the 'Protocols of the Elders of Zion,' and their present conduct is the best proof of what we are saying." The charter goes on to blame the Jews for World War I, World War II, and every global revolution. "With their money, they took control of the world media, news agencies, the press, publishing houses, broadcasting stations, and others," the charter goes on.

It was around this time that Sheikh Yassin, Hamas's spiritual leader, became close with a young man who prayed at his mosque in Gaza City. Born in the Khan Yunis refugee camp in 1962, Yahya Sinwar was a 25-year-old student at the Islamic University of Gaza, which Sheikh Yassin had cofounded. Sinwar was a founding member of Hamas's student movement, and helped Yassin create Hamas's security service, al-Majd. Its primary concern was punishing Palestinians suspected of collaborating with Israel and violating codes of morality. Finding and eliminating collaborators quickly became Sinwar's specialty. He earned such a reputation for brutality that he was known as "the butcher of Khan Yunis." In 1988, Israeli forces arrested Sinwar for the abduction and killing of 2 Israeli soldiers, and the killing of 4 Palestinians he suspected of working with Israel. Sinwar was sentenced to four life terms. Sheikh Yassin was rearrested the following year, and sentenced to life in prison for ordering the murder of Palestinian collaborators.[4]

According to the transcript from Sinwar's interrogation, he enjoyed killing collaborators, sometimes using a machete. Coldly recounting the details, Sinwar described forcing one Hamas fighter to bury his own brother alive. Most of the time, however, he preferred to kill them with his own hands. In the case of a man named Ramsi, he recalled, "I put him inside a large grave and strangled him with a keffiyeh I had. After strangling him, I wrapped him in a white shroud and closed the grave. I was sure that Ramsi knew he deserved to die." Sinwar continued to hunt down collaborators inside prison. Over the next two decades in jail, he also devoted his time to studying his enemy. He became fluent in Hebrew, read Israeli newspapers and books on Israeli politics, and took classes in Jewish history.

When Sinwar walked into the clinic at his high-security prison near Beersheba complaining of neck pain in 2004, medical staff discovered he had a life-threatening brain tumor. Surgeons at Soroka Medical Center in Beersheba operated on Sinwar immediately, saving his life.[5] *Pikuach nefesh.* Sinwar would go on to mastermind the deadliest attack in Israel's history.

The Qassam Brigades

In 1992, members of Hamas established a new military wing: the Izz ad-Din al-Qassam Brigades, named after the Islamic preacher-turned-warrior whose followers sparked the Great Arab Revolt in 1936. From the outset, the Qassam Brigades were primarily focused on derailing the peace negotiations related to the Oslo Accords. At the height of the peace process, Hamas carried out scores of suicide bombings and other deadly attacks, killing hundreds of Israeli civilians. Their stated goal was to undermine the peace talks underway between Yasser Arafat and Israeli prime minister Yitzhak Rabin. Hamas viewed any agreement with the Jewish state, and any relinquishing of Muslim claims to the land, as an affront to Islam.

Hamas was not alone in its crusade against peace. Palestinian Islamic Jihad, another Gaza-based militant offshoot of the Muslim Brotherhood, also took part in this wave of suicide bombings, shootings, and other attacks on Israeli civilians. The First Intifada that began in 1987 was technically still underway. It ended with the signing of the first Oslo Accord in September 1993. Those accords were meant to pave the way for Palestinian self-rule in Gaza and parts of the West Bank in 1994. But in 1994, Hamas's campaign of terror intensified.[6]

Promising the Israelis and the Americans that he would rein in the terror, Arafat delivered an entirely different message to his own people. As part of the Oslo negotiations, Israel allowed the Palestinian leader to return from three decades of political exile. Having been deported by the Jordanians, then by rival guerilla forces in Lebanon, Arafat had been living in Tunisia for twelve years before he made his triumphant return to Gaza in July 1994. Upon his return, he not only smuggled in weapons, but wanted terrorists. Riding into Gaza in the back of a Mercedes, Arafat was sitting on top of Jihad Amarin, the man who had allegedly planned the 1974 Ma'alot Massacre, in which 22 children were killed. Arafat also created a new militant group, Tanzim, to rival Hamas and Islamic Jihad.[7]

Despite Hamas's terror campaign and Arafat's duplicity, Israeli prime minister Yitzhak Rabin continued peace negotiations. In September 1995, he and Arafat signed the second Oslo Accords. By then they had both been awarded the Nobel Peace Prize. Two months later, at a pro-peace rally in Tel Aviv on November 4, Rabin was assassinated by a Jewish extremist, Yigal Amir. His assassination delivered a heavy blow to the peace process, as did the campaign of terror that led many Israelis to lose faith in that process. In 1996, Benjamin Netanyahu won his first term as prime minister, having campaigned on his strong stance against terrorism and the Oslo Accords.[8]

Nevertheless, Israelis remained hopeful, and in 1999, a new peace-seeking leader was elected. Prime Minister Ehud Barak vowed to continue the peace talks that had been stalled by Rabin's assassination. Those talks culminated at the Camp David Summit in July 2000, overseen by President Bill Clinton. In exchange for peace, Israel agreed to a demilitarized Palestinian state encompassing 92 percent of the West Bank and 100 percent of the Gaza Strip. Israel would withdraw from sixty-three settlements, with the exclusion of large settlement blocs such as the Etzion Bloc and Kiryat Arba, which Israel would retain through land swaps to the Palestinians. In Jerusalem, Israel offered the Palestinians full control of the Temple Mount as well as the city's Muslim and Christian quarters, and all Islamic and Christian holy sites. Israel would retain control over the Western Wall and the Jewish neighborhoods in East Jerusalem. As for the controversial Palestinian demand for the right of return, Barak agreed to absorb 100,000 Palestinian refugees within Israel. The rest would settle in the newly created Palestinian state and other Arab countries. Israel offered to pay for their resettlement and absorption, and to establish a $30 billion international fund that would manage compensation for Palestinian property. Arafat rejected the offer, and presented no alternative to it.[9]

As each side blamed the other, Israelis and Palestinians grew increasingly frustrated. Those tensions erupted on September 28, 2000, when right-wing opposition leader Ariel Sharon visited the Temple Mount surrounded by Israeli police. He went during normal tourist hours and did not pray, as non-Muslims are forbidden from praying on the Temple Mount. Sharon, Ehud Barak's rival, was drawing attention to this lack of religious freedom for Jews at their holiest site. His ascent to the Temple Mount enraged Palestinians, who interpreted the move as a sign of Israel's intent to take over Al-Aqsa. A cleric used the mosque's loudspeaker to call on Muslims to defend it. Hundreds of young Palestinians rushed the police lines in Sharon's direction. "Allahu Akbar!" (God is great), they screamed. "With our soul and blood we will redeem you, Al-Aqsa!"[10]

Echoing the rumors that sparked the rampage of 1929, the Palestinian riots that began on September 28, 2000, were the first embers of the Second Intifada, also known as the Al-Aqsa Intifada. After Friday prayers at Al-Aqsa the next day, chaos descended upon Jerusalem. Over the following days, riots ricocheted through the West Bank, Gaza, and Arab cities inside Israel. In its first month, the Second Intifada claimed the lives of 141 Palestinians and 12 Israelis. For the next five years, the uprising turned everyday life in Israel into a war zone. Suicide bombings and terror attacks carried out by Hamas and other Islamist groups became a near-daily routine. Suddenly, no place was safe. In Jerusalem, Tel Aviv, and other cities in Israel, cafés, restaurants, night clubs, buses, and shopping malls became regular targets of suicide bombers. Parents feared that when their children left home in the morning, they might not return home.

By the time the Second Intifada ended in 2005, more than 3,000 Palestinians and 1,000 Israelis had lost their lives to that violence, and Israel's crushing response to it. The collapse of the Israeli peace camp and the country's drift rightward over the next two decades was a byproduct of those five bloody years that followed Israel's most significant offer of Palestinian statehood.

What ended the uprising was the Sharm el-Sheikh Summit of 2005. Arafat, who had encouraged Palestinian security forces to participate in the intifada, had died of natural causes in 2004. He was succeeded by his deputy, a pragmatist named Mahmoud Abbas. At the summit in the Egyptian resort city, Abbas vowed to end Palestinian violence against Israelis. Ariel Sharon, the right-wing former general who had since replaced Ehud Barak as prime minister, agreed to cease all military action against Palestinians. Both leaders affirmed their commitment to the Roadmap for Peace established by the Middle East Quartet, an alliance between the UN, the EU, Russia, and the US to reach a peaceful resolution of the conflict. Those efforts culminated in 2008 with another proposal for a Palestinian state alongside Israel. Sharon, who had suffered a stroke, had been replaced by a new prime minister, Ehud Olmert, who offered Abbas a return to Israel's pre-1967 borders and a Palestinian capital in East Jerusalem. Abbas never responded to the offer. It would be Israel's last.[11]

At the time of Israel's proposal of a Palestinian state in 2000, there were approximately 177,000 Israeli settlers living in the occupied territories. Today there are half a million.[12]

The Withdrawal

Before the Second Intifada ended, the man who touched it off made another decision that would transform the region. In 2003, Prime Minister Ariel Sharon proposed a unilateral disengagement from the Gaza Strip. Approved by the Knesset in 2004 and carried out between August and September 2005, Israel withdrew all its forces, dismantled every settlement, and removed more than 8,000 Israeli citizens from their homes in the Gaza Strip, handing control of the territory to the Palestinian Authority.

The decision tore Israeli society in two. Many on the center and left supported the withdrawal from Gaza, believing it was an important step toward peace and a two-state solution. They also wanted to prevent more young Israeli soldiers from being killed on duty in Gaza, where they were stationed to protect the settlers. On the right, Israelis were appalled, especially since Sharon was a right-wing leader. Sixty percent of his Likud party had opposed the plan. In the months before their evacuation, thousands flocked to the Gaza settlements to stand in solidarity with those who faced eviction. Two Israelis in Gaza burned themselves alive in protest. When the time came to carry out the eviction orders, soldiers were forced to physically remove hundreds of Israelis in an emotionally painful last stand.[13]

Datya Itzhaki, the former spokeswoman for Gush Katif, a bloc of seventeen settlements in southern Gaza, was one of the last settlers to leave. On the morning of her eviction, she and her husband climbed onto their roof with their 3 young children. Their house on the coast was surrounded by 500 soldiers who arrived by boat, helicopter, and armored cars. "You can still refuse your orders!" Itzhaki cried out to them by megaphone. "This will be on your conscience! The price of leaving Gaza is going to be heavy! This is going to become Hamastan!" she shouted.

For Itzhaki, leaving Gaza was not difficult for religious reasons. Like nearly half of the settlers in Gaza, she was secular. "We knew that the moment we left, Hamas was going to take over," she told me from Neve Yam, the kibbutz in northern Israel where she now lives. "I thought to myself, if leaving will save one Israeli life, I would have done it easily. But we saw what Hamas did during the Intifada. We saw their barbarity against their own people. We knew that the people of Israel were going to pay the price in blood." Itzhaki recalled how a Palestinian friend from Rafah had been killed by Hamas. He was a driving instructor. "Everyone from Gush Katif went to him," she said. "They put a burning tire over his head."[14]

Left behind in Gaza were the vestiges of one of Israel's greatest assets: its highly advanced agricultural industry. The settlements of Gush Katif housed thousands of greenhouses owned by 200 farmers. Together they produced 15 percent of Israel's agricultural exports and 70 percent of its organic produce. In August 2005, a group of pro-Israel Jewish American philanthropists purchased more than 3,000 of those greenhouses for $14 million and donated them to the Palestinian Authority.[15]

The last settlement was evacuated on September 12. On September 13, Palestinians looted hundreds of greenhouses, walking away with expensive water pumps, irrigation hoses, and plastic sheeting. The Palestinian Finance Ministry estimated that 30 percent of the greenhouses had been damaged. President Abbas was horrified. In discussions with Israeli officials before the pullout, those greenhouses were the centerpiece of plans to develop Gaza's fledgling economy. The PA had high hopes for the greenhouses to provide much needed jobs and income to Gaza's impoverished residents. In a televised speech that day, Abbas said immediate steps would be taken to impose order. "We have one law for everyone and no one is above the law," he said. "We are not going to tolerate chaos after today." As he spoke, thousands of masked Hamas gunmen marched through the streets of Gaza wielding guns and grenade launchers.

As one man from Khan Yunis rummaged through the remnants of Kibbutz Neve Dekalim, he told a reporter for the *New York Times*, "The lesson I've learned, and I will pass it on to my sons, is that no matter how long it takes, the occupiers will leave because of resistance." Behind him stood a smoldering synagogue, built in the shape of a Star of David. Smoke billowed through the edges of the star. Standing atop its embers was the green flag of Hamas. Below the Hamas flag was the black flag of Palestinian Islamic Jihad, and below that, a small Palestinian flag that was soon removed. On the wall of another synagogue someone had scrawled, "Yes for freedom! No for Jews!—Hamas."

Hamas and Islamic Jihad fired rockets into southern Israel that very day. The occupation, they said, had not ended. After all, Israel maintained control of Gaza's land borders, its sea crossings, and its airspace. Before its withdrawal, Israeli security officials had tried to convince the Palestinian Authority to disarm the various militant groups jockeying for power in Gaza. The PA refused. Dan Halutz, the IDF chief of staff, said Israel expected the PA to maintain order. Speaking at a military ceremony marking the end of Israel's military presence in Gaza, Halutz said, "This is their true test. . . . They will not be able to shirk their responsibility."[16]

The first few days after Israel's withdrawal did not bode well for Gaza's future. It was about to get much worse.

The Image of Victory

Hamas claimed victory, declaring Israel's withdrawal from Gaza as vindication for its ruthless approach. When Palestinian elections were held on January 25, 2006, Hamas won by a landslide, securing 76 out of the 132 seats in the legislative council of the Palestinian National Authority. Hamas had long been designated a terrorist organization by the United States, the European Union, Canada, the UK, and many other countries. The group had no experience governing, but residents of Gaza were fed up with the corruption of the Palestinian Authority. Virtually overnight, Western governments cut off direct aid to the Hamas-led government, crippling the enclave's already battered economy. Israel refused to negotiate with Hamas so long as it failed to meet certain conditions, including recognizing Israel's right to exist and renouncing violence. Hamas would not meet those conditions. Between September 2005 and May 2007, close to 3,000 rockets were fired from Gaza.[17]

After a year of bitter infighting, in June 2007, Hamas fighters violently seized control of Gaza from the Palestinian Authority. Over the course of six days, Hamas imprisoned, executed, or expelled hundreds of Fatah officials, ushering in an era of deep division in Palestinian politics that continues to this day. No Palestinian national election has been held since. The West Bank remains ruled by the secular Fatah and its 88-year-old leader, Mahmoud Abbas, while Gaza is ruled by the Islamists of Hamas.[18]

In the aftermath of Hamas's bloody takeover of Gaza, both Israel and Egypt placed a blockade on the narrow strip of land that is sandwiched between them. The blockade of Gaza remains in place today. The densely populated strip, spanning 140 square miles and housing 2.2 million people, has no airport. Of the three land crossings into Gaza, two are controlled by Israel and one by Egypt. Both countries heavily restrict the entry of construction materials and computer equipment—"dual use" items that could be used for militant purposes—permitting them only as part of international donor projects. Israel also limits exports from Gaza, stifling the strip's economic development.[19]

Hamas, however, found ways to work around these blockades, smuggling in enough concrete and other material to build what it has described as a 500-kilometer (310-mile) network of underground tunnels. What it did not do was build bomb shelters to protect Gazans from the Israeli air strikes that often met Hamas's rocket attacks, or create a working economy for its residents. Before the October 7 massacres, unemployment in Gaza was 45 percent.

In the seventeen years since it seized power, Hamas has initiated four wars and dozens of skirmishes with Israel. While those battles have wrought devastation upon Gaza, Hamas has emerged from each one more powerful and more popular, both within Gaza and the West Bank. Most Palestinians blame Israel, not Hamas, for the suffocating blockade, the thousands killed, and the housing and infrastructure turned to rubble over the course of those wars. Hamas has seen few major demonstrations against its rule. Those who have dared to protest have been violently suppressed, jailed, or tortured. Meanwhile, Palestinians accused of working with Israel have been executed by firing squad. Homosexuality in Gaza is outlawed, as is abortion.[20]

Some Israeli and American officials hoped that Hamas's transition from a terrorist group to a government with responsibility for a civilian population would serve as a moderating force. Yet Hamas has shown little interest in reform.

When the Obama Administration revived the stalled peace process in 2009, Hamas worked to end it. On June 4, 2009, President Obama delivered a historic speech in Cairo, calling for a two-state solution and a "new beginning" for relations between the US and the Muslim world. Ten days later in his own speech at Bar Ilan University, Prime Minister Netanyahu endorsed a "demilitarized Palestinian state." In November of that year, Netanyahu initiated a ten-month construction freeze on settlements in the West Bank, in what he described as "a painful step that will encourage the peace process." When direct talks between Netanyahu, Abbas, and Secretary of State Hillary Clinton began in September 2010, Hamas led a coalition of thirteen Palestinian militant groups to disrupt them. "We will not let these negotiations go on," said Hamas spokesman Abu Obaida. Peace talks with Israel, he said, were "a stab in the back of the Palestinian people." After waging shooting attacks that killed 4 Israelis near Hebron, Hamas vowed to step up its attacks. Rockets and mortar shells rained down on southern Israel from Gaza for months. After Israel's settlement freeze ended, direct negotiations fell apart. Hamas continued its missile attacks, which were no longer indiscriminate. On April 7, 2011, an anti-tank missile fired at a clearly marked school bus driving near the Gaza border killed a 16-year-old boy.[21]

Hamas has tried to soften its image in recent years, issuing a revised charter in 2017. The new charter, however, differs little from the original. The most obvious distinction is that the word "Jew" has been replaced with the word "Zionist." The 2017 charter reiterates the group's mission of jihad for the liberation of all historic Palestine. Perhaps the most shocking element of the new charter is this clause, which has nothing to do with Israel: "Hamas believes in, and adheres to, managing its Palestinian relations on the basis of pluralism, democracy, national partnership, acceptance of the other and the adoption of dialogue." Hamas has ruled Gaza with an iron fist since 2007, forbidding elections, and jailing and torturing dissidents.[22]

CHAPTER 24

A Day at the Museum

THE HADASSAH HOUSE IN HEBRON TODAY LOOKS MUCH LIKE IT did a century ago. In the center of the Old City, just outside what was once the Jewish ghetto, stands the majestic three-story building, separated from the road by a stone footbridge. The face of the sand-colored structure, made of Jerusalem stone, is a latticework of Stars of David, regal columns, and grand archways. A Hebrew inscription above the main entrance reads Chesed L'Avraham, Kindness of Abraham. Built by Hebron's Sephardic community in 1893, it served as a charitable hospital, with donations from Jews of North Africa, India, and Iraq. Two decades later it became the Hadassah clinic.

Today there is no clinic. In its place are the apartments of a dozen Jewish families.

The Hadassah House sits at the end of Martyrs Street. Its Palestinian residents are forbidden from driving there, and only those with permission can walk on this street. The military order that closed the road to Palestinians was issued during the Second Intifada.[1] Near a playground less than a minute's walk from the Hadassah House is a memorial to one of the youngest victims of that uprising. Atop a bed of flowers, on a wall of ancient stone, is a ceramic rendering of a flame rising from a bassinet. It is in memory of Shalhevet Pass, a 10-month-old who was shot dead in her stroller in 2001 by a Palestinian sniper from a militant wing of Fatah.[2]

Walking through the Israeli side of Hebron toward the Hadassah House, it felt as if the memory of 1929 hovered over every corner. Atop one of the empty buildings was a large banner that read: THESE BUILDINGS WERE CONSTRUCTED ON LAND PURCHASED BY THE

HEBRON JEWISH COMMUNITY IN 1807. THIS LAND WAS STOLEN BY
ARABS FOLLOWING THE MURDER OF 67 HEBRON JEWS IN 1929. WE
DEMAND JUSTICE! RETURN OUR PROPERTY TO US! The structure the
sign hung from was, until 1994, the busy Arab market. This is where
that stalled building project is supposed to rise.

Down the footbridge and a stone stairway that descends to a
serene courtyard of palm trees is the museum on the bottom floor
of the Hadassah House. The cavernous, single-floor museum
depicts the arc of Jewish history from biblical times to the present
day. The walls of its cavelike rooms are painted with biblical land-
scapes and scenes of ancient Hebron by Shmuel Mushnik, a painter
whose home gallery is adjacent to the museum. Born in Moscow
in 1955, Mushnik moved to Israel with his family in 1970 as part
of a wave of Soviet Jews fleeing repression under the Communist
regime. After moving into the former home of the Hadassah clinic's
murdered pharmacist, Ben-Zion Gershon, Mushnik began to paint
the walls of the bottom floor, slowly transforming it into the tribute
it is today.

I first toured the museum in November 2019. My guide was
the curator, Tzipi Schlissel, a local author who lives in Hebron. A
58-year-old mother of 11, Tzipi is a seventh-generation Israeli whose
great-grandfather, Abraham Isaac Kook, served as the first Chief
Rabbi of British Mandate Palestine. As the founder of the world's
most influential Religious Zionist yeshiva, Mercaz Harav, where
Rabbi Levinger and many other settler leaders studied, Kook is considered the spiritual father of Religious Zionism.

Tzipi speaks with a permanent smile, no matter how dark the
subject she is discussing. Dressed in a purple sweater, purple-framed
glasses, a long black skirt, brown work boots, and a lilac scarf to
cover her hair, she led me through the maze of dimly lit rooms. The
first was a hallway devoted to the late Rabbi Levinger, who died in
2015. "It is thanks to him that we are here," she said, looking at a photograph of Levinger and his wife, Miriam, who died in 2020.

The next room told the story of ancient Hebron. A timeline descending from the ceiling began with Abraham's arrival in Hebron nearly 4,000 years ago, after God promised him the Land of Israel for his descendants. It continued through King Herod's construction of the Tomb of the Patriarchs and Matriarchs, and the destruction of the Jewish community during the Bar Kokhba revolt against the Romans. An entire wall was devoted to the biblical tale that settlers cling to, for it traces the Jewish inheritance of the Land of Israel to the first Jewish purchase of land in ancient Israel. According to the story in Genesis, when Abraham's wife, Sarah, died in Hebron, Abraham insisted on paying full price for the cave he wished to bury her in. The owner of the land, Ephron the Hittite, tried to give Abraham the cave as a gift. Abraham, the sages say, predicted that one day the Jewish peoples' claims to the land would be challenged. He paid far more than the land was worth to prevent anyone from contesting its ownership in the future.

Telling the Whole Story

The timeline of Hebron's history unfolded into the next room of the Hadassah House, through the return of the Jewish community to Hebron under Byzantine rule, the Islamic conquest of the city, its fall to the Mamluks and the Crusaders, and the arrival of Jewish exiles from Spain. Through all their years of exile, Hebron was one of the four holy cities where a small community of Jews always remained, tethered to the burial place of Abraham. And yet, under both Christian and Muslim rule, freedom of worship for Jews was heavily restricted. Tzipi showed me a letter written by Rabbi Yaakov Yosef Slonim in 1922 to her great-grandfather, Rabbi Kook. In the letter, Slonim asked Kook to appeal to British authorities for the protection of Jews who wished to pray outside the Tomb of the Patriarchs and Matriarchs. "It is truly indescribable the amount of sorrow and suffering and the magnitude of the insult," wrote Slonim. "They will not let any Jew or Jewess pour out what is in their soul without being terribly sorry . . . by throwing stones and dirt and pouring water and imitating, mocking shouts, and hurling difficult, immodest insults at women."[3]

This was before the arrival of the Slabodka Yeshiva and its students from Europe and the US. Tzipi recalled the stories of her great uncle, who had attended the yeshiva. "The students would come every month to pray there, and they would pay an Arab to protect them, to make sure rocks weren't thrown at them," Tzipi said, smiling. "Even though this place became a symbol to humiliate Jews, the Jewish people never stopped coming."

Tzipi's own life story is intricately intertwined with Hebron's. While most settlers there have no direct connection to the massacre, no immediate family members who lived there prior to the exile of 1929, the story of the Hebron massacre is the story of her life. Tzipi is named after her grandmother. Tzipora was a 13-year-old girl living with her parents in Jerusalem when she went for a long visit at her sister Leah's house in Hebron in the summer of 1929. Leah was married to Yaakov Shapira, a student at the Hebron Yeshiva. Leah and Yaakov lived next door to Rabbi Slonim.

When the riots broke out on Friday, August 23, Yaakov was in Jerusalem and could not get back to Hebron. Leah had just given birth six weeks earlier to their first child. On Saturday morning, as the rioters went from house to house in Hebron, Tzipora, Leah, and her baby took shelter in the home of Rabbi Slonim. Hearing the anguished cries of their neighbors, Tzipora was sure they would be slaughtered. But just as the mob arrived, their elderly landlord returned from the vineyards on his white horse. As Tzipi told me this story, I immediately recognized it from the testimonies I had read from survivors. "Abu Shaker?" I asked her. "Yes," she replied, smiling. "He saved all the people that were in the rabbi's house. Because of this old Arab man, my family survived, and I am here today."

Tzipi's great-grandfather, Rabbi Kook, had been pivotal in helping Slabodka Yeshiva relocate from Lithuania to Hebron. In 1924, he traveled to the United States with the yeshiva's leader, Rabbi Moshe Mordechai Epstein, to raise funds for the yeshiva and others in Europe and Palestine.[4] Six months after the massacre, Rabbi Kook led a memorial service in Jerusalem, where he delivered a message that still echoes in Hebron today: "Despite the terrible tragedy that took place in Hebron," he declared, "we will not abandon our holy places and sacred aspirations." Referring to the efforts by the city's exiled Jews to return to their homes, and the refusal by British and Zionist officials to allow them to, he said, "He who refuses to reestablish Hebron, undermines the deepest roots of our nation. . . . Jewish Hebron will be rebuilt, for honor and glory!"[5]

Tzipi and I stood in the darkest room of the museum, dedicated to the memory of the massacre. A dimly lit wall of faces stood beside a pile of stones. Among the black-and-white photographs of the massacre's 67 victims was one of David Shainberg, smiling beside his closest friend in Hebron, Bill Berman.

The broken stones, illuminated from below by a red light, were fragments of the desecrated graves from the ancient Jewish cemetery. Destroyed during Jordanian rule, they were salvaged by Jewish volunteers after Israel took control of Hebron. David's original gravestone, among those of other victims', was discovered as part of a fence that an Arab family had built around their home. The cemetery has since been renovated using new stones, leaving the originals on display in the museum.

A brief film narrated the story of the massacre, including the heroes of that day. "Among the thousands of rioters were also Arabs who protected their Jewish neighbors from the attackers," said the narrator, dressed to portray a survivor. Quoting the man who rescued his family, he said, "You are under my roof, and you are here under my protection. I assure you that if the rioters come here to harm you, I will protect you."

The space that was given to the Muslim heroes of Hebron took me by surprise. Given the extreme opinions of many of Hebron's settlers, I was not expecting this kind of recognition. Having heard the widespread denials of both Jewish history and the massacre on the other side of Hebron, it struck me that here, in the museum established by people who are among the most nationalist of all Israelis, there is an ability to recognize not only the Islamic history in Hebron, but the humanity on the other side, and the heroic role many Arabs played in 1929. The settlers understood that they could honor the suffering of their own people while also appreciating the courage and humanity of the good people who refused to be engulfed by hatred. The truth, they understood, did not need to be hidden. During my time on the Palestinian side of Hebron, I often tried to imagine how different life would be for Palestinians and Israelis if that kind of recognition could exist in Palestinian society. Their suffering, and their history, could be honored without erasing the history of the Jewish people in this land. Any such effort would sadly be seen as traitorous. But what if? Is it too naïve to wish?

The dark room dedicated to the destruction of Jewish Hebron led directly into a bright room devoted to its rebirth. On one wall were photos of what the Jewish Quarter looked like shortly after the Jordanian occupation ended. "What we found when we came to Hebron after the Six-Day War was very hard to see," said Tzipi, born in 1965, as if she herself had been there. Several photographs showed the ruins of the Avraham Avinu Synagogue, which had become an animal pen. One, from around 1968, showed Jews and Arabs standing around a giant pit piled with goats and sheep. It was Arabs in Hebron who helped Jews find the ruins of the synagogue and other Jewish properties. For nearly a decade, Jewish activists worked to rehabilitate Avraham Avinu, battling against the Israeli government. Wary of provoking Palestinian violence, and waiting for a treaty that would see it return the land in exchange for peace, the government sought to maintain the status quo. Leading the clandestine effort to rebuild it was Ben Zion Tavger, a Soviet physicist who emigrated to Israel in 1972. He worked as a professor at Tel Aviv University before moving to Kiryat Arba and dedicating his life to rehabilitating historic Jewish sites in Hebron. It was Tavger who collected the broken gravestones at the ancient Jewish cemetery and initiated efforts to restore it. When he began his work on the synagogue, the government and the military tried to stop him. Arrested on many occasions, he was put on trial and issued military orders limiting his movement in Hebron. It wasn't until the attack on the Hadassah House in 1980 that Tavger received government permission to complete his renovation. When the synagogue reopened in 1981, the dedication ceremony featured an eleventh-century Torah scroll rescued from the riots of 1929. It was dedicated by Yosef Ezra.

Tzipi pointed out the various landmarks of Jewish Hebron that had been renewed over the last four decades. "This decision came after the murder of Shalhevet Pass," she said, "and this one after the murder of Aharon Gross." Among the leading settlers in Hebron, Tzipi is a relatively new arrival. It was another tragedy that brought her, in yet another iteration of this morbid cycle of renewal. While Tzipi's grandmother was saved in Hebron by a courageous Muslim who rejected incitement to hatred in 1929, her own father was murdered in Hebron by a Muslim who believed that incitement seventy years later.

Rabbi Shlomo Raanan worked at the research institute of Mercaz Harav,* the Jerusalem yeshiva his grandfather founded. In 1992, he and his wife, Chaya, moved from Jerusalem to Tel Rumeida, Hebron's most ancient neighborhood, dating back to at least the Chalcolithic period. Like the six other Jewish families residing in Tel Rumeida, they lived in a trailer, waiting for more permanent housing.

On the night of August 20, 1998, the 63-year-old rabbi attended a wedding at the Tomb of the Patriarchs and Matriarchs, ate dinner with his wife, and went to bed.

---

* I would discover while writing this book that my own grandfather, Yisroel Schwartz, who lived in Brooklyn and died long before I was born, had worked as a fundraiser for the yeshiva. I also discovered that as a boy he had attended Torah Vodaath, the Brooklyn yeshiva established by Rabbi Wolf Gold.

Chaya was still in the dining room when she heard her husband's screams. As she ran to their bedroom, Shlomo stumbled out, covered in blood. The Palestinian man who had scaled a 10-foot wall, climbed through their bedroom window, and stabbed her husband in the neck, was standing before her. Holding a blood-soaked butcher's knife in one hand, he used his other hand to drag Shlomo away. Chaya tried to pull her husband out of his grip, but the man continued to stab Shlomo, then hurled a Molotov cocktail across the room, setting the house on fire. As Chaya cradled her dying husband in her arms, the intruder escaped through the bedroom window and took cover on the Palestinian side of town, eluding capture.

Benjamin Netanyahu was serving his first term as prime minister. One year earlier, he had signed the Hebron Protocol that handed 80 percent of Hebron's territory to the Palestinian Authority. Much as they had protested the 1993 Oslo Accords, which created the Palestinian Authority, settlers had vehemently opposed the Hebron Protocol of 1997. Fury at the government erupted in Hebron in the wake of the rabbi's murder. Settlers heckled government ministers who came to pay their respects, accusing authorities of doing too little to protect the enclave of 450 settlers from the 130,000 Palestinians living around them. There were no checkpoints or soldiers outside their homes then. When Prime Minister Netanyahu and his wife, Sara, visited the grieving Raanan family, Netanyahu promised them that the trailers in Tel Rumeida would be replaced with permanent structures. Announcing the plan on Israeli television, Netanyahu explained that its purpose was "one, to protect the settlement there, and two, to emphasize the permanence of a Jewish and Israeli settlement in Hebron."[6]

Two months later, Salem Rajab Sarsour, a 29-year-old father of 5 from Hebron, confessed to murdering Rabbi Raanan. He was arrested after hurling two grenades into a crowd at the central bus station in Beersheba, wounding 67 people, most of them civilians. The Izz ad-Din al-Qassam Brigades, Hamas's armed wing, took responsibility for the attack, calling it a "heroic operation" by "one of our heroic fighters."

Sarsour, a longtime member of Hamas, was known by his neighbors as "Sheikh Salem" for his religious fervor. He wore a white prayer cap, and his wife covered her face with a black veil. Speaking to a reporter after her husband's arrest, she sat beneath a poster of Sheik Ahmed Yassin, Hamas's spiritual leader. Her husband, she said, was "a fighter for the sake of God."[7]

Sarsour's attack at the crowded bus station was the tenth terror attack in three months. It seemed designed by Hamas to derail the peace talks that were underway in Maryland, with negotiations between Netanyahu and Palestinian president Yasser Arafat, led by then US president Bill Clinton. Hamas had declared its opposition to those talks and to any peace with Israel.

Salem Rajab Sarsour was sentenced to three life terms in prison. In 2011, he was released as part of yet another prisoner agreement in which Israel set free more than 1,000 security prisoners in exchange for 1 Israeli soldier. Held by Hamas in Gaza since 2006, Gilad Shalit had been kidnapped from his base near the Gaza border. Among the 1,000 released prisoners were 300 who were serving life sentences for planning or executing deadly attacks. Ahmed Jabari, a leader of Hamas's military wing who oversaw Shalit's kidnapping, boasted that the freed detainees had collectively killed 569 Israelis. Israel assassinated Jabari in a drone strike the following year.

Dozens of the men who were freed soon resumed terrorist activities, assuming leadership positions within Hamas, and operating terror cells in Gaza and the West Bank.[8] One of those men was Yahya Sinwar, whose brother had organized Shalit's abduction. Upon his release, Sinwar called for the capture of more Israelis to secure the release of every imprisoned Hamas member. In 2017, he became the leader of Hamas in Gaza. His election raised fears of escalation, as Sinwar was known for opposing any reconciliation with Israel. After another round of cross-border fighting in 2021, Sinwar made clear that he was preparing for a wider war. "This was just a rehearsal, nothing but a tiny drill," he declared in a victory speech carried live on Al-Jazeera. After thanking the Qatari network for being "the best pulpit to give the accurate voice to our position," Sinwar said, "We must be ready to defend Al-Aqsa. Our whole nation needs to be ready to march in a raging flood in order to uproot this occupation from our land."[9]

Little attention was paid to that speech at the time. In retrospect, it was a chilling warning.

Never Enough

In the twenty-five years since Netanyahu's promise to her grieving family during his first term as prime minister, Tzipi said little had changed. When she told me this in November 2019, Netanyahu was serving his fifth term as prime minister. As of this writing, he is in his sixth. And though he leads the most far-right, nationalist government in Israel's history, many settlers believe he and his government are constrained by Israel's Supreme Court.

In 2011, Israel's Supreme Court ruled that the Jews of Hebron have no right to land owned by Jews prior to 1948.[10] This ruling, and others like it, have led Netanyahu and his right-wing base to pillory the Supreme Court as a left-wing bastion. Annexing the West Bank, the policy change most settlers want, would allow the government to do what it wishes in Hebron and other parts of the West Bank. Israel's Supreme Court is one of the greatest obstacles standing in the way of annexation.

Of the seventeen housing units that were approved for construction after the murder of Tzipi's father just seven have been built. One of those buildings is home to her mother, Chaya, and the Ohr Shlomo Torah Study Center, which Chaya founded in her husband's memory. Tzipi's husband, Yisrael, runs the center. Until 2002, he commuted to work from their home in Jerusalem. Then, after several incidents in which his car was stoned and shot at by Palestinians on his drive to Hebron, they decided it would be safer to live there.

Three months after my tour of the museum, I came to see where Tzipi lives. I was surprised to discover that she lived in a trailer, just like the one in which her father was killed. To this day, she does not understand why Netanyahu has failed to fulfill his vow. It is a combination of the legal, political, military, and diplomatic challenges that arise from Hebron being located outside the borders of Israel.

"Everyone knows this land belonged to the Jewish community," said Tzipi, showing me a photocopy of the nineteenth-century deed to the land upon which the trailers stand. "All around us, the hills are covered with houses for Arab residents," she said. "When I look out my window at the Arab side of Hebron, I see construction projects, a massive shopping mall, high-rise apartment buildings. Only we, the Jews, have to fight for every housing unit. Even though we have clear ownership papers proven in court, we are forbidden from entering our property."

"A Bubble of Paradise"

It was a cold, rainy day in February of 2020, a week after heavy clashes between Palestinians and Israeli soldiers in Hebron. Just a few days earlier, a soldier was filmed with his face on fire after being hit with a Molotov cocktail by Palestinian protesters. Several Palestinians were killed in those clashes. They took place just outside the checkpoint down the street from Tzipi's house.

Tzipi's trailer was freezing, but it was filled with the warm aroma of vegetable soup on the stove. The kitchen was filled with pans of food left over from Shabbat. I was seven months pregnant, and Tzipi poured me a hot bowl of soup. Over the stove hung the artwork of her children and grandchildren. She had just baked cookies out of wheat one of her young sons had grown in the yard. I asked her and her husband what it was like to raise children and grandchildren in this atmosphere, and how it felt to live surrounded by soldiers, checkpoints, and people who would prefer you lived elsewhere. "I feel like we're in a bubble of paradise," said Tzipi. "It's very special to live in

Hebron. We have a beautiful community that has been through a lot together. We are like family."

Her husband, Yisrael, noted that his wife was nearly killed in 2015 when a Palestinian tried to stab her in the back as she walked down their street. Fortunately, he said, an armed Jewish passerby shot the man before he could reach Tzipi.

"If they didn't do these things, we wouldn't need all these soldiers here," said Yisrael. "The checkpoints aren't something we asked for." There are more effective ways the state could protect Jews in Hebron, he said. The measure favored by Yisrael and other settlers is the Israeli annexation of the West Bank, and the eviction of all Palestinians who support terrorism.

Aside from his car being shot at on the road, Yisrael said that multiple Molotov cocktails had been launched at him over the years. "All our kids have been attacked by Arabs in the street here," he said. Those attacks ranged from punches to stone-throwing, to the girls being cursed or spat at. "Everyone has rocks thrown at them. That's the way we live," he laughed. "You get used to it. We have soldiers protecting us and we trust in God that He's watching over us."

I asked them what they would like the army to do differently. "I think they have to get rid of all the terrorists and all the people who support the terrorists," said Yisrael. "The mayor of Hebron is a terrorist. So obviously there is widespread support for terrorism. Once we get rid of terrorism we won't need protection." I pointed out that with this math, he was essentially suggesting that Israel "get rid of" the majority of Palestinians in Hebron.

I wondered if Tzipi and Yisrael truly believed that Hebron's Jewish and Muslim residents could live together peacefully. Could they not see the repercussions of living among people whose rights were being suppressed for them to feel safe? Did the checkpoints, the restrictions on Palestinian movement, and the random searches of Palestinian homes actually make them safer? When I touched on these subjects with the Schlissels, they both kept coming back to the same point.

"We don't want to be surrounded by guns and checkpoints any more than they do," said Yisrael. "All they need to do is stop trying to kill us. All we want is to live here in peace," said Tzipi. "Is it so much to ask?"

"Of course not all Arabs in Hebron are terrorists," clarified Tzipi. "I think the moment when they stop inciting to kill and stop making the killers heroes, everything can change. But they cannot continue to say how good it is to kill Jewish people and then complain about having checkpoints. They should take responsibility for what they are doing and choose a different path."

Before I left that day, I asked Tzipi what living in Hebron meant for her on a spiritual level. "On a regular day," she said, "it's like living anywhere else in the world. You have your family, you have the laundry." But every time she goes to the Tomb of the Patriarchs and Matriarchs, she said, "I can't help but think what a privilege it is to live here, in the place where Abraham, Isaac, and Jacob were. It's something amazing. It's like you're not just a person but part of a nation, and that gives you a lot of meaning. I feel like a messenger of the nation of Israel."

CHAPTER 25

A Tale of Two Hebrons

Down an ancient stone alleyway in Jerusalem's Old City, just past the fourth-century Church of the Holy Sepulchre, stands the modest jewelry shop of Ibrahim Bader, its windows bursting with turquoise and coral stones. It was February 2020, and Christmas lights were still strung across the Christian Quarter, which, as Ibrahim explained, is mostly populated by Muslims.

I had come to find something elusive I had been searching months for with no success: descendants of the courageous Arab families who risked their lives to save their Jewish neighbors in 1929. I wanted to understand what kind of lives their descendants were living and why they were so hard to find.

Born in Hebron in 1965, Ibrahim was just 2 years old when Israeli troops arrived there. He was raised on his father's stories, and through those memories, he too recalls that day in 1967, when his father showed the letter of gratitude from Hebron's elders to the soldiers. Ibrahim still holds those wilted papers in a red leather satchel. It is with him wherever he goes. His father, Adnan, did the same. "He kept them in his car, and any time Israeli soldiers or border police gave him trouble, he would pull out these papers and say, 'My family saved your people!' It always worked."

Ibrahim recounted with pride the role his family played in Hebron in 1929. "My grandfather saved the Jews," he said, his kind brown eyes twinkling. He stood up, reached for a dusty box on the shelf, and opened his red satchel, carefully unfolding the decades-old letters. "It wasn't just my grandfather," Ibrahim said gently. He pointed to another piece of paper, testifying to how on August 24, 1929, four different members of the Bader family rescued 37 Jewish men, women, and children. Members of the Slonim, Mizrachi, Gozlan, and Castel families, and their descendants, owe their lives to Ibrahim's ancestors.[1]

Ibrahim's parents moved the family to Jerusalem when he was 6, but he still has family in Hebron. He lamented that few if any Arabs living in Hebron today would speak openly of their ancestors' rescue of Jews. "Some people in Hebron, less educated people, call us collaborators," he said. In Palestinian society, being labeled a collaborator with Israel is a death sentence. In Gaza, collaborators have been thrown from buildings and dragged through the streets by motorcycle. In the West Bank, they have been hung from lampposts—as recently as October 2023. In Israeli jails, Palestinian prisoners suspected of collaborating with Israel are often murdered by fellow inmates. Speaking of prison, Ibrahim told me, one of his cousins had just been released. "He's former Hamas, now Fatah. Everyone welcomed him home like a hero."

Ibrahim was born in a house near Hebron's ancient Jewish cemetery, where his cousins still live. "I love going to Hebron," he said. "But going there is also very sad because of the problems with the Israeli settlers." Restrictions on Palestinian movement in H2, the part of Hebron controlled by Israel, require Ibrahim to park his car far from his childhood home, on the opposite side of a checkpoint. Unlike their Jewish neighbors in H2, Arabs living under Israeli control are not Israeli citizens. Like all Palestinians in the West Bank, they live under a separate system of laws. While their Israeli neighbors live under civilian law, Palestinians living under Israeli control are subject to military law. In essence, Israelis in Hebron are innocent until proven guilty, while the opposite is true for their Palestinian neighbors. Settler violence and harassment of Palestinians in Hebron almost always go unpunished. Meanwhile, according to IDF veterans, many Palestinians in Hebron undergo midnight raids of their homes by Israeli soldiers who require no search warrant to enter their property. "What do you think happens to children who see soldiers hitting their parents, coming into their house at night?" Ibrahim asked me. "This will never encourage peace."

Ibrahim's father has since passed, but he was alive in 1929. "The Al-Buraq Rebellion," said Ibrahim, using the Arabic term for the riots, began on August 23, 1929. "Muslims were praying at Al-Aqsa, and when they came out, they had to go through the area of Al-Buraq, and Jews began to attack them." Never mind the established facts of that day, detailed in newspaper reports and in the thorough British investigation of the riots—this is the version of history he and other Palestinians are taught.

Living in Jerusalem, a city with a mixed population of Jews and Arabs, Ibrahim has met several Israelis who might not be alive today had it not been for his ancestors. He recalled the day in 1985 when an Israeli woman approached his booth at a Jerusalem arts festival. Seeing the name Bader, she asked if his family was from Hebron. When he said yes, she placed a hand on his shoulder and told him, "Your grandfather protected us when I was a little girl in Hebron." Ibrahim sent his son to fetch the red satchel from his car. He showed her the papers, and she burst into tears. Her name was Rivka Slonim. She was just a child in 1929, but the bravery and humanity of Ibrahim's grandparents had left an indelible mark. Her own mother had died in childbirth. Rivka considered Ibrahim's grandmother a second mother, bringing her to life by rescuing her from death.[2]

Since that chance encounter with Rivka, Ibrahim forged an unlikely friendship with her grandson, Itzik, an Israeli tour guide who brings tourists to Ibrahim's shop. He also became acquainted with Rivka's son, Avraham Burg, a peace activist and former speaker of Israeli Parliament.

"From the perspective of Zionist, Israeli, and Palestinian history, the Hebron massacre was a formative moment," Burg wrote in *Days to Come*, a memoir of his own life and Israel's. "It marked the end of good relations between neighbors, between peoples, between members of different faiths. That was where the violent path we have all walked down was first laid and paved. It is part of everyone's historical memory."[3]

Since the massacre, he wrote, his family has been torn in two. "Half of them will never trust an Arab." The other half, of which he is part, "will always be seeking out Abu Shaker, that lone righteous man, kind-hearted and courageous, with whom we can start the dialogue anew, restart a better life, and seek to set it all right."[4]

The Separation Barrier

Of nearly two dozen Muslim families who saved Jews in 1929, I could find only one of their descendants living in Hebron today who was willing to speak about it. As Ibrahim and other Palestinians told me, saving Jews is not something many Palestinians today are proud of. Even if they are, those living in Hebron fear the consequences of speaking openly about it.

The man who agreed to speak with me was 60-year-old Tayseer Abu Aisheh. His grandfather, Hamed, owned the Hebron dairy factory with Yaakov Ezra, and saved his family during the massacre. Today, I have more freedom on Tayseer's own street than he does. While I could drive and park my car there, Tayseer, like all Palestinians in H2, cannot. To get to his house, he parks on the opposite side of a checkpoint in H1. It takes him about ten minutes to walk from that parking spot to his house. "What if you have heavy groceries to carry?" I asked him. He smiled, shrugged his slender shoulders, and put both hands in the air. "He's used to it," said my friend Mahmoud, who was serving as my translator that day. It had been this way for more than two decades.

The Second Intifada, and the counter-terror measures that followed, had not just remade the landscape of Hebron, but the entire West Bank. The barrier that separates the West Bank from Israel was erected in response to the suicide bombings in Israel that characterized those bloody years. Long criticized by Palestinians and humanitarian organizations as a violation of Palestinian freedom of movement, most Israelis see it as an unfortunate but necessary means of protection. Though the barrier is often referred to as a wall, it is 90 percent chain-link fence and 10 percent concrete wall. Most of it was built in late 2003. In the three years before its construction, there were seventy-three suicide bombings carried out in Israel by terrorists from the West Bank. In the three years after, there were twelve.[5]

I drove to Hebron on April 10, 2022, from my home in the desert city of Beersheba, about 25 miles south. After passing through a checkpoint, I entered the hills of the West Bank, its beautiful landscape punctured by military watchtowers, guard posts, and garbage-strewn Palestinian villages filled with half-built concrete structures. Garbage collection in Palestinian villages is overseen by the Palestinian Authority. The red-roofed, manicured settlements are perched on the hills, and the Palestinian villages are nestled in the valleys. Marking the entrance to every Palestinian town in the West Bank is a bright red sign posted by the Israeli government. Written in Arabic, Hebrew, and English, it warns drivers, "This road leads to 'Area A' under the Palestinian Authority. The entrance for Israeli citizens is forbidden, dangerous to your lives."

No warning signs stand outside of Jewish settlements, where Palestinians regularly enter for work. The men who build the homes and clean the streets in Jewish settlements are most often Palestinians, attracted by the higher wages they receive compared to similar work in Palestinian towns. The first time I saw those red warning signs years earlier, I thought they were over the top. Then I learned the history behind them.

On the morning of October 12, 2000, two weeks after the Second Intifada began, two Israeli reservists were reporting for duty at an army base near the settlement of Beit El. Unfamiliar with the roads of the West Bank, Yossi Avrahami, a 38-year-old father of 4, and

Vadim Nurzhitz, 33 and newly married, took a wrong turn. Driving in Vadim's Ford Escort and wearing civilian clothes, they ended up in Ramallah, headquarters of the Palestinian Authority. Pulling up to a PA roadblock, Palestinian policemen detained them and brought them to a police station. Word quickly spread that undercover Israeli soldiers were there. A crowd of 1,000 Palestinian men gathered outside, calling for their death. Some policemen tried to hold back the crowd, while others took part in what followed.

Rioters stormed the station, beating and stabbing both Israelis to death. In a photograph that is seared into Israeli memory of the Intifada, one of the attackers proudly raised his blood-soaked hands out the open window of the station for all to see. The crowd outside roared with cheers. Yossi and Vadim's bodies were then tossed out the window and brutalized. One of them was set on fire, his head beaten. Their mutilated bodies were then dragged to the town square.[6]

Today, Israelis do not need a reminder that entering a Palestinian town is dangerous. The first time I reported from a Palestinian village, several months after moving to Israel, I received a call from an Israeli source and made the mistake of answering in Hebrew. I was very quickly scolded by the Palestinian I had come to interview. "Never speak Hebrew in a Palestinian town," he warned me.

The Cage House

Tayseer Abu Aisheh lives in Tel Rumeida, the oldest part of Hebron, across the street from Tzipi's trailer. Tel Rumeida is perched on a hill in H2. After parking my car several houses down the hill from Tayseer's, I met him at the checkpoint in H1. The street leading up the hill was a battle of graffiti. Blue Stars of David were crossed out in black. Black Arabic insignias of the Ibrahimi Mosque were crossed out in blue. When we reached the top of the hill, there was a young, sunburned Israeli soldier standing across the street from Tayseer's

View of Palestinian H1 from Israeli H2, 2019.

house. His guard post stood near a large blue sign that read, WEL-
COME TO BIBLICAL HEBRON.

Like all Palestinians in H2, Tayseer is not permitted to have visitors unless their name appears on a preapproved list submitted to the
military in advance. When I arrived to meet him, my name was not
on this list.

"IDs," said the soldier, stationed there to check the papers of every
Palestinian who passes by, including those who live there. The soldier, who looked about 18, checked Tayseer's name against a list of
residents. Then he turned to me and Mahmoud. "What are you doing
here? Did you get the army's permission?"

I was unaware of this list and this requirement of permission. Tayseer had never mentioned it to me or Mahmoud, who is from the
Palestinian side of Hebron. I had been on this street many times before
to interview Jewish settlers who live there. They are not required to

preapprove their visitors with the army. When I had come to interview them, soldiers never questioned me. Then they had smiled and said hello.

I handed the soldier my government-issued press card. "I'm a journalist," I told him. "This is Mahmoud, my translator."

"You need permission to be here," he said. "I don't make the rules." He gave us back our ID cards and told us we couldn't go any farther. Only Tayseer had permission to enter his home.

We stood there, trying to decide what to do, when a settler who was taking out her trash approached us. "They're not allowed to be here," she commanded the soldier. He mumbled that he was trying to get us to leave. "Get them out of here," she shouted, pointing her finger at us. I tried to reason with her, explaining that I didn't know about this rule. I had been here before to interview Jewish residents without needing preapproval.

"Well, now you're here with Arabs," she snapped.

The West Bank, and Israel in general, was on edge. Just that morning, a Palestinian woman had stabbed a soldier outside the Tomb of the Patriarchs and Matriarchs (not the same woman as my visit in 2019). The previous night, dozens of Palestinians had broken into Joseph's Tomb in Nablus, setting fire to the ancient shrine, and breaking the tombstone of the biblical figure. Joseph is also holy to Muslims, who consider him a prophet. Two nights before that, a Palestinian from Jenin had gone on a mass shooting spree on one of the busiest streets in Tel Aviv, killing 3 civilians, wounding 6 others, and placing residents under lockdown until the gunman was found hiding in a mosque the next morning. Two weeks earlier, a supporter of ISIS killed 4 people in a car-ramming and stabbing attack in Beersheba.

Perhaps this woman in Hebron was genuinely afraid. To Mahmoud and Tayseer, both gentle and peaceful men, her behavior was typical.

"Every settler here is a government in his- or herself," said Tayseer. The settlers, he said, were a bigger problem than the soldiers. "Settlers will tell new soldiers who come to serve here that I don't live here, just to cause problems. It's always a different soldier stationed here, so they don't know who lives here and who doesn't."[7]

I had wanted to see Tayseer's house because I had already heard so much about it. Locals and soldiers called it the Cage House because it is fully encased in iron bars. Tayseer covered his home in metal to protect his family from young settlers whose favorite pastime seems to be hurling stones at Palestinian homes. "They still throw stones at our house, but it doesn't cause as much damage," said Tayseer.

After a call to the government press office, I received a call from an IDF spokesperson. I could enter Tayseer's house, she said, but Mahmoud could not. "Because he's Palestinian, he needs special permission," she explained. Tayseer does not speak English, and I do not speak Arabic. Interviewing him without Mahmoud was not an option. It was a sunny, eighty-degree day during Ramadan, a month when Muslims fast from sunrise to sunset, without so much as a sip of water. We walked down the hill and sat on the sidewalk, where we spoke for hours.

Soon after we sat down, Tayseer's 86-year-old father, Muhammad, shuffled down the street, a traditional keffiyeh on his head, wooden walking stick in hand. He was on his way to pray at the Ibrahimi Mosque, about a mile down the road. "My father has lived here all his life," said Tayseer. "My grandfather lived here, my great-grandfather lived here, we are many generations here." The house where Tayseer's grandfather lived was declared a closed military zone ten years earlier, after a Palestinian gunman opened fire from outside the house. The man had no connection to Tayseer's family, but that didn't matter. "We've tried to reopen the house and renovate it, but every time we are stopped by settlers. They harass us, don't let us do our work."

One day a few months earlier, he and his wife, Reema, were walking home with their 14-year-old son, Haitham, when a teenage settler walked up to Haitham and punched him in the face. They went to the police and filed a report against Yitzhak, the boy who punched him, but nothing happened. This wasn't their first run-in with Yitzhak. Another time Tayseer and Haitham were walking down the street, Yitzhak came up behind Haitham, wrapped his arm around his neck, and put him in a headlock. When Tayseer removed Yitzhak from his son, a soldier rushed over, grabbed Tayseer, and threw him to the ground.

"Sometimes the soldiers try to help," Tayseer said. When Haitham was punched in the face, a soldier shared the surveillance video with the police to back up Tayseer's report of the incident. The police did nothing. Yitzhak isn't the only settler who has harassed his family. Once, said Tayseer, his then 13-year-old niece came to visit. Tzipi Shlissel, who was outside, hit her, said Tayseer. "She didn't want her entering," he said. Five years after filing a police report against Tzipi, the family took her to court in Jerusalem. Tayseer said that Tzipi cried on the stand. "I don't want people who don't live here to come here," he said she told the court, explaining what had happened to her father. She was not charged. A month before our meeting, Tayseer said, one of Tzipi's sons threw rocks at his house. He showed me the video on his cell phone, shot from inside the house, as rocks pelted the windows.

The Abu Aisheh family is sadly not an outlier. A survey conducted by the United Nations Office for the Coordination of Humanitarian Affairs in 2018 found that 70 percent of Palestinian families living near Jewish enclaves in Hebron had been affected by settler violence. I witnessed that violence myself on several occasions.

Shortly after my first meeting with Tzipi Schlissel, I came to Hebron for Shabbat Chayei Sarah, the annual celebration of the Torah portion of that name. In Hebron, that Shabbat is a massive festival, where the chapter of Genesis in which Abraham purchased the cave to bury his wife, Sarah, is read in that very place. The Friday I arrived, Hebron's Jewish population had swelled from 800 to more than 40,000 people, many of whom slept outside in tents. The air and the words on people's lips carried a messianic tone. Just four days earlier, then secretary of state Mike Pompeo had announced that the US did not consider settlements in the West Bank a violation of international law, reversing nearly four decades of American foreign policy and removing a chief obstacle to the annexation of the West Bank. On the steps leading to the Tomb of the Patriarchs and Matriarchs that Friday, two dozen men and women held up a giant banner that read, PRESIDENT TRUMP & ADMINISTRATION: THANK YOU FROM HEBRON!

During the festival, part of Palestinian H1 was open to Jews so they could visit the burial site of Othniel, a biblical figure who was the first judge of Israel. I watched as hundreds of Jewish teenagers and young men marched through the streets where Palestinians live, singing Hebrew songs and waving Israeli flags. Some cursed or gave the middle finger to Arabs watching from their windows. Others vandalized cars. After 2 teenagers tore off the sideview mirrors of a Palestinian car and scratched the side of it, I asked them, "Why are you doing this?" They looked at me as if I were deranged. "They're killing us, and you worry about *their cars?*"

It struck me that the young religious men who were vandalizing Palestinian property and cursing Palestinian residents were doing so on the Sabbath, in one of their holiest cities, just after they had prayed at the Tomb of the Patriarchs and Matriarchs. Many of them were yeshiva students. For a group of people who seek to embody the teachings of the Torah, these young men had either misunderstood or forgotten some of its most fundamental teachings.

In that moment, I wondered, if David were a yeshiva student in Hebron today, which side of this scene would he be on? I hoped he would be one of the many people, like myself, who were looking on in horror, wondering what they could do to stop it. Soon enough, soldiers cleared the crowds out of the street and sent them back to H2. Several of the young men tried to fight the soldiers off, and were dragged away, kicking and shouting.

That evening, another group of teenagers was throwing stones at Palestinian homes. One of those stones broke through a window, barely missing the head of a sleeping baby.[8]

The Cost of Security

Reema and Tayseer have 4 sons and 4 daughters. Haitham, the youngest, was supposed to have a twin brother. When Reema went into labor, the ambulance took too long to arrive because it had to coordinate its arrival with the Israeli army. One baby died, and Haitham lived. A year before Haitham was born, they lost another baby when Reema went into labor. They had walked to the hospital, which was on the other side of the checkpoint in H1. Shortly after their arrival, they discovered that the baby had died during their long walk. One month before Haitham's birth, Tayseer had called the Palestinian Red Cross to arrange for an ambulance to prevent another tragedy. Because of the checkpoints and the bureaucracy, it still took too long.

The hypnotic melody of the Muslim call to prayer wafted through the air. We paused as the muezzin called out "Allahu Akbar." God is great.

"What does Hebron mean to you?" I asked Tayseer. "What makes you want to stay here?"

"I was born here," he said. "The prophet Ibrahim is buried here. I've never considered leaving. I'm not causing any problems. Why should I leave my home? They're the ones attacking me."

At their core, the Jews and Muslims of Hebron have so much in common. They love this place for the very same reasons. They cling to the memory of Abraham, and worship at his burial site nearly every day on opposite sides of the same shrine. And as they fight over whose right it is to live here, both see themselves as the one being threatened by the other. Neither is going anywhere. I told Tayseer what every settler I had met in Hebron had told me: that they simply wanted to live there in peace. "If they wanted to live in peace, they could," said Tayseer. "Long ago, during my grandfather's time, Jews lived here peacefully."

That was before they were violently expelled, I said.

"The settlers know my family saved Jews in 1929," Tayseer continued. "Life then was normal. We were neighbors. They attended our weddings and funerals and we attended theirs."

Yosef Ezra, who lives in Jerusalem, still calls Tayseer and his family to see how they are doing. Occasionally, when the security situation allows, he visits them. Before the Second Intifada, he would visit every week.

Tayseer's father, Muhammad, was now on his way home from the mosque, and joined us on the sidewalk. Hearing us talk about 1929, he said, "In 1929, there was an issue between the Jews and the British, so the British incited the Arabs to kill Jews."

Tayseer's uncle Radi came walking down the street and sat down with us. He used to own a supermarket on Martyrs Street. It's been closed since Goldstein's massacre. "They killed us, and we were punished. We live here, they live there," he said, pointing across the street. "We live under military law, they live under civilian law."

"How would you fix Hebron?" I asked Tayseer.

"They must remove the settlers," he said. "Not because they're Jews. Not out of hatred. We have visited Jewish peace activists in Israel, and they have visited us. It's not us who don't want to live with them. It's they who don't want us to live here."

In my interviews with settlers, they had said almost exactly the same thing about Palestinians.

After sitting on the ground for nearly three hours, my friend Mahmoud had to head home. Now that we no longer needed to speak, Tayseer showed me his house, which lived up to its name. We communicated through nods, hand gestures, laughter, and the few words we imagined the other might understand. Tayseer opened an iron door, and we climbed up a long flight of stone stairs to his two-story home. Reema, her head covered in a black-and-white floral hijab, showed me the living room. One of the stained-glass windows was still missing from a stone-throwing incident. Theirs is not the only Palestinian home in H2 that is stoned by young settlers, or whose windows are covered in metal bars, but it is the only one that looks like an iron fortress. If radical settlers hope their attacks will lead Tayseer and Reema to leave, they are mistaken. Not only does it convince them that they

The author in Hebron in 2022, far right; with Tayseer Abu Aisheh, second from right; his uncle, second from left; and his father, far left.

should stay, but that the settlers must go—much like Palestinian violence only hardens the Israeli stance.

Tayseer and Reema then showed me their garden, where they kept two chicken coops, one filled with chickens and another with pigeons. While Reema knelt down to collect the eggs her hens had laid that day, Tayseer proudly showed me the pigeon eggs, and introduced me to a pigeon baby he cupped in his hands. Beside their feathered friends was a row of ancient olive trees, estimated by Tayseer to be 1,000 years old.

I wondered, what if instead of fighting over narratives and victimhood, the Jews and Muslims of Hebron put their energy into harvesting Hebron's olive groves or growing Hebron's famous grapes, using their shared reverence for Abraham as a source of strength rather than hatred?

I said good-bye to Tayseer and Reema, feeling uplifted by their warm smiles, their clucking chickens, and their determination to live the life they had chosen. Yet the moment I stepped out of their home I was brought back to reality. Someone had parked their car directly in front of Tayseer's house, blocking the entrance. I squeezed myself out the door and around the car, thankful I wasn't pregnant this time.

The Profits of Perpetual Conflict

According to that same UN survey conducted in Hebron in 2018, 75 percent of Palestinian homes located near checkpoints and Jewish enclaves had been searched by Israeli forces at least once since 2015. In 97 percent of those cases, searches involved threats and intimidation. One-third reported at least 1 member of the household being physically assaulted. While a similar survey has not been conducted since, I met several Palestinian families with firsthand experience.

In the most combustible part of Hebron, next to the Bab Al Zawiyah checkpoint that separates Palestinian H1 from Israeli H2, lives Umm Salah, a 58-year-old mother of 6 whose husband sells produce at the nearby market. Just outside her home in H1, clashes break out between young Palestinians and Israeli troops on a regular basis. When Palestinian boys throw rocks at the soldiers, the soldiers respond with tear gas, which often seeps into Umm Salah's stone-walled home. Soldiers have entered her house more times than she could count. One evening, while looking to punish stone-throwers, they grabbed her 15-year-old son, Hamza, who was not involved, and beat him with their guns before dragging him from the house. Hamza returned hours later, battered and bruised. He needed 27 stitches in his head. Umm Salah surprised me by saying she does not blame the young Israeli soldiers, or the stone-throwing Palestinians, but Palestinian officials, who she said pay boys to throw stones. I would later hear about these payments from other Palestinians, not only in Hebron.

"The Palestinian Authority cares little about the Palestinian people," said Umm Salah. The conflict, she said, is perpetuated by the political and financial interests of Palestinian leaders, who receive billions of dollars in aid from the international community, yet give little of it to the Palestinian people. "Our government doesn't want peace," she explained. "When there is peace, foreign aid will stop," said her son Ali. Umm Salah lamented that only a minority of Palestinians want peace. When I asked her why, her son Mustafa answered for her. "Because the Jews took the lands of the Palestinians," he said. "It is the Jews who want peace," said his mother.

As I left Umm Salah's home, I noticed a massive banner on the building next door, depicting Mahmoud Abbas and Yasser Arafat with the Tomb of the Patriarchs and Matriarchs behind them. Above the official logo of the Hebron Municipality, it read, WITH OUR BLOOD WE WILL DEFEND IBRAHIMI MOSQUE.

CHAPTER 26

Kahane Lives

ACROSS THE STREET FROM TAYSEER ABU AISHEH'S HOUSE, IN THE leafy yard of a children's playground, a red tricycle stood outside a yellow trailer whose unassuming exterior, decorated with flowers, belied the man who lives there. A small Hebrew sticker on the front window offered a hint: RABBI KAHANE WAS RIGHT, it declared. The slogan, a common refrain on Israel's far right, is in reference to the late Meir Kahane, who was banned from Israeli Parliament in the 1980s. Kahane's ideology made him a pariah in Israeli politics. Yet his beliefs now have a powerful platform through his political offspring.

Baruch Marzel, one of Kahane's closest disciples, greeted me with pursed lips and what sounded like a grunt. The Muslim call to prayer, sounded five times a day, was so loud that Marzel had not heard me knocking at his front door, though he was seated 10 feet away from it. He came to the door after I called his cell phone.

"They do it this loud so we know they're here," he said. "Does it bother you?" I asked him. "The sound doesn't bother me," he said. "It bothers me that those who want to destroy us are still here."

In a city that harbors some of the most radical settlers, Baruch Marzel holds a special place at the top of that list. Among soldiers in Hebron, he is known for buying a pizza pie for anyone who shoots a suspected terrorist. Marzel inherited Kahane's Kach party after Kahane's assassination in 1990. He served as the party's spokesman until Kach was outlawed in 1994, following the massacre perpetrated by his friend and fellow Kach supporter, Baruch Goldstein. In 2012, Marzel cofounded the far-right political party Otzma Yehudit, whose name literally means "Jewish Power." As the reincarnation of Kach, Jewish

Power is led by some of Kahane's most ardent followers, including Marzel's former attorney and spokesman, Itamar Ben-Gvir, who lives in Kiryat Arba, the settlement just outside of Hebron. As national security minister, Ben-Gvir is one of the most powerful members of Israeli parliament. By welcoming Ben-Gvir into his government, Netanyahu has brought Kahanism and its extremist ideology from margins of Israeli society to the center of Israeli politics.

The first time I met Marzel was in December of 2019. Wearing wireframe glasses and a long gray beard, the 62-year-old showed me to a seat at his dining table, beside a pink toy stroller and a plastic highchair. The floors of his home were littered with the toys of his grandchildren. The dining room was a shrine to Meir Kahane. In front of me was a bookshelf lined with books written by and about Kahane. Behind me was a wall adorned with framed photos of Kahane, a young Marzel and Kahane, and Baruch Goldstein, holding a Torah scroll.

"Baruch Goldstein was a very good man. I knew him as a great tzadik before the attack," said Marzel, using the Hebrew word for a righteous soul. "I don't know if there was ever in the world such a great doctor. I can't understand what he did or why he did it," Marzel went on, caressing the curls of his beard as he spoke. He immediately proceeded to justify Goldstein's actions. In a version of history I heard from many settlers, Marzel explained that Goldstein had prevented a massacre of Jews. Goldstein, a Hebron medic, had been told by the IDF a day before his rampage that he should prepare one hundred hospital beds, said Marzel. His justification of Goldstein's attack reminded me of the way in which Palestinians portray the massacre of 1929. The difference was that Marzel's view is not representative of mainstream Israeli society.

"They had intelligence that there was going to be a major attack on Jews in Hebron." The night before, said Marzel, Jews praying at the Tomb of the Patriarchs and Matriarchs reported hearing Muslim worshippers shouting, "Death to the Jews."

How could shooting a room full of Muslim worshippers prevent a massacre of Jews? I asked Marzel. He paused, and seemed to be contemplating his response, when his phone rang. Marzel was repeatedly interrupted by phone calls from political operatives and reporters, asking him about his party's plans for the upcoming election in March 2020. Israel was in the throes of a political crisis, preparing for its third parliamentary election in less than a year, after Prime Minister Netanyahu had failed to muster the votes to cobble together a stable coalition. Israelis were deeply divided over Netanyahu's future. Three weeks earlier, he had been indicted in three separate corruption cases. The charges against him included bribery, fraud, and breach of trust. Ignoring widespread calls to step down and relinquish his leadership of the Likud party, Netanyahu remained.

Since its establishment, the Jewish Power party had lived on the very fringes of Israeli politics. Regarded as too extreme even by most right-wing Israelis, it had always failed to win enough votes to enter the Knesset. That threshold is just 3.25 percent. The party was bound to meet that fate in the elections of April 2019, with polls projecting it winning just 1 percent of votes. Then, Netanyahu proved, not for the first or the last time, that there was no string he was unwilling to pull to remain in power. Fighting for his political survival, he did what many analysts had deemed unthinkable. To strengthen the right-wing bloc of parties he needed to build a ruling coalition, in February 2019 he brought Jewish Power into mainstream Israeli politics, orchestrating its merger with two other right-wing parties. To seal the deal, Netanyahu promised the newly formed Union of Right-Wing Parties two cabinet posts if he won reelection.

The leader of Jewish Power at the time was a man named Michael Ben Ari. When I spoke with Ben Ari on March 17, 2019, he described the ethos of Jewish Power by telling me, "Kahane was right. . . . The time is over for those who think that Jews will not fight back when we are attacked."

Just a few hours after we spoke, Israel's Supreme Court disqualified both Ben Ari and Baruch Marzel from appearing on the ballot
due to incitement to racism. The ruling followed unprecedented criticism from American Jewish organizations, including AIPAC, which
rarely criticizes Israel in public, but felt Netanyahu's embrace of Jewish Power had crossed a line.

Responding to the criticism of his party, which AIPAC called
"racist and reprehensible," Ben Ari said, "There is no greater chutzpah
than to sit there in America and preach morality to me. When the
anti-Semitism in America leads them here to live free as Jews, it will
be my sons, IDF combat soldiers, who will protect them."

While its leaders were disqualified, Jewish Power was not. The
party chose a new leader: Itamar Ben-Gvir, a man who had been
indicted, by his own count, fifty-three times. In a country where military service is mandatory, Ben-Gvir had the unique distinction of
being banned from enlisting due to his extremism. Largely unknown
outside of Israel back then, Israelis knew Ben-Gvir as the go-to attorney for Jewish extremists. In 2015, Ben-Gvir defended Marzel after
he was charged with entering the home of a Palestinian activist and
attacking him when he was asked to leave. At the time of the attack,
which took place in 2013, the activist, Issa Amro, was arrested. Ben-
Gvir also represented Marzel in 2015 before Israel's Central Election
Committee, which had disqualified him for incitement to racism.
Ben-Gvir argued that Marzel's statement on the issue of African
asylum-seekers, which he labeled "a cancer," was not racist, because
Marzel "never said their race was what made them a cancer."[1]

In July 2019, Benjamin Netanyahu replaced Israel's founding
leader, David Ben-Gurion, as the nation's longest-serving prime
minister—having done so by embracing a party that calls openly for
the segregation of Jews and Arabs, the imposition of Jewish law, and
economic incentives to rid Israel of its Arab citizens, who make up
20 percent of the population.[2]

Sitting at Marzel's dining table in December 2019, Ben-Gvir and his party were not yet part of the Israeli government. Between phone calls from party operatives, I asked Marzel to tell me about his relationship with Kahane. "Rabbi Kahane was at my bar mitzvah," he said with pride. He then stood up, took a prayer book off the shelf, and opened it to the inside of the front cover. The book was a gift from Kahane, with a hand-written note to a 13-year-old Marzel, wishing him a fruitful life of good deeds, filled with Torah, justice, and love for Israel. Marzel was just 12 when he became a student of the rabbi. Marzel, born in Boston, moved with his family to Israel when he was 6 weeks old. He grew up in Jerusalem, where he attended the Mercaz Harav Yeshiva. After marrying his wife, Sarah, they became one of the first Jewish families to move to Tel Rumeida in 1984. They live in the trailer next to Tzipi's.

The Power of Memory

The driving force behind Kahane's ideology, said Marzel, was the 1929 Hebron massacre. "If you ask about one specific thing that made Rabbi Kahane into Rabbi Kahane, it was the massacre of 1929." Kahane advocated against coexistence between Jews and Muslims, or in Kahane's words: "There is no coexistence with cancer." Like Kahane, Marzel believes it was Jewish pacifism that led to the slaughter in Hebron. Today the memory of the massacre motivates Marzel's very existence. "We are here to continue what they tried to stop," he said. "We need to be here to not allow the murderers of 1929 to win."

When I confronted him about his extremist history, Marzel called the criticism hypocritical. To demonstrate, he took me outside to his porch, which overlooks H1. The windows of his home were framed by bullet holes. *This is what violent extremism looks like*, he was saying.

"The same people who condemn me won't condemn Jews getting killed by Arabs nearly every day," he said. "People continue to fund the Hebron mayor even though he carried out an attack like Baruch's. Think of what would happen if Kiryat Arba had made Baruch Goldstein mayor. The whole world would be against it."

By the time I returned to Marzel's house four years later, Itamar Ben-Gvir, a man with a criminal record, was Israel's minister of national security. Netanyahu had given him the powerful position, putting Ben-Gvir directly in charge of the very police force that had so many times arrested him.

After three failed election campaigns, Ben-Gvir had managed to pass the electoral threshold by toning down his messaging to win over mainstream right-wing voters. He took down his framed photo of Baruch Goldstein and changed his rallying cry of "death to the Arabs" to "death to the terrorists."[3]

While Ben-Gvir is considered one of the most radical figures in Israeli politics, Marzel feels his former comrade is not extreme enough. "He has lost his way," said Marzel. "I'm Jewish Power. He's not." Speaking in 2022 at the annual memorial honoring Kahane in Jerusalem, Ben-Gvir was booed for saying, "I don't support expelling all Arabs, and I won't make laws creating separate beaches for Jews and Arabs."[4]

Prior to becoming a government minister, Ben-Gvir had called for the expulsion of Arab citizens of Israel who were not "loyal" to the state, a policy Marzel also advocates. Since taking office in 2022, Ben-Gvir has avoided such literal expressions of his ideology. Instead, he has relied on code words, such as his campaign slogan that asked, "Who are the landlords here?" which could also be interpreted as, "Who owns this land?" Ben-Gvir's time in the Knesset has been defined by controversy and provocation, including several visits to the Temple Mount, and his defense of vigilante attacks by settlers.[5]

When I sat down at Marzel's dining table in April 2023, it was a day after Holocaust Remembrance Day. Marzel lamented that Israel had not learned the lessons of the Holocaust. "What lesson is that?" I asked him. "When someone says he wants to kill you, believe him." He showed me a newspaper article about a plan by Hamas to destroy Israel. "No one is speaking about this," he said incredulously. "Hamas plans are dismissed as nonsense. But we know it's not nonsense."

CHAPTER 27

Warning Signs

SHIELDING HIS EYES FROM THE SUN AS IT REFLECTED ON THE SAND dunes, Eyal Naveh looked out at the hundreds of new recruits gathered at an army base in central Israel. He felt his stomach churn as he looked into the earnest eyes of the 18-year-olds who peered up at him, exhausted by the morning's training exercises. Naveh is a 48-year-old veteran of Sayeret Matkal, Israel's most prestigious special-forces unit. As part of his reserve duty in late January 2023, he was training a new generation of fighters.

Normally, when instructing recruits, Naveh beams with pride for his country. But on that day, he told me, he thought to himself, *What kind of country would they go on to serve?* During their lunch break, Naveh took a seat with 5 reservist friends. Newspapers on the table carried disturbing headlines. Netanyahu was pushing ahead with a vast judicial overhaul that would give his government unprecedented control over the country's courts, including a greater say in the appointment of judges, and limitations on the Supreme Court's powers. In a country with no other system of checks and balances, many Israelis worried that this effort to weaken the Supreme Court would give the government the power to do virtually anything it wished. Prominent legal experts warned that Israel would become a de-facto dictatorship. Some feared that Netanyahu, who was on trial for corruption, had a clear motive for shaping the judiciary in his interests.

"This is no reform," Naveh said to his friends. "This is a coup. We have to do something." The soldiers started a WhatsApp group to figure out what they could do to thwart the government's plan. They called themselves Brothers in Arms. Within a day, the group had 800 members.

They came from across the spectrum of Israeli politics. None had ever protested against the government before. Within two months, Brothers in Arms was at the forefront of what would become the largest protest movement in Israel's history. By the time I met Naveh in March 2023, his group encompassed 30,000 men and women. Now they were threatening to stop serving reserve duty unless the judicial overhaul was scrapped. That prospect would deliver a serious blow to the armed forces. While the IDF does not disclose its figures of active duty or reserve soldiers, an army spokesperson told me that the "tens of thousands" of combat reservists outnumbered those in active duty. The Israeli army "cannot win a war" without these reservists, he said.

Reservists were not the only ones leading the battle against Netanyahu's efforts to weaken the Supreme Court—a policy push that was largely driven by the settler movement, which views the Supreme Court as its greatest obstacle. More than a dozen retired security chiefs were also vocal forces in the movement to prevent the reforms from passing. Dan Halutz, the former head of the IDF, was among the most prominent former security officials leading the protest movement. "We see this as our second war of independence," he told me. Other former heads of the IDF, the Shin Bet, and the Mossad warned that Israel risked becoming a dictatorship if the reforms passed. They also worried that the deep rifts the overhaul was causing within society and the military presented a grave threat to Israel's national security.

In February 2023, 400 former Israeli security chiefs published an open letter to Israel's president, Isaac Herzog, urging him to oppose any laws that would undermine Israeli democracy. In March, a letter to Netanyahu and Defense Minister Yoav Gallant from all 10 living former commanders of the Israeli Air Force warned of "severe and concrete danger to national security." Also in March, IDF chief of staff

Herzi Halevi warned Netanyahu that the legislation and the resulting protests of reservists "could harm the IDF's operational capacity."[1] Neither Netanyahu nor his coalition members heeded those warnings.

As anti-government protests intensified, National Security Minister Ben-Gvir lamented that the police were not handling them harshly enough. Then, on March 1, police deployed water cannons and stun grenades against thousands of Israelis who were chanting "Democracy!" as they blocked a highway in Tel Aviv. Ben-Gvir praised the officers for their severe response, saying, "The right to protest is not the right to commit anarchy."

Meanwhile, Ben-Gvir had refused to condemn a deadly rampage perpetrated by settlers in the West Bank just days earlier. Hours after two Israeli brothers were killed by a Hamas gunman as they drove past the Palestinian town of Huwara on February 26, hundreds of settlers descended on the town. Over the course of several hours that night, settlers attacked Palestinians at random, and set fire to dozens of businesses, cars, and homes, some of them with children inside. More than 200 Palestinians were wounded, and one man was killed.

As police wrestled peaceful protesters to the ground in Tel Aviv, demonstrators chanted "Where were you in Huwara?" While Ben-Gvir defended the violent police tactics, Netanyahu defended him. "I fully support National Security Minister Ben-Gvir, the police commission, and the Israel police officers, who are working against lawbreakers who are disrupting the daily lives of Israeli citizens," Netanyahu said that day. Hours earlier, the Knesset had advanced a bill that would make it more difficult to declare the prime minister unfit to serve, and another, backed by Ben-Gvir, to enforce the death penalty for convicted terrorists. That same day, Ben-Gvir's political partner, the far-right finance minister Bezalel Smotrich, a settler who oversees civilian affairs in the West Bank, condemned those who "took the law into their own hands." Huwara, said the leader of the Religious Zionist party, "needs to be wiped out. I think the State of Israel should do it."

When Eyal Naveh asked himself what kind of country his recruits would go on to serve, it was statements like these that worried him most.[2]

On March 15, President Isaac Herzog announced that he had formulated a compromise in the hope of avoiding a civil war. Netanyahu rejected the president's plan within an hour. Three days later, Brothers in Arms escalated their rebellion. Merely threatening not to serve wasn't working. Now, the group called on all reservists to sign a petition committing them to refusing reserve duty. More than 30,000 signed immediately. Hundreds began skipping their duty in protest, risking fines and military prison.

Israel had never felt so divided. On March 15, President Isaac Herzog unveiled a compromise to the judicial reforms, in the hope of avoiding a civil war. "Those who think that a real civil war, with human lives, is a border we won't cross, have no idea," he told the country in a primetime address. In Tel Aviv that afternoon, demonstrators were met by water cannons and mounted police. Later that day, in a primetime televised address, Netanyahu announced that the primary components of the judicial overhaul would be ratified the following week. On March 25, Defense Minister Yoav Gallant issued the most forceful warning yet. "The legislative process should be halted," Gallant declared in his own primetime address to the nation. "We face unprecedented security challenges," he said, citing rising Palestinian attacks from Gaza and the West Bank, threats from the Lebanese terror group Hezbollah, Iranian proxies in Syria, and Iran's nuclear program. "The growing rift in our society is penetrating the IDF and security agencies. This poses a clear, immediate, and tangible threat to the security of the state," he said, adding, "For the sake of Israel's security, for the sake of our sons and daughters, the legislative process should be stopped now."[3]

Right-wing ministers, including Itamar Ben-Gvir, assailed Gallant, calling for Netanyahu to fire him—which he did, the very next day. The firing of Gallant, himself a right-wing politician, solidified the fear among many Israelis that Netanyahu—who had for decades campaigned as Mr. Security—cared more about his own political survival than he did about Israel's safety. The following evening, 600,000 Israelis—roughly 6 percent of the population—took to the streets in furious protests, blocking traffic across the country and setting fires on highways. After union leaders held a general strike and Netanyahu saw his popularity in the polls plummet, the prime minister reinstated Gallant as defense minister.[4]

Yet in the face of even more dire warnings, Netanyahu refused to back down from his quest to neuter the Supreme Court. In April, the military intelligence directorate warned Netanyahu that Israel's enemies sensed the country was in a divided, vulnerable state.[5]

The government planned to pass the first part of its judicial overhaul on Monday, July 24. On Friday, July 21, more than 1,000 air force reserve officers, including pilots and navigators, vowed that they would no longer report for duty if the bill passed. The air force would not be functional if they were to follow through. The next day, roughly 100 former senior officers and commanders of the IDF, police, Mossad, and Shin Bet published an open letter to Netanyahu in support of the protesting reservists. Netanyahu and his quest to reshape the nation's democratic order, they declared, was singularly responsible for the "severe damage" to Israel's security. "Prime Minister," they implored, "this legislation is crushing the shared basis of Israeli society, tearing the people apart, disintegrating the IDF, and causing fatal damage to Israeli security." The security officials signed off, "We, veterans of Israel's wars, feel we are on 'the eve of the Yom Kippur War,' and raise a bright red stop sign in front of you and your government."[6]

Their reference to the Yom Kippur War—what was, until October 2023, the greatest military and intelligence failure in Israeli history—was clear. Israel was more vulnerable to attack than ever before. On Monday, July 24, IDF Chief of Staff Halevi sought to hold a security briefing with Netanyahu ahead of the highly anticipated vote. Netanyahu refused to meet with him. The legislation passed, and Netanyahu's far-right coalition partners celebrated "With God's help, this will be just the beginning," Ben-Gvir told reporters after the vote.[7]

Hundreds of thousands of Israelis took to the streets in the fierc-est protests yet. On July 28, Israel's air force chief, Tomer Bar, warned that the country's enemies could exploit the political crisis that was distracting the political echelons. "It is possible that at a time like this," Bar said in a prophetic address to his forces, "they will try to test the frontiers, our cohesion, and our alertness."[8]

Nevertheless, Netanyahu and his government vowed to press forward with more bills tied to their vast judicial overhaul. Security officials, in turn, continued to issue their warnings. Those warnings continued to be ignored.

On Friday, October 6, the chief of IDF intelligence analysis, Brig-adier General Amit Saar, wrote a letter warning that Iran and its proxies, Hamas and Hezbollah, recognized in the country's historic political crisis a unique opportunity to attack Israel. Based on infor-mation gathered by the military's intelligence division, Saar wrote that senior officials in the "Iranian axis" believed the time had come to inflict severe damage. The letter had already reached IDF Chief of Staff Halevi, and was meant to be delivered to Prime Minister Net-anyahu immediately after the holiday of Simchat Torah, which would end the night of October 7.[9]

CHAPTER 28

The Al-Aqsa Flood

Saturday morning, October 7, 2023, began like so many mornings in the desert oasis of Kibbutz Be'eri. The songs of sparrows mixed with explosions in the sky.

Avida Bachar sprang from his bed at 6:30 a.m. A 50-year-old farmer who was born and raised on the kibbutz, he was accustomed both to waking early and to the sound of rockets from Gaza. The agricultural collective of Be'eri, where Avida oversaw the cultivation of wheat, sunflowers, avocados, and mangos was just 3 miles from the border. Avida couldn't count the number of times he had been woken by Hamas rockets. Normally, he wasn't all that worried. Israel had the Iron Dome, a missile defense system that intercepted rockets before they reached their targets. His home, like all homes along the border, had a safe room that operated as a bomb shelter.

But almost immediately after he awoke, Avida knew this time was different. The explosions were so powerful that the ground shuddered. Still in their pajamas, Avida and his wife, Dana, grabbed their children from their beds, ran downstairs, walked outside, and gazed up at the sky. The horizon glowed with the glimmers of daybreak as rockets hissed through the skies above like shooting stars. The rockets from Gaza were raining down with such intensity that the Iron Dome could not keep up. In nearby Bedouin villages in the desert, where tents and ramshackle homes do not have bomb shelters, 7 Arab citizens of Israel were killed by these rockets. Hamas claimed to have fired 5,000 that day. Avida and his family, like most Israelis, did not yet know this.[1]

Avida looked at his wife, the love of his life since they were teenagers. "It's never been like this," Dana said softly. Air raid sirens pierced the air, still sweet with the scent of morning dew. The words *Tzeva Adom*—"Code Red"—blared incessantly through the kibbutz loudspeakers. Normally, these warnings ceased when a rocket barrage ended. Now they were relentless. The warnings told them they had fifteen seconds to take shelter before a Qassam rocket could reach Be'eri.

Heading to their safe room, Avida and Dana forced themselves to remain calm for their 13-year-old daughter, Hadar, and 15-year-old son, Carmel. "It will be OK," assured Dana, the head of the kibbutz nursery. She had such a special way with children that she was known as the baby whisperer of Be'eri.

They had just celebrated the weeklong harvest festival of Sukkot. October 7 was Simchat Torah, marking the end of the annual reading of the Torah and the beginning of a new cycle. Dana thought of her two older children, who were away that weekend, celebrating the holiday with friends. "I'm sure the army will come soon," said Avida. Then came sounds he had never heard in his fifty years on the kibbutz: rapid gunfire coupled with shouts in Arabic. Avida employed several Palestinians from Gaza and understood some Arabic. There were two words he kept hearing, coupled with machine gunfire: "Allahu Akbar!"[2]

God is great. The same words that accompany the Muslim call to prayer.

Avida and Dana's phones pinged with messages flooding the kibbutz WhatsApp groups.

Terrorists have infiltrated the kibbutz.

Lock your doors and windows.

Get inside your safe rooms.

In another corner of the kibbutz, past cypress and eucalyptus trees, Dekel Shalev huddled on the floor of her children's bedroom, which, like that of most young families, was the house's safe room. Dekel and her husband, Oshri, had been up since 6:15, awakened not by rockets but by their 3-year-old daughter, Daria, and 5-year-old son, Lenny. That was when the paradise they knew was lost, and the nightmare in which they have lived since began.

Seven-year-old Goni, their eldest, was still asleep in his bed when everyone gathered in the safe room and closed the heavy iron window that was normally open, waking him. Lenny had to pee. Dekel waited for a pause in the air raid sirens, but a pause never came. She swept Lenny up, ran to the bathroom, and ran back. Thinking they would be able to leave the room soon and eat a proper breakfast, she grabbed some chocolate pudding from the fridge to hold the kids over until the rockets ceased. Then she saw the WhatsApp messages and heard the gunshots.

The doors of the Shalev home, like most homes on the kibbutz, were never locked. Thirty-four-year-old Dekel was born in Be'eri and had lived there all her life. As the kibbutz secretary, she knew every one of the village's 1,100 residents. She locked the doors and returned to the safe room. Daria and Lenny were restless and hungry. "Don't worry, this will be over soon," Dekel told them, certain that if the kibbutz had been infiltrated, there were likely just a few terrorists. The kibbutz's emergency response team, or the army, would take care of them quickly.

Minutes later, the sounds of gunfire drew closer. "We need to be quiet," she told her petrified children, speaking as calmly as she could. "There are bad people outside and if they hear you, they will come inside and hurt us."

The children understood. Oshri sat on the bed with Lenny. Goni stayed under his covers. Daria sat quietly on her bed. Dekel, nine weeks pregnant, sat on the floor.

Paradise Lost

Five miles south, more than 4,000 young people were dancing euphor-
ically in a dusty field in the Negev Desert. DJs had arrived from around
the world. Revelers from across the country had poured in throughout
the night and early morning for a rave hosted by the Tribe of Nova, a
community dedicated to "spreading light and love" through the unifying power of music.

Nova raves were held on Israeli holidays at different sites around
the country. Few attendees seemed concerned about the location, 3
miles from the Gaza border, just outside Kibbutz Re'im—until the
skies lit up at 6:29 a.m.

"Fireworks!" some partygoers exclaimed in those initial moments
of confusion. Many of the young men and women dancing at the Nova
festival were high on various drugs.

"It's not fireworks! They're rockets! They're firing at us!" shouted
a young man who filmed the scene on his phone. "It's not a hallucina-
tion!" shouted another.

The music stopped. Nova organizers took to the DJ stand, shouting, "Code Red! Code Red!"

Aviv Eliahu, the festival's security director, announced through
the microphone: "Lie on the floor. Put your hands over your heads."

Dima Fleiman, an attendee filming the chaotic scene, muttered to
himself, "OK, explosions. We have a strong army." An alert appeared
on his phone, and his tone changed. "Oh. Rockets over Tel Aviv, too.
Wow." Qassams near the Gaza border were common. Qassams over
Tel Aviv were not.

"The event is over," Eliahu announced to a resounding "Noooo!"
from the festivalgoers. They thought this was just another missile
attack from Gaza, something many had experienced at least once a
year for most of their young lives.

Thousands made their way to their cars. A long line of traffic
accumulated, as cars inched slowly out of the parking lot.

Eliahu would soon lose his life protecting the festivalgoers who tried to escape.

Let Thousands Die for Islam

On the back of a motorcycle, a young man filmed his euphoric ride down a desert road. The knotted tie on the green Hamas headband on the driver's head before him fluttered in the wind. The camera tilted down to reveal a rocket-propelled grenade launcher strapped across the driver's back. They were in Gaza, making their way toward Israel's vaunted border fence, a high-tech concrete barrier built above and below ground over the course of nearly four years at a cost of more than $1 billion. As he drove into the sunrise, thousands of his comrades were doing the same.

Roughly 3,000 militants, led by Hamas, breached thirty different points along the 37-mile-long border. They scaled it by foot, drove through it with bulldozers, and set off explosives to break through. Some flew over in paragliders. Others came by sea, washing up on the shores of Zikim beach, where another overnight rave was just coming to an end. More than a dozen of those partygoers would soon be dead.

Triumphant images ricocheted through the Muslim world, posted to Telegram by Hamas, and broadcast on Al-Jazeera. The world's most widely viewed Arabic news channel, based in Qatar, portrayed Hamas as heroic freedom fighters and its civilian victims as soldiers of the "occupation army." In one video, a bulldozer plunged through the border fence as crowds of young men cheered, "Allahu Akbar!" Inside Israel, a row of motorcycles and white pickup trucks overflowing with gunmen in green headbands celebrated an almost unbelievable victory: they were deep within Israeli territory, and the army was nowhere to be found.[3]

In the months that Hamas terrorists had spent training for what they termed Operation Al-Aqsa Flood, they had not imagined it would be this easy. Fifty years earlier, almost to the day, Israel had suffered what was until October 7 the worst surprise attack in its history. That attack, on Yom Kippur in October 1973, had led to years of investigations, political fallout, and decades of hand-wringing—lessons that had seemingly been forgotten.[4]

Like the assault by a coalition of Arab states led by Egypt and Syria on Yom Kippur in 1973, Hamas timed its rampage to a holiday when many soldiers were home with their families. Military bases and crossings along the border were operating at minimum capacity. The Gaza border crossings were closed for the holiday. Six days earlier, the head of Israel's National Security Council, Tzachi Hanegbi, had stated confidently, "Hamas is very, very restrained." That same week, senior military and security officials assessed that Hamas was neither interested in war nor preparing for it. The Israel Defense Forces, shockingly, had *no plan* for how to respond to an invasion by the Islamist militant group that rules Gaza, which had made clear its mission to destroy Israel.[5]

The IDF was more concerned with the West Bank, which was experiencing historic levels of violence by Palestinians and vigilante attacks by settlers. In the days before what Israelis now call the Black Sabbath, three battalions were moved from the Gaza border to the West Bank to protect settlers during Sukkot. The number of IDF battalions stationed in the West Bank had already been doubled in June.[6] Though the government and the upper echelons of the IDF were confident that Hamas was not interested in escalation, soldiers stationed along the border had been sounding the alarms for months. Many soldiers, most of them female, repeatedly told their higher-ups of suspicious activity they witnessed over the border. Hamas appeared to be training for an unprecedented, large-scale attack that Israel was unprepared for. Those female soldiers, whose job it was to monitor the border, were among the first to die that morning. Others were taken to Gaza.

After storming the border, Israel's next line of defense, the military bases, were quickly overrun. Communications systems were shut down, preventing troops from reporting the assault or calling in for reinforcements. Unsuspecting soldiers, many of them just 18 or 19 years old, were gunned down in their beds or hiding beneath them. The Erez crossing, the primary avenue for UN personnel, medical patients, and Gazans with permits to work in Israel, became the gateway to a killing field. The Kerem Shalom crossing, where before October 7, an average of 500 commercial and aid trucks entered Gaza from Israel every day, was destroyed.[7]

"God is great! There is no god but Allah!" sang a jubilant convoy of gunmen as they drove into the horizon on motorcycles and white Toyota pickup trucks. The man who was filming panned to the other side of the road. "There's someone there!" he shouted. "Shoot!"

The passenger behind him shot into the trees on the other side of the road.

Seconds later, they pulled up to two cars that had sped out of the Nova festival's parking lot, spraying the passengers with bullets, cheering as they fired into the cars.[8]

Elsewhere on that same road, Route 232, which runs parallel to Gaza and leads to the various kibbutzim near the border, another militant filmed himself approaching Kibbutz Re'im in a car full of elated gunmen. "We're inside!" he shouted in ecstasy. "Everyone take someone!" shouted another man in the car. "Let thousands die for Islam! Let tens of thousands die for Islam!"[9]

The driver honked his horn in celebration.[10]

In the hundreds of hours of videos uploaded to social media by Hamas fighters and other militants that day, no one was calling for an end to the blockade of Gaza or the occupation of the West Bank. They were not crying, "Free Palestine." Much like their predecessors in 1929, they were praising Allah, defending Islam, fighting for Al-Aqsa. They did not refer to their victims as Israelis, but *Yahud*. Jews.

In Kibbutz Mefalsim, a man named Mahmoud called his parents from the phone of a *Yahudia*, a Jewish woman. "Dad!" Mahmoud shouted into the phone ecstatically. "Look how many I killed with my own hands! Your son killed Jews!"

"God is great," his father replied. "May Allah protect you."

"I'm calling you from a Jewish woman's phone, Dad. I killed her and her husband. I killed 10 with my own hands!"

"God is great," his father kept repeating.

In the background, his mother was weeping. "God bless you, my son," she said. Mahmoud told his parents to open WhatsApp to see photos of his victims. "Your son is a hero!" Mahmoud exclaimed.[11]

Here Are the Dogs

Squads of heavily armed men surrounded the Nova site. Seeking maximum carnage, they choked off most of the viable escape routes, blocking the road from north and south, and swarming the sprawling festival grounds on foot from three directions.

With traffic leaving the festival at a standstill, panicked young men and women ran in every direction. Hundreds huddled in bomb shelters along the road, as rockets rained down from Gaza. Others lay beneath trees and bushes, buried themselves in ditches, or covered themselves in dried grass. Dozens stayed at the Nova site, hiding behind the bar, beneath the stage, inside dumpsters and latrines. Many more ran through open fields with nowhere to hide.[12]

It was 7:56 a.m. when several white pickup trucks with mounted machine guns surrounded a bomb shelter on Route 232. The squat concrete shelter was painted over with a blue bird. Inside stood 24 young men and women. Gunmen leaped out of the trucks and truck beds. Some wore military fatigues, stolen IDF uniforms, and black face masks. On their green Hamas headbands were white Arabic letters. THERE IS NO GOD BUT ALLAH, MUHAMMAD IS THE MESSENGER OF GOD, they read, atop THE AL-QASSAM BRIGADES, the name of Hamas's military wing. In the center was the Islamist group's emblem: a gunman's keffiyeh-covered head, and Al-Aqsa in the background. The men who infiltrated Israel that day were led by Hamas, but they included members of five other Palestinian armed groups, including

Islamic Jihad. None of them were Hamas leaders, but foot soldiers carrying out Operation Al-Aqsa Flood, the most brazen mission in Hamas history, the deadliest attack in Israel's history, and one of the largest terror attacks in modern history, spanning more than two dozen towns, cities, and military bases.[13]

What unfolded at the bomb shelter was captured on the dash cam of Osama Abu Asa's car. A 36-year-old Arab citizen of Israel, Abu Asa had worked the night shift guarding shops at Kibbutz Re'im. He was on his way home to Tel Sheva, the Bedouin town where his wife and 2 children were waiting for him. He had just called his wife to say that he was on his way home when the air raid sirens led him to pull over and take shelter. When militants pounded at the door, he told them, "There are Muslims here." Forced out at gunpoint, a dozen armed men surrounded Osama, ordering him to remove his shirt and to give them his wallet and his watch. Slumped on the ground outside the bomb shelter, his back against the concrete wall, Osama was beaten relentlessly. In his final moments, he implored the gunmen in Arabic. The people inside are innocent civilians, he told them. Please, don't hurt the women. There is a family here, he said, referring to 33-year-old Or Levy and his 32-year-old wife, Einav. Their 2-year-old son, Almog, was at the home of his grandparents.

The gunmen did not care that Osama was Muslim or that the Israelis inside the shelter were civilians. In Hamas's eyes, Osama was worse than an Israeli. He was a collaborator. They executed Osama and fired into the bomb shelter. Standing near the Levys were 23-year-old Hersh Goldberg-Polin, an American Israeli who was born in Chicago and lived in Jerusalem, and his best friend, Aner Shapira. A 22-year-old native of Jerusalem who served in an elite IDF unit, Aner, like many soldiers that day, was on leave. His military base had been overrun by Hamas gunmen.

Aner stood closest to the doorway. When the terrorists lobbed a grenade into the shelter, Aner picked it up and tossed it back. They tossed in another, and he threw that one too. After ejecting seven grenades, the eighth exploded in Aner's hand, killing him. Hersh's left arm was blown off from the elbow down. Einav Levy was shot. When the smoke cleared, the gunmen went in and took stock of their carnage. Just 7 people had survived.

"Here are the dogs!" bragged one gunman as he dragged a bloodied girl by the hair and brought her to his friends. Her legs were badly wounded. "No, we will keep this one," a man off camera told him. The girl was led out of view, and 3 wounded young men were thrown onto the back of a pickup truck. One of them was Hersh. He sent his last text message to his parents at 8:11 a.m. "I love you," he wrote, followed by, "I'm sorry." Perhaps he knew that whatever happened to him from that moment would bring his family tremendous pain.

Lying beside Hersh on the truck bed was Or Levy. In the chaos of that day and those that followed, Or's wife, Einav, was presumed to have been taken to Gaza. She was declared dead four days later, after her remains were identified among the 1,200 dead bodies lying across southern Israel.

Or and Einav's son, Almog, now lives between the homes of his grandparents. "We told him that his mother won't come back," Or's brother, Michael Levy, told me. "How do you tell a 2-year-old boy such a thing?" They told Almog that his father is missing and that they are looking for him. In the weeks and months that followed, Almog spent many hours in his grandparents' bomb shelters while Hamas continued to fire rockets at Israeli towns and cities. He often cried for his mother and father. One day, his uncle read him a book about a girl who hugs her mother at the end. Almog took the book and hugged it tight.[14]

Where Is the Army?

Back at the festival grounds, militants shot anything that moved. Some of the gunmen were teenagers, dressed in civilian clothes and sandals, machine guns strapped across their backs. Gunmen fired into the row of yellow latrines, killing the people hiding inside.

Dozens who had remained at the Nova site escaped into the surrounding brush. Seemingly everyone was asking each other the same question: "Where is the army?"[15]

The police officers guarding the festival that morning were tragically unprepared and exponentially outnumbered. In the fierce gun battles that ensued, most of the officers were killed. Some of those who survived rescued hundreds. Officer Remo Salman El-Hozayel, a Muslim citizen of Israel, arrived for his shift six minutes before the rampage began. His car, hit by an RPG, was engulfed in flames. Crouching through a field where many had abandoned their cars to run, El-Hozayel climbed into an unlocked Nissan and gunned the ignition. He spent the next three hours shuttling back and forth between the Nova site, dodging bullets and grenade fire as he rescued dozens of festivalgoers, dropping them off at a cement barricade manned by another policeman.[16]

Others who did the same were not as fortunate. Among the 367 people who were slain at the Nova festival was Ben Shimoni, a 31-year-old who ferried at least 9 people to safety in Beersheba. He had just picked up 3 more when his car came under fire from militants on the highway. Everyone in the car was killed.[17]

The Face of an Angel

From their hiding places on and around the festival grounds, survivors witnessed scenes they wish they could unsee.

Sapir, who told her story to the New York Times but asked that her last name not be published, was shot in the back as she fled the rave.[18] The 26-year-old accountant kept running until she found a bushy tamarisk tree near Route 232. She hid beneath the tree, covered herself in dried grass, and lay as still as she could. Around 8:00 a.m., she saw cars, white pickup trucks, and motorcycles pull over about 50 feet away. Dozens of armed men congregated in a makeshift assembly point, handing each other weapons and young wounded women. The first had long brown hair. Her pants were gathered around her knees, and blood trickled down her back. As one of the men forced her to bend over, another violently penetrated her, stabbing her in the back every time she recoiled in pain. Soon she was motionless. The next woman was raped by one terrorist, then passed to another, and another. Her final assailant shot her in the head. Another young woman was raped by one gunman as another cut off her breast. Her face was slashed, and she fell out of Sapir's view. Before the terrorists drove away, Sapir saw them rape 2 other women, and carry away the severed heads of 3 others.[19]

Shoam Gueta, a fashion designer, was hiding in a dried-up stream bed off Route 232, about a mile from the Nova site, with his friend Raz Cohen. About 100 feet away, they told the *New York Times*, a white van pulled over. Five men, dressed in civilian clothing, carrying knives and a hammer, dragged a young woman across the ground. Laughing, they gathered in a half circle around her. While one of the men raped her, another raised his knife and stabbed her repeatedly. She screamed, and the men laughed. It was unclear to Gueta and Cohen whether these men were militants or civilians.[20] In the aftermath of Hamas's border infiltration, hundreds of Gazans had poured through the openings in the fence.

Yoni Saadon, a 39-year-old father of 4, hid beneath the festival stage and watched, helpless, as a beautiful young woman was beaten and raped by as many as 10 fighters. She had "the face of an angel," Saadon told a journalist weeks later. "I kept thinking it could have been one of my daughters," he said.

"Stop it," he heard her scream in agony as the men laughed. "I'm going to die anyway from what you are doing, just kill me!" she cried. The last one to torture her shot her in the head. When the terrorists walked away, Saadon pulled her body over his, smearing himself with her blood so he would be mistaken for dead. "I will never forget her face," said Saadon. "Every night I wake to it and apologize to her."[21]

Yinon Rivlin, one of the producers of the Nova festival, had gone to the rave with 3 of his brothers. Two of them were killed. Rivlin spent hours lying in a ditch off Route 232. When the gunfire around him ceased, he emerged, and headed toward the parking lot. The road was lined with dead bodies. One of them was a young woman, lying on her stomach, naked from the waist down, her legs spread open. Her vaginal area was torn apart. When emergency response teams reached the ravaged kibbutzim hours later, they discovered dozens of bodies of women and teenage girls with similar, unmistakable signs of sexual abuse.[22]

Mommy Doesn't Feel Pain Anymore

Avida Bachar sat closest to the reinforced safe room door. Carmel, his 15-year-old son, sat on the couch, clutching four kitchen knives he had grabbed on his way to the safe room. "I don't think we will be able to fight them off," Avida lovingly told his son, a surfer who now looked like a ninja. "We just need to survive." Outside the cinder block walls of their home, dozens of terrorists roamed the pastoral village, entering homes and killing men, women, and children methodically and sadistically.

For four hours, the Bachar family waited. They watched the massacre of Be'eri unfold through the panicked messages sent by their friends and neighbors.

"They're in our house"

"Help! They're shooting"

"They're going to kill us"

"Where is the army???"

"Where is the fucking army!!"[23]

Sitting in silence, the Bachars heard gunmen prowling their neighborhood, laughing, and shouting "God is great!" as they fired machine guns and grenade launchers. Around 10:00 a.m., they reached the Bachar home. While the family's bomb shelter, like the bomb shelters in most Israeli homes, could sustain the force of a rocket attack, it was not designed for home intrusions. The door was not bulletproof. It had no lock. Avida placed his weight against the steel door, holding the handle as tightly as he could. Gunmen fired at the door, piercing Carmel in the hand and stomach. With bullets in both of his legs, Avida fell to the ground. Unable to hold the door, he assumed the terrorists would enter. Instead, the room filled with smoke. As they were doing in homes across Be'eri and other kibbutzim, they set the house on fire to lure them out.

Gasping for air, Dana and 13-year-old Hadar opened the iron shutters of the safe room window. Minutes later, grenades and gunfire poured through. Dana was shot in the chest. Hadar and Avida were sprayed with shrapnel. Carmel was bleeding profusely from his stomach. Hadar, who often helped her mother at the nursery, tended to her parents and her brother, placing whispered calls to emergency services. Minutes later, Avida told his daughter through tears, "Mommy doesn't feel pain anymore."

Carmel was slowly bleeding to death. "Abba," he winced, gasping for air as he told his father his dying wish. "Bury me with my surfboard."[24]

Live-Broadcasting a Massacre

Early that morning, in her apartment in a suburb of Tel Aviv, 50-year-old Maayan Zin frantically texted her ex-husband, Noam Elyakim.

Noam lived in Nahal Oz, just 650 yards from the Gaza border, with his partner, Dikla, and her 17-year-old son, Tomer. Zin's daughters, 8-year-old Ella and 15-year-old Dafna, were at their father's house for the holiday.

"Are you in the safe room? How are the girls?" she asked Noam.

"We're OK, in the safe room."

"Is Ella afraid?"

"No."

Two hours later, Zin texted again, asking if she could speak to her daughters. She waited and waited, but Noam never responded.

This is so like Noam, she thought, annoyed, but not too worried. Nahal Oz had been on the front line of Hamas rocket attacks for more than two decades. As always, Zin assumed, Ella and Dafna would stay in the safe room with their father until the rockets stopped falling. They would be fine.

Then came the photograph from her sister. It was from a Telegram channel where Hamas was posting an endless cascade of horrifying photos and videos, documenting their atrocities, and broadcasting them to Israelis for maximum impact. If they couldn't physically harm every Israeli, they would terrorize those they couldn't reach.

At first, Zin thought the photo of her daughters was fake. It was simply too unfathomable to be real. Dafna, her long curly brown hair framing her almond-shaped eyes, sat barefoot on a mattress on a floor in Gaza, looking blankly into the distance. The pajamas she was wearing, covered in red hearts and the word *LOVE*, were not hers.

Panicking, Zin called Tomer. He sent her a video that was even more disturbing. In the video, a Hamas fighter was using Dikla's phone to livestream the family's capture.

"Talk with your country," the man instructed Noam, whose leg was bleeding. Next to him was Dikla, her arms wrapped tightly around Ella, who was in her underwear.

"Hamas is here, in our home in Nahal Oz, and they have shot me in the leg," Noam said to the camera, which then panned to show gunmen roaming the house. Doe-eyed Ella, sitting on Dikla's lap, looked up at the camera, terrified. Sitting next to her father, holding his left arm with both hands, Dafna wept. Her legs were covered in a white sheet. The floor was a pool of blood.

Horrific thoughts careened through Zin's mind. *What are they doing to them? Is their father still alive? What did they see?* In another photo posted to Telegram by Hamas, Ella was sitting on a different mattress on the floor in Gaza, across from her big sister. Two of the fingers on Ella's right hand were wrapped in a bloodied bandage. Both the girls' clothes had been changed since they left their home. Zin tried not to imagine who had changed them.

Hamas fighters took Dafna and Ella to Gaza after murdering their father and stepmother. Threatened at gunpoint, Tomer was forced to escort Hamas gunmen to the homes of his neighbors and convince them to open their doors.[25]

When he arrived at the home of the Idan family, they were hiding in their safe room. Tsahi Idan was holding the door handle. His wife, Gali, and their 3 children huddled behind him. Hamas filmed Tomer, who was barefoot, dressed in a white tank top and beige shorts, knocking on the safe room door.

"Open the door," Tomer said in Hebrew, repeatedly and unconvincingly. Tsahi didn't listen. The terrorists fired on the door. The room went black, and Tsahi screamed in anguish.

"Maayan! No! Maayan!"

Tsahi let go of the door handle. His 18-year-old daughter, Maayan, who had tried to help him keep the door closed, was shot in the head. Tsahi was covered in his daughter's blood, cradling her in his arms. Hamas fighters entered the room. "She is OK," one of the gunmen said in English. "She is with Allah," he said, pointing above.

The gunmen took Tsahi; his wife, Gali; their 11-year-old daughter, Yael; and 9-year-old son, Shachar, into the living room. "Do what they say, so they won't hurt you," Tomer whispered to Gali before he was taken to another house. Hours later, when his help was no longer needed, Tomer was killed.

One of the terrorists took Gali's phone, forced her to enter her password, and livestreamed the family's suffering on Facebook Live. For twenty-six excruciating minutes, the family was shown cowering on the floor. Yael and Shachar sobbed uncontrollably, failing to understand what had happened to their big sister. Tsahi, shell-shocked, his hands covered in his daughter's blood, was silent, staring at the ground. Gali held her children tight, trying to soothe them.

"Dad, are you OK?" asked Shachar, between sniffles. "Is Maayan really dead?"

"What did we do that they are shooting at us?" Yael asked through sobs.

Maayan's lifeless body was just meters away. They had just celebrated her eighteenth birthday. Balloons were all over the house.

"Let's pray to Al-Aqsa," said one of the gunmen hovering over the family.

For several hours, Hamas terrorists used the Idan home as their base, shooting at members of the kibbutz's rapid-response team, at soldiers and police. They brought in captured neighbors: Omri Miran, his wife, and their 2-year-old and 6-month-old daughters; then Judith Raanan and her daughter Natalie, American citizens who were visiting family on the kibbutz.

Around 1:30 p.m., the terrorists decided to head back to Gaza. "Get up," they told Tsahi. They tied his hands behind his back with zip ties, then did the same to his neighbor, Omri, and the 2 American women.

"Don't take them! Don't take them!" screamed Yael and Shachar.

"We love you," Gali told her husband. "Don't be a hero. Come back to us alive."

Yael and Shachar begged the gunmen not to kill their father. Omri's wife and young daughters cried.

"Relax," said one of the terrorists. "They will be back."

As they left, another gunman told the family, "Don't move, or you will die."

When soldiers arrived at the house around 5:30 that evening, the children refused to leave.

"We can't get up or we will die," Shachar told them. "We don't want to leave," said Yael. "They will kill us."[26]

Taken by foot to Gaza, hands tied behind their backs, Judith and Natalie Raanan were brought to a hospital, where they saw other hostages. Jubilant nurses cheered their arrival.[27]

Using Facebook as a tool of psychological warfare was part of the Hamas playbook that day. Bracha Levinson's grandchildren discovered what happened to their 74-year-old grandmother through her Facebook page, which Hamas used to broadcast her murder. Levinson was seen lying on her living room floor in Kibbutz Nir Oz, clutching her chest, bleeding to death. Hamas gunmen stood over her body.[28]

Horrifying videos flooded the homes of Israelis across the country. Filmed by Hamas gunmen and Palestinian civilians who followed them over the border, they were posted on social media platforms such as Facebook and Telegram. Some videos were aired on Israeli TV.

In one video, a nearly naked young woman was dragged through the streets of Gaza on the back of a motorcycle as young men and boys cheered in celebration. The lifeless, disfigured body of another barely dressed young woman was splayed across the bed of a pickup truck. Her dreadlocked head, caked in blood, lay beneath the legs of several proud militants who paraded her like a souvenir through the streets of Gaza. A mob of unarmed young men surrounded the truck, spitting on her and shouting, "God is great!" Her name was Shani Louk, a 22-year-old German Israeli tattoo artist who had attended the Nova festival. In another video, a pretty girl was dragged by her hair from a bomb shelter by one Hamas gunman as another delivered instructions. "That one is not a prisoner," he said. "She is for rape. Put her over there."[29]

In one of the more disturbing videos, 19-year-old Naama Levy was pulled by her hair from the trunk of a black jeep and forced into a side door at gunpoint. The backside of her gray sweatpants was stained with blood. Both her Achilles tendons had been slashed to prevent her from running. Blood streamed from her face, and her hands were tied behind her back. Crowds of Palestinian men and boys watched, cheering and shouting, "God is great!"

In a video that became emblematic of the hostage crisis that began that day, 25-year-old university student Noa Argamani was forced onto a motorcycle in a field outside the Nova festival. "Don't kill me!" she screamed in horror as she reached out for her boyfriend, who was also taken to Gaza. In another video that is painful to watch, 32-year-old Shiri Bibas clutched her 2 redheaded sons in her arms as they were abducted. Ariel Bibas was 4 years old at the time. His baby brother, Kfir, was just 9 months old. They were separated from their father, 34-year-old Yarden, who was also kidnapped.[30]

The End of Days

Thirty-year-old police officer Oriel Uzan was at his parents' house outside Jerusalem with his wife and 9-month-old son when he received the call from his commander. It was 7:30 a.m., and even his commander couldn't grasp what was happening. Police were being called up from across the country to head south. Uzan's team gathered at a police station in the coastal city of Ashkelon, where Hamas rockets set cars and buildings ablaze. They made their way south in armored cars to the various towns and villages that had been infiltrated.

Uzan's unit of 9 men was the first to arrive at Kibbutz Be'eri. It was already 1:00 p.m. Normally, the drive from Ashkelon to Be'eri took thirty minutes. That day, it took hours. Bodies of men, women, and children were strewn across the highway beside the smoldering carcasses of burned-out cars. Uzan drove slowly to avoid the corpses. Entire families had been shot or burned alive. He felt as if he had entered the apocalypse. *Is this what the end of days is supposed to look like?*

As Uzan approached the yellow gate that leads into Be'eri, smoke and the unmistakable stench of death filled his lungs. He could already see gunmen crouching behind bushes, standing on rooftops, behind buildings, running in and out of homes. Some of them wore stolen IDF uniforms. Others wore T-shirts and sandals. Uzan drove into the kibbutz and took a right. The first thing he saw was the body of a young child covered in blood. The child, who looked not much older than his own infant son, lay beside the body of a half-naked woman, also covered in blood. Presumably the child's mother, she lay topless, on her stomach, her shorts torn. Oriel instinctively pulled to a stop. "Keep going," urged his commander, seated beside him. As he drove, they passed more bodies.

In the ensuing battle between the militants and Uzan's unit of 9 policemen, Uzan was the only one who survived. Seven months later, he remains a shell of the man he was before that day, barely summoning the energy to play with his son, whose cries bring him back to the scene in Be'eri.

They're Here

On the other side of the kibbutz, Dekel Shalev had been hiding in the safe room with her husband and 3 young children for six hours. Safe rooms have no bathroom. They relieved themselves in plastic bags. Dekel, nine weeks pregnant, was excruciatingly nauseous. Her bathroom bag had filled quickly, leaking on the floor around her. Her children were hungry and terrified. They hadn't eaten in six hours. Three-year-old Daria wouldn't stop crying. Dekel lay helpless on the floor in her pajamas. The overwhelming smell of urine and feces, coupled with unbearable anxiety, made her vomit.

Then came knocks at the windows and doors, followed by silence. Somehow, the kids fell asleep. Soon the men returned and jiggled the safe room door. The Shalevs had put a lock on the door years ago, one of the best decisions they had ever made.

Gunmen screamed in Hebrew to open the door. The family was silent, and the men left. Minutes later, Daria's doll stroller was thrown at the door. Dekel heard people going in and out of the house, digging through their belongings, filling bags with clothes, jewelry, electronics, everything they could take. During and after Hamas's rampage,

Gazans looted the homes of residents who were hiding in their safe rooms.

In her WhatsApp group of other young moms on the kibbutz, Dekel's friends begged for help, unaware that their entire kibbutz, and their country, was under attack. *Help! I'm having contractions,* wrote Dekel's sister, who was six months pregnant. *They are burning our house.*

They're here, wrote Dekel's friend Rinat Even, a social worker and mother of 4 who lived near the Bachar house. Then came a cryptic message from Sandra Cohen, a mother of 3 who lived just three doors down from Dekel.

Mila is dead.

Dekel and other moms in the group couldn't understand. *What do you mean?* asked one mother. *What happened?* wrote another. Sandra did not respond. Mila was just 9 months old.

Sandra Cohen, a 38-year-old pediatric nurse, was in the safe room with her husband, Ohad; their daughter, Mila; and their sons, 3-year-old Dylan and 9-year-old Liam. Sandra was cradling Mila in her arms when militants broke into their home and fired into the safe room. Mila was shot in the head, dying in her mother's arms. The round of gunfire that killed Mila ripped through Sandra's arm. Liam suffered head trauma from grenade shrapnel. Smoke filled the room. Desperate to keep their sons alive, Ohad and Sandra climbed out the window. Militants waiting outside tied up Ohad and executed him before his wife and children. They continued to shoot Ohad and Mila to ensure they were dead.

In her home on the edge of the kibbutz, Ohad's 73-year-old mother, Yona Cohen, was also bound and executed. Sandra and her young boys were taken captive, along with an elderly woman in a wheelchair and her Filipino aide. Terrorists were marching them out of the kibbutz when Israeli troops appeared. Sandra, Dylan, Liam, and the elderly woman were rescued by the IDF soldiers who had just arrived, replacing another battalion that had been quickly overpowered. Gracie, the Filipino caretaker, was taken to Gaza.[31]

Dekel's friend Rinat Even was sweating inside her safe room with her husband, Chen; their four sons; and their dog, Marco. As their home burned, they stripped down to their underwear. Like many that day, they were forced to decide between suffocating or burning alive in their safe room, or risk being gunned down outside. "We have to get out," Rinat wrote to a friend. She jumped from the safe room window with Chen, 8-year-old Nir, 11-year-old Tomer, 14-year-old Idan, and 16-year-old Ilan. They laid beneath a row of bushes and nestled their bodies together in the cool soil. "With God's help," Rinat wrote to a friend, "this will all be over soon."[32]

As homes around them smoldered, plumes of smoke rose over Be'eri and the skies above the other kibbutzim that hug the Gaza border.

In Kibbutz Kfar Aza, Avihai Brodutch, a 42-year-old farmer, heard a gentle knock on the door and the sound of a crying child. He opened the door to find 3-year-old Avigail, the daughter of his neighbor and close friend, photojournalist Roi Idan. Avigail was covered in her father's blood. Roi had been killed while clutching her in his arms. Avigail had also witnessed the murder of her mother, Smadar. Her 6- and 9-year-old brother and sister hid in a closet for fourteen hours.[33] Avihai whisked Avigail into the safe room to take shelter with his wife, Hagar, and their 3 children, Ofri, Yuval, and Uriah. He went outside to find a gun. When he returned ten minutes later, his wife and the children were gone. Ofri had just turned 10. Yuval was 8, and Uriah was 4. Avihai would discover the following day that his wife and children, and Avigail, had been taken to Gaza.[34]

Chaim Peri, an 80-year-old artist and peace activist, stood behind the door of his safe room nearby. His wife, Osnat, hid behind baskets of yarn and fabric. Chaim and Osnat were well-attuned to the suffering of Palestinians in Gaza. As 1 of 3,000 volunteers with the Israeli nonprofit organization Road to Recovery, Chaim had helped dozens of Palestinians from Gaza receive medical treatment in Israel, where hospitals are ranked among the best in the world. Throughout the years, Chaim had driven to the Erez border crossing—destroyed by Hamas that morning—to pick up Palestinian parents and children, drive them to Israeli hospitals, wait for them to receive treatment, then drive them back to the border. Road to Recovery was established in 2010 by Yuval Roth, a peace activist whose brother was kidnapped and killed by Hamas terrorists in Gaza one month after the signing of the first Oslo Accord in 1993.[35]

Osnat watched from behind the baskets as her husband was dragged away by Hamas fighters. "Don't resist," she heard them tell Chaim. "We won't hurt you."

Chaim was among the founders of the utopian village, a haven of like-minded peace activists and left-wing Israelis. Many of those who were killed and kidnapped that day, in Nir Oz and other kibbutzim, had spent years building bridges with Palestinians, seeking to forge peace from the ground up.

The Peris' friends, Yocheved and Oded Lifshitz, were also peace activists who volunteered with Road to Recovery. They too were kidnapped. Out of Nir Oz's 400 residents, more than 100 were either killed or kidnapped.[36]

Not Your Enemy

Dekel Shalev, who had never been political, had a lot of time to think that day. In her mind, she asked the gunmen, "Why us?"

Established in 1946 on uninhabited land in the Negev Desert, Kibbutz Be'eri was founded on the idealistic vision of a collective, egalitarian farming community, much like most other kibbutzim. Its residents were secular.

Like most kibbutzim, Be'eri was home to some of the most left-wing members of Israeli society. Many of Dekel's friends had spent the previous ten months protesting Netanyahu and his government's plans to erase the only checks and balances on the most right-wing government in Israeli history. Inside homes that were turned into charred rubble that day were the telltale symbols of the protest movement: banners declaring LOYALTY TO THE DECLARATION OF INDEPENDENCE, Israel's equivalent of the constitution. Dekel's grandmother Chana, who also lived in Be'eri, was a member of Women Wage Peace and Road to Recovery. Dekel's stepmother was in a political party representing Arabs and Jews. "We are the most left-wing you can get," she told me.

Be'eri had a special fund that provided financial aid to Gazans who worked on the kibbutz. The gunmen who stormed Israeli military bases and residential communities carried detailed maps that were informed, at least in part, by Gazans with Israeli work permits. Dekel, her grandmother Chana, Avida Bachar, and many thousands of kibbutz residents felt betrayed on October 7—not only by the Palestinians with whom they sought peace, but by their own leaders.[37]

The military and the government had not only ignored clear and repeated warnings from soldiers and security officials, failing to prevent Hamas's onslaught and protect civilians from the massacres that unfolded. Government decisions had also left civilian-operated emergency response teams powerless to defend the kibbutzim. After the supposedly impenetrable high-tech border fence was completed in 2021, the IDF took weapons away from the Gaza border communities' local defense teams to prevent gun theft. Many kibbutzim were left with one or two rifles in all. In villages closest to Gaza, the guns were locked in a vault. By October 7, the number of weapons in all the southern towns, from Ashdod to Eilat, dropped to just 800. Meanwhile, settlements in the West Bank, home to a fraction of the population, were given more weapons. By July 2023, there were at least 2,600 guns in West Bank settlements, according to official statistics. A state comptroller report estimated the figure to be 40 percent higher than that.[38]

In Be'eri, the head of the emergency team was killed almost immediately after the kibbutz was invaded. Without their leader, the team's surviving volunteers could not open the vault where their guns were kept. Some defended the kibbutz unarmed. Among the 11 members of the rapid-response team who fought off militants that day was Shachar Zemach, a 39-year-old peace activist. As a member of Breaking the Silence (see page 9), Shachar had led tours of Hebron for activists and journalists, highlighting the plight of Palestinian residents. After guarding the kibbutz clinic where wounded residents were being cared for, he ran out of ammunition and retreated inside. "Please, I'm not your enemy!" survivors heard Shachar shout in English before he was killed.[39]

The Lucky Ones

"Open! It's the army!"

Twelve hours into her living nightmare, Dekel Shalev refused to open the door. How could she trust that the men pounding on it were not Hebrew-speaking militants, or an Israeli who Hamas was holding at gunpoint?

"Your house is burning," said the soldier at the door. "If you don't come with us now, you will burn to death."

Still wearing her pajamas, covered in her own vomit, Dekel reluctantly emerged. She held Daria in her arms, Oshri held Lenny, and Goni followed the soldiers.

But their nightmare was still not over. In many ways, it had just begun.

Following the soldiers to the home of a friend, they crouched down, shielding themselves and their children from the Molotov cocktails and gunfire that lit up the ground around them, illuminating the dead bodies strewn across their neighbor's yards. They covered their children's eyes as they ran. A shard of glass sliced through Oshri's leg. He didn't notice until an hour later.

In a dark corner out of their view, beneath a row of bushes, lay the bodies of their friends, Rinat and Chen Even, and their 2 eldest sons, curled up in the fetal position. They had all been shot dead. Their 2 younger sons had managed to escape.

Dekel and Oshri's phones had died while they were in their safe room. When they got to their friend's house, they did not know that any other town in Israel had been infiltrated. They inhaled bowls of cornflakes, their first meal of the day. Their phones turned back on, and they began to absorb the greatest catastrophe in Israel's history. Five of Dekel's best friends were now widows. In Lenny's class of 20 children, 5 no longer had fathers. Many of the couple's friends were kidnapped to Gaza. Some of them are still there.

Dekel's house was the only one in her entire neighborhood where no one was murdered. Her mother, father, pregnant sister, and grandparents had all survived. They were the lucky ones.

All told, close to 1,200 men, women, and children were murdered that day—more than in all five years of the Second Intifada. Close to 6,000 more were wounded. Dozens of Israeli Muslims were among those killed, kidnapped, or wounded by the Hamas-led attack. Among them were those who risked their own lives to rescue others, much like the courageous Arabs in Hebron in 1929. One of them was Awad Darawshe, a 23-year-old paramedic who was working at the Nova festival and refused to flee when the attack began. As he bandaged the wounded, Hamas gunmen killed Darawshe, took his ambulance, and drove it to Gaza. "This is what we would expect from him and what we expect from everyone in our family," said Awad's cousin, Mohammad Darawshe, a leader in efforts to bridge the divides between Israel's Arab and Jewish population. "To be human, to stay human, and to die human."[40]

The vast majority of the casualties that day were civilians, including 40 children. The youngest was a newborn, killed fourteen hours after birth. The eldest was 94. Nearly one-third of the dead were slain at the Nova festival. Hamas and its allies kidnapped more than 250 men, women, and children.[41]

No Israeli town suffered more bloodshed than Kibbutz Be'eri, where an estimated 100 people were killed and 30 kidnapped. With 200 of the village's 350 buildings damaged in Hamas's assault, the kibbutz became uninhabitable.[42]

Yet these figures, and the sheer scale of the destruction, were not known in Israel for days. It would take weeks for a full tally of the dead, the abducted, and the unaccounted for. Dozens of bodies were so charred or mutilated that they were unidentifiable for months. After October 7, Israelis lived in a state of suspended animation. Each day brought new pronouncements of death for those who had until then been missing, new revelations of the atrocities, and seemingly endless discoveries of warnings ignored by the government. While many military and security officials have apologized and taken responsibility, as of this writing, Prime Minister Benjamin Netanyahu has yet to do either.

At 9:00 the night of October 7, Dekel, Oshri, and their children were on the move again, running through gunfire to an armored jeep that took them to an open field outside the kibbutz. The smell of smoke and dead bodies was suffocating. Dekel and Oshri laid on the ground with hundreds of traumatized kibbutz survivors, covering their children's bodies with their own. Rockets from Gaza whizzed overhead and sirens rang in their ears. When buses came to shuttle them to safety, one of the buses came under fire from terrorists on the road.

Hotel of the Living Dead

The Shalev family would continue their escape until around 2:00 that morning, when they and the rest of the survivors of Be'eri and other kibbutzim reached a hotel at the Dead Sea. Its location, on a body of water at the lowest point on earth that cannot sustain life, seemed a cruel metaphor for their new existence in a post–October 7 world.

With the outbreak of war that Hamas initiated, some 200,000 Israelis were evacuated from their homes, both in the south, where terrorists remained for days and where rockets rained down for months, and in the north, where the Lebanese terror group Hezbollah fired at Israeli towns in solidarity with Hamas.[43]

On their second day at the hotel, Oshri placed his hand on Dekel's stomach. She had not thought about the new life growing inside her since the morning of October 7, when the tectonic plates of her life shifted. She looked at Oshri. They both knew. This was not a world they wanted to bring another child into. Two days later, under rocket fire from Gaza, Dekel drove to Jerusalem to end her pregnancy.

CHAPTER 29

Hostage Nation

AS THE DEADLIEST DAY THE JEWISH PEOPLE HAVE SUFFERED SINCE the Holocaust, October 7, 2023, will live in the darkest corner of collective Jewish consciousness. Since then, Israelis have lived in freefall, in a world turned upside down. There were no words to describe what they had suffered, no historical comparisons that captured the horror they had endured. Some likened Hamas's attack to 9/11, but even that did not capture the scale of the atrocities. With 1,200 Israelis killed in a country of 9.9 million, this was the equivalent of more than 41,000 Americans killed in one day. In a nation so small, everyone knew someone who had been affected somehow. For Jews around the world, October 7 was painfully personal.[1]

Two of my husband's young cousins were killed on their military bases on October 7. On October 8, I took my daughter to Hebrew school at our synagogue in New York's Hudson Valley. We had, coincidentally, left Israel in July, moving to the United States to be closer to my family. My daughter's Hebrew teacher, Maurice Shnaider, was born in Peru, and had spent much of his life in Israel. He walked into synagogue that morning in tears, explaining that he would not be able to teach the children. "We can't find my sister," he said, shaking. "We think they took her to Gaza. She has Parkinson's. She needs her medicine." Maurice showed me a picture on his phone of his missing sister, Margit, and her husband, Yossi. Then another photo of Margit's daughter, Shiri Bibas, and her 2 red-headed boys, 9-month-old Kfir and 4-year-old Ariel. My 2 children were about the same age. I hugged Maurice, as tears rolled down my cheeks. Grasping for comforting words, all I could summon was silence. Two weeks later,

Margit Shnaider Silberman and Yossi Silberman were declared dead, their bodies discovered in their kibbutz. Their daughter, Shiri; her husband, Yarden; and their sons had all been kidnapped to Gaza.[2]

Part of what made October 7 so viscerally traumatic was the intimacy of the attack. The men, women, and children who lost their lives were not felled by airstrikes or faraway snipers whose faces they could not see. The young and the old were hunted down and shot at point blank. Terrified men, women, and children were paraded through the streets of Gaza before exuberant crowds. The sheer cruelty of the attack was unfathomable, as if transported from a bygone era. The only comparable event was so barbaric it had seemed destined to live on only in the footnotes of history, never to be repeated. But on October 7, history came knocking, surpassing the massacre of 1929 in both scale and scope.

The echoes of 1929 on October 7 were haunting and inescapable. Hamas did not hide its weaponization of Al-Aqsa. It named the attack Al-Aqsa Flood. Even after October 7, Hamas used Al-Aqsa to galvanize support. Hamas declared October 13 "Friday of the Al-Aqsa Flood," calling on Muslims around the world to take to the streets, and on Arabs in Israel to unite at Al-Aqsa "to protect its Islamic character." In February 2024, when the war in Gaza had already claimed more than 30,000 Palestinian lives, displacing more than 1.5 million people from their homes, Hamas used Al-Aqsa in an effort to open new fronts in its war with Israel. On the eve of Ramadan, Hamas leader Ismail Haniyeh called on Palestinians in the West Bank and Arab citizens of Israel to march to Al-Aqsa during the holy month that in previous years had seen violent clashes between worshippers and Israeli forces. Fortunately, the escalation Hamas had hoped for at Al-Aqsa never materialized. In the wake of October 7, Arab Israelis reported a deeper sense of belonging to the state of Israel, and largely ignored Hamas's entreaties. While Itamar Ben-Gvir sought to place tight restrictions on Muslim visits to the Temple Mount, including barring Israeli Arabs from visiting, he was overruled by the prime minister.[3]

Just as the atrocities committed against innocent Jews in Hebron were both justified and denied in 1929, the same was true in 2023. Hamas's attack was not only cheered in the streets of Gaza, but across the West Bank. Crowds of Hamas supporters marched in celebration through the streets of Hebron. Palestinian polls showed widespread support for Al-Aqsa Flood, and a rise in support for Hamas itself. One poll conducted in late November by a Ramallah-based research group found that three-quarters of Palestinians approved of the attack. The same poll found that support for Hamas in the West Bank had tripled since October 7. Surveys by another Palestinian pollster reached similar findings. The opinions of Palestinians living in Gaza and the West Bank stood in stark contrast to those living in Israel. According to one survey of Israel's Arab citizens, 80 percent opposed Hamas's attack. In another, 56 percent agreed that Hamas's actions on October 7 "do not reflect Arab society, the Palestinian people, and the Islamic nation."[4]

In late October, senior Hamas official Ghazi Hamad vowed to repeat the attacks of October 7 "again and again" until Israel is destroyed. "The Al-Aqsa Flood is just the first time, and there will be a second, a third, a fourth," he said on a Lebanese news program. "Does that mean the annihilation of Israel?" the news anchor asked. "Yes, of course," Hamad replied. In a claim that would be echoed by self-described liberal people in months to come, Hamad added, "We are the victims of the occupation. . . . Nobody should blame us for the things we do."[5]

In interviews, many Palestinians, including journalists, denied the widespread accounts of sexual violence and murder of children. They were simply stating what they had been told: In Palestinian media and on the world's largest Arabic news network, Al-Jazeera, Hamas fighters were portrayed as heroic freedom fighters who killed only military targets.[6] On October 9, Basem Naim, the head of International Relations for Hamas, falsely claimed that no civilians were killed on October 7. Accusations of murdered civilians were "Israeli propaganda," Naim asserted on Sky News. Echoing the lies spread by

Arab leaders in 1929, Naim argued that Israel had killed thousands of its own citizens. Palestinian officials repeated those claims, refuting accounts of rape and other atrocities as "lies spread by Israel," as one Palestinian diplomat put it. Not a single Palestinian official condemned the horrors of October 7. The Palestinian Authority, seen by Western governments as the most viable replacement for Hamas in Gaza, insisted that Israel fabricated Hamas atrocities to justify a "genocide" in Gaza.[7]

As a journalist writing about October 7, I experienced the direct impact of these false claims. One editor I was working with on a story about Israeli hostages two weeks after October 7 objected to my reference to Hamas atrocities. Those "reports," she wrote, were "laying the ground" for Israel to "exterminate the Palestinians." One of her edits to my text described Hamas's attack as "stunning." She ultimately decided to kill my story.

Just as the victims in Hebron in 1929 were not Zionists, the victims of October 7 were not settlers. And yet, just as they were then, the victims were blamed. In 1929, Israel did not exist, nor did the occupation or the settlements. Back then, the supposed cause of the massacre was Jewish immigration and the peaceful demonstration of Jews at the Western Wall. By October 7, 2023, it was clear to anyone interested in truth that the cause of both massacres was an age-old hatred that had simply found new justification. As the writer Bari Weiss would observe months later, Jews around the world now understood that our brief vacation from unbridled anti-Semitism had ended.[8]

Demonstrators in cities around the world were already accusing the Jewish state of committing genocide in October. A letter cosigned by 33 Harvard student groups on October 7 held "the Israeli regime entirely responsible for all unfolding violence." On October 8, the national wing of Students for Justice in Palestine called Hamas's attack "a historic win for the Palestinian resistance." In an article published that day, Joseph Massad, a professor of Arab politics and intellectual history at Columbia University, my alma mater, called the massacre "awesome," "incredible," and a "stunning victory of the Palestinian resistance." Massad described the peaceful kibbutzim near the Gaza border as "settler-colonies." A week later, Russel Rickford, a professor of history at Cornell, called October 7 "exhilarating." Anyone who did not feel the same, he said, "would not be human." As of this writing, Massad and Rickford are still employed at Columbia and Cornell. They are just two examples of many. In cities across North America, students who sought to call attention to the plight of the hostages were assaulted. Posters bearing the faces of Israeli women, children, and toddlers held captive in Gaza were torn down or defaced.[9]

Jews around the world, but particularly the families of hostages, suffered another layer of shock as supposedly peace-seeking protesters called not for Hamas to release innocent men, women, and children, but for Israel to end its war against the Islamist terrorist organization that had deliberately sparked that war. In January 2024, senior Hamas official Khaled Mashal said that American and European students chanting "From the River to the Sea, Palestine will be free" was proof of global support for Hamas's goal of eradicating Israel. Calls to globalize the Intifada and praise for Hamas at protests on college campuses across the United States made Jewish students fear for their safety, and Jews around the world feel as if we had entered an alternate universe. How, so many, including myself, wondered, could liberal students and faculty support a militant Islamist organization that has outlawed homosexuality, subjugated women's rights, and both explicitly and violently opposed peace for decades?[10]

In another theater of the absurd, South Africa accused Israel of genocide at the International Court of Justice. South Africa was not a neutral bystander. Its government had long maintained friendly relations with Hamas, an internationally recognized terrorist organization. Ten days after October 7, South Africa's foreign minister called Hamas leader Ismail Haniyeh to express her country's "solidarity and support" for the Palestinian people, and "sadness and regret for the loss of innocent lives on both sides." Weeks before the trial at the Hague began, South Africa's government hosted a delegation of Hamas leaders, including Basem Naim, the Hamas official who claimed that no civilians were killed on October 7.[11]

In his opening statement at the ICJ on December 29, Israeli legal adviser Tal Becker elucidated the irony and hypocrisy of South Africa's case against Israel. The term genocide, Becker noted, was coined by Raphael Lemkin, a Polish Jew who had witnessed the horrors of the Holocaust. "The existing legal lexicon was simply inadequate to capture the devasting evil that the Nazi Holocaust unleashed," said Becker. Now the term was being weaponized against the world's only Jewish state to end a war of self-defense that it had neither started nor wanted, yet had to fight to protect its citizens from the future massacres that Hamas promised to execute. "If there have been acts that may be characterized as genocidal," said Becker, "then they have been perpetrated against Israel. If there is a concern about the obligations of States under the Genocide Convention, then it is in relation to their responsibilities to act against Hamas's proudly declared agenda of annihilation, which is not a secret, and is not in doubt."[12]

Every Day Is October 7

In 1929, the denials of the atrocities in Hebron were called out by leading newspapers for what they were: lies. But in the post-factual world of 2023, in a war clouded by misinformation and disinformation, many people did not know who or what to believe. That confusion was fueled by the traditional arbiters of truth—news organizations that recycled Hamas claims while presenting Israeli statements as unverified.

When a blast erupted outside Gaza's al-Ahli Hospital on October 17, the Hamas-controlled Gaza Health Ministry immediately reported that an Israeli airstrike had killed nearly 500 people and injured more than 300 others. Despite this suspicious, impossible ability to count hundreds of dead bodies in minutes, and the lack of

evidence of an airstrike—the building was not damaged—news organizations around the world parroted the claims. "Israeli Strike Kills
Hundreds in Hospital, Palestinians Say," read the headline at the top
of the *New York Times* homepage, above a photo of an entirely different destroyed building in another part of Gaza. Israeli officials
immediately denied striking the hospital. The blast had been caused,
they said, by a rocket fired by Islamic Jihad from a cemetery behind
the hospital. That rocket had fallen short and landed in the hospital's parking lot. Israeli officials noted that in the ten days prior to the
blast at the hospital, roughly 450 rockets fired from Gaza had landed
inside Gaza. In previous wars with Hamas and Islamic Jihad, as many
as one-third of their rockets had misfired.

On October 23, the *New York Times* published an Editor's Note
on page 15, admitting it had "relied too heavily on claims by Hamas."
The paper's initial reporting "left readers with an incorrect impression
about what was known and how credible the account was." The *New
York Times* was not the only respected news organization to parrot
Hamas's claims. NPR, Reuters, CNN, the BBC, and nearly every other
major news outlet had carried similar headlines and news reports
accusing Israel of bombing the hospital.[13]

In late November, an investigation by Human Rights Watch—a
frequent critic of Israel—confirmed Israel's claims, including that the
death toll was far lower than initially reported. But the damage had
already been done. The outrage had led Jordan to cancel a summit
between President Biden and Palestinian and Egyptian leaders, and
fueled anti-Semitic attacks in Europe, and riots across the Middle East.[14]

Despite this massive error, and the lessons that should have been
learned from it, similar journalistic failures characterized war coverage in the months that followed. When Israeli forces entered Gaza's
Shifa Hospital on November 14 to rout out militants who were operating there, many news organizations framed the military raid as an
unwarranted attack on a medical facility. This would of course be
a war crime, had Hamas and other groups not committed the war

crime of turning a hospital into a military base. After Israel withdrew its forces from Northern Gaza in February 2024, hundreds of militants returned to al-Shifa Hospital. When Israel raided the hospital again in March 2024, killing dozens of Hamas fighters and arresting hundreds more, the crisis was again depicted as unwarranted Israeli aggression. In news reports, from NPR, the *New York Times*, CNN, and many others, the presence of militants in the hospital was barely mentioned. When they were mentioned, the arrested militants were framed as men who "Israel claims" were "terrorists"—wording seemingly designed to shed doubt on those claims. Yet the presence of militants at Shifa was confirmed by patients, widely available video evidence, and Hamas itself, which acknowledged its "martyred" warriors. Similar cases of media failure emerged throughout the war at other Gaza hospitals used by Hamas and Islamic Jihad, along with mosques, residential buildings, schools, and kindergartens. When militants' use of civilian infrastructure was mentioned, it was almost always framed as "Israeli claims," including Hamas tunnels and weapons discovered at Shifa and other hospitals.[15]

News organizations also diligently repeated Hamas claims that most of the people killed in Gaza were innocent women and children. All civilian deaths in war are a tragedy, but several facts undermined the narrative of most war coverage: Gaza's health ministry is an arm of Hamas, the same group that deliberately embeds itself among civilians. According to Israeli and American military assessments, nearly half the casualties in Gaza were combatants. That fact was rarely mentioned in news reports, leading millions of people to think that Israel was committing genocide. In fact, according to various military experts, Israel was doing everything in its power to mitigate civilian casualties. Despite Hamas's tactic of wearing civilian clothing and fighting from civilian infrastructure, the ratio of civilian to combatant deaths in Gaza was lower than any war in the history of modern urban warfare.[16]

For many Israelis and Jews in the Diaspora, just as painful as the attack itself was the silence of so many human rights organizations in the face of Hamas's atrocities. Israeli women felt especially neglected by the international community, which seemed to be saying that women should always be believed, unless they are Israeli. For nearly two months after October 7, there was no mention or condemnation from the United Nations of Hamas's use of sexual violence. In the weeks after October 7, UN Women, the women's rights agency of the United Nations, issued more than a dozen statements and press releases concerning the plight of Palestinian women and girls. Yet only on November 27 did UN Women publish its first social media post condemning Hamas's attack. Within hours, that post was deleted. It was not until December that UN Women issued its first statement concerning sexual violence on October 7. "We thought we had made so much progress," said Miriam Schler, director of the Tel Aviv Crisis Center for Sexual Assault, whose organization collected testimonies of Hamas's sexual violence. "We didn't think we need to provide such graphic details to be believed. It's another form of abuse," she told the Israeli news channel i24. At protests outside UN headquarters in New York, demonstrators chanted, "Me too, unless you're a Jew."[17]

Even after the United Nations published a report in March that found "reasonable grounds to believe that conflict-related sexual violence—including rape and gang rape—occurred across multiple locations of Israel," Reem Alsalem, the UN's Special Rapporteur on violence against women and girls, continued to deny Hamas's use of rape. Instead, Alsalem coauthored a salacious report featuring lurid claims of sexual abuse by Israeli soldiers and kidnapping of Palestinian babies, citing no sources. She repeated those unsubstantiated claims on international media, telling journalists she could not disclose the sources of her information. In one interview, she said she was unaware of rocket attacks against Israel by Hamas and Hezbollah.[18]

The horrors of October 7 did not end that day. Months later, gruesome stories were emerging daily. An Israeli father, David Tahar, was told that his son, Adir, was missing. Weeks later, first responders identified Adir's body. When David received it for burial, he was warned not to look, but he did, and found that Adir, 19, had been beheaded. David spent the next two months searching for his son's head. It was discovered by the IDF in January, in an ice cream shop in Gaza, through information gleaned from an interrogation. A captured Hamas operative confessed to trying to sell Adir's head for $10,000. According to interrogations of other militants, Hamas had promised that amount for every Israeli brought to Gaza.

Then came the revelation that UN employees in Gaza had participated in the abduction of several hostages. In one intercepted phone call, an UNRWA teacher was heard boasting to a friend that he was in Israel, with the *sabaya*—the sex slaves.[19]

In this endless cascade of horror stories, with hostages still in Gaza, and many in the international community unthinkably sympathizing with Hamas, many Israelis felt—and still feel—as if October 7 never ended.

Once, Twice, Forever Abandoned

Israel's fundamental purpose was to be the one place in the world where Jews would be free from persecution. That existential identity was shattered on October 7. Dekel Shalev's grandfather, who survived October 7, had also survived the Holocaust in a ghetto in Hungary. After cowering in a safe room with his son and grandson on October 7, 88-year-old Chaim Raanan said he felt he had lived through a second Holocaust. He had never imagined that Jews would be hunted down in Israel. Raanan has barely stopped crying since that day. "I ask myself, which number is worse? Six million or 107?" he said, referring to the number of dead in Be'eri. "For me, 107 is worse. Because those 107, I felt them with my flesh. The 6 million, I only learned about them years later when I grew up."

In 1929, Jews in Palestine were neglected by the British, whose failure to protect them led to the transformation of Zionism. In 2023, the betrayal was both more shocking and more painful, as Israel's own government had failed in its most essential duty. The trauma of that failure will take years, if not generations, to overcome.

"We were completely abandoned," Dekel told me when we spoke in December, echoing the sentiment of hundreds of thousands of Israelis. Netanyahu, Ben-Gvir, and other right-wing politicians had for years derided left-wing Israelis as traitors. Most of the residents of Gaza border towns who lost their homes and loved ones were left-wing Israelis. Today they feel a stinging sense of betrayal.

"We're the traitors?" asked Sofie Berzon MacKie, an artist and mother of 3 from Kibbutz Be'eri. "They left us to die. They're the traitors," she cried on Israel's Channel 12. "The blood of all the children is on their hands."

The scale of the government's failure to prevent or respond to the worst attack in Israel's history is almost beyond comprehension. The government, most notably Prime Minister Netanyahu, did not just ignore the warnings that Hamas was planning an attack, that Israel was more vulnerable than ever, and that the judicial overhaul was causing dangerous divisions in Israeli society that threatened national security. If that was not enough, according to news reports, Netanyahu also worked to strengthen Hamas for more than a decade, allowing and even encouraging Qatar to prop up Hamas with billions of dollars. Those cash payments, Netanyahu believed, could buy quiet and order. Netanyahu and his nationalist allies viewed Hamas as a key to staving off the emergence of a Palestinian state, maintaining the paralyzing rift in Palestinian leadership that divided Gaza from the Fatah-controlled West Bank. Bezalel Smotrich, the far-right finance minister who now oversees settlements in the West Bank, explained that outlook plainly in 2015. "The Palestinian Authority is a burden," Smotrich said on an Israeli news program, referring to the PA's legitimacy and its ability to lead to a Palestinian state. "Hamas is an asset."[20]

Netanyahu was warned that allowing Qatar to finance Hamas would lead to catastrophe. Former defense minister Avigdor Lieberman, himself a former right-wing ally of Netanyahu, resigned in 2018 in protest of those payments. At the time, Lieberman accused Netanyahu of "buying short-term peace at the price of serious damage to long-term national security." Speaking to the *New York Times* in November 2023, Lieberman called October 7 a direct result of those policies. "For Netanyahu, there is only one thing that is really important," he said. "To be in power at any cost."[21]

Bring Them Home

As weeks passed and their loved ones remained in captivity, the families of the hostages felt their government had not only abandoned them on October 7, but was now forsaking them in Gaza. "You cannot make war at the expense of children and babies," cried Hadas Calderon, whose 12-year-old son, Erez, and 16-year-old daughter, Sahar, were being held hostage. "Time is critical!" she said. "We have a very small window of opportunity now and we must use it."

It was October 19, and Calderon was speaking at a Tel Aviv press conference organized by the newly formed Hostages and Missing Families Forum, a group comprised of thousands of family members and volunteers supporting them. Many felt neglected by their government.

Before Prime Minister Netanyahu met with families of hostages for the first time on October 16, American officials at the highest levels had already met with them. On October 12, US secretary of state Antony Blinken met with families in Tel Aviv. On October 13, President Joe Biden met with them at the White House. Those who met with leaders of both governments said they received more empathy from the White House than from their own government.

The emotional speech Biden delivered from the White House on October 10 was more heartfelt and more compassionate than any speech Netanyahu has delivered to his own nation since October 7.[22]

"This attack has brought to the surface painful memories and the scars left by millennia of anti-Semitism and genocide of the Jewish people," said President Biden, pledging to stand with Israel against Hamas. "A lot of us know how it feels," he said of the grieving families. "It leaves a black hole in your chest when you lose family, feeling like you're being sucked in. The anger, the pain, the sense of hopelessness. This is what they mean by a 'human tragedy'—an atrocity on an appalling scale."[23]

Netanyahu, who rose to prominence after his brother Yoni was killed in the hostage rescue operation at Entebbe in 1976, and who is known for his oratory skills, had a simpler message for his people. In a brief televised address to his country on the most difficult day in its history, Netanyahu said coldly, "We are at war and we will win it."[24]

As their military retaliated for the most painful attack in its history, families of the hostages found themselves at the center of a moral crisis. Like most Israelis, they wanted their leaders to destroy Hamas, which had until then been allowed to thrive in their backyard. They recognized that October 7 had changed everything, and that the mistakes of the past—releasing thousands of terrorists, tolerating Hamas in Israel's backyard—had all led to this moment. But as Israel worked to eradicate Hamas, flattening entire neighborhoods in the process, many feared the hostages could become collateral damage. Hamas had long used Palestinian civilians as human shields. Now, Israelis feared their own family members had become human shields.[25]

"The world needs to help us get out all the innocent civilians from Gaza and destroy Hamas once and for all," said Maayan Zin, the mother of Ella and Dafna Elyakim, who were taken to Gaza after witnessing the murder of their father, stepmother, and stepbrother. Maayan could not understand how the world could possibly be calling for a ceasefire after what Hamas had done. "We are always agreeing to ceasefires," she said, struggling to speak through her tears. It was late October, and her daughters were still in Gaza. "We are treating Hamas as people," said Maayan. "They are not people. They planned this abuse of women and children. Enough. The world needs to help us get rid of them."

Maayan did not want any innocent Gazans to suffer. The international community, she said, should get all the civilians out of Gaza, so that the Israeli military could focus on fighting Hamas. "We need the world to help us with this," she told me. "We can't be fighting in the north, south, and taking care of Gaza's innocent people."

Many Israelis and Palestinians had hoped that Egypt would offer shelter to Gazans fleeing the war. Yet Egypt quickly sealed its border with Gaza in October, placing concrete blocks at its border crossing. Claiming to be acting in Gazans' interest to prevent their forced displacement, Egyptian president Abdel Fattah el-Sisi explained that leaving Gaza would mean "an end to this cause of all causes." The people of Gaza, he said, must "remain steadfast and present on their land." Jordanian king Abdullah II echoed those sentiments. Apparently Arab leaders believed that Gazans preferred to die than to obtain refuge in an allied nation until the war ended. And yet, in the weeks that followed Sisi's statement, thousands of upper-class Gazans—including government officials, professors, Palestinians with foreign citizenship, and less fortunate residents who crowdfunded their escape—received refuge in Egypt. They did so only after paying as much as $10,000 per person to Egyptian authorities, a bribery scheme confirmed by numerous media outlets, including *The Guardian* and Al Jazeera.[26]

Better Than Their Leaders

On October 7, the divisions that threatened to engulf Israel in civil war one day earlier melted away. In the first week, 360,000 reservists reported for duty, with thousands flying in from abroad. In an instant, Brothers in Arms morphed from a vast protest movement to a herculean civil assistance effort. With the government and the army caught off guard, members of the group drove to the besieged border towns to battle terrorists, rescue panicked residents, and help them find shelter. The organization, since renamed Brothers and Sisters in

Arms, established a massive hub in Tel Aviv, managing the collection and delivery of thousands of tons of donated clothing, toiletries, toys, medical supplies, and other needs for the country's 250,000 displaced residents. They organized meals for soldiers, helped businesses whose owners were on reserve duty, and set up hundreds of hotel-based kindergartens and activities for uprooted children. Within six months, the group raised $36 million. They weren't the only ones. With the government paralyzed, Israeli civilians filled the vacuum. In the first two weeks of the war, nearly half the population—Jews and Muslims alike—volunteered in some way, providing care for traumatized children, tending to neglected farms near the Gaza border, and raising funds for soldiers and evacuees.[27]

While the trauma of October 7 briefly unified Israel, the rifts of October 6 were just beneath the surface. Netanyahu's conduct after the war revived them. While other members of his government, including Finance Minister Smotrich, took responsibility for the failures that led to October 7, Netanyahu, who had led the country for thirteen of the previous fourteen years, did not. Instead, the man who for years campaigned as Mr. Security placed the blame on the security establishment. "At no stage was Prime Minister Netanyahu warned of Hamas's war intentions," he posted in a since-deleted tweet. "On the contrary, all the security officials," Netanyahu continued, "assessed that Hamas had been deterred and was looking for a settlement." By then, the IDF chief of staff Herzi Halevi, Shin Bet chief Ronen Bar, and the head of military intelligence, Aharon Haliva, had all taken responsibility for failing to prevent the attack. Haliva later became the first high-level government or military official to resign over those failings. Netanyahu, meanwhile, made clear he had no plans to resign or apologize. Such issues, he has maintained, would be investigated after the war. Polls showed that between 75 to 85 percent of Israelis wanted him to resign. Knowing that elections would not be held in wartime, Netanyahu told local officials in January 2024 that the war would likely continue through 2025.[28]

Netanyahu's Hostages

On October 15, the seeds of a new anti-government protest were planted when a grief-stricken father camped himself outside IDF headquarters in Tel Aviv. Sitting quietly on a folding chair with coffee and his dog, Avihai Brodutch held a small handwritten cardboard sign. MY FAMILY IS IN GAZA, it said. Brodutch, whose wife and 3 young children were kidnapped along with their orphaned 3-year-old neighbor, vowed to stay there until all the hostages returned. Hours later, hundreds had joined him. Within weeks, thousands were demonstrating on the streets of Tel Aviv and Jerusalem for their return.

Many of the hostages' families felt the government had mistaken its priorities. While the goals of the war were to eliminate Hamas and free the hostages, they believed the hostages had to come first if they were to come home alive. "We have the rest of our lives to fight Hamas," said Maurice, the uncle of Shiri Bibas, who was sitting shiva for his sister, Shiri's mother. "The hostages have no time."

Finally, in late November, Israel and Hamas reached an agreement. In exchange for a ceasefire and Israel's release of 240 Palestinian prisoners, Hamas released 105 hostages. While their release brought tremendous relief to their families, their joy was fleeting. The husbands and fathers of many of the women and children who were freed remained in Gaza, along with more than a dozen young women. While all the abducted children were released in November—including Maayan's daughters, Ella and Dafna, 2 children remained in Gaza: Kfir and Ariel Bibas. Hamas claimed the boys and their mother had been killed in an Israeli airstrike. Israeli officials said that fact could not be confirmed. Hamas had played this game before, stating that 1 elderly hostage had been killed, only to release her during the ceasefire. For the Bibas family, the uncertainty was unbearable. Yarden Bibas, separated from his wife and children, was forced by Hamas to film a heartbreaking propaganda video, blaming Israel for their death. If he was alive, Kfir Bibas would have marked his first birthday in

Gaza. Abducted at the age of 9 months, he has spent most of his life in captivity.[29]

When Hamas announced that Shiri and her boys had been killed, Maurice said, "I was sad, but there was also a feeling of relief. I thought I could finally turn the page, live my life again, be there for my wife again. But the army wouldn't confirm it. We don't know if they are dead or alive. It is this not knowing that keeps us in agony. . . . I want to start a new book, but I am stuck on that last page." The families of more than 120 hostages who remained in Gaza felt a similar agony. Not knowing if their loved ones were dead or alive, they tried not to imagine what they were enduring in captivity.

While Hamas claimed to have treated the hostages with humanity, released hostages told a different story. Children were beaten and forced to watch horrific videos from October 7. Adults and children alike were fed so little that many lost ten to thirty pounds. Children and toddlers were threatened at gunpoint when they cried. Emily Hand, kidnapped when she was 8, could barely speak above a whisper in her first few weeks home, and could only sleep beside her father. Having lost her biological mother when she was 2, Emily discovered upon her release that her stepmother had been killed on October 7. Several captives reported being kidnapped or held in the homes of UNRWA staffers. Others were held in cages and subterranean tunnels with little oxygen.[30]

In 2021, Yahya Sinwar boasted that Hamas had built 500 kilometers (310 miles) of underground tunnels in Gaza. During Israel's ground operation, the first since 2014, Israel discovered these claims were true. While Hamas had managed to build a tunnel network that is roughly half the length of the New York City subway system—despite the blockade of Gaza—they never bothered to build bomb shelters for civilians caught in the wars they started. The material Hamas used to construct tunnels could have also built much-needed water treatment plants. Even before October 7, water contamination was the cause of 12 percent of child deaths in Gaza, and more than 25 percent of all illnesses. While 70 percent of Gazans were dependent on international aid before October 7, Hamas leaders amassed vast wealth, with several reported to be worth millions of dollars.[31]

When Sinwar and other leaders of Hamas planned October 7, they expected a crushing response from Israel. They did not care that thousands of innocent Gazans would die, and said so openly. In his interview on Lebanese TV in late October, Hamas official Ghazi Hamad said, "We are called a nation of martyrs, and we are proud to sacrifice martyrs." Asked about the rising death toll in Gaza, Khaled Mashal told another journalist, "In all wars, there are some civilian victims. We are not responsible for them." Another senior Hamas official, Moussa Abu Marzouk, told Russian TV that the tunnels were built to protect Hamas fighters. As for Palestinian civilians, he said, it was the obligation of Israel and the UN to protect them. None of these leaders were willing to pay the price themselves. Weeks before October 7, Ghazi Hamad left Gaza for Lebanon. Hamas's political leaders, including Ismail Haniyeh and Khaled Mashal, have lived in Qatar, whose government funds Al-Jazeera, for years. Sinwar, Hamas's military leader, has spent the war deep underground, reportedly surrounded by Israeli hostages.[32]

At first, few of the released hostages spoke publicly of their physical abuse. With more than 130 still held hostage, and the expectation of another ceasefire agreement soon, they did not want to endanger those left behind, or cause more pain to those whose loved ones were still being tortured in Gaza. But as months passed, and hostage negotiations faltered, that silence was broken. Several women spoke of witnessing or enduring sexual assault at gunpoint and being tortured and beaten by their captors. Others reported that both male and female hostages still in Gaza had been sexually abused.[33]

At a Knesset hearing in which hostages shared their testimony, the daughter of released hostage Aviva Siegel could not contain her anger. "Right now there is someone being raped in a tunnel in Gaza!" Shir Siegel shouted in exasperation. "Where are the really important people?" she asked, outraged that no cabinet ministers were at the hearing. The same had been true for other hearings devoted to the hostages. Shir's father remains in Gaza.[34]

As Passover approached in April, hostage negotiations were still ongoing, with no breakthrough in sight. While Netanyahu and other Israeli officials blamed Hamas for the lack of progress, many Israelis perceived their own leader as the greatest obstacle to an agreement. The weekly anti-government rallies that were a mainstay in Tel Aviv and Jerusalem before the war returned. The prime minister, protesters believed, was holding up a hostage deal for political reasons. Many protesters called for elections to replace Netanyahu and his government, which had overseen the worst failure in Israel's history, and was now overseeing a war that had still not accomplished its goal of defeating Hamas. At some of these demonstrations, family members of hostages were treated with brutality by the police force overseen by Itamar Ben-Gvir. Netanyahu, members of his government, and many Israelis opposed ending the war and releasing hundreds of Hamas members from prison. These were among the conditions Hamas had insisted upon for months. At a demonstration outside IDF headquarters in Tel Aviv on April 13, the Hostages and Missing Families Forum issued a desperate plea.

"If getting our loved ones back alive means ending the war, agree to it now!" they said. "Bring them home now. Take care of the threats in Gaza after." Netanyahu, the organization stated, "is responsible for the release of the captives. Because of him, women are raped, men are tortured, and abductees are murdered." Protesters were referring to what was now the fulfillment of many family members' fears. As the war dragged on, hostages in Gaza were murdered by Hamas, and tragically killed by Israeli forces who mistook them for militants. Among those who were killed in captivity was Chaim Peri, the peace activist from Kibbutz Nir Oz. Ministers Ben-Gvir and Smotrich had repeatedly threatened to bring down Netanyahu's fragile government if he agreed to end the war. Many believed the prospect of his government falling apart—which would prompt new elections—was preventing Netanyahu not only from agreeing to a ceasefire and hostage deal, but to formulating a "day after" plan for who would rule Gaza after the war. Smotrich and Ben-Gvir openly expressed the goal of resettling Gaza—a policy opposed by a majority of Israelis, but favored by many in places like the Jewish community of Hebron.

With the hostages still in Gaza more than six months after their abduction, many Israelis felt the entire country was being held hostage, not only by Hamas, but by Netanyahu and his far-right government.

The Limits of Compassion

In the shadow of the war in Gaza, tensions in the West Bank soared. On October 7, curfews were enforced in Palestinian towns and cities, new travel restrictions were introduced, and hundreds of suspected militants were detained. In the immediate aftermath of Hamas's massacre, National Security Minister Ben-Gvir announced the purchase of 10,000 assault rifles to arm civilian security teams. He would soon begin distributing those weapons in West Bank settlements and Israeli towns. In March 2024, he celebrated the approval of 100,000 new gun licenses since October 7, declaring, "weapons save lives."[35]

With the world's focus on Gaza, vigilante attacks by settlers became rampant. When Israelis were killed in terror attacks, groups of young settlers responded by setting fire to Palestinian homes and cars. By March, 9 Palestinians had been killed by armed settlers in the West Bank. By March 2024, more than 1,000 Palestinians from 19 herding communities had been displaced by settler violence and threats. According to the Israeli monitoring group Kerem Navot, settlers seized more than 37,000 acres of land from Palestinians in the West Bank in the months after October 7.[36]

In the past, violent attacks by settlers were widely condemned by mainstream Israeli society. When settlers rampaged through the Palestinian town of Hawara in February 2023, setting fire to homes and cars, Israelis from across the political spectrum denounced the attack as a "pogrom." In the aftermath of October 7, the violence on the West Bank was of little concern to most Israelis. Even the suffering in Gaza was rarely discussed in the Israeli media. The images of Palestinians pulling bodies from the rubble of buildings in Gaza and burying children—the images that shocked the world and led to global condemnation of Israel's conduct during the war—were barely visible in Israeli news coverage, which focused on Israeli suffering. There was no longer room for Palestinian suffering.

It is now difficult for even left-wing Israelis to access compassion for Palestinians. For those who suffered the attacks directly, the trauma was too raw. For those who had not experienced the attacks first-hand, the images of Palestinians cheering the atrocities and crowding around the hostages in Gaza were forever seared into their minds. When the hostage Mia Schem was interviewed after her release and spoke of being held captive in the home of a family, she told her interviewer, "There are no innocents in Gaza." That was the feeling of many Israelis after October 7.[37]

Until that day, Dekel Shalev told me, "I had sympathy for the people of Gaza, and the children who were born there. Now I have no sympathy. They supported it, they cheered it," she said. She noted how, despite the catastrophic consequences of Hamas's attack on the people of Gaza, polls showed steady support for the attack and for Hamas.[38] "Their children are educated on this hatred for Jews," Dekel lamented. Before October 7, Dekel's grandmother was an ardent peace activist, volunteering with Road to Recovery and Women Wage Peace. Those days are over, said Dekel.

When President Biden and Secretary Blinken pressed Israel to agree to a path to a two-state solution in January, many Israelis were stunned. Israeli president Isaac Herzog, no right-wing nationalist, responded to the renewed push for a two-state solution by saying, "Nobody in his right mind is willing" to think about that. What concerned Israelis now, Herzog said, was that they "will not be attacked in the same way from north or south or east."[39] If withdrawing from Gaza had led to the rise of a terror state whose leaders were now even more popular in the West Bank than they were in Gaza, how could Israelis consider repeating the same process in the West Bank, whose far longer borders with Israel would place millions more Israelis at risk?

In a world that seems indifferent to Israeli suffering, many Israelis have experienced a drastic shift rightward. Avida Bachar, like many kibbutz residents, considered himself left-leaning before October 7. He supported easing Israeli restrictions on Gaza and allowing more Gazans to work in Israel. "I thought if they have hope for peace, they will just want to live in peace," he told me. We spoke several weeks after the funeral of his wife and son, who was laid to rest with his surfboard. Avida, who also lost a leg on October 7, believes he and millions of others dangerously misunderstood this conflict. "Radical Islam has no place in this world," he said. "It's us or them."

It struck me that not just Avida, but so many formerly left-wing Israelis, were now sounding a lot like settlers from Hebron. In waging the deadliest attack in Israeli history, Sinwar's alleged goal was to scuttle an imminent peace agreement between Saudi Arabia and Israel, and to bring the Palestinian cause to the forefront of global attention. Some analysts believed it was also meant to galvanize Palestinian support in the wake of anti-Hamas protests in Gaza in the summer of 2023. All those targets were met. Yet seeing this rightward shift in Israeli society, and knowing how much Sinwar had studied the Israeli psyche, I wondered, was this stifling of Israelis' compassion also one of his goals?[40]

Much like every other explosion of violence Hamas has initiated, the suffering of Palestinians has only worsened since October 7. In Hebron, Tayseer Abu Aisheh's "cage house" has taken on new meaning. He and his family have barely left their home since Hamas's massacre. Traveling between H1 and H2, already challenging, is now often impossible. With his shop located over the checkpoint in H1, Tayseer has barely worked a day since October 7. His son, Haitham, has not been able to attend school, which is also in H1. Like many Palestinians in Hebron, Tayseer's family is suffering an acute loss of income. With restrictions on who can and cannot visit them, they have not seen their family members who live in H1.

Meanwhile, settlers in Hebron say that Israel should retake control of Gaza, rebuild the settlements, and facilitate what they refer to as the "voluntary" transfer of Palestinians to other countries, such as Egypt, Turkey, and Qatar.

The End of Refuge

Almost immediately after their arrival at the hotel for evacuees at the Dead Sea, Dekel Shalev and her husband decided that they had to leave Israel. The choice was both obvious and heartbreaking. Dekel had lived her entire life in Kibbutz Be'eri. Her husband had also grown up in the area known as the Gaza Envelope. They had never wished to live anywhere else.

"Be'eri was paradise," said Dekel.

But after October 7, living in Israel meant reliving the trauma of October 7 every day. The rockets from Gaza would not cease, the horror stories from that day would never fade, and the faces of the hostages were plastered across the country. Dekel could no longer hear Arabic without feeling shivers of fear course through her body. A simple knock at the door made her heart pound. "I never thought for a moment I would leave Israel, but my world has been turned upside down," she told me. "I don't think my children can live a safe life in Israel."

Through her Hungarian grandfather, Dekel and her children have European passports. Deliberating where they could move, she and her husband first considered Europe. Then, just days after Hamas's rampage, she saw videos on Facebook of pro-Hamas rallies in Europe, and news of Jewish schools being forced to close. When her father's cousin offered to house them in Denver, Colorado, Dekel asked him, "How safe is it for Jews?"

That was once a straightforward question. But in the aftermath of October 7, anti-Semitic attacks in the United States rose by nearly 400 percent. While Jews account for 2 percent of the American population, they are the targets of 60 percent of religious-based hate crimes. According to FBI figures, Jews are the victims of six times the number of attacks compared to Muslims in America.[41]

Nevertheless, three weeks after the morning that forever changed her life and the lives of millions of Israelis and Palestinians, Dekel, her husband, and their 3 children were on a plane to Denver. She feels relatively safe in her new home, she said, but is careful not to appear outwardly Jewish. She often worries who will hear her children speaking Hebrew. In public spaces like supermarkets, Dekel tells them to speak quietly. The armed guards outside the local Jewish community center only make her feel less safe, as if under siege.

"It seems I will never feel safe in this world," she said. "But I hope that my children will."

Avida Bachar now lives in a hotel on the Dead Sea, but he plans to return to Be'eri. Two of his 3 surviving children already have. "We will rebuild it all," he told me. "This is where I was born, this is where I will live, and we will always work to make it even better."

CHAPTER 30

To the Grave

JILL NOTOWICH LOOKED OUT HER WINDOW, MESMERIZED BY THE lush vineyards and rocky hillsides rolling past her bulletproof bus through the winding roads of the West Bank. She could not wait to see, for the first time in her life, the city her uncle David had loved so dearly. It was the summer of 2011, and the entire Shainberg family was in Israel to celebrate the bat mitzvah of Jill's daughter, Deena, one of many family members who is named after David. Most of the Shainberg family had never been to Hebron. Now they were going to visit the grave of the late uncle they had never known.

"This is the story of a young man who followed his heart and pursued his dream," Jill's cousin, Cindy Shainberg, said over the tour bus microphone. Jill's mother, Suzie, had just discovered David's letters two years earlier. Jill wondered if Hebron was still as beautiful as David had described. "Sadly, the terrible events of 1929 still hang over Hebron, and the fear that triggered it lives on," Cindy said as they pulled into Hebron.

The bus parked just outside the Tomb of the Patriarchs and Matriarchs, and Jill stepped off, along with her mother and father; her husband, Scott, and their three children; Jill's brother and sister-in-law; and her nieces, nephews, and cousins. Jill took a deep breath and looked around, understanding almost instantly that everything had changed since David lived there.

The panoramic views were marred by barbed wire. The ancient stone homes were falling apart. The peaceful serenity had been replaced by soldiers, machine guns, guard posts, and checkpoints. The Hebron before her bared no resemblance to the elegant portrait of the city David had painted for his family. As they walked solemnly to the cemetery with their armed tour guide, Jill noticed a young Jewish boy watching them from the side of the road. He looked about 8 years old. In his hand was a toy gun, which he lifted and aimed at them, pretending to shoot. Is he afraid, Jill thought to herself, or is he simply doing what he sees all around him? Her heart ached for that little boy. She would never forget him.

Reciting the Mourner's Kaddish at David's grave was one of the most powerful experiences of Jill's life. As she stood there, she wondered, what would David think of Hebron today? She was not sure. But surely, she thought, it would pain him that a century after his death, his family needed a bulletproof bus and an armed guard to simply visit Hebron.[1]

Between Memphis and Hebron

During Jill's decade-long journey to learn more about her Uncle David and the massacre that took his life, she befriended an unlikely ally in Memphis: Waheed AlQawasmi, a Palestinian-Jordanian immigrant who shared her visceral connection to the Hebron massacre.

Waheed is a 37-year-old Emmy Award–winning filmmaker who emigrated to Memphis when he was 13. Born and raised in Jordan, his father's side of the family was originally from Hebron. They were among the Muslim families who risked their lives to save their Jewish neighbors on August 24, 1929.

Today Waheed's family is scattered between Hebron and Amman. The Qawasmi clan is among the most prominent in Hebron politics and business. Some 30 percent of the city's Muslim population bears the Qawasmi name, which is spelled in English as Kawasmeh, Qawasmeh, and other variations. Fahed Qawasmeh was the owner of the Park Hotel who rented rooms to Rabbi Moshe Levinger in 1968. He then served as mayor of Hebron before Israel deported him. In 1984, he was assassinated by Fatah militants in Jordan. Members of the

Qawasmeh family are affiliated with both Fatah and Hamas, including Marwan Qawasmi, a Hamas member who was killed by Israeli forces in 2014. Marwan was one of the primary suspects in the kidnapping and murder of 3 Israeli teenagers, sparking the 2014 war in Gaza. Another Qawasmeh member of Hamas was arrested in March 2024 during the raid of Shifa Hospital in Gaza City.[2]

Waheed has never spoken to his cousins in Hebron about the massacre of 1929, or his family's courageous actions that day. "People my age in Hebron don't even know what happened in 1929," he said. If his cousins did know about the massacre, Waheed told me, they would not be proud of their ancestors' role in it. "They know better. If anyone finds out you're a collaborator, they will hang you." Growing up in Jordan, Waheed learned not to talk about it."[3]

But what if more people could share those stories? Waheed wonders. "What if you were able to get those families to talk to one other today?"

Jill met Waheed in 2017, following the premier of his 2016 film, *Lives Restarted.* His documentary chronicled the lives of Holocaust survivors who settled in Memphis after liberation. Waheed's father refused to see *Lives Restarted.* "Why are you perpetuating this lie?" was his reaction when Waheed told him he was making the documentary. The Holocaust is a taboo subject in the Muslim world, particularly among Palestinians, who see it as the sole reason for Israel's existence.

Ever since they first met, Jill and Waheed have maintained a close bond. During the Covid pandemic, Jill helped Waheed bring to life one of his most ambitious film projects. *Jacir,* starring Academy Award–nominee Lorraine Bracco of *Goodfellas* and *Sopranos* fame, looks at the divided US political system through the eyes of a young Syrian refugee on the streets of Memphis, and his conservative neighbor, played by Bracco. Jill served as executive producer. Their friendship has endured the greatest test of all: October 7. Aside from her close friends in Israel, Waheed was the first person who Jill reached out to that day. She asked how his family was doing, and he asked about hers. They reassured one another that their loved ones were alive, the best anyone in Israel or Palestine could be those days. Two days later, Waheed was already finding humor in the pain. He sent Jill a video posted to social media parodying the LGBTQ activists and "Queers for Palestine" who were demonstrating in support of Hamas. "I'm sure the Islamic terrorists would love you, queer intellectual feminists," joked the star of the video. The irony was too much for Waheed, who could not understand how anyone—but especially so-called liberals—could support the mass murder of innocent men, women, and children by a patriarchal group of radical Islamists.

Weeks after October 7, Jill remained in a state of shock that made it difficult for her to accomplish the simplest of things. "I didn't even know how to put my clothes on," she said.

Seeing the astonishing rise in anti-Semitism that immediately followed October 7, Jill asked herself, "Are we like those Jews living the good life among the gentiles before the Holocaust? Didn't you always feel in some part of your body that it could happen? Were we just sitting here waiting?"

Horrified by the displays of anti-Semitism at American college campuses, Jill was grateful that all three of her children had already graduated. But she worried for her granddaughter and future grandchildren. She heard from friends and family members with kids in college who were asking their non-Jewish friends if they would hide them if they needed to.

Jill feels as if the world in which she raised her children has crumbled. She cannot stop worrying about the one in which her grandchildren will live. "I fear for the generational trauma," said Jill. "What will we teach them, and how will they learn to be unoppressed, free Jews?"

Jill, who speaks with a thick Southern twang, sees herself as carrying on David's legacy of love for the Land of Israel and the Jewish people. Her husband, Scott, is president of the Memphis Jewish Federation, a nonprofit organization whose philanthropic work contributes millions of dollars to Israel each year. In the six weeks after October 7, the Memphis Federation raised $4 million to help the victims of the massacre. If any light has emerged from the darkness of that day, Jill says it's the clarity it has brought to the Jewish community, which feels more unified. "This is a galvanizing moment for the Jewish world," she told me in November, just after she returned from a massive pro-Israel demonstration in Washington, DC. It's not that Jill had never experienced anti-Semitism before. As a young girl in Memphis, other children sometimes threw pennies at her. Others told her that she would go to hell for being a Jew. As a business owner, suppliers told me they could "Jew down the prices" for her. And yet, she said, this new wave of anti-Semitism is different, and far more terrifying.

For the first time in their lives, Jill and Scott are talking about "red lines." What will be the red line when they decide it's time to leave the country? Jill is still not sure, nor does she know where they would go. Before October 7, Israel was the most obvious destination for a Jew fleeing antisemitism. Given the government's failure to protect its citizens, that is no longer the case.

In the days after October 7, one of Jill's close friends in Israel, an oral surgeon, was called in to identify bodies. "I had to put my phone down because she was sending me information about beheadings," said Jill. "She told me, 'show the world that these beheadings happened.' Now, who goes from living the life of almost retirement to being thrown in to identify burned bodies, raped bodies, segments of bodies? She's doing this horrifying work, and being forced to tell the world about it because people don't believe it happened."

Hope for Hebron

The same day Jill visited David's grave in Hebron, she prayed at the Tomb of the Patriarchs and Matriarchs, where she experienced the deepest spiritual awakening she had ever felt. After spending years learning about David and the Hebron he knew, Jill was both deeply moved by her time there and deeply conflicted. What Jill witnessed in Hebron that day did not fit with her vision of what Israel is or should be. And yet, she did not know what Hebron should look like, given the circumstances.

Jill believes Jews have every right to live in Hebron, and should be able to live there in peace. Yet she cannot condone young Israeli soldiers being forced to risk their lives to protect the settlers, or Palestinians being oppressed for the sake of their security. At the same time, she told me, "I don't think we should give up on Hebron. I don't want to ever not have the opportunity to visit David's grave and pay my respects. But at the cost of other people's lives to protect us?" She paused, contemplating the question she had just asked herself. "There comes a point," she said, "when you don't want to risk another person's life to protect a building, or a space, however sacred it is."

If only a Jewish presence in Hebron did not require such a choice.

Knowing that Waheed descended from Muslims who saved Jews in Hebron, and ended up in Memphis of all places, gives Jill hope. "It has to be a sign," she said. Maybe, one day, Palestinians and Israelis will know peace. Even in Hebron.

EPILOGUE
The Lessons in the Echoes

I WRITE THESE WORDS IN EARLY JUNE 2024, JUST AFTER A LONG visit to Israel, where the mourning has not ended. It is a nation shattered, still living with one foot in October 7. In Tel Aviv, nearly every street is covered in posters bearing the faces of hostages still held in Gaza, and graffiti that cries BRING THEM HOME. Normally overflowing cafés, bars, and restaurants are emptier, the music they play more subdued. The unbridled joy and passion for life—once so pervasive that living here felt like a long vacation—has been replaced by a sorrow and hopelessness that hovers over everything.

With 120 hostages still held in Gaza, including 43 who have been declared dead in captivity, Israelis cannot move forward.[1] And with leaders on both sides of the battlefield who appear more interested in their own political survival than the lives of the people they are meant to lead, there seems to be no path toward a brighter future. One of the longest, bloodiest, most challenging wars in Israel's history is being overseen by what is arguably the most incompetent government in its history. The families of the hostages feel the government has forsaken them, prioritizing a devastating, protracted war with no end in sight over the return of their loved ones. Military leaders say the government's refusal to formulate a plan for who will govern Gaza after Hamas is defeated has hamstrung the war effort and created a power vacuum, enabling Hamas to regroup.

Eight months into the war, with none of its goals met, Itamar Ben-Gvir continues to feed into the hands of Hamas. The minister of national security declared in June that his policy was to allow Jews to pray on the Temple Mount. Though Prime Minister Netanyahu immediately clarified that the status quo—a ban on Jewish prayer—had not changed, Ben-Gvir's police force has, in fact, been allowing Jews to pray at the bitterly contested site.[2] All of this makes it easier for Hamas to perpetuate the false claim that Israel seeks to conquer Al-Aqsa.

And so it is that the people whose ideology was formed by the massacre of 1929 are the same people who are now failing the victims of Hamas's massacre, and whose provocations promise only more bloodshed.

Writing about the Hebron massacre before October 7, I never imagined that something even remotely similar could happen again. Nor could I imagine that so many would hold Israel responsible for such a gruesome attack. Yet the outrage against Israel that exploded so soon after October 7 has brought a clarity we did not have previously. Lurking behind much of the legitimate criticism of Israel is a more sinister opposition to the very existence of a Jewish state. In a world with dozens of Muslim and Christian states, including many Muslim states that do not tolerate religious minorities, the source of this opposition is clear. The Jewish state is the only country in the world that is constantly defending its right to exist.

When I moved to the United States with my husband and our two young children in July 2023, it was to be closer to family. Yet I also imagined that our children's lives would be easier, far away from the incessant terror attacks in Israel and rockets from Gaza that led us to run to bomb shelters with our babies more times than I can count. When we came to the US, I never once contemplated whether my children being Jewish or born in Israel might one day be a problem.

Growing up in New Jersey, and attending Columbia University, I never experienced anti-Semitism. Now, Jewish students across the country are being harassed by protesters who supposedly seek peace though many openly support Hamas—a group that is diametrically opposed to peace.

•••

The seeds of the war in Gaza were planted in 1929. And while nearly everything has changed since, the forces behind the holy war that began that year have not. The lessons in the echoes of 1929 are a guide—not only to how we could prevent another massacre, but forge a path forward for the millions of Israelis and Palestinians who wish to live in peace in their homeland. So long as Palestinian leaders refuse to accept the right of a Jewish state to exist, and continue their detrimental history of incitement and disinformation, this endless cycle of carnage will continue. If protesters and world leaders truly wish for peace, their focus should be on ending this century of armed resistance, which has only bred more extremists and more suffering on both sides.

The heroism displayed by so many Muslim citizens of Israel on October 7 demonstrates that this conflict is not between Islam and Judaism. It is between extremists. The only way out is to empower the moderate, peace-seeking Israelis and Palestinians whose voices have been sidelined for far too long. For if the massacre of 1929 set the stage for the world's most intractable conflict, what will the long-term impact of October 7 be?

Somehow I remain hopeful that lessons will be learned to bring peace to this tortured land and its people, who are destined to share it. There is no other way. Neither side has any intention of abandoning their homeland. In the face of the devastation this war has wrought, I hope that those who seek a more peaceful future will prevail.

As Maayan Zin told me when her young daughters were still being held hostage by Hamas, "I have no choice but to hope for good." Maayan did not know if Ella and Dafna were dead or alive, or what they were suffering in captivity. I asked her how she remained so optimistic. "This is how I stay OK," she said. "It is because of hope."

ACKNOWLEDGMENTS

My deepest appreciation goes to my angel of a husband, Shachar. *Ghosts of a Holy War*, and my sanity while writing it, would not exist without your endless support and encouragement. Thank you for giving me the time and space to write while also giving birth to two babies. My gratitude for you is endless.

A tremendous thank you to my tireless and impeccable editor, Claire Wachtel. Your faith in me from the very beginning of this winding journey has taken me places I could only dream of. I am beyond grateful for your honesty, and your ability to improve my drafts even after your eighteenth time reading them.

My heartfelt thanks to the entire team at Union Square & Co. for your tremendous enthusiasm for and work on *Ghosts of a Holy War*, including Christina Stambaugh, Marina Padakis Lowry, Patrick Sullivan, Erik Jacobsen, Lisa Forde, Kevin Ullrich, Sandy Noman, Blanca Oliviery, and Elke Villa, as well as publicist Moshe Schulman. Special thanks to Barbara Berger for your dedication to helping produce this book as beautifully—and as quickly!—as you did.

To my agent, Richard Abate, who recognized the value of this book to tell a different kind of story: thank you for persevering to find it the perfect home at Union Square.

To the magnificent Jill Notowich, who devoted a decade to archiving and digitizing David's letters, and entrusted me with the telling of his story. Thank you for opening your home and family to me, and for granting me the creative independence to write this story as I felt it should be written. It has been the greatest honor of my life. I wish your fabulous mother could be with us now to see what her discovery of that box in the attic led to. To the entire Shainberg family: thank you so much for your tremendous support.

Of the many people who set *Ghosts of a Holy War* in motion, I cannot thank Yossi Klein Halevi enough for serving as the conduit through which it came to me. Thank you for believing in me and enabling me to fulfill a lifelong dream, and for the many hours you devoted to mentoring me these last five years.

To my friends, the talented writers and journalists Ruth Margalit, Jaclyn Goldis, Ben Sales, Adam Rasgon, Melissa Weiss, and Leron Kornreich: thank you for reading my drafts and providing such invaluable feedback. I am blessed to call you my friends.

Oren Kessler, you have my profound gratitude for your incomparable research skills, your sage advice and edits, your thoughtful responses to all my questions, and the exceptional resource that was your gem of a book, *Palestine 1936*.

Special thanks to Matti Friedman for the early meeting in Jerusalem that helped me envision how I would write this book, and for your exemplary writing that is a constant inspiration.

To everyone who generously provided blurbs, thank you so much for your support.

My enormous gratitude to the descendents of survivors of the Hebron massacre who shared their family's stories with me, including Noit Geva and Yosef Ezra.

A massive thanks to Manar, my brilliant Palestinian translator, who not only enabled me to spend dozens of hours speaking with Palestinians in Hebron, but also served as a window into the Palestinian experience.

I'm not sure how I would have navigated many of my days in Hebron, or my writing of this book, without the camaraderie and unique perspective of Mahmoud Jabari, who began as a source of insight and a resource for connecting with Palestinians in Hebron, but quickly became a dear and trusted friend. Thank you.

To Tayseer Abu Aisheh, Umm Salah, Tzipi Schlissel, Dekel Shalev, Maayan Zin, Avida Bachar, and the many others who opened their worlds to me: thank you for sharing some of the most painful moments of your lives, and for allowing me to tell your stories. I am humbled by your trust.

My deepest appreciation to the Paul E. Singer Foundation for the generous support of my research. To Professor Shlomo Tikochinski, whose scholarship on the Slabodka Yeshiva in Hebron was pivotal. Thank you to Hillel Cohen for your instrumental book, *Year Zero of the Arab-Israeli Conflict*, and for sharing some valuable research materials. Special thanks to Rabbi Akiva Males of Memphis for your brilliant work transcribing and adding context to many of David's letters, and for answering my questions about Jewish life in 1929. Thank you to Gilbert Jacobson for your insight into the Memphis Jewish community in David's time, and for your detailed genealogy of the Shainberg family. Tremendous thanks to Dan Chill for helping me out of a black hole as I searched for the mysterious "bride" David left behind in New York, sitting with me for hours to share your family's fascinating story. My immense gratitude to Chaim Gold, the grandson of Wolf Gold, who helped me fill in so many missing pieces of David's story. Thank you to Noam Arnon, my human encyclopedia of Hebron's Jewish community, past and present.

To G. Wayne Dowdy, the Memphis author, historian, archivist, and senior manager of the Memphis Public Libraries history department, thank you for sharing your knowledge and the archival newspaper clippings that helped me bring the Memphis aspect of this story to life. Thank you to Jennifer Kollath at the Temple Israel Archives for making sure I had all of David's letters, photographs, and diary entries, and for aiding me in years of sleuthing. Thanks to Lynnie Mirvis of the Jewish Historical Society of Memphis and the Mid-South for assisting in my archival research, and Rabbi Micah Greenstein, for taking me on an unforgettable tour of Jewish Memphis and teaching me about the community's history of civil rights activism. My sincere gratitude to Dan Smith, grandson of Rabbi David Genuth, whose remarkable archival skills helped me identify and describe numerous illusive names mentioned in David's letters. Special thanks to Daniel Price at the Shalom Hartman Institute, for reviewing early drafts of my chapters with an eye on religious details. To Shimon and Orly at SOL café and gallery in Beersheba, thank you for the beautiful space where much of *Ghosts of a Holy War* was written.

Thank you to my saba, Ken Cohen, whose passion for a good story, discovering new people and places, and seeking out different opinions made me who I am. I wish you were here to see my greatest story come to life. I miss you so much, and know that wherever you and Savta are, you're both kvelling.

To my abba, Raphael Schwartz, where would I be without you? Thank you for nurturing my love of reporting, serving as my first and best editor, agent, and manager, and consistently helping me be a better journalist. Thank you to my mother, Abby Cohen, for raising me with the confidence that I could be anything I wanted to be, achieve anything I dreamed, and for setting an example of perseverance. To my aunt Shelley Nutkis, thank you so much for connecting me with so many of the people who either appear in this book or assisted in my research. Your love for Hebron imbued me with a deeper understanding and appreciation of its history. To my brothers, Yonah and Rishon, and to my Aunt Judy and Uncle Paul, for supporting and cheering me on. And finally, saving the best for last, thank you to my children, Ayala and Lior, for bringing me boundless joy, hope, and purpose, reminding me each day what truly matters.

NOTES

Abbreviations for frequently mentioned publications:

AP   *Associated Press*   JP   *Jerusalem Post*   UPI   United Press International
CO   Colonial Office (British)   JTA   Jewish Telegraphic Agency   WP   *Washington Post*
CZA   Central Zionist Archives   NLI   National Library of Israel
ISA   Israeli State Archives   NYT   *New York Times*
JA   Jewish Agency (JA for Palestine,   TI   *Times of Israel*
      and later, JA for Israel)

Chapter 1: The Floating Palace

1 Sept. 12, 1928, *NYT*, "Outgoing Passenger and Mail Steamships," 55; David's letters.

2 *Sefer Zikaron L'Kodshei Yishivat Hevron* (Memorial Book for the Fallen of the Hebron Yeshiva) (Jerusalem, 1930), 78.

3 *Sefer Zikaron*, 78, and David's letters.

4 *Memphis Press-Scimitar*, May 9, 1956 and May 19, 1965; *Memphis Commercial Appeal*, June 15, 1995.

5 Sam Shankman, *Baron Hirsch Congregation: From Ur to Memphis* (Memphis, TN: Baron Hirsch Synagogue, 1957), 38–39.

6 *Sefer Zikaron*, 77; Shankman, *Baron Hirsch Congregation*, 64–65.

7 A. Z. Benzin and Shabtai Weiss, *Let the People of Israel Remember the Saints of 1929* (Jerusalem, 1930), 143 (Hebrew); Shankman, *Baron Hirsch Congregation*, 64–65.

8 *Sefer Zikaron*, 77–78; Yizkor, 143.

9 David's letter; Mark Chirnside, RMS *Aquitania: The Ship Beautiful* (Cheltenham, UK: The History Press, 2008), 8, 10, 13, 88; Cunard Line, Aquitania: *The Ship Beautiful* (Cunard Line, 1914); "My Favorite Things: RMS *Aquitania*—Her Story and Her Ship's Wheel," Nova Scotia Museum, tinyurl.com/4h52y3ph; "RMS *Aquitania*," *Titanic* and Co.: The Legacy of the Liners, www.titanicandco.com/aquitania/aquitaniaindex.php.

Chapter 2: The All-Too-Promised Land

1 "Mandate for Palestine and Memorandum by the British Government Relating to Its Application to Transjordan, Geneva, League of Nations," 1922. League of Nations Archives, 144 of Jewish National Home in "Palestine: Hearings Before the United States House Committee on Foreign Affairs, 78th Congress, Second Session" (Washington, DC: US Government Printing Office, 1944).

2 Vincent Sheehan, "Holy Land 1929," in *From Haven to Conquest: Readings in Zionism and the Palestine Problem until 1948*, ed. Walid Khalidi (Washington, DC: Institute for Palestine Studies, 1971).

3 Israel State Archive ᴨ19/333 B3 & C6.

4 Tom Segev, *One Palestine, Complete: Jews and Arabs Under the British Mandate* (New York: Macmillan, 2000), 21–22; Oren Kessler, *Palestine 1936: The Great Revolt and the Roots of the Middle East Conflict* (Lanham, MD: Rowman & Littlefield, 2023), 11.

5 "Palestine Commission on the Disturbances of August 1929," vol. 1, 550, evidence heard Dec. 5, 1929 (London: Colonial Office, 1930).

6 Cmd. 3530, Report of the Commission on the Disturbances of August 1929 ("Report of the Shaw Commission") (London: His Majesty's Stationery Office, 1930), 8; Confidential letter to Haim Arlosoroff from David Gurevich. Subject: Statistics of Land Transactions. Jerusalem, Sept. 18, 1931. CZA S25/1335; Douglas V. Duff, *Bailing with a Teaspoon* (London: John Long, 1959), 98–99.

7 Segev, *One Palestine Complete*, 273–75; Kessler, *Palestine 1936*, 23.

8 Duff, *Bailing with a Teaspoon*, 98–99.

Chapter 3: The Grand Mufti

1 ISA, P-3051/26; Kessler, *Palestine 1936*, 7; Philip Mattar, *The Mufti of Jerusalem: Al-Hajj Amin Al-Husayni and the Palestinian National Movement* (New York: Columbia Univ. Press, 1988), 1, 6.

2 Kessler, *Palestine 1936*, 10; David G. Dalin and John F. Rothmann, *Icon of Evil: Hitler's Mufti and the Rise of Radical Islam* (New York: Random House, 2008), 8.

3 Dalin and Rothmann, *Icon of Evil*, 7.

4 Neville J. Mandel, *The Arabs and Zionism Before World War I* (Berkeley: Univ. of California Press, 1976), 41; Kessler, *Palestine 1936*, 10.

5 Kessler, *Palestine 1936*, 13; "Herbert Samuel's Secret 1937 Testimony on the Infamous Mufti of Jerusalem Revealed," *TI*, Aug. 19, 2023, tinyurl.com/45whaw4d.

6 Shaw Commission Evidence, Testimony of Haj Amin Al Husseini, vol. 1, 498–500; Dalin and Rothmann, *Icon of Evil*, 8–9.

7   Rivka Gonen, *Contested Holiness: Jewish, Muslim, and Christian Perspective on the Temple Mount in Jerusalem* (Brooklyn, NY: Ktav, 2003), 138; Moshe Ma'oz, *Studies on Palestine during the Ottoman Period* (Jerusalem: Magnes Press, 2011), 358; Segev, *One Palestine Complete*, 2001, 132.
8   Kessler, *Palestine 1936*, 17.
9   Segev, *One Palestine Complete*, 127–28; Khalil Sakakini, *Kadha Ana ya Dunya* [Such Am I, O World] (Beirut: Al-Ittihad, 1982), 193–94; Howard Sachar, *A History of Israel: From the Rise of Zionism to Our Time* (New York: Alfred A. Knopf, 2006), 123.
10 Segev, *One Palestine Complete*, 128–36; Kessler, *Palestine 1936*, 17.
11 Report of the Shaw Commission, 71; Segev, *One Palestine Complete*, 139; Michael Bar-Zohar and Eitan Haber, *The Quest for the Red Prince* (New York: William Morrow, 1983), 34–35.
12 Haganah Archives, Tel Aviv, Testimony of Sigmund Nesher (date unknown), File 84.50; Zev Golan, *Free Jerusalem: Heroes, Heroines and Rogues Who Created the State of Israel* (Jerusalem: Devora, 2003), 26; Segev, *One Palestine Complete*, 132–37.
13 Dalin and Rothmann, *Icon of Evil*, 16.
14 Segev, *One Palestine Complete*, 156, 159; Kessler, *Palestine 1936*, 20; "Herbert Samuel's Secret 1937 Testimony," *TI*; Rashid Khalidi, *The Iron Cage: The Story of the Palestinian Struggle for Statehood* (Boston: Beacon Press, 2006), 63; Mattar, *The Mufti of Jerusalem*, 25; Elie Kedourie, "Sir Herbert Samuel and the Government of Palestine," in *The Chatham House Version and Other Middle Eastern Studies* (Chicago: Ivan R. Dee, 1984), 63.
15 Dalin and Rothmann, *Icon of Evil*, 8.
16 Pierre Van Paassen, *Days of Our Years* (New York: Hillman-Curl, 1939), 363–64; Steven Wagner, "On Brand: The Fashion Choices of Hajj Amin journaal-Husayni," Cornell Univ. Press, tinyurl.com/2kzmwj8e.
17 Baruch Kimmerling and Joel Migdal, *The Palestinian People: A History* (Cambridge, MA: Harvard Univ. Press, 2003), 81–86; Segev, *One Palestine Complete*, 271–72; Hillel Cohen, *Year Zero of the Arab-Israeli Conflict 1929* trans. Haim Watzman (Waltham, MA: Brandeis Univ. Press, 2015), 82–83.
18 Palestine Royal Commission, 67th Meeting (Private), "Notes of Evidence taken in London," Feb. 12, 1937, 460 (witness Sir John Chancellor, former High Commissioner of Palestine).
19 Kessler, *Palestine 1936*, 163; Duff, *Bailing with a Teaspoon*, 97.
20 Weldon C. Matthews, *Confronting an Empire, Constructing a Nation: Arab Nationalists and Popular Politics in Mandate Palestine* (London: I.B. Tauris, 2006), 32; Gonen, *Contested Holiness*, 137–38; Segev, *One Palestine Complete*, 159; Palestine Royal Commission, 67th Meeting (Private), "Notes of Evidence taken in London," Feb. 12, 1937, 468.

Chapter 4: Memphis Meets Palestine

1   Immigration figures: archive.jewishagency.org/historical-aliyah/content/28841.
2   Moshe Sherman, *Orthodox Judaism in America: A Biographical Dictionary and Sourcebook* (Westport, CT: Greenwood Press, 1996), 78.
3   Dov Cohen, *To Rise Above: A Journey to Greatness Against All Odds* (New York: Feldheim, 2016), 99–100; "1921 Jaffa Riots 100 Years On," *TI*, May 1, 2021, tinyurl.com/yazhzkw5.
4   Segev, *One Palestine Complete*, 183–84; Shaw Commission Evidence, vol. 1, 20.
5   Report of the Shaw Commission, 7.
6   Jerold S. Auerbach, *Hebron Jews* (Lanham, MD: Rowman & Littlefield, 2009), 30.
7   Report of the 1930 Western Wall Commission, International Commission for the Wailing Wall, Dec. 1930, 7, 8, 10, 11; Cohen, *Year Zero*, 64.
8   Cohen, *Year Zero*, 68; Report of the Shaw Commission, 28; Benny Morris, *Righteous Victims: A History of the Zionist–Arab Conflict, 1881–1998* (New York: Knopf Doubleday, 1999), 112; Kessler, *Palestine 1936*, 25.
9   Philip Mattar, "The Role of the Mufti of Jerusalem in the Political Struggle over the Western Wall, 1928–29," *Middle Eastern Studies*, 19(1) (Jan. 1983), 108–10; Segev, *One Palestine Complete*, 296–97.
10 Duff, *Bailing with a Teaspoon*, 172–73.
11 Segev, *One Palestine Complete*, 305–6; Duff, *Bailing with a Teaspoon*, 174.
12 Duff, *Bailing with a Teaspoon*, 174.
13 "View Wailing Wall Incident Yom Kippur Infringement of Jewish Rights," JTA, Sept. 27, 1928, tinyurl. com/772ut6c8; Segev, *One Palestine Complete*, 298.
14 Report of the Shaw Commission, 8.
15 Duff, *Bailing with a Teaspoon*, 97.
16 Segev, *One Palestine Complete*, 278–79, 303–4; Mattar, "The Role of the Mufti of Jerusalem," 108–10.
17 *Palestine Bulletin*, Sept. 27, 1928, 1, 3 (NLI).
18 Ilan Pappe, "Haj Amin and the Buraq Revolt," *Jerusalem Quarterly* (18) (June 2003), 9; "New Attacks on Worshippers at Wailing Wall," JTA, Oct. 2, 1928, 1.
19 Segev, *One Palestine Complete*, 272; Philip Mattar, "The Role of the Mufti of Jerusalem," 106–8.
20 Mattar, "The Role of the Mufti of Jerusalem," 108–10; Segev, *One Palestine Complete*, 303–4; Shaw Commission Evidence, Testimony of Haj Amin Al Husseini, vol. 1, 498–500; Report of the Western Wall Commission, 7, 8, 10, 11; Cohen, *Year Zero*, 64.

21 Report of the Shaw Commission, 31.

22 Mattar, "The Role of the Mufti of Jerusalem," 105, 108; Supreme Muslim Council, *A Brief Guide to Al-Haram Al-Sharif* (Jerusalem: Moslem Orphanage Press, 1930, 1935, 1950).

23 Cohen, *Year Zero*, 53–54; Report of the Shaw Commission, 32.

24 Segev, *One Palestine Complete*, 304; Cohen, *Year Zero*, 87; CO 733/160/57540/11, Va'ad Le'umi letter of Oct. 10, 1928; Report of the Shaw Commission, 30.

25 Cohen, *Year Zero*, 70; CO 733/98, W. Ormsby-Gore to Brigadier General Clayton, 2 May 1918, encloses Weizmann letter of 1 May 1918; CO 733/98, Muslim dignitaries to Storrs, 2 May 1918; Mattar, "The Role of the Mufti of Jerusalem," 109.

26 Steven E. Zipperstein, *Law and the Arab-Israeli Conflict: The Trials of Palestine* (Abingdon, UK: Routledge, 2020); Mattar, "The Role of the Mufti of Jerusalem," 110–11.

27 Mattar, "The Role of the Mufti of Jerusalem," 110–11. | 28 Ibid., 111–12.

29 Steven E. Zipperstein, "Revealed: An Arab Prince's Secret Proposal to Sell the Western Wall to the Jews," *TI*, Jan. 9, 2020.

Chapter 5: City of Abraham

1 David's letters; Cohen, *To Rise Above*, 227.

2 David's letters; Cohen, *To Rise Above*, 248.

3 Segev, *One Palestine Complete*, 316–17.

4 Isaac Shemer, *The Shmerlings: Six Generations in Eretz-Israel* (Herzliya, ISR: Malo Pub., 2004), 30; Saeed Al-Bitar, *The Guard*, documentary produced by the Gaza Palestinian Women's Information & Media Center, 2006, www.youtube.com/watch?v=-uOVMwefB_c.

5 Cohen, *Year Zero*, 137–39.

6 Shemer, *The Shmerlings*, 29; Cohen, *To Rise Above*, 231.

7 Segev, *One Palestine Complete*, 318.

8 Auerbach, *Hebron Jews*, 1, 29–30.

9 Ibid., 36; Menachem Klein, *Lives in Common: Arabs and Jews in Jerusalem, Jaffa and Hebron* (Oxford, Oxford Univ. Press, 2014), 91–92.

10 "Ambassador Henry Morgenthau in the Promised Land," *NYT*, July 12, 1914, 6, tinyurl.com/k2rdjd2j.

11 Leo Gottesman, *The Martyrs of Hebron* (New York: Printed by the author, 1930), 21–22; Cohen, *Year Zero*, 150–51; Segev, *One Palestine Complete*, 318; Cohen, *To Rise Above*, 253.

12 Auerbach, *Hebron Jews*, 60; Cohen, *To Rise Above*, 231.

13 Shlomo Tikochinski, *Torah Scholarship, Musar and Elitism: The Slabodka Yeshiva from Lithuania to Mandate Palestine* (Jerusalem: Zalman Shazar Center, 2016), 194 (Hebrew).

14 Cohen, *To Rise Above*, 127, 132; Rabbi Shimon Yosef Meller, *Prince of the Torah Kingdom* (Nanuet, NY: Feldheim, 2010), 61.

15 Tikochinski, *Torah Scholarship, Musar and Elitism*, 194.

16 Ibid., 197–99.

17 Ibid., 216–19; *Haaretz*, July 20, 1924.

18 Oded Avissar, *Sefer Hevron* [The Book of Hebron] (Jerusalem: Keter, 1970), 71–72; Cohen, *Year Zero*, 135–36; Tikochinski, *Torah Scholarship, Musar and Elitism*, 246.

19 Avissar, *Sefer Hevron*, 62.

20 Cohen, *To Rise Above*, 137.

21 Auerbach, *Hebron Jews*, 66; David's letters.

22 *Sefer Zikaron*, 115–16.

23 Cohen, *Year Zero*, 148–49; *Sefer Zikaron*, 115–16.

24 Meller, *Prince of the Torah Kingdom*, 87.

25 "Chicagoans Dead in Hebron Massacre," *Chicago Sentinel*, Aug. 30, 1929, 15.

26 Interview with Moshe Gold's son, Chaim, 2019.

27 From Gottesman, "The Martyrs of Hebron," 63; Dovi Safier, "A Bond Sealed in Blood," *Mishpacha Magazine*, Sept. 23, 2020, 77–78; Yizkor, 128–29 and *Sefer Zikaron*, 91–92; *The Forward* (Yiddish), Aug. 28, 1929.

28 *Sefer Zikaron*, 81–84; Yizkor, 140–41.

Chapter 6: Breathing Holy Air

1 Yizkor, 143; David's letters.

2 Meller, *Prince of the Torah Kingdom*, 81.

3 *The Forward*, Aug. 28, 1928, and David's letters.

4 Ibid.; *Sefer Zikaron*, 91, 79; Cohen, *To Rise Above*, 217–18.

5 *The Forward*, Aug. 28, 1929; Gottesman, *The Martyrs of Hebron*, 52–55; Safier, "A Bond Sealed in Blood," 82; *Sefer Zikaron*, 73–75.

6 Yizkor, 143; *Sefer Zikaron*, 77–78.

7 Tikochinski, *Torah Scholarship, Musar and Elitism*, 246; Cohen, *To Rise Above*, 255.

Chapter 7: A Premonition

1 *The Palestine Bulletin*, May 5, 1929, 3.

2 Maoz Azaryahu, "Tel-Aviv's Birthdays: Anniversary Celebrations of the First Hebrew City 1929–1959," *Israel Studies* 14(3) (Oct. 2009), 3.

3 Auerbach, *Hebron Jews*, 30.

4 "10,000 Jews Guarded at the Wailing Wall," *NYT*, Aug. 16, 1929, tinyurl.com/2xxw4w7r.

5 Ibid.

6 Shaw Commission Evidence, vol. 1, 305; Report of the Shaw Commission, 46; Cohen, *Year Zero*, 72.

7 Report of the Shaw Commission, 38–39; Shaw Commission Evidence, vol. 1, 280.

8 Report of the Shaw Commission, 42.

9 Ibid., 49–50; Mattar, "The Role of the Mufti of Jerusalem," 113.

10 Report of the Shaw Commission, 48.

11 Doar Hayom, Aug. 12 1929, quoted by the Report of the Commission on the Palestine Disturbances of August, 1929. Cmd. 3530, 1930, 49–50.

12 March on August 15: Report of the Shaw Commission, 54; "Jewish Daily Bulletin," JTA, Aug. 16, 1929, tinyurl.com/yf82vdv2.

13 Martin Kolinsky, "Premeditation in the Palestine Disturbances of August 1929?," *Middle Eastern Studies* 26(1) (Jan. 1990), 26; Report of the Shaw Commission, 41; Pappe, "Haj Amin and the Buraq Revolt," 11–13.

14 Mattar, "The Role of the Mufti of Jerusalem," 113; Pappe, "Haj Amin and the Buraq Revolt," 15; Report of the Shaw Commission, 53–54; Morris, *Righteous Victims*, 113.

15 Kolinsky, "Premeditation in the Palestinian Disturbances," 28; Report of the Shaw Commission, 54; "Diaries Reveal Overwhelmed British Officials in Palestine Wanted to Go Home," *TI*, June 13, 2020, tinyurl.com/2t6p2ddr.

16 "Arab Mob Invades Wailing Wall Lane," *NYT*, Aug. 17, 1929; Report of the Shaw Commission, 55; Cohen, *Year Zero*, 73; Mattar, "The Role of the Mufti of Jerusalem," 113; Segev, *One Palestine Complete*, 295–313; Morris, *Righteous Victims*, 113; Martin Kolinsky, *Law, Order and Riots in Mandatory Palestine 1928–35* (London: St. Martin's Press, 1993), 43–44; Zipperstein, *Law and the Arab-Israeli Conflict*, 118.

17 Report of the Shaw Commission, 55; Segev, *One Palestine Complete*, 310.

18 Segev, *One Palestine Complete*, 310; Report of the Shaw Commission, 56–57; "Jews Allege Arabs Desecrate Wall," *NYT*, Aug. 25, 1929, 5.

19 *Haaretz*, Aug. 23, 1929.

20 Report of the Shaw Commission, 58–59.

21 *Palestine Bulletin*, Aug. 23, 1929.

22 Report of the Shaw Commission, 58–59; Kolinsky, "Premeditation in the Palestinian Disturbances," 25.

23 "Contemplated Avoiding Arab Outbreaks When Original Draft of Braude Proclamation Was Introduced," *Jewish News of Northern California*/JTA, Nov. 29, 1929, tinyurl.com/54yj6mjx.

24 Report of the Shaw Commission, 59

25 Kolinsky, "Premeditation in the Palestine Disturbances," 18–34. Segev, *One Palestine Complete*, 312.

26 Report of the Shaw Commission, 60.

27 Ibid., 64.

Chapter 8: It Won't Happen Here

1 Haganah Archives, Testimony of Aharon Chaim Cohen, File 27.16.

2 Gottesman, "The Martyrs of Hebron," 21; Haganah Archives, Testimony of Aharon Chaim Cohen, File 27.16, and Testimony of Saadia Kirschenboim, File 120.30; Documentary film featuring testimonies of survivors: *What I Saw in Hebron*, Jerusalem Cinematheque, Israel Film Service, 1999.

3 Report of the Shaw Commission, 79.

4 "Evidence of Mufti's Responsibility for Arab Outbreak Piles Up in Jerusalem Trial," JTA, Oct. 17, 1929, 3–4, tinyurl.com/3k4xv4j3.

5 Haganah Archives, Testimony of Aharon Chaim Cohen, File 27.16; Testimony of Saadia Kirschenboim, File 120.30.

6 Haganah Archives, Testimony of Baruch Katinka, File 120.27; Testimony of Sigmund Nesher, File 84.50.

7 Segev, *One Palestine Complete*, 317–18; Shaw Commission Evidence, Cafferata Testimony, vol. 1, 154.

8 Haganah Archives, Testimony of Baruch Katinka and Sigmund Nesher.

9 Haganah Archives, Testimony of Yaakov Pat, June 2, 1949, File #139.15.

10 Shaw Commission Evidence, Testimony of Haj Amin Al Husseini, vol. 1, 520–521.

11 Testimony of Rabbi Meir Franco, Sept. 1, 1929, Central Zionist Archives, L59/148; Shaw Commission Evidence, Testimony of Rabbi Franco, Dec. 23, 1929, vol. 2, 851; Testimony of David Gozlan, Sept. 1, 1929, NLI Archives, V722/01/10.

12 Testimony of Shifra Ben-Gerson, Central Zionist Archives, L59/148; Shulamit Ezrachi, *The Mashgiach: The Life and Times of Rabbi Meir Chodosh* (Brooklyn, NY: Mesora, 2006), 207.

13 Shaw Commission Evidence, Report by Cafferata, vol. 2, 984; Shaw Commission Evidence, Testimony of Haim Bajayo, vol. 2, 854; David's letters; Avissar, *Sefer Hevron*, 325–26; Moshe Ehrenwald, "Hebron in the Riots of 1929," *Mechkarei Eretz Yehuda* (Land of Judea Studies) B, (2018), 94.

14 David's and Sylvia's letters, from interviews with Sylvia's nephew, Dan Chill, 2020.
15 "Last Letter Home from Yeshiva Student," Jewish Community of Hebron, May 28, 2006: en.hebron.org.il/history/519.
16 Memorandum to the High Commissioner from the Jewish Community of Hebron, Sept. 5, 1929, CZA, A245\135\3; Testimony of Rabbi Slonim, CZA L59/149; Shaw Commission Evidence, Testimony of Rabbi Meir Franco, vol. 2, 852.
17 Shaw Commission Evidence, Testimony of Rabbi Slonim, vol. 2, 833; Testimony of Rabbi Yaakov Yoseph Slonim, CZA L59/149 and Testimony of Rabbi Meir Franco, CZA L59/148.
18 "Arabs Opened Attack after Noon Prayers," NYT, Aug. 25, 1929, 5.
19 Report of the Shaw Commission, 61; Edward Keith-Roach, Pasha of Jerusalem: Memoirs of a District Commissioner Under the British Mandate (London: Radcliffe, 1994), 122–23.
20 Report of the Shaw Commission, 61–62; Mattar, "The Role of the Mufti of Jerusalem," 114.
21 Keith-Roach, Pasha of Jerusalem, 122–23.
22 Report of the Shaw Commission, 61–62; Segev, One Palestine Complete, 314; Keith-Roach, Pasha of Jerusalem, 123; "Arabs Opened Attack after Noon Prayers," NYT.
23 Morris, Righteous Victims, 113; Segev, One Palestine Complete, 314–15.
24 Report of the Shaw Commission, 63; Segev, One Palestine Complete, 316.
25 Segev, One Palestine Complete, 314–16; Report of the Shaw Commission, 63; Morris, Righteous Victims, 119; Papers Relating to the Foreign Relations of the United States 1929, Telegram from Knabenshue to the Secretary of State, Aug 24, 1929, 47; Cohen, Year Zero, 96–97; Keith-Roach, Pasha of Jerusalem, 122–23.

Chapter 9: Prelude to a Massacre

1 Testimony of Haim Abushdid, CZA L59/148—Evidence heard from A–I from Hebron by the JA's Central Legal Committee after the riots of 1929.
2 "Nine Jews, Three Arabs Killed, 110 Injured, in Clash Blamed on Moslems in Jerusalem," NYT, Aug. 25, 1929, 1, tinyurl.com/y4eetffh.
3 Testimony of Yehuda Leib Schneerson, 8/28/29; CZA L59/149: Evidence heard from K–Z from Hebron by the JA's Central Legal Committee after the riots of 1929; Cohen, To Rise Above, 228.
4 Cohen, To Rise Above, 268; CZA, Testimony of Benjamin Sokolovsky and Dr. Zvi Kitayin, L59/149: Evidence heard from K–Z from Hebron by the JA's Central Legal Committee after the riots of 1929; Yisrael Amikam, Hahatkafa Al Hayishuv Hayehudi b'Eeretz Yisrael B'Tarpat [Hahatkafa: The Attack on the Jewish Community in the Land of Israel in 1929] (Haifa: Dfus Omanut, 1930), 51.
5 David left the yeshiva, went home, and locked the doors: Harbater interview with reporters—NYT, Aug. 27, 1929; Trial of Sheikh Taleb Marka, 10/15/29; Testimony of Raymond Cafferata; NLI, 41, tinyurl.com/5n9aycky.
6 Testimony of Rabbi Slonim, Yehuda Leib Schneerson, Fanny Sokolover, Ephraim Sokolover, Dr. Leib Levit, collected in August and September 1929. CZA L59/149.
7 Testimony of Y. L. Grodzinsky, in Amikam, Hahatkafa, 5–56; Ezrachi, The Mashgiach, 208; Testimony of Zecharia Ben Meshail, Rabbi Slonim, Fanny Sokolover, Ephraim Sokolover, Collected in August and September 1929, CZA L59/149; Cohen, To Rise Above, 269.
8 Avissar, Sefer Hevron, 67; Testimony of Zecharia Ben Meshail, CZA L59/148—Evidence heard from A–I from Hebron by the JA's Central Legal Committee after the riots of 1929.
9 Testimony of Dr. Zvi Kitayin, CZA L59/149: Evidence heard from K–Z from Hebron by the JA's Central Legal Committee after the riots of 1929; Sefer Zikaron, 77.
10 Testimony of Rabbi Slonim, Dr. Kitayin, CZA L59/149; Testimony of Zecharia Ben Meshail, L59/148.
11 Ezrachi, The Mashgiach, 208; Testimony of Slonim, Franco, Schneerson, Sokolover, CZA L59/49; Avissar, Sefer Hevron, 67–68.
12 Vincent Sheehan, "New York Student Tells of Arab Raids on Defenseless Jews," New York World, Aug. 27, 1929.
13 Shaw Commission Evidence, Report by Cafferata, vol. 2, 984.
14 Ibid.

Chapter 10: Black Sabbath

1 Ezrachi, The Mashgiach, 208; Avissar, Sefer Hevron, 68; Testimonies of Rabbi Franco, Rabbi Slonim, and Yehuda Lieb Shneerson, CZA L59/148 and CZA L59/149; Amikam, Hahatkafa, 45; Shaw Commission Evidence, vol. 2, 833–37, 851–54; Shaw Commission Evidence, Cafferata testimony, vol. 1, 154–66, and vol. 2, 983–84; "The Massacre at Hebron," Palestine Bulletin, Sept. 2, 1929, 1–2.
2 Avissar, Sefer Hevron, 73; National Archives—London—C.O. 733/181/4— 8–35. Part IV—Palestine Disturbances—Death Sentences—1930 (testimonies from the trials); CZA A245\135\3: Memorandum to the High Commissioner from the Jewish Community of Hebron, Sept. 5, 1929; "A Visit to Hebron: Evidence of the Massacres," Reuters, Sept. 2, 1929.
3 Amikam, Hahatkafa, 46, 53 (what happened to the Abushdid and Gozlan families); Memorandum to the High Commissioner for Palestine by the Jewish Community of Hebron, Sept. 5, 1929, 7, Middle East Center, St. Antony's College, Oxford.

4 Sarah Castel testimony—National Archives—London—C.O./733/181/1— 80–101. Part IV—Palestine Disturbances—Death Sentences—1930; Memorandum to the High Commissioner for Palestine by the Jewish Community of Hebron, Sept. 5, 1929, 6, Middle East Center, St. Antony's College, Oxford.

5 "The Massacre at Hebron," *Palestine Bulletin*, Sept. 2, 1929, 1–2; Amikam, *Hahatkafa*, 40.

6 Zmira Mani, "What I Saw in Hebron," *Haaretz*, Sept. 12, 1929; Documentary film by Noit and Dan Geva, "What I Saw in Hebron," 1999; interview with filmmaker Noit Geva, Zmira Mani's granddaughter, 2019.

7 Testimony by survivor Shalom Goldschmidt: tinyurl.com/5n874s3e; Testimony of Mina Goldschmidt: CZA L59/148—Evidence heard from A–I from Hebron by the JA's Central Legal Committee after the riots of 1929; M. Levine, *The Palestine Massacres of August 1929, the Wounded at Bikur Holim Hospital, Their Statements and Medical Reports* (Jerusalem: Solomon Press, 1929), 13–14; *Sefer Zikaron*, 123.

8 Cohen, *To Rise Above*, 277.

9 Testimony of Mina Orlinsky, sister of Slonim's wife, Hannah, who witnessed their murder: CZA L59/149: Evidence heard from K–Z from Hebron by the JA's Central Legal Committee after the riots of 1929; Avissar, *Sefer Hevron*, 70; Cohen, *To Rise Above*, 279.

10 Auerbach, *Hebron Jews*, 70.

11 Description of the massacre at Slonim's house from Amikam, *Hahatkafa*, 52, and from testimonies of survivors Mina Orlinsky, Y. L. Grodzinsky, Joseph Rachelson, Eliezer Tuker, CZA L59/148 and 149.

12 Cohen, *To Rise Above*, 278.

13 Ibid., 279; Rechavam Ze'evi, *Tarpat: The Hebron Massacre of 1929* (Jerusalem, 1994), 51.

14 Ezrahi, *The Mashgiach*, 213; Testimony of Haim Kostanovitch, CZA L59/149: Evidence heard from K–Z from Hebron by the JA's Central Legal Committee after the riots of 1929.

15 CZA A245\135\3: Memorandum to the High Commissioner from the Jewish Community of Hebron, Sept. 5, 1929.

16 Testimony of Joseph Rachelson and Eliezer Tucker, CZA L59/149: Evidence heard from K–Z from Hebron by the JA's Central Legal Committee after the riots of 1929; Ze'evi, *Tarpat*, 52–55.

17 Slonim family story: Avraham Burg, *In Days to Come: A New Hope for Israel* (New York: Nation Books, 2018), 184–88; Avissar, *Sefer Hevron*, 73.

18 National Archives—London—C.O. 733/181/1— 126–48. Part IV—Palestine—Disturbances—Death Sentences—1930 (trial testimonies).

19 Sheehan, "New York Student Tells of Arab Raids," *New York World*; Meller, *Prince of the Torah Kingdom*, 87–88; CZA S25/4472-37.

20 Ezrahi, *The Mashgiach*, 214–15.

21 Segev, *One Palestine Complete*, 317–18; Shaw Commission Evidence, Cafferata testimony, vol. 1, 154.

22 Sources for the details of the attacks: Avissar, *Sefer Hevron*, 66–74; Shaw Commission Evidence, Cafferata testimony, vol. 1, 154–66, and vol. 2, 983–84; Testimony of Rabbi Franco, vol. 2, 851–854; Testimony of Rabbi Slonim, vol. 2, 833–37; Testimony of Y. L. Grodzinsky: Ze'evi, *Tarpat*, 51.

Chapter 11: Mourner's Kaddish

1 Avissar, *Sefer Hevron*, 74.

2 Ezrachi, *The Mashgiach*, 215–216; Testimony of Rabbi Franco, Sept. 1, 1929: CZA L59/148—Evidence heard from A–I from Hebron by the JA's Central Legal Committee after the riots of 1929; *Memphis Press-Scimitar*, Aug. 27, 1929.

3 Auerbach, *Hebron Jews*, 70; Amikam, *Hahatkafa*, 59.

4 CZA S25/4472-23, 27, 34.

5 Meyer Greenberg, "Hebron Massacre of 1929: A Recently Revealed Letter of a Survivor," hebron1929.info/Hebronletter.pdf; Testimony of Dr. Kitayin: CZA L59/149: Evidence heard from K–Z from Hebron by the JA's Central Legal Committee after the riots of 1929.

6 Testimony of Dr. Levit: CZA L59/149: Evidence heard from K–Z from Hebron by the JA's Central Legal Committee after the riots of 1929.

7 Avissar, *Sefer Hevron*, 74–75.

8 Testimony of Benjamin Berkai, Sept. 8, 1929: CZA L59/148—Evidence head from A–I from Hebron by the JA's Central Legal Committee after the riots of 1929.

9 Avissar, *Sefer Hevron*, 75; *Sefer Zikaron*, 87.

Chapter 12: The List

1 "Palestine Death Toll Mounts Hourly, with Fifteen Americans Among Slain . . . ," 1–2, "British Troops Are Attacked Landing at Jaffa," 1, "18 British Warships Are Speeding to Palestine," 2, *NYT*, Aug. 27, 1929, tinyurl.com/4ymd9su8; "2,000 Tribesmen Menace Jerusalem," 1, "British Troops Fight Moslems in Haifa . . . Arabs Reporting Massing on Borders," 1–2, "Riot Death Total Now Placed at 119," 3, *NYT*, Aug. 28, 1929, tinyurl.com/mvwhxta3; "Danger for Arab Jewry Growing as Attacks Multiply on Fifth Day of Arab-Jewish Warfare," *Jewish Daily Bulletin*/JTA, Aug. 28, 1929, tinyurl.com/4e6tf2h9.

2 "2,000 Tribesmen," "British Troops Fight Moslems," "Riot Death Total," *NYT*.

3 "Palestine Death Toll Mounts Hourly," "British Troops Are Attacked," "18 British Warships," *NYT.*
4 Ezrachi, *The Mashgiach*, 216; Testimony of Rabbi Yaakov Yosef Slonim, CZA L59/149; Evidence heard from K–Z from Hebron by the JA's Central Legal Committee after the riots of 1929; Avissar, *Sefer Hevron*, 75.
5 *The Commercial Appeal*, Memphis, Aug. 27 and 28, 1929; *Memphis Press-Scimitar*, Aug. 27 and 28, 1929.
6 Letters from the Shainberg family; *Memphis Press-Scimitar*, Aug. 26 and 27, 1929.
7 *The Jewish Forum*, New York, Oct. 1929, 406.
8 *The Commercial Appeal*, Memphis, Sept. 2, 1929.

Chapter 13: Red Tuesday

1 "Situation Reported Quieter," *NYT*, Aug. 27, 1929, tinyurl.com/3zsv85x4.
2 "Palestine Death Toll Mounts Hourly," *NYT*; "Sixteen Jewish Dead of the Total of Eighteen," JTA, Aug. 27, 1929, tinyurl.com/yc56ff85.
3 "British Troops Fight Moslems in Haifa," *NYT*, Aug. 27 and 28, 1929, tinyurl.com/cs57tbzk; Klausner's home destroyed: Mattar, *The Mufti of Jerusalem*, 48.
4 Gaza: Cohen, *Year Zero*, 28; "Palestinian Jews Protest Government's Juggling with Figures," JTA, Aug. 28, 1929, tinyurl.com/2wv48yfv. Number of families living in Gaza at the time: Michael R. T. Dumper and Bruce E. Stanley, *Cities of the Middle East and North Africa: A Historical Encyclopedia* (Santa Barbara, CA: ABC CLIO, 2007); "2,000 Arabs Marched toward Jerusalem," JTA, Aug. 28, 1929, tinyurl.com/y5ky8wyj.
5 "Palestinian Jews Protest," JTA, Aug. 28, 1929; *NYT*, Aug. 28, 1929.
6 Story of first Jew killed, and that most were Mizrahi: Cohen, *Year Zero*, 193, 194, 197; Safed accounts of brutality: David Hacohen, *Time to Tell: An Israeli Life, 1898–1984* (Plainsboro Township, NJ: Associated Univ. Presses, 1985), 38; "Reign of Terror in Safed," *The Glasgow Herald*, Sept. 14, 1929, 10.
7 "British Troops Fight Moslems in Haifa," *NYT.*
8 Archive of the NLI—Arab Executive Proclamation 1929, tinyurl.com/mtz5mzns.
9 CZA S25/4472-4.
10 "Horrifying Evidence in Hebron Examinations," *Palestine Bulletin*, Sept. 25, 1929, 1, tinyurl.com/mr3vbb8v.
11 "Chief Rabbi Kook Appeals to Moslem World," *Palestine Bulletin*, Sept. 2, 1929, tinyurl.com/cfa8zf8p.
12 Mufti letter: Cohen, *Year Zero*, 203–4.
13 NLI Archive—High Commissioner Proclamation, Sept. 4, 1929.
14 CZA A245\135\3-10, 3-11, 3-12.
15 Memorandum to His Excellency the High Commissioner for Palestine by the Jewish Community in Hebron, Sept. 5, 1929; Middle East Centre, St. Antony's College, Oxford.
16 Shaw Commission Evidence, vol. 1, 163.
17 High Commissioner's Telegram no. 204, Sept. 19, 1929, attached in appendix to "Palestine—Situation In. Report by the Chiefs of Staff Sub-Committee" (Dec. 1929), CAB 24/209, National Archives, UK, 5.
18 High Commissioner Sir John Chancellor's Diary, Bodleian Library, Oxford.
19 Haganah Archives, Tel Aviv, Testimony of Naftali Rubinshtein, File 124.14, taken July 13, 1966.
20 ISA 758 / 4 - ‫ב‬ Justice Louis Brandeis Report on the Judicial Proceedings Consequent upon the August 1929 Riots, 15–18, 98–100.
21 "Testimony of Orphaned Jewish Children Moves Hebron Court," JTA, Sept. 27, 1929, tinyurl.com/5d6xzxr3.
22 "Evidence of Mufti's Responsibility," JTA.
23 Report of the Shaw Commission, 4–5.
24 Shaw Commission Evidence, vol. 1, 154–57, 160–61.
25 Auerbach, *Hebron Jews*, 72; Cohen, *Year Zero*, 125; Segev, *One Palestine Complete*, 331, 341, 472–74.
26 "New Attacks Disturb Palestine Peace; Jew Stabbed to Death," JTA, Sept. 27, 1929, tinyurl.com/yyn4prwb; "General Feeling of Insecurity Among Jews as Series of Assaults Continues in Palestine," JTA, Nov. 19, 1929, tinyurl.com/ypr69d7b; "Isolated Incidents of Violence Reveal All Not Yet Quiet in Palestine, JTA, Nov. 15, 1929, tinyurl.com/2stz8b4y.
27 "Arabs Threaten to Deny Jews All Rights at Wailing Wall," JTA, Nov. 20, 1929, tinyurl.com/34ynzkun.
28 Shaw Commission Evidence, vol. 1, 494, 499; vol. 2, 527–28.
29 Ibid., vol. 1, 506–7, 509; vol. 2, 534–36.
30 Ibid., vol. 1, 510; vol. 2, 536.| 31 Ibid., vol. 1, 514.
32 Kessler, *Palestine 1936*, 145.
33 Shaw Commission Evidence, vol. 1, 515–16.
34 Ibid., vol. 2, 523–24.
35 Cohen, *Year Zero*, 218–20, 247.
36 Shaw Commission Evidence, vol. 2, 539; Secret testimony of John Chancellor, Palestine Royal Commission 67th meeting, Notes of Evidence Taken in London on Friday, February 12, 1937, 468.
37 "Strike on Balfour Starts Tomorrow," *NYT*, Mar. 24, 1925, tinyurl.com/284uuprr; "Balfour Sees Work of Jewish Farmers," *NYT*, Mar. 28, 1925, tinyurl.com/5ckepmxm.
38 Shaw Commission Evidence, vol. 2, 539.
39 Ibid.
40 Shaw Commission Closing Remarks by Boyd Merriman (Jerusalem: Steimatsky, 1929), 31–34.

41 Report of the Shaw Commission, 63.
42 Ibid., 151, 163, 169. | **43** Ibid., 169. | **44** Ibid., 174.
45 Ibid., 172–73. | **46** Ibid., 182–83.
47 Auerbach, *Hebron Jews*, 72; Shaw Commission Evidence, vol. 1, 157.
48 Kolinsky, *Law, Order and Riots in Mandatory Palestine*, 31; Morris, *Righteous Victims*, 116.
49 Haganah Archive, Testimony of Naftali Rubinshtein.
50 Cohen, *Year Zero*, 239.
51 Ibid., 239–40; "Al-Buraq Revolution," Samidoun (Palestinian Prisoner Solidarity Network), tinyurl.com/ycy5khns.
52 Ahmad Alami, *Thawrat al-Buraq* [The Buraq Revolt] (Jerusalem: Published by author, 2000).
53 Cohen, *Year Zero*, 238. | **54** Ibid., 246.
55 "Steal What You Will from the Blueness of the Sea and the Sand of Memory," *Al-Jazeera*, Nov. 21, 2012, tinyurl.com/2cbfykfb; "Al-Buraq Revolution," Samidoun.
56 *Arabic Language (1): Reading, Grammar, Presentations and Expression*, vol. 2, Grade 11, Palestinian Education Ministry, 2019, 34–38; K. Tabibian, *History, Grade 9, A Journey to the Past: The Modern World in Crisis* (Tel Aviv: Center for Educational Technology, 2011), 224.

Chapter 14: Revolution
1 Cohen, *Year Zero*, 52, 53, 56, 257.
2 Shaw Commission Evidence, vol. 2, 853.
3 Cohen, *Year Zero*, 55–56.
4 Haganah Archive 103/23.
5 Cohen, *Year Zero*, 52, 53, 56, 257.
6 Zeev Tzahor, "The Struggle Between the Revisionist Party and the Labor Movement, 1929–1933," *Modern Judaism* 8(1) (Feb. 1988), 15–25.
7 CZA S25/4472 222-225; CZA 172, 174, 235, 236; CZA S25/4472 144.
8 Cohen, *Year Zero*, 165; Auerbach, *Hebron Jews*, 75.
9 Kessler, *Palestine 1936*, 31–32.
10 Segev, *One Palestine Complete*, 341; Kessler, *Palestine 1936*, 32–33.
11 Kessler, *Palestine 1936*, 45.
12 Ibid., 47–48. | **13** Ibid., 49.
14 Ibid., 44. | **15** Ibid., 46. | **16** Ibid., 225.
17 Ibid., 49–50, 53–55.
18 Auerbach, *Hebron Jews*, 76; interviews with Yosef Ezra, 2019.

Chapter 15: The First Two-State Solution
1 Kessler, *Palestine 1936*, 75, 76, 104.
2 Francis R. Nicosia, *Nazi Germany and the Arab World* (Cambridge, UK: Cambridge Univ. Press, 2014), 72.
3 Julias Mayer, "The Constantine Pogroms," *The Sentinel*, Aug. 23, 1934, 6, tinyurl.com/2v2cz36p; James McDougall, *A History of Algeria* (Cambridge UK: Cambridge Univ. Press, 2017), 116–17; Joshua Cole, "Constantine before the Riots of August 1934: Civil Status, Anti-Semitism, and the Politics of Assimilation in Interwar French Algeria," *Journal of North African Studies* 17(5) (2012); JTA, Aug. 8, 1934.
4 Kessler, *Palestine 1936*, 45–46.
5 Al-Difa, Apr. 20, 1936; Cmd. 5479: Report of the Palestine Royal Commission ("Peel Commission"), His Majesty's Stationery Office, London, July 1937, 96–97; Kessler, *Palestine 1936*, 58; Mattar, *The Mufti of Jerusalem*, 147.
6 Kessler, *Palestine 1936*, 59, 66.
7 Ibid., 63, 66, 67 (Jewish and British death toll).
8 Ibid., 72–73. | **9** Ibid., 79. | **10** Ibid. | **11** Ibid., 81. | **12** Ibid., 90.
13 Ibid., 78. | **14** Ibid., 84–85. | **15** Ibid., 71. | **16** Ibid., 72, 78.
17 Secret testimony of John Chancellor, Palestine Royal Commission 67th meeting, Notes of Evidence Taken in London on Friday, Feb. 12, 1937, 468–69.
18 Cmd 5479, Palestine Royal Commission, London, 1937, 394–95.
19 Ibid., 395. | **20** Ibid.
21 Kessler, *Palestine 1936*, 98–99.
22 Ibid., 101–2. | **23** Ibid., 103–4.

Chapter 16: The Mufti and the Führer
1 Yehuda Taggar, *The Mufti of Jerusalem and Palestine Arab Politics, 1930–1937* (London: London School of Economics, 1973), 451.
2 Kessler, *Palestine 1936*, 102; Henry Laurens, *La question de Palestine*, vol. 2: *Une mission sacrée de civilization, 1922–1947* (Paris: Fayard, 2002), 373; Haim Levenberg, *Military Preparations of the Arab Community in Palestine: 1945–1948* (London: Frank Cass, 1993), 8; *Daily Telegraph*, July 29, 1937; "Mufti Muffed," *Time*, Nov. 3, 1941.
3 Kessler, *Palestine 1936*, 109–11.

4 Matthew Hughes, *Britain's Pacification of Palestine: The British Army, the Colonial State, and the Arab Revolt, 1936–1939* (Cambridge, UK: Cambridge Univ. Press, 2019), 422–523; Kessler, *Palestine 1936*, 111–12; Zvi Elpeleg, *The Grand Mufti: Haj Amin Al-Hussaini, Founder of the Palestinian National Movement* (London: Frank Cass, 1991), 48.

5 Yoav Gelber, *Jewish-Transjordanian Relations 1921–1948* (Abingdon, UK: Routledge, 1997), 133–35; Neil Caplan, *Futile Diplomacy: A History of Arab-Israeli Negotiations, 1913–1956* (Abingdon, UK: Routledge, 2015), 238–39.

6 Walid Khalidi, *From Haven to Conquest: Readings in Zionism and the Palestine Problem until 1948* (Beirut: Institute for Palestine Studies, 1987), 846–49; Hughes, *Britain's Pacification of Palestine*, 245–48, 375–84; Yehuda Slutsky, *Sefer Toldot Hahaganah*, vol. 2 (Tel Aviv: Zionist Library, 1963), 801 (Hebrew).

7 Ruth Wodak and John E. Richardson, *Analysing Fascist Discourse: European Fascism in Talk and Text* (Abingdon, UK: Routledge, 2013), 56; video of his speech: encyclopedia.ushmm.org/content/en/article/1939-key-dates; J. Arieh Kochavi, "The Struggle against Jewish Immigration to Palestine," *Middle Eastern Studies* 34(3) (July 1988), 146.

8 Cmd. 6019, Statement of British Policy in Mandatory Palestine (The 1939 White Paper).

9 Kessler, *Palestine 1936*, 212.

10 Cmd. 6019, Statement of British Policy.

11 Kessler, *Palestine 1936*, 222.

12 Issa Khalaf, *Politics in Palestine: Arab Factionalism and Social Disintegration, 1939–1948* (Albany, NY: SUNY Press, 1991), 283; Benny Morris, "The Tangled Truth," *New Republic*, May 7, 2008; Taggar, *The Mufti of Jerusalem*, 447; Morris, *Righteous Victims*, 159.

13 "Mufti Muffed," *Time*; Kessler, *Palestine 1936*, 228.

14 The Expulsion that Backfired: When Iraq Kicked Out Its Jews," *Times of Israel*, May 31, 2016, tinyurl.com/mwb8hzam.

15 Record of the Conversation Between the Führer and the Grand Mufti of Jerusalem on November 28, 1941 . . . in Berlin, Documents on German Foreign Policy, 1918–1945, Series D, Vol. 13 (London, 1964); Stefan Wild, "National Socialism in the Arab Near East between 1933 and 1939," *Die Welt des Islams* 1/4(25), (1985), 126–73; Jeffrey Herf, *Nazi Propaganda for the Arab World* (New Haven, CT: Yale Univ. Press, 2009), 24–26; video of their meeting: tinyurl.com/ywr8yb3x; "Hajj Amin Al-Husayni Meets Hitler" (film), Holocaust Museum, tinyurl.com/ynxzvp8u; Jan Friedman, "New Research Taints Image of Desert Fox Rommel," *Der Spiegel*, May 23, 2007, tinyurl.com/ynxzvp8u; Dalin and Rothmann, *Icon of Evil*, 4.

16 "Full Official Record: What the Mufti Said to Hitler," *TI*, tinyurl.com/ysmd7hn8; David G. Dalin, "Hitler's Mufti," *First Things*, Aug. 2005, www.firstthings.com/article/2005/08/hitlers-mufti.

17 Record of the Conversation Between the Führer and the Grand Mufti; Friedmann, "New Research Taints Image of Desert Fox Rommel," Freda Kirchwey,*The Arab Higher Committee: Its Origins, Personnel, and Purposes* (a report of the Nation Associates, May 10, 1947); Wolfgang G. Schwanitz, "Photographic Evidence Shows Palestinian Leader Amin al-Husseini at a Nazi Concentration Camp," *Tablet*, Apr. 7, 2021, tinyurl.com/ym2jusv6; Chen Malul, "Revealed: SS Chief Heinrich Himmler's Warm Wishes to Mufti Haj Amin al-Husseini," *The Librarians*, Nov. 6, 2017, blog.nli.org.il/en/himmler/.

18 Norman Cameron and R. H. Steven, *Hitler's Table Talk, 1941–1944* (New York: Enigma Books, 2000), 547; Dalin and Rothmann, *Icon of Evil*, 47–48; Adolf Hitler, *Hitler's Secret Conversations, 1941–1944*, trans. Norman Cameron and R. H. Stevens (New York: Farrar, Straus and Young, 1953), 443–44.

19 J. C. Hurewitz, *The Struggle for Palestine* (New York: Norton, 1951), 154; Richard Breitman and Norman J. W. Goda, *Hitler's Shadow: Nazi War Criminals, US Intelligence, and the Cold War* (Washington, DC: National Archives and Records Administration, 2011), pg. 19.

20 "Hajj Amin al-Husseini: Wartime Propagandist," Holocaust Encyclopedia, tinyurl.com/3dyjft8v; Moshe Pearlman, *Mufti of Jerusalem: The Story of Haj Amin El Husseini* (London: Victor Gollancz, 1947), 68.

21 Pearlman, *Mufti of Jerusalem*, 51; Kessler, *Palestine 1936*, 228–29; Kenneth R. Timmerman, *Preachers of Hate: Islam and the War on America* (New York: Crown Forum, 2003), 109–10.

22 Telegram from Heinrich Himmler to Haj Amin al-Husseini: NLI: blog.nli.org.il/en/himmler_/.

23 Gilbert Achcar, *The Arabs and the Holocaust: The Arab-Israeli War of Narratives* (New York: Henry Holt, 2010), 157.

24 Pearlman, *Mufti of Jerusalem*, 68; Achcar, *The Arabs and the Holocaust*, 148, 150–58; Amin Husseini, *Mudhakkirat al-Hajj Muhammad Amin al-Husayni* [The Memoirs of Haj Amin al-Husseini], ed. Abd al-Karim al-Umar (Damascus: Al-Ahali, 1999), 123–24, 127–28, 194.

25 Record of the Conversation Between the Führer and the Grand Mufti; Friedmann, "New Research Taints Image of Desert Fox Rommel."

26 Friedmann, "New Research Taints Image of Desert Fox Rommel."

27 Bernard Lewis, *The Middle East: A Brief History of the Last 2,000 Years* (New York: Scribner, 1997), 311; Klaus-Michael Mallmann and Martin Cüppers, *Nazi Palestine: The Plans for the Extermination of the Jews in Palestine* (New York: Enigma Books, 2010), 201; Friedmann, "New Research Taints Image of Desert Fox Rommel."

28 Mallmann and Cüppers, *Nazi Palestine*, 201; Ronen Bergman with Gil Meltzer, Shahar Alterman, ed., *And Authority Is Given: Where Did We Go Wrong? How the Palestinian Authority Became an Assembly Line of*

Corruption and Terrorism (Tel Aviv: Yedioth Ahronoth Pub., 2002, 59 (Hebrew); Ronen Bergman, *Rise and Kill First: The Secret History of Israel's Targeted Assassinations* (New York: Random House, 2019), 641; Sean McMeekin, *The Berlin-Baghdad Express: The Ottoman Empire and Germany's Bid for World Power* (Cambridge, MA: Harvard Univ. Press, 2010), 362.

29 "United Nations Information System on the Question of Palestine: The Origins and Evolution of the Palestine Problem: 1917–1988, PART II 1947–1977," tinyurl.com/3necthzd.

30 Breitman and Goda, *Hitler's Shadow*, 21–22; JTA, "Ex-mufti of Jerusalem Placed on War Criminals List; Indicted by Yugoslav Government," July 20, 1945; Jeffrey Herf, *Haj Amin al-Husseini and the French Government: May 1945–May 1946* (Cambridge, UK: Cambridge Univ. Press, 2022).

31 *Palestine: A Study of Jewish, Arab and British Policies* (New Haven: Yale University Press, published for the Esco Foundation for Palestine, 1947), 1214; Dalin and Rothmann, *Icon of Evil*, 83.

32 The Nobel Peace Prize 1994, "Yasser Arafat: Facts," www.nobelprize.org/prizes/peace/1994/arafat/facts/; Dalin and Rothmann, *Icon of Evil*, 82; Robert S. Wistrich, *A Lethal Obsession: Anti-Semitism from Antiquity to the Global Jihad* (New York: Random House, 2010), 701; Schwanitz, "Photographic Evidence."

33 Husseini, *Mudhakkirat*, 164; Achcar, *The Arabs and the Holocaust*, 155–58; David Patterson, *Judaism, Antisemitism, and Holocaust* (Cambridge, UK: Cambridge Univ. Press, 2022), 165–84; Kessler, *Palestine 1936*, 229.

34 Wistrich, *A Lethal Obsession*, 701–2; "PA President 'Abbas Commemorates 'Martyrs,'" MEMRI, tinyurl.com/rk6f9ya4; Facebook photo: tinyurl.com/7nueau33.

35 *NYT*, Mar. 26, 2000; "Wiesenthal Center Asks ICRC to Cut Ties to Red Crescent," JTA, Dec. 20, 1990, tinyurl.com/whtpphnp.

36 "Palestinian Holocaust Denial," Washington Institute, tinyurl.com/4ywhufbb; "Palestinian Leader's Comments on Holocaust Draw Accusations of Antisemitism from US and Europe," AP, Sept. 7, 2023, tinyurl.com/mr3earfj; "The Holocaust Wasn't Fueled by Antisemitism," *Haaretz*, Sept. 7, 2023, tinyurl.com/2s3erf83; "Holocaust Row: Abbas Accused of Anti-Semitism," BBC, May 1, 2018, tinyurl.com/4sk486bb; "Abbas Claims Link between Nazis and Zionists," JTA, Jan 22, 2013, tinyurl.com/ymz6s4dy; "Palestinian Leader Incites Uproar with Speech Condemned as Anti-Semitic," *NYT*, May 2, 2018, tinyurl.com/mrr3ar6w.

Chapter 17: Army of the Holy War

1 Yehudit Kleiman and Nina Springer-Aharoni, *The Anguish of Liberation: Testimonies from 1945* (Jerusalem: Yad Vashem, 1995), 54–55.

2 Palestine Royal Commission Report, 242, 291; Moshe Auman, "Land Ownership in Palestine 1880–1948," in Michael Curtis et al., *The Palestinians* (Piscataway, NJ: Transaction Books, 1975), 25.

3 "Cyprus Detention Camps," Holocaust Encyclopedia; Aharon Cohen, *Israel and the Arab World* (New York: Funk and Wagnalls, 1970), 174.

4 "Jerusalem Bomb Kills 41 in Attack on British Offices," *NYT*, July 23, 1946, 1, 3, tinyurl.com/4p5twth7; "Zionist Terrorists Say They Set Bomb," *NYT*, July 24, 1946, 1, 5, tinyurl.com/5ct3kmry.

5 "Jerusalem Bomb Kills 41," *NYT*; "Zionist Terrorists Say They Set Bomb," *NYT*.

6 House of Commons, July 23, 1946, "Terrorist Outrage Jerusalem (1946)," Parliamentary Debates (Hansard), tinyurl.com/47rf4282.

7 "Zionist Terrorists Say They Set Bomb," *NYT*.

8 Eric H. Cline, *Jerusalem Besieged: From Ancient Canaan to Modern Israel* (Ann Arbor: Univ. of Michigan Press, 2005), 260.

9 Bruce Hoffman, *Anonymous Soldiers: The Struggle for Israel, 1917–1947* (New York: Alfred A. Knopf, 2015).

10 Richard Andrew Cahill, "'Going Berserk': 'Black and Tans' in Palestine," *Palestine Studies* 38 (2009), tinyurl.com/4f2xacxt; "Lt. Raymond Oswald Cafferata," The Auxiliaries, tinyurl.com/bddnmzk6.

11 Bernard Reich, *A Brief History of Israel* (New York: Checkmark Books, 2005), 39–40.

12 Artur Patek, *Jews on Route to Palestine 1934–1944* (Krakow: Jagiellonian Univ. Press, 2012), 54–55; "Exodus 1947," Holocaust Encyclopedia, tinyurl.com/4nzfyju9; Elisabeth Åsbrink, *1947: Where Now Begins* (New York: Other Press, 2017), 139–40; Alexander Crosby Brown, *Steam Packets on the Chesapeake* (Cambridge, MD: Tidewater Publishers, 1961), 121–22.

13 Anglo-American Committee of Inquiry—Appendix IV, Palestine: Historical Background.

14 "Arabs See U.N. 'Murdered,' Disavow Any Partition Role," 1, 60, "Zionist Audience Joyful After Vote," 67, *NYT*, Nov. 30, 1947, tinyurl.com/mu6nwue9.

15 Interview with Yosef Ezra, 2019.

16 "Palestine's Arabs Kill Seven Jews, Call 3-Day Strike," *NYT*, Dec. 1, 1947, 1, 8, tinyurl.com/mtffeccz.

17 "Jerusalem Torn by Rioting, Arabs Use Knives, Set Fires . . . ," *NYT*, Dec. 3, 1947, 1, 4, tinyurl.com/w85hbh7s; "Palestine Strife Widens . . . Toll Climbs to 24," *NYT*, Dec. 4, 1947, 1, 4; tinyurl.com/5tu53wnp; *Facts on File Yearbook 1948*, vol. 8, Jan. 1, 1949, 231.

18 "Arab States Call Meeting; Riots over Palestine Go On," *NYT*, Dec. 2, 1947, 1, 10, tinyurl.com/mmav47dp; "Moslem Sages Ask Holy War as Duty to Bar Palestine Split" *NYT*, Dec. 3, 1947, 1, 6, tinyurl.com/w85hbh7s; "A Timeline of Jews in Egypt," *NYT*, June 24, 2015, tinyurl.com/58a99xuy; "How Egypt's Last Jews Will Mark Hanukkah," CBS News, Dec. 15, 2022, tinyurl.com/yc28dtxs.

19 Mallmann and Cüppers, *Nazi Palestine*, 200, 201; "Nazis Planned Palestine Subversion," BBC, July 5, 2001, tinyurl.com/yx7baztj; "Kurt Wieland, alias Heinz Hecht, Frederick Baksen, Abu Yassin," London: National Archives, KV 2/401.
20 Danny Rubenstein, *The Mystery of Arafat* (New York: Steerforth Press, 1995), 38; Dalin, "Hitler's Mufti"; Herf, *Nazi Propaganda for the Arab World*, 241–45; Said K. Aburish, *From Defender to Dictator* (New York: Bloomsbury, 1998), 7–32.
21 "35 Deaths in Day Set Palestine Peak," *NYT*, Dec. 12, 1947, 1, tinyurl.com/22tsr86n; Interview with Yosef Ezra, 2019; "British, Jews Foil Invasion by Arabs in North Palestine," *NYT*, Jan. 10, 1948, 1, 3, tinyurl.com/yc85yy6f.

Chapter 18: Between Independence and Catastrophe

1 "Zionists Proclaim New State of Israel . . . Egypt Orders Invasion," *NYT*, May 15, 1948, 1–2, tinyurl.com/2u7sddba.
2 Israel's declaration of independence: avalon.law.yale.edu/20th_century/israel.asp.
3 "One Day That Shook the World," *JP*, Apr. 30, 1998, tinyurl.com/k5pu93ut.
4 "Cunningham Goes as Mandate Ends," *NYT*, May 15, 1948, 1, 2, tinyurl.com/2u7sddba.
5 "Air Attack Opens," *NYT*, May 15, 1948, 1, 2, tinyurl.com/2u7sddba; "Arab Armies Invade Palestine; Reach Gaza, Bomb Tel Aviv Again," *NYT*, May 16, 1948, 1, 4, tinyurl.com/yc54yfkj; Benny Morris, *1948: A History of the First Arab-Israeli War* (New Haven, CT: Yale Univ. Press, 2008), 185.
6 Benny Morris, *The Birth of the Palestinian Refugee Problem Revisited* (Cambridge, UK: Cambridge Univ. Press, 2004), 16.
7 Matti Friedman, *Spies of No Country* (Chapel Hill, NC: Algonquin, 2019), 119; Morris, *1948: A History of the First Arab-Israeli War*, 404–6; Adam M. Garfinkle, *Politics and Society in Modern Israel: Myths and Realities* (Armonk, NY: M.E. Sharpe, 2000), 61.
8 Memorandum on the Palestine Refugee Problem, May 4, 1949, Foreign Relations of the United States, *1949*, 973, 984; Sachar, *A History of Israel*, 332; "British Halt Jerusalem Battle," *Pittsburgh Press*, May 3, 1948, 1; Morris, *Righteous Victims*, 252–58; Morris, *The Birth of the Palestinian Refugee Problem Revisited*, 262; Hussein Ibish, "A 'Catastrophe' That Defines Palestinian Identity," *The Atlantic*, May 14, 2018; Friedman, *Spies of No Country*, 105.
9 Cohen, *Year Zero*, 165; "Cabinet Report Says Jordan Destroyed 56 Old City Synagogues," *JTA*, Nov. 2, 1967, tinyurl.com/fr5kbab7.
10 Auerbach, *Hebron Jews*, 79.
11 "The Arabs of Palestine," *The Atlantic*, Oct. 1961, tinyurl.com/39u766bd.
12 Spencer C. Tucker and Priscilla Mary Roberts, *The Encyclopedia of the Arab-Israeli Conflict: A Political, Social, and Military History* (Santa Barbara, CA: ABC-CLIO, 2008), 464; Walter Laqueur and Barry Rubin, *The Israel-Arab Reader: A Documentary History of the Middle East Conflict*, 7th ed. (New York: Penguin, 2008); Raja Shehadeh, *From Occupation to Interim Accords* (Alphen aan den Rijn, The Netherlands: Kluwer Law International, 1997), 77–78; Yitzhak Oron, ed. *Middle East Record*, vol. 1 (Jerusalem: Jerusalem Post Press, 1960), 128; Khalaf, *Politics in Palestine*, 129–30.
13 "The Invisible Community: Egypt's Palestinians," Al-Shabaka, June 11, 2011, tinyurl.com/553tazat; "The Palestinians' Long Wait in Lebanon," *NYT*, Mar. 3, 2011, tinyurl.com/ydeytddm; "Palestinians in Lebanon: A Forgotten People," *Time*, Feb. 25, 2009, tinyurl.com/3bk6npwn, "A Palestinian Seat in Lebanon's Parliament?" Al Jazeera, Mar. 19, 2018, tinyurl.com/yc6em3xc; "Nationality, Documentation, and Statelessness in Syria," Inst. on Statelessness and Inclusion, tinyurl.com/2388mxbb.
14 "Who We Are," United Nations Relief and Works Agency, www.unrwa.org/who-we-are; "Meet Our People," UNHCR, www.unhcr.org/en-us/meet-unhcr-staff.html; "Update on Budgets and Funding (2022 and 2023)," Executive Committee of the High Commissioner's Programme, Feb. 17, 2023, tinyurl.com/54wrmvca; "Palestinian Schools Have a Problem," *Foreign Policy*, Nov. 5, 2021, tinyurl.com/3sya4k57.
15 "Palestinian Schools Have a Problem," *Foreign Policy*; "How We Spend Funds," UNWRA, tinyurl.com/yezhemua; "The 2020–21 Palestinian School Curriculum Grades 1–12," IMPACT-se, tinyurl.com/yeyjwd5k; "Report on Palestinian Textbooks," Leibnitz-Institut für Bildungsmedien, tinyurl.com/vh2rvtm6.

Chapter 19: Ingathering of the Exiles

1 "The Mass Migration to Israel of the 1950s," My Jewish Learning, tinyurl.com/yc5pvhmk; "400 Olim Arrive in Israel Ahead of Independence Day," June 5, 2008, YNet, tinyurl.com/3zz8ahwt; Spencer Tucker, ed. "Cyprus Detention Camps," *Encyclopedia of the Arab-Israeli Conflict*, vol 1 (Santa Barbara, CA: ABC-CLIO, 2008), 280.
2 International Protection of Human Rights: Hearings Before the Subcommittee on International Organizations and Movements, 93-1, 1974, 313; Carole Basri, "The Jewish Refugees from Arab Countries: An Examination of Legal Rights—A Case Study of the Human Rights Violations of Iraqi Jews," *Fordham International Jaw Journal* 26(3) (2002), 657, tinyurl.com/4tty22eh; Israel's Central Bureau of Statistics; "The Expulsion that Backfired," *TI*; "On Passover 2021, Iraq's Jewish Community Dwindles to Fewer than Five," *TI*, Mar. 28, 2021, tinyurl.com/bdyudm4c.
3 Hadass Tesher, "Jewish Population Rises to 15.3 Million Worldwide," *JA*, tinyurl.com/272zny53.

Chapter 20: The First Settler

1 Cohen, *Year Zero*, 154.

2 Yossi Klein Halevi, *Like Dreamers: The Story of the Israeli Paratroopers Who Reunited Jerusalem and Divided a Nation* (New York: HarperCollins, 2013), 4.

3 Interview with Ibrahim Bader, whose father was one of those men who showed the soldiers the letter of gratitude, 2020; Auerbach, *Hebron Jews*, 82 (Sheikh Jaabari).

4 Interview with Yosef Ezra, 2019, and Shlomo Hasson, who met with Jaabari soon after this, 2024.

5 Rabbi Moshe Levinger, "How It Happened," en.hebron.org.il, date unknown (article link since discontinued); "The Settlers in Hebron Held a Passover Seder," *Maariv*, Apr. 15, 1968, tinyurl.com/48shk67y.

6 "Rabbi Franco, Survivor of Hebron Massacre, Dies," JTA, tinyurl.com/4rr9uyxy; "Franco, Avraham," encyclopedia.com, tinyurl.com/536xw3w7; Shaw Commission Evidence, vol. 2, 851; Burg, *In Days to Come*, 193; interview with Moshe Levinger's daughter, Atiya, 2023.

7 *What We Saw in Hebron* (documentary); Auerbach, *Hebron Jews*, 83–85; Burg, *In Days to Come*, 192; interviews with Yosef Ezra, 2019.

8 "Six Day War: The East Jerusalem Controversy," NPR, tinyurl.com/y43brbtb.

9 "Stop Waiting for the Phone to Ring," *Haaretz*, Mar. 29, 2006, tinyurl.com/5n7bvhdt; "This Week in History: The Arab League's Three No's," *JP*, tinyurl.com/2extk8zz.

10 "Hebron Settlers May Stay in Town," *NYT*, May 16, 1968, 13, tinyurl.com/sry73mvw.

11 Knesset transcript, Oct. 30, 1967; Shlomo Gazit, *The Carrot and the Stick: Israel's Policy in Judaea and Samaria, 1967–68* (Tel Aviv: Kineret Zmura-Bitan, 1985), 170 (Hebrew).

12 Avissar, *Sefer Hevron*, 399; Gazit's letter to the lawyers of Franco and Hasson: IDF Archive 47/2845/1997 183.

13 Auerbach, *Hebron Jews*, 89.

14 Jeffrey Goldberg, "Among the Settlers," *New Yorker*, May 31, 2004, www.newyorker.com/magazine/2004/05/31/among-the-settlers.

15 Ruth Kark and Michal Oren-Nordheim, *Jerusalem and Its Environs; Quarters, Neighborhoods, Villages 1800–1948* (Jerusalem: Hebrew Univ. Magnes Press, 2001), 338, 342–45, 358.

16 Auerbach, *Hebron Jews*, 86–88.

17 Levinger, "How It Happened"; "The Settlers in Hebron Held a Passover Seder," *Maariv*; "Recalling a Historic Seder" (Miriam Levinger interview), *Jewish Press*, Apr. 18, 2019, tinyurl.com/yckr2c9v; interview with Shachar Levinger, their granddaughter, and their daughter, Atiya, 2023.

18 "Recalling a Historic Seder," *Jewish Press*; Levinger, "How It Happened"; "The Settlers in Hebron Held a Passover Seder," *Maariv*; Halevi, *Like Dreamers*, 151–52; "After 42 Years, Jews Are Part of Hebron," *NYT*, July 24, 1971, tinyurl.com/2wafjcnr.

19 Ibid.

20 "Cabinet Member Tells Religious Group They Can Remain in Hebron," JTA, May 14, 1968, tinyurl.com/mrxdm3uz; "Hebron Settlers May Stay in Town," *NYT*, May 16, 1968, tinyurl.com/29z48uyh; Auerbach, *Hebron Jews*, 92.

21 Avissar, *Sefer Hevron*, 15; Auerbach, *Hebron Jews*, 94; "Recalling a Historic Seder," *Jewish Press*.

22 "Cabinet Member Tells Religious Group They Can Remain in Hebron," JTA; "Hebron Settlers May Stay in Town," *NYT*.

23 "The Israel of Amos Oz," *New Yorker*, Jan. 5, 2019, tinyurl.com/49upjk65; Auerbach, *Hebron Jews*, 96; "Hebron Settlers May Stay in Town," *NYT*; "After 42 Years, Jews Are Part of Hebron," *NYT*.

24 Auerbach, *Hebron Jews*, 95.

25 Halevi, *Like Dreamers*, 151; "Hebron Youth Admits Throwing Grenade," JTA, Oct. 10, 1968, tinyurl.com/2b5wsh84; "Hand Grenade Hurled by Arab Terrorists Explodes at Tomb," JTA, Oct. 11, 1968, tinyurl.com/mswmrhxz.

26 Cohen, *Year Zero*, 154.

27 Noam Arnon, Hebron *4000 Years & 40: The Story of the City of the Patriarchs* (Kiryat Arba, ISR: Shilo & Barkats, 2008), 30.

28 "After 42 Years, Jews Are Part of Hebron," *NYT*.

29 "Jewish Defense League," Southern Poverty Law Center, tinyurl.com/bdf69mwn.

30 "Man Convicted in Terrorism Conspiracy Is Denied New Trial," *NYT*, Jan. 13, 2012, tinyurl.com/mvm3bmwa; Greg B. Smith, "Bin Laden Bankrolled Kahane Killer Defense," *New York Daily News*, Oct. 9, 2002.

31 Interviews with Levinger's daughter Atiya in 2023, with Yehudit Katsover, who was there with her children in 2023, and Sarah Nachshon, 2020; "Recalling a Historic Seder," *Jewish Press*; Levinger, "How It Happened"; "The Settlers in Hebron Held a Passover Seder," *Maariv*.

32 Interviews with Yehudit Katsover, 2023; Auerbach, *Hebron Jews*, 105.

33 Interviews with Levinger's daughter Atiya, who was there, 2023, and Yehudit Katsover; Auerbach, *Hebron Jews*, 105.

34 Auerbach, *Hebron Jews*, 105; "The Women and Children Prepare for Another Shabbat at 'Hadassah' in Hebron," *Maariv*, May 4, 1979, 3, tinyurl.com/mr3kb86n (Hebrew).

35 "Arab Women Offered Food to 'Settlers' in 'Hadassah' in Hebron; PM Demands the Women Leave the Place," *Maariv*, Apr. 30, 1979, 4, tinyurl.com/2p8sanyu (Hebrew); "Women and Children Prepare for another Shabbat," *Maariv*.

36 "Rabbi Kahana and His Followers Removed by Force from Hebron," *Maariv*, Feb. 27, 1978, 6, tinyurl. com/3nykksmb (Hebrew); "Rabbi Kahana Removed from Roof of Hadassah in Hebron," *Maariv*, Mar. 24, 1978, 63, https://tinyurl.com/yme7d7at (Hebrew); "Women and Children Prepare for Another Shabbat," *Maariv*; "Residents of Kiryat Arba Held Prayers at Hadassah House in Hebron," *Davar*, Aug. 18, 1976, 3, tinyurl. com/4f4zbbzk (Hebrew); "Yeshiva Students Removed from Old Jewish Quarter of Hebron," *Davar*, Aug. 17, 1976, 1, tinyurl.com/e4pek7k5 (Hebrew); interviews with Noam Arnon, Yehudit Katsover, Tzippi Shlissel, Sarah Nachshon; 2019–23.

37 Auerbach, *Hebron Jews*, 106–7.

38 Auerbach, *Hebron Jews*, 106–7; interviews with Yehudit Katzover; "Arab Women Offered Food," *Maariv*.

39 "Arab Women Offered Food," *Maariv*.

40 Hebron population figures: Auerbach, *Hebron Jews*, 110; "5 Are Killed in Palestinian Attack on Jewish Settlers in West Bank," *NYT*, May 3, 1980, tinyurl.com/3rmfk2jv.

41 Auerbach, *Hebron Jews*, 109; *NYT*, Mar. 24, 1980; "Hebron under Tight Security Following Murder of Yeshiva Student," *JTA*, Feb. 4, 1980, tinyurl.com/3zsbmvyr; "Murder of Yeshiva Students Spurs Calls for Jewish Presence in Hebron," *JTA*, Feb. 5, 1980, tinyurl.com/knf8drsh.

42 Auerbach, *Hebron Jews*, 109; *NYT*, Mar. 25, 1980; "West Bank Deportations Are Ordered," *WP*, May 4, 1980, tinyurl.com/3tkh3zs7; "Arab General Strike on West Bank Is Only Partially Successful," *JTA*, Mar. 26, 1980, tinyurl.com/3fnc8wku..

43 "The Hebron Raid: Tension Rising in Israel," *NYT*, May 5, 1980.

Chapter 21: Revenge of Renewal

1 Details of the attack and the attackers: "Israel Charges 10 Palestinians in Hebron Ambush," *WP*, Sept. 17, 1980, tinyurl.com/3a5c2zkv; "Palestinian Guerrillas Put Aside Differences to Train in USSR," *WP*, Nov. 17, 1980, tinyurl.com/3647v45p; "Israel Holds 10 Arabs for Hebron Slaying of 6 Jews in May," *NYT*, tinyurl.com/2hdf5rm2.

2 The Palestinian National Charter: Resolutions of the Palestine National Council July 1–17, 1968, avalon.law. yale.edu/20th_century/plocov.asp.

3 Dalin and Rothmann, *Icon of Evil*, 134–35; Wistrich, *A Lethal Obsession*; "In a Ruined Country," *The Atlantic*, Sept. 2005, tinyurl.com/57mwfp4v.

4 Details of the attack and those who were killed are from my interviews with survivors Yerachmiel and Simcha Elyashiv, 2020, and from newspaper reports: "The Hebron Raid: Tension Rising in Israel," *NYT*, May 5, 1980, tinyurl.com/y2t23dja; "Palestinian Guerrillas Put Aside Differences to Train in USSR," *WP*; "Virginia Man's Violent World Ends in West Bank," *WP*, May 7, 1980, tinyurl.com/3sac4ame; "Israel Holds 10 Arabs for Hebron Slaying of 6 Jews in May," *NYT*; "West Bank Deportations Are Ordered," *WP*.

5 "The Hebron Raid," *NYT*.

6 "A Deadly Spiral on the West Bank," *NYT*, May 4, 1980, tinyurl.com/2dbrdehm; "West Bank Deportations Are Ordered," *WP*.

7 "West Bank Deportations Are Ordered," *WP*.

8 Trudy Rubin, "A Voice of Moderation Is Silenced in Jordan," *Philadelphia Inquirer*, Jan. 4, 1985, 1; "Tale of Two Mayors," *WP*, Dec. 8, 1980, tinyurl.com/4uub83e6; "A Deadly Spiral," *NYT*; "Arafat Defends Ambush of Israeli Settlers in Hebron as Resistance to Occupation," *NYT*, May 8, 1980, tinyurl.com/2z6dkxhn.

9 "West Bank Deportations Are Ordered," *WP*.

10 "Israeli Defense Minister Quits," *WP*, May 26, 1980, tinyurl.com/mrkkh3pk.

11 Interviews with Noam Arnon, 2019–20; Auerbach, *Hebron Jews*, 110.

12 "Israeli Student Is Slain in Hebron," *NYT*, July 8, 1983, tinyurl.com/5n6z5emv; "Kiryat Arba Settler Stabbed," *JTA*, Nov. 2, 1981, tinyurl.com/ymjfn5m5.

13 Auerbach, *Hebron Jews*, 112; "Hebron under Curfew after Arabs Fatally StabYeshiva Student," *JTA*, July 8, 1983, tinyurl.com/yk4u4e53.

14 "Arens Indicates the Government Has Ambitious Plans for Restoring the Jewish Quarter in Hebron," *JTA*, July 14, 1983, tinyurl.com/2hxua6ze.

15 Auerbach, *Hebron Jews*, 112; "Israeli Student Is Slain in Hebron," *NYT*.

16 "Israelis Arrested in Bomb Plot," *WP*, Apr. 29, 1984, tinyurl.com/ckxps9jk; "Key Rabbi Reported Arrested in Israeli Terror Investigation," *NYT*, May 14, 1984, tinyurl.com/3v55bf7w.

17 "Key Rabbi Reported Arrested," *NYT*; "25 Are Indicted as Jewish Terrorists in Israel," *NYT*, May 24, 1984, tinyurl.com/5n93mcjd.

18 "Israeli Court Sentences 15 Jewish Terrorists," *NYT*, July 23, 1985, tinyurl.com/4skb47uj; Edward Alexander, *The Jewish Idea and Its Enemies: Personalities, Issues, Events* (Piscataway, NJ: Transaction Publishers, 1988), 177; "Israeli Debate on Amnesty Moving to the Streets," *Los Angeles Times*, June 1, 1985, tinyurl.com/2vjn9kjr; "Marcher Is Killed in Israeli Protest," *NYT*, Feb. 11, 1983, tinyurl.com/ej25ex6t; "Revisiting Peace Activist Emil Grunzweig's Murder," *Haaretz*, Feb. 16, 2016, tinyurl.com/bdm2mnd4.

19 "Jewish Settlers Are Convicted in Terror Cases," *NYT*, July 11, 1985, tinyurl.com/yc4c9e23; "Israeli Court Sentences 15 Jewish Terrorists," *NYT*.
20 "15 Israelis Convicted for Terrorism," *WP*, July 11, 1985, tinyurl.com/yc7npx24.
21 "Israeli Court Sentences 15 Jewish Terrorists," *NYT*; "Jewish Terrorist in Israel is Sentenced to 10 Years," *NYT*, June 22, 1984, tinyurl.com/nnm9euch.
22 "How a Group of Jewish Terrorists Ended Up in Israel's Halls of Power," *Haaretz*, July 5, 2018, tinyurl.com/3uz7jvtf; "Ethnic Cleansing in God's Name," *Haaretz*, Jan. 29, 2024, tinyurl.com/yv8pj78a.
23 "Israeli Leader Commutes Jewish Terrorists' Terms," *WP*, Mar. 28, 1987, tinyurl.com/2ddeexwd; "Aging Extremist Laments Violence Now Used against Palestinians," *NYT*, Aug. 22, 2015, tinyurl.com/2e4yvzfk.
24 Goldberg, "Among the Settlers," *New Yorker*, May 31, 2004; "Law Enforcement vis-a-vis Israeli Civilians in the Occupied Territories," B'Tselem, Mar. 1994, 22, 23, 102, 107, 108, tinyurl.com/yv6jy6d2.
25 "NGO Says Only 6% of Police Probes of Settler Violence It Was Party to Ended in Charges," *TI*, Jan. 22, 2024, tinyurl.com/29anrf3e.

Chapter 22: The Mayor

1 "List of Military Checkpoints in the West Bank and Gaza Strip," B'tselem, Nov. 11, 2021, tinyurl.com/sr62hbp9.
2 "Irreconcilable Hebron," *New York Review*, Apr. 21, 2021, www.nybooks.com/online/2021/04/21/irreconcilable-hebron/.
3 "Playing the Security Card," B'tselem, Sept. 2019, tinyurl.com/4rewryaj; "In Israeli-Occupied Hebron, Palestinians Describe Living in 'a Prison,'" *WP*, Feb. 28, 2024, tinyurl.com/3287brfe.
4 "Legal Affairs: The House that Rajabi Built," *JP*, Nov. 20, 2008, tinyurl.com/3su4x2k9; "Palestinians Lose Appeal over Hebron House Ownership," *Haaretz*, Mar. 11, 2014, tinyurl.com/4v6xu97c; "Jordan, PA Arrest 2 Palestinians for Selling Hebron House to Jews," *Haaretz*, Mar. 30, 2007, tinyurl.com/2zefvue; "200 Jews Enter New Building in Hevron: 'Peace House,'" Israel National News, Mar. 20, 2007, www.israelnationalnews.com/news/121891; Rabbi Moshe Levinger, "How It Happened"; "The Settlers in Hebron Held a Passover Seder," *Maariv*.
5 "Ya'alon: Settlers Can Move into Hebron Jouse," *JP*, Apr. 13, 2014; tinyurl.com/2jed3w7f; "200 Jews Enter New Building in Hevron," Israel National News.
6 "UNESCO Declares Hebron's Core as Palestinian World Heritage Site," *NYT*, July 7, 2017, tinyurl.com/2spddth5.
7 Supreme Muslim Council, *A Brief Guide to Al-Haram Al-Sharif*.
8 "Top Palestinian Muslim Cleric Okays Suicide Bombings," Scholars for Peace in the Middle East, Oct. 23, 2006, tinyurl.com/vfwsva5p.
9 "Israeli Police Arrest 2 Protesting Palestinian Legislators," *NYT*, Jan. 24, 2012, tinyurl.com/242kmtb3.
10 "Israel's Y2K Problem," *NYT*, Oct. 3, 1999, tinyurl.com/yht6y3zn; "Israel Allows Palestinian Cleric Probed for Incitement to Fly to Morocco," *TI*, Jan. 24, 2023, tinyurl.com/yeydv2bw.
11 Peter Wehner, "Erasing Jewish History Will Not Help Palestinians," *The Atlantic*, Jan. 19, 2024.

Chapter 23: Heirs to the Mufti

1 "Israel Frees 1,150 to Obtain Release of Last 3 Soldiers," *NYT*, May 21, 1985, 1, 6, tinyurl.com/4u6v65s4.
2 Zaki Chehab, *Inside Hamas: The Untold Story of Militants, Martyrs and Spies* (London: I.B. Tauris, 2007), 15–16; "Obituary: Sheikh Ahmed Yassin," *The Guardian*, Mar. 23, 2004, tinyurl.com/bdhbb39p.
3 Mustafá Kabahā, *The Palestinian People: Seeking Sovereignty and State* (Boulder, CO: Lynne Rienner, 2014), 324; "Hamas Covenant 1988," avalon.law.yale.edu/20th_century/hamas.asp.
4 Beverley Milton-Edwards and Stephen Farrell, *Hamas: The Islamic Resistance Movement* (Hoboken, NJ: John Wiley & Sons, 2013), 116; "Who Is Hamas Leader Yehiya Sinwar?," *WP*, Dec. 11, 2023, tinyurl.com/yvhcm365; "Behind Hamas's Bloody Gambit to Create a 'Permanent' State of War," *NYT*, Nov. 8, 2023, tinyurl.com/28huy2kk; "Who Are Hamas's Top Leaders in Gaza?," *NYT*, Mar. 12, 2024, tinyurl.com/3p5594cm; "Hamas Elects Hardliner Yahya Sinwar as Its Gaza Strip Chief," *The Guardian*, Feb. 13, 2017, tinyurl.com/5fhynk48; "Yahya Sinwar: Who Is the Hamas Leader in Gaza?," BBC, Nov. 21, 2023, tinyurl.com/t57wmeec.
5 "Saving Sinwar," *Tablet*, Mar. 19, 2024, tinyurl.com/3j47kz94; "'I Strangled Them with My Own Hands,'" Israel Hayom, Nov. 9, 2023, tinyurl.com/367rvyze; "Who Is Hamas Leader Yehiya Sinwar?," *WP*; "Hamas Leader Yahya Sinwar's Confession Transcript," *Haaretz*, Nov. 8, 2023, tinyurl.com/mten7ff2.
6 Richard Davis, *Hamas, Popular Support and War in the Middle East: Insurgency in the Holy Land* (Abingdon, UK: Routledge, 2016), 68; Daniel Byman, *A High Price: The Triumphs and Failures of Israeli Counterterrorism* (Oxford: Oxford Univ. Press, 2011), pg. 79; William L. Cleveland, *A History of the Modern Middle East* (Boulder, CO: Westview Press, Boulder, 1999), 494; "The Oslo Accords Held Promise: Extremists Derailed Them," Washington Institute, Sept. 1, 2023, tinyurl.com/ycj47smt; US Department of State, *1995 April: Patterns of Global Terrorism*, 1994 Department of State Publication 10239; "What Was Hamas Thinking?: For over Three Decades, It Has Had the Same Brutal Idea of Victory," AP News, Oct. 12, 2023, tinyurl.com/jwt9fyav.
7 "Exile Ends as Arafat Leaves Tunisia for Gaza," *Los Angeles Times*, July 12, 1994, tinyurl.com/mud65r78; Byman, *A High Price*, 81–85.
8 Byman, *A High Price*, 80.

9 Byman, *A High Price*, 81–85; "Two Decades Ago, Bill Clinton Threw a Hail Mary for Middle East Peace," *WP*, July 5, 2023, tinyurl.com/bdzn8y33; "Lost in the Woods: A Camp David Retrospective," Carnegie Endowment, July 13, 2020, tinyurl.com/2smyr8ac; "Bill Clinton: Israel Offered Temple Mount to Palestinians in 2000," *TI*, May 1, 2014, tinyurl.com/55hcnr5c.

10 "Rioting as Sharon Visits Islam Holy Site," *The Guardian*, Sept. 29, 2000, tinyurl.com/ymtunt9m; "Sharon Touches a Nerve and Jerusalem Explodes," *NYT*, Sept. 29, 2000, tinyurl.com/5ay3tv3e; "Palestinians and Israelis in a Clash at Holy Site," *NYT*, Sept. 28, 2000, tinyurl.com/59azru8z.

11 "Mahmoud Abbas and the Years of Terror," *The American Interest*, July 13, 2017, tinyurl.com/yfbny3ss; "Full Text of Abbas Declaration," BBC, Feb. 8, 2005, tinyurl.com/3m84zxet; "Full Text of Sharon Declaration," BBC, Feb. 8, 2005, tinyurl.com/2p9r6m48; "A Plan for Peace that Still Could Be," *NYT*, Feb. 7, 2011, tinyurl.com/mr2pzfhs.

12 "Israeli Settler Population in West Bank Surpasses Half a Million," Israel's Central Bureau of Statistics, tinyurl.com/yc4uf2sj.

13 "For the Land She Loved to Death," *Haaretz*, Aug. 30, 2005, tinyurl.com/yc3tthy7; "Young Man Who Set Himself on Fire Because of the Withdrawal Dies of His Wounds," Ynet, Sept. 6, 2005, tinyurl.com/44psreca (Hebrew); "Plan to Pull Out of Gaza Rejected in Likud Vote," *WP*, May 2, 2004, tinyurl.com/2tun5ve7.

14 Interview with Datya Itzhaki, Nov. 2023.

15 Andy Newman, "How Old Friends of Israel Gave $14 Million to Help the Palestinians," *NYT*, Aug. 18, 2005; "Gush Katif: Past and Future," Israel National News, July 15, 2010, tinyurl.com/36bxwexd.

16 "Gazans Revel as They Sift through Ex-Settlements," *NYT*, Sept. 13, 2005; "Looters Strip Gaza Greenhouses," NBC News, Sept. 13, 2005, tinyurl.com/mw5hmv3z; Dina Kraft, "Synagogue Razings Stoke Fear of Gaza Chaos," *JTA World Report*, Sept. 13, 2005; "Rocket on Sderot," *JTA News Brief*, Sept. 13, 2005.

17 "Indiscriminate Fire," Human Rights Watch, 2007, tinyurl.com/3wnccfzm; "Hamas Wins Huge Majority," Al Jazeera, Jan. 26, 2006, tinyurl.com/bdefyywx.

18 Taghreed El-Khodary and Ian Fisher, "In Aftermath of Gaza Battle, Grim Realities," *NYT*, June 16, 2007.

19 Gisha—Legal Center for Freedom of Movement: Gaza Up Close, June 28, 2023, features.gisha.org/gaza-up-close/.

20 "Hamas Executes Two Accused of Aiding Israel," *NYT*, Apr. 15, 2010, tinyurl.com/r7rsm2aj.

21 "Addressing Muslims, Obama Pushes Mideast Peace," *NYT*, June 4, 2009, https://tinyurl.com/2p9satmm; "Netanyahu Backs Palestinian State, with Caveats," *NYT*, June 14, 2009, https://tinyurl.com/bdh4c3x8; Fares Akram, "Gaza: Militant Groups Promise More Attacks," *NYT*, Sept. 2, 2010; "Gaza Mends, but Israelis See Signs of Trouble," *NYT*, Dec. 16, 2010, tinyurl.com/es5km2mx; "Rockets, Mortars Fired at Southern Israel," UPI, Sept. 15, 2010, tinyurl.com/4x2matxk; "Palestinians Hunt the Killers of 4 Israelis," *NYT*, Sept. 2, 2010, tinyurl.com/mrx9k8za; "Boy, 16, Badly Hurt after Hamas Fires Missile at School Bus," *JP*, Apr. 8, 2011, tinyurl.com/y9rxbjdv; "Daniel Viflic, 16, Injured in Hamas Bus Attack, Dies," *JP*, Apr. 17, 2011.

22 "Hamas Covenant 1988"; "Understanding Hamas's Genocidal Ideology," *The Atlantic*, Oct. 10, 2023, tinyurl.com/a32jc2ct; "Gaza Rights Groups Denounce Hamas Crackdown on Protests," Al Jazeera, Mar. 19, 2019, tinyurl.com/mpcbpbdp; "Hamas Tortured Me for Dissent. Here's What They Really Think of Palestinians," *Newsweek*, Jan. 2, 2024, tinyurl.com/u6sndm25.

Chapter 24: A Day at the Museum

1 "Army, Settlers Have Turned Hebron into a Ghost Town, Report Charges," B'tselem, May 14, 2007, tinyurl.com/79cw2j4v; "Ghost Town," B'tselem, May 2007, btselem.org/download/200705_hebron_eng.pdf; "The Isolation of Palestinians in the Israeli-Controlled Area of Hebron City Continues," UN Office for the Coordination of Humanitarian Affairs, Apr. 13, 2017, tinyurl.com/2zhkkmed; "Hebron, Area H-2: Settlements Cause Mass Departure of Palestinians," B'tselem, Aug. 2003, tinyurl.com/3epwauap.

2 Deborah Sontag, "Israeli Baby's Funeral Becomes Focus of Settler Militancy," *NYT*, Apr. 2, 2001; Peter Bouckaert, "Center of the Storm: A Case Study of Human Rights Abuses in Hebron District," Human Rights Watch, 2001, 64–65.

3 Noam Arnon, *Hevron B'Ayin Hareiya* [Hebron in the Eye of the Rabbi . . . Rabbi Abraham Isaac Kook and the Jewish Community in Hebron] (Jerusalem: Rabbi Kook House, 2023), 29 (Hebrew).

4 Joshua Hoffman, "*Rav Kook's Mission to America*," originally printed in *Orot: A Multidisciplinary Journal of Judaism* 1 (5751/1991), 78–99.

5 Simcha Raz, *An Angel among Men: Impressions from the Life of Rav Avraham Yitzchak Hakohen Kook* (Jerusalem: Kol Mevaser, 2003), 40, 46, 200–203.

6 Interviews with Tzipi Schlissel (2019, 2020); "Rabbi Slain at Home in Hebron," *WP*, Aug. 22, 1998, tinyurl.com/ytdsf9yv.

7 "Grenades Wound 67 in Israeli Bus Station," *NYT*, Oct. 20, 1998, tinyurl.com/4f4e8xnh; "Beersheba Suspect Confesses to Other Terrorist Attacks, Israeli Army Aides Say," *NYT*, Oct. 21, 1998, tinyurl.com/y5vtmx4x.

8 "Terrorists Freed in Shalit Deal Resume Terror Activity, Data Shows," Ynet, Oct. 17, 2012, tinyurl.com/2u6c8hps; "Shalit's Captors: He Wasn't Tortured, He Received Medical Care and Watched TV," *Haaretz*, Oct. 20, 2011, tinyurl.com/mtfmun96.

9 "Terrorist Designations of Yahya Sinwar, Rawhi Mushtaha, and Muhammed Deif," US Dept. of State, Sept. 8, 2015; "Hamas Elects Hardliner Yahya Sinwar as Its Gaza Strip Chief," *Guardian*; "Hamas Actually Believed It Would Conquer Israel and Divided It into Cantons," *Haaretz*, Apr. 5, 2024, tinyurl.com/mkhujujz; "Hamas Leader Yahya Sinwar, Israel's Most Wanted—in His Own Words," MEMRI, Dec. 22, 2023, tinyurl.com/9kwmsh46.

10 "Israeli Supreme Court Rules Hebron Jews Can't Reclaim Lands Lost after 1948," *Haaretz*, Feb. 18. 2011, tinyurl. com/yn8s67wu.

Chapter 25: A Tale of Two Hebrons
1 Interview with Ibrahim Bader, 2020; Avissar, *Sefer Hevron*; CZA S25/4472–23, 27.
2 Ibid.
3 Burg, *In Days to Come*, 194.
4 Ibid., 188–89.
5 Dion Nissenbaum, "Death Toll of Israeli Civilians Killed by Palestinians Hit a Low in 2006," McClatchy DC, Jan. 10, 2007, tinyurl.com/www5tenx; Double Bombing Kills 23 in Israel," *WP*, Jan. 5, 2003, tinyurl.com/5cs4k7w3; "38 Hurt as Suicide Bomb Rocks Netanya Again," *WP*, Mar. 31, 2003, tinyurl.com/59ud7hck; "Jerusalem Suicide Bombing Kills 7," *WP*, May 17, 2003, tinyurl.com/333vr266; "Suicide Bomber Kills 15 on Bus in Northern Israel," *WP*, Mar. 5, 2003, tinyurl.com/ynvsufuy; "Car Bomb in Jerusalem Kills 2 as Call for Truce is Delayed," *NYT*, Nov. 2, 2000, tinyurl.com/3yxedb79; Israel's Ministry of Foreign Affairs, "Suicide and Other Bombing Attacks in Israel Since the Declaration of Principles (Sept. 1993)."
6 Mark Seager, "I'll Have Nightmares for the Rest of My Life," *Chicago Sun-Times*, Oct. 22, 2000, tinyurl. com/5n7nyfxm; Alan Philps, "A Day of Rage, Revenge and Bloodshed," *Daily Telegraph*, Oct. 13, 2000; Sharon Waxman, "On Both Sides, Toll Is Personal," *WP*, Oct. 14, 2000; "Lynch Mob's Brutal Attack," BBC Oct. 13, 2000, tinyurl.com/7tenyknb.
7 Interview with Tayseer Abu Aisheh (2020), throughout chapter.
8 "The Humanitarian Impact of Israeli Settlements in Hebron City," OCHA, tinyurl.com/yexv8mv5; "The Humanitarian Situation in the H2 Area of Hebron City," OCHA, Apr. 2019, tinyurl.com/2p8j3apt; interview with Imad Abu Shamsieh, the man whose home was stoned (2019).

Chapter 26: Kahane Lives
1 "Ben-Gvir: Marzel Charges 'Stink of Tampering,'" Israel National News, Mar. 11, 2015, tinyurl.com/yaruu386; "Zoabi, Marzel Banned from Running for Knesset," *JP*, Feb. 12, 2015, tinyurl.com/yc6fc2vf.
2 "Netanyahu's Trumpy Reelection Bid Divides America's Jewish Community," *Politico*, Mar. 25, 2019, tinyurl. com/4c44942y; "Netanyahu Officially Makes Israeli History as Longest-Serving Prime Minister," *TI*, July 20, 2019, tinyurl.com/5suyshvx.
3 "Itmar Ben-Givr, Israel's Minister of Chaos," *New Yorker*, Feb. 20, 2023, tinyurl.com/ymww9nww.
4 Ibid.
5 "Far Right's Rise in Israel Driven by Anxiety and Fear," *NYT*, Nov. 5, 2022, tinyurl.com/mr2cn5ua; "Far-Right Minister Says Israel 'In Charge' on Visit to Jerusalem Holy Site," *The Guardian*, May 21, 2023, tinyurl. com/2rhhftuz; "Israel's Ben-Gvir Rebukes Police Over 'Collective Punishment' of Settlers," Reuters, June 25, 2023, tinyurl.com/bdesha5f.

Chapter 27: Warning Signs
1 "Israel Is Hurtling Toward Dictatorship, Former Shin Bet Chief Warns," *Haaretz*, Mar. 17, 2023, tinyurl. com/67f3v6e2; "400 Ex-Security Chiefs Urge Herzog Not to Sign Laws that Negate Israel's Core Values," *TI*, Feb. 16, 2023, tinyurl.com/39r3zs7r; "Former Israeli Air Force Commanders Call on Netanyahu to Halt Judicial Legislation," *Haaretz*, Mar. 6, 2023, tinyurl.com/2aaph8nh; "Hundreds of Mossad Pensioners Petition the Government: 'We Are Horrified by the Accelerated and Uncontrolled Legislative Process,'" *Haaretz*, Mar. 1, 2023, tinyurl.com/4x9xuyv8 (Hebrew); "IDF Chief Said to Warn PM of Deepening Military Crisis if Judicial Overhaul Approved," *TI*, Mar. 23, 2023, tinyurl.com/26vk77nh.
2 "Israeli Police Violently Crack Down Protest on Judicial Overhaul," *WP*, Mar. 1, 2023, tinyurl.com/tmen9trd.
3 "Warning of Civil War, Herzog Unveils Framework for Judicial Reform; PM Rejects It," *TI*, March 15, 2023, tinyurl.com/y82b73dh; "Gallant Calls to Pause Judicial Overhaul, Citing Tangible Danger to State Security," *TI*, Mar. 25, 2023, tinyurl.com/mpapns8r.
4 Ibid.; "Netanyahu Fires Defense Minister Gallant for Calling to Pause Judicial Overhaul," *TI*, Mar. 26, 2023, tinyurl. com/5n79uy6v; "Netanyahu Reverses Firing of Israeli Defense Minister," *NYT*, Apr. 10, 2023, tinyurl.com/4ay7nkah.
5 "Military Intelligence Directorate in an Unusual Warning: Israel's Deterrence against Its Enemies Is Eroding," *Israel Hayom*, Apr. 4, 2023; tinyurl.com/4tsvwc9a (Hebrew).
6 "Former Heads of the IDF, Mossad and Shin Bet: We Support the Threat Not to Report to Reserve Duty, Netanyahu Is Hurting the IDF" *Haaretz*, July 22, 2023, tinyurl.com/2p9bne3m (Hebrew).
7 "Netanyahu Refuses to Meet Israeli Military Chief before Key Judicial Overhaul Vote," *Haaretz*, July 24, 2023, tinyurl.com/5e2tnysj.
8 "Israeli Air Chief Warns of Security Threat after Judicial Reform Vote," Reuters, July 28, 2023, tinyurl.com/ ydxz6auw.
9 "Exposed: Military Intelligence Directorate's Warning Letter on the Eve of October 7," Mar. 5, 2024, tinyurl. com/42f6ejnx (Hebrew); "Could October 7 Have Been Prevented?," *JP*, Mar. 5, 2024, jpost.com/israel-hamas-war/article-790374.

Chapter 28: The Al-Aqsa Flood

1 "October 7, 2023: Israel Says It Is 'at War' after Hamas Surprise Attack," CNN, Oct. 7, 2023, tinyurl.com/5649zc5m.

2 Interviews with Avida and Dekel (2023), "Hunted by Hamas: 27 Hours of Slaughter and Survival Inside Israel's Kibbutz Be'eri," Reuters, Nov. 3, 2023, tinyurl.com/5hymadxk.

3 "A Deadly Cascade: How Secret Hamas Attack Orders Were Passed Down at Last Minute," *The Guardian*, Nov. 7, 2023, tinyurl.com/5n7mcxrj; "How Hamas Duped Israel as It Planned Devastating Attack," Reuters, Oct. 8, 2023, tinyurl.com/2p9tbjc3; "Behind Hamas's Bloody Gambit," *NYT*; "Israel-Hamas War: Timeline and Key Developments," ABC News, Nov. 22, 2023, tinyurl.com/58m2xccb; "A Handful of Israeli Officers Saved 90 New Recruits from Hamas Terrorists," *Haaretz*, Oct. 20, 2023, tinyurl.com/ypshwnkc; "For Most Palestinians, October 7's Savagery Is Literally Unbelievable," *TI*, Jan. 19, 2024, tinyurl.com/38ya24a4; interviews with Palestinians, i.e., Mhaimer Abu Sada, Mahmoud Jabari (2023).

4 "What Happened in Israel: A Breakdown of How the Hamas Attack Unfolded," *Al Jazeera*, Oct. 7, 2023, tinyurl.com/2naz4vjm.

5 "Where Was the Israeli Military?" *NYT*, Dec. 30, 2023, tinyurl.com/dp4f74y2.

6 "How West Bank Settlements Led to the Conflict in Gaza," *American Prospect*, Oct. 20, 2023, prospect.org/world/2023-10-20-west-bank-settlements-conflict-gaza/; "IDF to Send 2 More Battalions to West Bank after Series of Settler Attacks," *TI*, June 25, 2023, tinyurl.com/mucphue2.

7 "The Sole Avenue of Coexistence that Became a Hamas Killing Field," *TI*, Nov. 23, 2023, tinyurl.com/eeuc6hxn; "Watch: This is How Hamas Terrorists Stormed Kibbutz Kerem Shalom in Southern Israel," All Israel News, Oct. 20, 2023, tinyurl.com/rsh9mdmd; "How Hamas Attacked Israel's Communications Towers," *NYT*, Oct. 20, 2023, tinyurl.com/36sasnwc; "Why Only a Trickle of Aid Is Getting into Gaza," CNN, Feb. 22, 2024, tinyurl.com/2ydbuuaz.

8 *#NOVA* (documentary), produced by YES, Dec. 24, 2023, segment: YouTube, youtube.com/watch?v=94GpyR5iYTY.

9 Ibid. | 10 Ibid.

11 "What I Saw When I Watched Videos of the Hamas Attack," *WP*, Nov. 1, 2023, tinyurl.com/yxytajx8.

12 "How a Rave Celebrating Life Turned into a Frenzied Massacre," CNN online, Oct. 14, 2023, tinyurl.com/5yrytrm9.

13 *#NOVA*; "A Deadly Cascade," *The Guardian*; Kan News interview with Osama's uncle on X: Nov. 7, 2023, tinyurl.com/5n7dsr5e (Hebrew).

14 "With Supreme Bravery Aner Shapira Saved Many Lives with His Bare Hands," *JP*, Dec. 11, 2023, tinyurl.com/52r2ykem; "Family of Hamas Attack Victim Offers $1 Million for Information on His Killers," Ynet, Nov. 8, 2023, tinyurl.com/ycyxnaxm; "Son of Chicagoans, Hersh Goldberg-Polin among Five Hamas Hostages with Illinois Ties," *Chicago Sun-Times*, Oct. 22, 2023, tinyurl.com/3m8smpvc; "Family of Man Murdered on the Black Sabbath: 'A Million Dollars for Whoever Finds the Terrorists,'" Walla, Nov. 6, 2023, news.walla.co.il/item/3620789 (Hebrew); *#NOVA*.

15 *#NOVA*.

16 "Bedouin Policeman Who Saved Lives at Nova Festival to Run Jerusalem Marathon," *Jewish Chronicle*, Mar. 7, 2024, tinyurl.com/4wfej98r; "Death Toll from Nova Music Festival Massacre on Oct. 7 Raised by 100 to over 360," *TI*, Nov. 18, 2023, tinyurl.com/5br3ay9n; "Heroic Police Commander Relives the Hardest Day of His Life," i24 News, Mar. 10, 2024, tinyurl.com/2nbduk5j.

17 "Ben Shimoni, 31: Music-Loving 'Angel' Who Saved 9 from Supernova," *TI*, Dec. 19, 2023, tinyurl.com/y3bajeeh.

18 "'Screams without Words,' How Hamas Weaponized Sexual Violence on Oct. 7," NYT, Dec. 28, 2023, tinyurl.com/46ym6fwx.

19 "The Scope of Hamas' Campaign of Rape against Israeli Women," *Haaretz*, Nov. 30, 2023, tinyurl.com/25ex4wvr; "'Screams without Words,'" *NYT*; November 28 Knesset meeting of the Women's Advancement Legislative Committee aired testimony of witness collected as part of the police investigation into sexual violence on Oct. 7, YouTube, tinyurl.com/bd9e8xua; testimony of Cochav Elkayam Levy, founding director of Civil Commission on Oct. 7th Crimes by Hamas against Women and Children, YouTube, tinyurl.com/zhf88jez; and "The Unspeakable Terror: Gender Based Violence on October 7," YouTube, tinyurl.com/3dtr5425; " USA: Hamas Will Not Release Women Who It Fears What They Will Say. Hard to Watch: The Rape Evidence Israel Exposed at the UN," Ynet, Dec. 5, 2023, ynet.co.il/news/article/byme0fssa (Hebrew).

20 "'Screams without Words,'" *NYT*.

21 "First Hamas Fighters Raped Her. Then They Shot Her in the Head," *Times UK*, Dec. 2, 2023, tinyurl.com/534bx26x.

22 "'Screams without Words,'" *NYT*; "Sexual Violence Crimes on October 7: Special Report by the Association of Rape Crisis Centers in Israel," Feb. 2024, tinyurl.com/4h5h5vu2; "The Deadly Hamas Rampage across Southern Israel," Reuters, Oct. 12, 2023, tinyurl.com/mf2a9ut4; "Special Report by the Association of Rape Crisis Centers in Israel."

23 "Where Was the Israeli Military?," *NYT*.

24 Interviews with Avida Bachar (2023).

25 Interviews with Maayan Zin (2023); "Israel's Hostage Families Feel Abandoned by Israel," *Foreign Policy*, Oct. 20, 2023, tinyurl.com/mrxvjevr; "Two Sisters Alone in Gaza: Dafna and Ella Elyakim Speak," Mako, Jan. 30, 2024, tinyurl.com/y4z8fs86 (Hebrew).

26 "'Hamas Said They Wouldn't Shoot, Then Murdered My Daughter,'" BBC, Oct. 23, 2023, tinyurl.com/4vavyybu; All Israel News interview with Gali Idan, Oct. 26, 2023, tinyurl.com/3ft7bc2b.

27 "Released American Hostage Says Nurses in Gaza Hospital 'Cheered' at Sight of Abductees," *TI*, Mar. 14, 2024, tinyurl.com/2wj9uadj.

28 "Why Can't Facebook Stop Hamas from Posting Grisly Videos of the Killing of Israeli Civilians?," NBC News, Nov. 1, 2023, tinyurl.com/348s6ttx.

29 "Families Were Reportedly Coerced by Hamas," i24 News, undated, YouTube, tinyurl.com/e5u2tdzk; testimony of ZAKA's Yossi Landau: "The Silence from International Bodies," *Newsweek*, Nov. 22, 2023, tinyurl.com/dwp8sbzp; testimony of Cochav Elkayam Levy, founding director of The Civil Commission on Oct. 7th Crimes by Hamas against Women and Children: "The Unspeakable Terror: Gender Based Violence on October 7," YouTube, tinyurl.com/4d6xt24c.

30 "Noa Argamani Became the Face of the Nova Music Festival Hostages," NBC News, Dec. 19, 2023, tinyurl.com/wkkfua9k; "Mother of Gaza Hostage Naama Levy Tells Her Story," DW, Jan. 25, 2024, tinyurl.com/2ep93wp8; "Mother of Naama Levy, from Harrowing Gaza Video," *TI*, Dec. 9, 2023, tinyurl.com/4w4r2yvr; "Taken Captive: Shiri Bibas and Her Redheaded Babies," *TI*, Jan. 22, 2024, tinyurl.com/56hvt4m9.

31 Background on Sandra Cohen: gofundme.com/f/sandras-tomorrow; "3 Generations of Israeli Family Killed by Hamas Laid to Rest at Kibbutz Be'eri," UPI, Oct. 23, 2023, tinyurl.com/bdu2kpdw; "One Community for the Cohen Family from Kibbutz Be'eri," undated, YouTube, tinyurl.com/5ehtjvta; "Three Generations Wiped Out by Hamas in Kibbutz Be'eri," Jewish News Syndicate, Oct. 23, 2023, tinyurl.com/2dhx3kb3; "Yona, Ohad, Mila Cohen, 73, 43, 9 Months: Three Generations Slain," *TI*, Oct. 31, 2023, tinyurl.com/8t7f93b7; and from my interview with Dekel Shalev (2023).

32 "The Day Hamas Came," *NYT*, Dec. 22, 2023, tinyurl.com/2ftmujyv.

33 Interviews with Avihai Brodutch (2023); "Aunt of 4-Year-Old Israeli Hostage Talks about Her Time in Captivity," *NYT*, Nov. 29, 2023, tinyurl.com/3s8cm66t; "Roee and Smadar Idan, 43 & 38: News Photographer and Shin Bet Employee," *TI*, Oct. 20, 2023, tinyurl.com/mrynwzf3.

34 "Hamas and Israel Complete 3rd Exchange of Hostages for Prisoners," *NYT*, Nov. 26, 2023, tinyurl.com/25f4y85u.

35 "An Israeli Charity for Palestinians Grapples with Oct. 7 Attacks," *NYT*, Jan. 31, 2024, tinyurl.com/4r94memx; "Yuval Roth Gives Palestinians a Lift," Christian Science Monitor, Mar. 10, 2016, tinyurl.com/57nb3d2j.

36 "Taken Captive: Oded Lifshitz, Drove Gazans to Hospitals," *TI*, Oct. 23, 2023, tinyurl.com/48a8mjke; "Hamas Took Her, and Still Has Her Husband," *NYT*, Mar 29, 2024, tinyurl.com/y4p95vvy.

37 "How Hamas Exploited Israel's Reliance on Tech to Breach Barrier on Oct. 7," *WP*, Nov. 17, 2023, tinyurl.com/5232fydh; "Behind Hamas's Bloody Gambit to Create a 'Permanent' State of War," *NYT*; interviews with Dekel, Avida, and other survivors (2023).

38 "The IDF Took Away Weapons from Gaza Border Communities," *Haaretz*, Oct. 20, 2023, tinyurl.com/4uht82p7.

39 "Shachar Zemach, 39: Peace Activist Defended Kibbutz until Last Bullet," *TI*, Feb. 19, 2024, tinyurl.com/bdfuu4pk; "The Day Hamas Came," *NYT*.

40 "Hamas Also Slaughters Muslims," *Jewish News Syndicate*, Nov. 23, 2023, jns.org/hamas-also-slaughters-muslims; "An Arab Paramedic Who Treated Israelis Injured by Hamas Militants Is Remembered as a Hero," Oct. 15, 2023, tinyurl.com/mw65hnuf.

41 "Hamas Hostages: Stories of the People Taken from Israel," BBC, May 8, 2024, tinyurl.com/452nfvth; "New Tally Puts October 7 Attack Dead in Israel at 1,163," *Barrons*, Feb. 1, 2024, tinyurl.com/mr2rkb3k; "14 Kids under 10, 25 People over 80," *TI*, Dec. 4, 2023, tinyurl.com/mpt4u27s.

42 "Hostage Families Return to Beeri as Pressure Builds for New Releases," *WP*, Dec. 20, 2023, tinyurl.com/ns5t2hkp; "The Day Hamas Came," *NYT*.

43 "About 200,000 Israelis Internally Displaced," *TI*, Oct. 22, 2023, tinyurl.com/mrxh2ktw.

Chapter 29: Hostage Nation

1 Population press release, Central Bureau of Statistics (CBS), Israel, May 9, 2024, tinyurl.com/24awbwn4.

2 "Margit & Yossi Silberman, 63 & 67: South Americans Put Down Kibbutz Roots," *TI*, Oct. 26, 2023, updated Feb. 11, 2024, tinyurl.com/2y2uas2n.

3 "Former Hamas Chief Calls for Protests, Neighbours to Join War against Israel," Reuters, Oct. 11, 2023, tinyurl.com/bdf4ufu5; "Former Hamas leader Khaled Meshaal Calls for Day of Jihad," *Daily Mail*, Oct. 12, 2023, tinyurl.com/rt77ub6y; "Hamas Raises Stakes in Gaza Truce by Calling for Ramadan March," Reuters, Feb. 28, 2024, tinyurl.com/45xm9a8s; "Most Arab Israelis: October 7 Does Not Reflect Islamic, Palestinian Society Values," Dec. 26, 2023, Israel Democracy Institute, en.idi.org.il/articles/52016; "Netanyahu Overrules Ben Gvir: Temple Mount Access on Ramadan to Be Like Previous Years," *TI*, Mar. 5, 2024.

4 "Public Opinion Polls: Gaza Survey 7th October," Arab World for Research & Development, Nov. 14, 2023, tinyurl.com/3zy35k9j; "Arab-Israelis Are Facing a Crisis. But There's a Way Out," Atlantic Council, Feb. 2, 2024, atlanticcouncil.org/blogs/menasource/arab-israelis-crisis; "Most Arab Israelis," Israel Democracy Institute; "Netanyahu Overrules Ben Gvir," *TI*.

5 "Hamas Official Ghazi Hamad: We Will Repeat the October 7 Attack," MEMRI, Nov. 1, 2023, tinyurl.com/3t8ar9p2; "Hamas Official Says Group Aims to Repeat Oct. 7 Onslaught," *TI*, Nov. 1, 2023, tinyurl.com/2p8akbw; "'No Place on Our Land,'" MSNBC, Nov. 2, 2023, tinyurl.com/4km5v5zz.

6 "Street Rallies Celebrate Hamas Onslaught in West Bank and Throughout the Middle East," *TI*, Oct. 8, 2023, tinyurl.com/mru5ufbe; "As Israel Fights to Destroy, Hamas, the Group's Popularity Surges among Palestinians," NPR, Dec. 21, 2023, tinyurl.com/pe8arwk8; "Public Opinion Poll No. 90," Palestinian Center for Policy and Survey Research, Dec. 2, 2023, pcpsr.org/en/node/963; "Gaza Survey 7th October," Arab World for Research and Development, Nov. 14, 2023, tinyurl.com/ycycdvky; "For Most Palestinians, October 7's Savagery Is Literally Unbelievable," *TI*.

7 "Hamas Official: 'We Have Not Killed Any Civilians,'" undated, YouTube, tinyurl.com/mr3rkhvp; "Palestinian Authority Claims Israel Fabricated Evidence of October 7 to Justify Its Attack on Gaza," *TI*, Nov. 19, 2023, tinyurl.com/y9j8488k; "Palestinian Diplomat: IDF Might 'Burn, Behead' Gaza Corpses to Claim Hamas Atrocities," *TI*, Jan. 11, 2024, tinyurl.com/2p8rrfkv.

8 Bari Weiss, "The State of World Jewry," 92nd Street Y, tinyurl.com/3duuhw2r.

9 "How a Pro-Palestinian Campus Group Became a National Lightning Rod," NBC News, Nov. 24, 2023, tinyurl.com/ry9nu4kb; "Day of Resistance Toolkit," DW, Oct. 12, 2023, tinyurl.com/mz6a7mkv; "Harvard Student Groups Face Intense Backlash," *Harvard Crimson*, Oct. 10, 2023, thecrimson.com/article/2023/10/10/psc-statement-backlash/; "Cornell Professor 'Exhilarated' by Hamas's Attack Defends Remark," *Cornell Sun*, Oct. 16, 2023, tinyurl.com/27znsm2m; "Growing October 7 'Truther' Groups Say Hamas Massacre Was a False Flag," *WP*, Jan. 21, 2024, tinyurl.com/8xyh8jmj.

10 "Hamas Leader Says Students Chanting 'From the River to the Sea' Is Proof of Western Support for the Destruction of Israel," *New York Sun*, Jan. 22, 2024, tinyurl.com/7ywkhfjz; "General Studies Student Allegedly Assaulted in Front of Butler Library," *Columbia Spectator*, Oct. 12, 2023, tinyurl.com/ykapch6u; "How Posters of Kidnapped Israelis Ignited a Firestorm on American Sidewalks," *NYT*, Oct. 31, 2023, tinyurl.com/3hyrc6cx; "Just Another Battle or the Palestinian War of Liberation?," Electronic Intifada, Oct. 8, 2023, tinyurl.com/z29fhftn.

11 "Hamas Officials Join Nelson Mandela's Family at Ceremony," AP News, Dec. 5, 2023, tinyurl.com/yfmvyjwj; "South African Foreign Minister's Phone Call with Hamas Sparks Ire," VOA News, Oct. 18, 2023, tinyurl.com/53ka63sf.

12 "Opening Statement of MFA Legal Advisor Tal Becker at ICJ Proceedings," Israeli Ministry of Foreign Affairs, Jan. 12, 2024, tinyurl.com/2uwhsjfv.

13 "Editors' Note: Gaza Hospital Coverage," *NYT*, Oct. 23, 2023, tinyurl.com/5yd3p64b; "French Intelligence Points to Palestinian Rocket, Not Israeli Airstrike, for Gaza Hospital Blast," AP News, Oct. 21, 2023, tinyurl.com/cfk7su6z; "*NYT* Admits Error in Gaza Hospital Report," Politico, Oct. 23, 2023, tinyurl.com/4ar9yuh4; "Gaza Hospital Blast: What We Know about the Explosion," Reuters, Oct. 18, 2023, tinyurl.com/45f5c9ah.

14 "Gaza: Findings on October 17 al-Ahli Hospital Explosion," Human Rights Watch, Nov. 26, 2023, tinyurl.com/8turzsrw; "Gaza Summit in Jordan Cancelled after Hospital Attack," *Wall Street Journal*, Oct. 18, 2023, tinyurl.com/efuu8jcu; "Angry Protests Flare Up across Middle East after Gaza Hospital Blast," *Guardian*, Oct. 18, 2023, tinyurl.com/yc8eyyze; "Gaza Hospital Explosion Sparks Anger and Protests in Arab Countries," CNN, Oct. 18, 2023, tinyurl.com/9m4syh54.

15 "Israel Seizes Gaza Hospital that Became Symbol of the War Itself," *NYT*, Nov. 15, 2023, tinyurl.com/3mt4y8h8; "'Floor by Floor Searches,'" *Haaretz*, Nov. 15, 2023, tinyurl.com/yc7ywf8z; "As Israel Withdraws from Raid on Shifa Hospital, Accounts from Military and Witnesses Differ Wildly," AP News, Apr. 2, 2024, tinyurl.com/thvm2jd6; "Witnesses Describe Fear and Deprivation at Besieged Hospital in Gaza," *NYT*, Mar. 24, 2024, tinyurl.com/mr3cmyyj; "Here's What We Found after Israel's Raid on Al-Shifa," NPR, Apr. 6, 2024, tinyurl.com/2frjsh5a; "Why Israeli Forces Are Raiding Gaza's Al-Shifa Hospital—Again," CNN, Mar. 28, 2024, tinyurl.com/543u4r9f; "Doctors Forced to Strip in Cold at Gaza's Nasser Hospital," CNN, Feb. 19, 2024, tinyurl.com/5xddbrea; "Searching for the Remains of Hostages," NPR, Feb. 16, 2024, tinyurl.com/zy9z45rn; "Israel Shows Videos of Gaza Hospital Basement It Says Was Used by Hamas," *NYT*, Nov. 14, 2023, tinyurl.com/yc2u4yv8.

16 "Israel Has Created a New Standard for Urban Warfare," *Newsweek*, Mar. 25, 2024, tinyurl.com/bdhjj2tx; "Gaza Fatality Data Has Become Completely Unreliable," Washington Institute, Mar. 26, 2024, tinyurl.com/4ysckk96; "Amid Outcry over Civilian Casualties in Gaza," ABC News, Dec. 15, 2023, tinyurl.com/33ye9ajr; "Israel Military Says 2 Civilians Killed for Every Hamas Militant Is a 'Tremendously Positive' Ratio," CNN, Dec. 5, 2023, tinyurl.com/5n6znjcp.

17 "UN Women Rapid Assessment and Humanitarian Response in the Occupied Palestinian Territory," UN Women, Oct. 2023, tinyurl.com/jph97knh; "Pres Release: UN Women Report Reveals Devastating Impact," UN Women, Oct. 2023, tinyurl.com/bdhz8utp; "Voices from Gaza: Hayam's Story," UN Women, Oct. 25, 2023, tinyurl.com/w23t29md; "Voices from Gaza: Amani's Story of Loss," UN Women, Nov. 1, 2023, tinyurl.com/zpcjbs83; "Voices from Gaza: Nourhan's Story of Survival amid Airstrikes," UN Women, Nov. 13, 2023, tinyurl.com/2s4yusu3; "'We Need an Immediate Humanitarian Ceasefire,'" UN Women, Nov. 5, 2023, tinyurl.com/2s4fp5ay; "After Backlash over Silence," JTA, Nov. 27, 2023, tinyurl.com/ycx5m48p; "Families Were Reportedly Coerced by Hamas," i24 News, undated, YouTube, tinyurl.com/e5u2tdzk; "UN Women Statement on the Situation in Israel and Gaza," UN Women, Dec. 1, 2023, tinyurl.com/3pcydtyc; "Accounts of Sexual Violence by Hamas Are Aired amid Criticism of UN," *NYT*, Dec. 4, 2023, tinyurl.com/2bkx4ymm; "After 7 Weeks of Silence, UN Chief Calls to Investigate Hamas Sex Crimes on Oct. 7," *TI*, Nov. 30, 2023, tinyurl.com/mr2yvyuz; "Jewish Women March on UN over October 7 Attacks," *Al-Monitor*, Dec. 2023, tinyurl.com/sxv8ucns.

18 "Official Visit of the Office of the Special Representative of the Secretary-General on Sexual Violence in Conflict," SRSG-SVC, Feb. 14, 2024, tinyurl.com/2p8mvsxu; "UN Official Won't Say Who Accused IDF of Rape, Sexual Abuse," Jewish News Syndicate, Mar. 6, 2024, tinyurl.com/mpktfp46; "UN Experts Appalled by Reported Human Rights Violations against Palestinian Women and Girls," Office of the High Commissioner for Human Rights, Feb. 19, 2024, tinyurl.com/3ubkw8rp; "UN Special Rapporteur 'Unaware' of Rocket Attacks on Israel," *JP*, Mar. 6, 2024, tinyurl.com/3t2y2sz7; "Why Is Hamas's Sexual Violence of October 7th Being Ignored?," Progressive Britain, Nov. 25, 2023, tinyurl.com/2trh3br6.

19 "Father of Fallen Soldier: Terrorist Decapitated My Son, Tried to Sell Head for $10,000," *TI*, Jan. 18, 2024, tinyurl.com/23e8yyyz; "Sgt. Adir Tahr, 19: Quiet Boy Who Fulfilled Dream of Joining Golani," *TI*, Feb. 18, 2024, tinyurl.com/226srcrr; "Israel Releases Video of Captured Hamas Militant," Business Insider, Oct. 24, 2023, tinyurl.com/yvtjacfy; "'I Captured One!,'" *TI*, Mar. 4, 2024, tinyurl.com/yjuafvd3.

20 "Buying Quiet: Inside the Israeli Plan that Propped Up Hamas," *NYT*, Dec.10, 2023, tinyurl.com/ryyhpthf; Bezalel Smotrich, "'Abu Mazen (Mahmoud Abbas) Is a Burden, Hamas Is an Asset", Knesset Channel, YouTube, Oct. 7, 2015, tinyurl.com/ycxaedva.

21 "Israel Defence Minister Lieberman Resigns over Gaza Ceasefire," BBC, Nov. 14, 2018, tinyurl.com/bdept292; "Buying Quiet; Inside the Israeli Plan that Propped Up Hamas," *NYT*.

22 "PM Meets with Families of Israelis Kidnapped to Gaza," *TI*, Oct. 16, 2023, tinyurl.com/2a8p48m6; "The History of Presidential Visits to War Zones, from Madison to Biden," *WP*, Oct. 17, 2023, tinyurl.com/mpa6pwst; "Biden Meets with Relatives of Americans Held Hostage by Hamas," Reuters, Dec. 13, 2023, tinyurl.com/56jzsj66; "Israel's Hostage Families Feel Abandoned by Israel", *Foreign Policy*; "Families of Soldier Hostages Says Netanyahu Offered 'Nothing New' in Meeting," *TI*, Mar. 29, 2024, tinyurl.com/yc84putd.

23 "Biden's Speech: Hamas Unleashed Evil," *TI*, Oct. 10, 2023, tinyurl.com/y6u67uh2.

24 Video: "We Are at War: Watch PM Netanyahu's Address to the Nation," *Israel Hayom*, Oct. 7, 2023, tinyurl.com/2pudpxr9.

25 "We Cannot Ignore the Truth that Hamas Uses Human Shields," *WP*, Nov. 14, 2023, tinyurl.com/54n2d2kk.

26 "The Last Remaining Exit for Gazans Is Through Egypt," CNN, Oct. 13, 2023, tinyurl.com/czd3we6z; "Jordan, Egypt Unwilling to Take Palestinian Refugees, King Says," The Hill, Oct. 17, 2023, tinyurl.com/53ypft4a; "Egypt's Sisi Rejects Transfer of Gazans," Reuters, Oct. 18, 2023, tinyurl.com/yjsp7zd5; "Palestinians Desperate to Flee Gaza Pay Thousands in Bribes to 'Brokers,'" *Guardian*, Jan. 8, 2024, tinyurl.com/2vfmb5v2; "Palestinians Paying Thousands in Bribes to Leave Gaza," Al Jazeera, Sept. 5, 2016, tinyurl.com/msbxkykh.

27 "With an Ambitious Civic Agenda, Brothers and Sisters in Arms Says It's Here to Stay," *TI*, Apr. 1, 2024, tinyurl.com/4tce2cjx; "In Stunning Response, 15,000 Volunteers Fill Leadership Vacuum to Help Victims of Hamas," *TI*, Oct. 22, 2023, tinyurl.com/y9zz3fr2; "Israel's Massive Mobilization of 360,000 Reservists Upends Lives," *WP*, Oct. 10, 2023, tinyurl.com/4wb5b9ab; "Study: Nearly 50% of Israeli Citizens Volunteered during First Weeks of War," *TI*, Nov. 3, 2023, tinyurl.com/3kmrkua7.

28 "Netanyahu Slammed for Post Blaming Intelligence Chiefs for Oct. 7 Failure," *TI*, Oct. 29, 2023, tinyurl.com/mtz83spp; "ABC's Muir Presses Netanyahu on Whether He Takes Responsibility for Oct. 7 Intelligence Failures," ABC News, Nov. 7, 2023, tinyurl.com/mr3c4tum; "Most Israelis Think Netanyahu Responsible for Failing to Prevent Hamas Attack," Reuters, Oct. 20, 2023, tinyurl.com/5enfw7az; "Israeli Military Intelligence Chief Resigns, Citing Oct. 7 Failures," Axios, Apr. 22, 2024, tinyurl.com/4brp28y9; "After Hamas Attack, Most Israelis Want Netanyahu to Resign," NPR, Nov. 11, 2023, tinyurl.com/k6rths2h; "Only 15% of Israelis Want Netanyahu to Keep Job after Gaza War," Reuters, Jan. 2, 2024, tinyurl.com/5apdt3fp; "Netanyahu Says War against Hamas Set to Continue into 2025," *TI*, Jan. 17, 2024, tinyurl.com/2s4dmbea.

29 "Hamas and Israel Complete 3rd Exchange of Hostages for Prisoners," *NYT*; "Hamas Releases Sick Propaganda Video of Heartbroken Hostage," *New York Post*, Nov. 30, 2023, tinyurl.com/456jr4jk.

30 "'I Captured One!,'" *TI*; "UNRWA Workers Accused of Kidnapping Woman, Taking Part in Kibbutz Massacre," *TI*, Jan. 29, 2024, tinyurl.com/ydk5jvhk; Emily Hand interview: "The Trauma of 9 Year Old Emily, Who Was Released from Hamas Captivity," YouTube, tinyurl.com/yc29ykuz; "Cages, Beatings, and Death Threats: Freed Hostages Tell Their Story," Jewish Chronicle, Dec. 1, 2023, tinyurl.com/avryup84; "Hamas Forced Hostage Kids to Watch Videos of Oct. 7 Atrocities," *TI*, Nov. 28, 2023, tinyurl.com/ycxrdr8j; "As Calderon Family Rejoices," *TI*, Nov. 28, 2023, tinyurl.com/4bft68xt.

31 "Inside the Tunnels of Gaza," Reuters, Dec. 31, 2023, tinyurl.com/3hvzysvh; "The 'Gaza Metro,'" CNN, Oct. 28, 2023, tinyurl.com/yzhka468; "Polluted Water Leading Cause of Child Mortality in Gaza," *Haaretz*, Oct. 16, 2023, tinyurl.com/23dnshvv; "Gaza Children Face Acute Water and Sanitation Crisis," UNICEF, Sept. 1, 2017, tinyurl.com/34yxjnn6.

32 "For Years, Two Men Shuttled Messages between Israel and Hamas. No Longer," *NYT*, Nov. 19, 2023, tinyurl.com/m6kpf3hv; "Top Hamas Official Declares Group Is Not Responsible for Defending Gazan Civilians," *TI*, Oct. 31, 2023, tinyurl.com/2vsdrf8b; "Mashaal: Hamas 'Well Aware of Consequences' of Attack," *TI*, Oct. 20, 2023, tinyurl.com/3v7m3adj; "Hamas Bigwig Rejects 2-State Solution," *TI*, Jan. 23, 2024, tinyurl.com/2dznsux3.

33 "Israeli Hostage Says She Was Sexually Assaulted and Tortured in Gaza," *NYT*, Mar. 26, 2024, tinyurl.com/4ntwm2wf; "Terrorist 'Sexually Assaulted Hostage at Gunpoint,'" *TI*, Feb. 13, 2024, tinyurl.com/2ubjawr3.

34 "'Right Now Someone Is Being Raped in a Tunnel,'" *TI*, Jan. 23, 2024, tinyurl.com/zhuk2ssn.

35 "Ben Gvir Says 10,000 Assault Rifles Purchased for Civilian Security Teams," TI, Oct. 10, 2023, tinyurl.com/mz9r4d7p; "Ben Gvir Celebrates Issuing 100,000 Gun Licenses Since October 7," Mar. 18, 2024, tinyurl.com/3329s972.

36 "UN Human Rights Chief Deplores New Moves to Expand Israeli Settlements in Occupied West Bank," OHCHR, Mar. 8, 2024, tinyurl.com/3n55n47v; "With the World's Eyes on Gaza, Attacks Are on the Rise in the West Bank," AP News, Nov. 20, 2023, tinyurl.com/4dsj8z6w; "How a Campaign of Extremist Violence Is Pushing the West Bank to the Brink," NYT, Nov. 2, 2023, tinyurl.com/5bx7s6hw; "In the West Bank, Guns and a Locked Gate Signal a Town's New Residents," NYT, June 1, 2024, tinyurl.com/bderrdch.

37 "Freed Israeli Hostage Mia Schem in First Interview," YouTube, tinyurl.com/kf62xz2x.

38 "Polls Show Palestinians Back Oct. 7 Attack on Israel," Reuters, Dec. 14, 2023, tinyurl.com/ycynkcb9; "Poll: Gazans Increasingly Happy with Oct. 7," TI, Mar. 21, 2024, tinyurl.com/3mhtkhvn; "Press Release: Public Opinion Poll No. 91," Palestinian Center for Policy and Survey Research, Mar. 20, 2024, pcpsr.org/en/node/969; "Public Opinion Poll No. 90," Palestinian Center for Policy and Survey Research.

39 "Herzog: 'No Israelis in Their Right Mind' Are Thinking about Peace Process Right Now," TI, Jan. 18, 2024, tinyurl.com/4vanht8b.

40 "Biden's Hopes for Establishing Israel-Saudi Relations Could Become a Casualty of the New Mideast War," AP News, Oct. 11, 2023, tinyurl.com/3ue4r3hz; "Hamas Aims to Kill Saudi Deal that Would Help Palestinians," YouTube, undated, tinyurl.com/2rervms2; "Biden Says Hamas Attacked Israel in Part to Stop a Historic Agreement with Saudi Arabia," AP News, Oct. 21, 2023, tinyurl.com/2suf8bhm; "Despite Hamas Crackdown, Gaza Protests Continue in Rare Defiance," Al-Monitor, Aug. 6, 2023, tinyurl.com/3v5kcwtn; "Gaza Protests Struggle to Gain Traction as Police Crack Down," NYT, Aug. 7, 2023, tinyurl.com/4df8ucsn.

41 "ADL Records Dramatic Increase in U.S. Antisemitic Incidents Following Oct. 7 Hamas Massacre," ADL, Oct. 24, 2023, tinyurl.com/2z46cj5d; "Jews Again Faced Most Hate Crimes of Any Religious Group in 2022, FBI Reports," TI, Oct. 17, 2023, tinyurl.com/38ehwc7t.

Chapter 30: To the Grave
1 Interviews with Jill Notowich (2019, 2020, 2023), throughout chapter.
2 "IDF Says It Detained Senior Hamas Operative," CNN, Mar. 2, 2024, tinyurl.com/5hbrce9u.
3 Interviews with Waheed Al-Qawasmi (2019, 2020, 2023), throughout chapter.

Epilogue
1 "Four More Hostages Have Died in Hamas Custody; Israel Says More Than a Third Are Dead," NBC News, June 3, 2024, https://tinyurl.com/yxuedmy4.
2 "Israel Police Quietly Gave Up on Enforcing the Temple Mount Status Quo, Despite Netanyahu," Haaretz, June 6, 2024, https://tinyurl.com/3rekr7jw.

PICTURE CREDITS

INDEX